CONSPIRACY
AT CARTHAGE

MARK GOODMANSEN

CONSPIRACY AT CARTHAGE

THE PLOT TO MURDER JOSEPH SMITH

CFI
An Imprint of Cedar Fort, Inc.
Springville, Utah

© 2016 Mark Goodmansen
All rights reserved.

No part of this book may be reproduced in any form whatsoever, whether by graphic, visual, electronic, film, microfilm, tape recording, or any other means, without prior written permission of the publisher, except in the case of brief passages embodied in critical reviews and articles.

This is not an official publication of The Church of Jesus Christ of Latter-day Saints. The opinions and views expressed herein belong solely to the author and do not necessarily represent the opinions or views of Cedar Fort, Inc. Permission for the use of sources, graphics, and photos is also solely the responsibility of the author.

ISBN 13: 978-1-4621-1850-2

Published by CFI, an imprint of Cedar Fort, Inc.
2373 W. 700 S., Springville, UT 84663
Distributed by Cedar Fort, Inc., www.cedarfort.com

LIBRARY OF CONGRESS CATALOGING-IN-PUBLICATION DATA

Names: Goodmansen, Mark, 1953- author.
Title: Conspiracy at Carthage / Mark Goodmansen.
Description: [Springville, Utah] : CFI, An imprint of Cedar Fort, Inc., [2016] | "2016 | Includes bibliographical references and index. | Description based on print version record and CIP data provided by publisher; resource not viewed.
Identifiers: LCCN 2015048597 (print) | LCCN 2015048085 (ebook) | ISBN 9781462126439 () | ISBN 9781462118502 (perfect bound : alk. paper)
Subjects: LCSH: Smith, Joseph, Jr., 1805-1844--Assassination. | Smith, Hyrum, 1800 1844--Assassination. | Church of Jesus Christ of Latter-day Saints--History--19th century. | Mormon Church--History--19th century.
Classification: LCC BX8695.S6 (print) | LCC BX8695.S6 G66 2016 (ebook) | DDC 289.3092--dc23
LC record available at http://lccn.loc.gov/2015048597

Cover design by Shawnda T. Craig
Cover design © 2016 Cedar Fort, Inc.

Printed in the United States of America

10 9 8 7 6 5 4 3 2 1

Printed on acid-free paper

Dedicated to my dear family, on both sides of the veil.

Contents

Introduction

Colonel Stephen Markham quickened his pace, his footsteps pounding up the stairs at Hamilton's Hotel in Carthage, Illinois. A posted sentry, realizing Markham's identity sounded the alarm to those in a secret council. The meeting dismissed abruptly. They scattered, not wanting to be identified as fellow conspirators in their bloody plot. In a stupor, they left the minutes memorializing their foul designs on the table. Dr. Wall Southwick, an invited guest had the presence of mind to seize the abandoned minutes amid the disruptive chaos.

After the frenzied tumult and finding Markham alone, Southwick confronted him and offered to share the minutes with him. He warned Markham of what had transpired. Dr. Wall Southwick likewise had also spent the previous night inside the jail with the Prophet and Markham. This Vigilance Committee of Safety for Hancock County had been called that afternoon of June 26, 1844, with representatives from all but three of the states of the Union.[1]

> The purport of said meeting was to take into consideration the best way to stop Joseph and Hyrum's career, as Joseph's view on Government was widely circulated and took like wild fire. He said that if he did not

> get into the Presidential chair this election, he would be sure to next, and if Illinois and Missouri would join together to kill them, they would not be brought to justice for it.[2]

Joseph's "Views on Government" were being circulated by hundreds of missionaries sent out in May. In this publication, Joseph incited the populace to "frustrate the designs of wicked men"[3] in reference to the nation's top party leaders. Dr. Southwick indicated Governor Ford and Captain Smith of the Carthage Greys had been in the meeting. The gathered representatives formed an odd assemblage of mostly Whig and some Democratic Party supporters united in their determination to rid the state of the Mormons. The Mormons had continued to thwart their efforts in realizing their greedy economic ambitions and political patronage.

Immediately, Markham returned to Carthage Jail and reported to the Prophet what Southwick had revealed. They intended to kill him. Joseph Smith simply responded, "Be not afraid."[4] Markham was unable to secure the minutes from Dr. Southwick, but fortunately notes were taken by another attendee, George T. M. Davis, working for an Alton newspaper. He later reported,

> There existed a secret tribunal in the county of Hancock, known as "The Vigilance Committee of Safety," all of whose members were old citizens of that county of the highest repute. They had determined that one of two results must occur. Either that immediately after the governor had taken up his line of march upon Nauvoo with the State Militia, the two Smiths must be shot by a detail from the Quincy Guards; or that, on the arrival of the State forces at "the City of the Beautiful," it must be laid in ashes, and its men, women, and children left to the disposal of the soldiers. This Committee decided that justice and mercy demanded that the lives of the two Smiths should be the penalty for the transgressions of their own dupes, and the people of Nauvoo should be shielded from bodily harm, and their property saved from infamy or destruction, upon condition that within a given period of time they would leave the State in a body, taking with them all their movable effects.[5]

George T. M. Davis and Colonel Enoch C. March rode with Governor Ford to Nauvoo. While in town, they met Jonathan C. Wright and had a lively discussion as to his impressions of the fate of his Mormon Prophet. In a serious and dramatic tone,

> Col. March replied, "Mr. Wright, you are mistaken, and I know it; you do not know what I know; I tell you they will kill Joe Smith before he leaves Carthage, and I know it, and you never will see him alive again." Said I, "Enoch, I do not believe it, he is in the hands of God, and God will deliver him." Says he, "I know better; when you hear of him again, you will hear he is dead, and I know it. The people at Carthage wanted permission from the Governor to kill you all and burn up your city, and Ford [the Governor] asked me if I thought it was best to suffer it." I replied, "No, no, for God's sake, Ford, don't suffer it, that will never do, no never. Just see for a moment, Ford, what that would do; it would be the means of murdering thousands of innocent men, women and children, and destroying thousands of dollars' worth of property, and that would never do, it would not be sanctioned, it would disgrace the nation. You have now got the principle men here under your own control, they are all you want, what more do you want? When they are out of the way the thing is settled, and the people will be satisfied, and that is the easiest way you can dispose of it; and Governor Ford concluded upon the whole that was the best policy, and I know it will be done."[6]

The Hancock County Vigilance Committee of Safety had its origins three years prior. Internally, the group was organized with a central corresponding committee of five members. But an inner circle, evolved with about ten members of the anti-Mormon Party, who volunteered or were assigned to various temporary or ad hoc positions. Unlike the other local participants, they were afforded a priority status by virtue of their various appointments as commissioners approved through the state legislature or county administrators. The inner circle was supported by the anti-Mormon Party precinct leaders, who were generally farmers and merchants located on the key roads being developed for commercial expansion, anxious to benefit from an expected increase in land values and commercial activity if the Mormons would leave.

George T. M. Davis was an attorney, a newspaper editor, and a Whig Party activist from Alton, Illinois. He also worked closely with Whig leaders and leading merchants in St. Louis in performing legal services and provided editorial support for their newspaper. He served as a primary liaison between the Missouri anti-Mormon groups and the Hancock County Vigilance Committee leadership. He and his friend Enoch Marsh were land speculators and promoters.

Conspiracy at Carthage

The next day, Joseph and Hyrum Smith were murdered by a mob. More than two hundred militia members from Illinois and Missouri had attacked the jail. As ordered by the committee, the local Carthage Grey's—the majority of who were sympathetic with the mob—fired intentionally over the heads of the charging mob attackers. The fatal bullet for Joseph Smith came from a deputy US Marshall from Hamilton, Ohio. Governor Ford later verified the acts of the conspirators as they carried out the plot to murder the Mormon Prophet:

> A communication was soon established between the conspirators and the company; and it was arranged that the guard should have their guns charged with blank cartridges, and fire at the assailants when they attempted to enter the jail. . . .
>
> The conspirators came up, jumped the slight fence . . . were fired upon by the guard, which, according to arrangement, was overpowered immediately, and the assailants entered the prison, to the door of the room where the two prisoners were confined.[7]

With the shedding of martyrs' blood, Joseph and Hyrum were gone. Following a brief respite, John Taylor, though emotionally distraught, returned to his duties in the *Times and Seasons* printing office. There, in the stock room, was a new publication printed during that fatal final month of June, 1844. "The Voice of Truth" had been intended as a means to articulate a message to all citizens and to promote Joseph's candidacy for President of the United States.

Included in "The Voice of Truth" was Joseph's "Views on Government": This pamphlet displayed the intensity of Joseph Smith's indictment of Van Buren, Benton, Boggs, Calhoun, Clay, and a few others. They had dishonored the core values of the Constitution, all to perpetuate their own lusts for power and to continue to provide political preferences for their favorites. Political parties were corrupting the integrity of public office.

> Democracy, Whiggery and Cliquery, will attract their elements and foment divisions among the people, to accomplish fancied schemes and accumulate power. . . .
>
> A still higher grade, of what the "nobility of nations" call, "great men," will daily with all rights in order to smuggle a fortune at "one

fell swoop;" mortgage Texas, possess Oregon, and claim all the unsettled regions of the world for hunting and trapping; and should a humble honest man, red, black, or white, exhibit a better title, these gentry have only to clothe the judge with richer ermine, and spangle the lawyer's fingers with finer rings, to have the judgment of his peers, . . . as a pattern of honesty, virtue and humanity, while the motto hangs on his nation's escutcheon: *"Every man has his price!"*. . . Now, oh! people! people! Turn unto the Lord and live; and reform this nation.[8]

These prophetic utterances were intended to identify those groups of corrupted officials and merchants who planned to smuggle their fortunes at the expense of the masses including the Native Americans. They had to be stopped. The Prophet went even further by directing attention to the corruptions of a few leaders by name. Their patrons and allies were thus also indicted.

Then why? Oh! Why! Will a once flourishing people not arise, phoenix like, over the cinders of Martin Van Buren's power; and over the sinking fragments and smoking ruins of other catamount politicians; and over the wind-falls of Benton, Calhoun, Clay, Wright, and a caravan of other equally unfortunate law doctors.

In this highly charged publication, Joseph drew attention to the political cliques that had permeated the ranks of county, state, and federal governments. Many of the targeted partisan leaders organized to quiet the Illinois Prophet leader's poignant alarms. His murder had been decreed. The clique managers in Missouri, Illinois, and the Iowa Territory guaranteed that those executing the cold-blooded murders would not experience any convictions.

In this work, Joseph left a critical message known as the "Four Main Pillars of Prosperity." In a clear tone of optimism and enlightenment, Joseph also noted in the pamphlet,

When the people are secure and their rights properly respected, then the four main pillars of prosperity, viz: agriculture, manufactures, navigation, and commerce, need the fostering care of government.

In the previous year, Joseph Smith inserted a forwarded letter into his journal and made note of a "corrupt conspiracy formed against me in Missouri and Illinois."[9] There were five groups of organized enemies of the Church that had evolved independently in Missouri, Illinois, and the Iowa Territory. The "Corrupt Conspiracy" the Prophet identified reached its apex of evil after all five groups assisted in the sinister plot to murder Joseph and Hyrum. The plot also included plans to force a complete Mormon exodus out of Illinois and Iowa. The groups were linked through Samuel Owens of Jackson County, Missouri, and John C. Bennett. All five groups were driven by greed, and then, when economic conditions worsened, they became desperate. Each committed serious acts they needed to keep secret. After four kidnapping attempts failed, they developed a plot to murder Joseph Smith.

The Prophet had dedicated his life to the building up of the kingdom of God and the establishment of Zion. In the beginning of the year, he had been charged to make a proclamation to the world of the coming of the new kingdom of God. Later, he finalized plans for "The Council of Fifty" to lead in this new kingdom. Herein, the prophetic leader of this, the final dispensation, revealed the keys to the building of an Enoch society, as a planned component to the New Jerusalem. But it was from this feared "Enoch Prophecy" that the enemies of the Saints would invoke their wrath against all who preached of Zion and the new kingdom of God.

On May 13, 1844, the Prophet responded back to Henry Clay, the Whig candidate:

> For the glory of America has departed, and God will set a flaming sword to guard the tree of liberty, while such mint-tithing Herods as Van Buren, Boggs, Benton, Calhoun and Clay, are thrust out of the realms of virtue as fit subjects for the kingdom of fallen greatness; *vox reprobi, vox diaboli!*[10]

So it seemed that this "Voice of Truth" was yet to expose the "Voice of Reprobates" and the "Voice of Devils." Further in the letter Joseph stated with plainness,

> Benton and Van Buren, who make no secret to say, if they get into power, they will carry on Boggs' exterminating plan to rid the country of Latter Day Saints.[11]

Of the hundreds actively involved in the Martyrdom, only five were charged with the murders of Joseph and Hyrum. Four of the ten inner circle members of the Vigilance Committee were on trial. These four were militia officers who took a leading role in the efforts of the "Council of Officers," demanding the hostile march to Nauvoo. Little attention was given to other members of the anti-Mormon Party supporting the Hancock County Vigilance Committee of Safety. Delegates, from Warsaw and Carthage, decreed their deaths and issued the orders to the Hancock County militia units. Twelve activist anti-Mormon Party members, or their direct associates, with state-sanctioned positions were directly involved in the murders.

At the trial, held in May 1845, Judge Richard M. Young presided. William Richardson, the defense attorney, opened with an unconventional motion to the presiding judge. Richardson requested the empanelled jury be entirely dismissed as the five defendants felt the jury might be prejudiced against them. The jury had been called according to law, from proportionate Mormon and non-Mormon Hancock County communities. This extreme request had never been used before in a criminal trial. Surprisingly, Judge Young ruled in favor on the motion. The duly authorized jurors were all dismissed. The judge ruled that new jurors would be selected from those attending the trial in Carthage, knowing that Mormons were not in attendance.

The judge, the five defendants, the six defense attorneys, and the two appointed elisors were directly or indirectly tied to what Joseph Smith had previously identified as a "Corrupt Conspiracy." Judge Young had an agenda, relationships, and a past he wanted to remain hidden. The six defense attorneys likewise were acting to protect the guilt of other collaborators and to divert attention from themselves and others seeking anonymity as to their culpability. The prosecutor also had a clouded past. All five defendants were acquitted. Everyone knew they were guilty. Next, the Hancock County Vigilance Committee of Safety and their allies plotted the forced exodus of the rest of the Mormons from Iowa and Illinois.

Earlier, after rallying the Saints to the cause of Zion, the Prophet Joseph Smith proclaimed he had been called to build the kingdom Daniel had spoken of, and he was laying the foundation for world revolution.[12] How much could he have achieved in developing the four pillars to create a world revolution if he had not been murdered then?

Conspiracy at Carthage

The conspiracy at Carthage was expanding. The battle for Zion continued between the Saints and their multiple enemy groups. This is their story.

1: Senator Benton and the St. Louis Junto

A letter, dated February 27, 1808, arrived at President Jefferson's home in Washington, DC.

> Sir, It was my intention to have presented myself before you & to have stated to you my wish of engaging in an extensive trade with the Indians . . . (that) may in time embrace the greater part of the fur trade on this continent the most of which passes now through Canada.[13]

With passionate enthusiasm, President Jefferson replied to John Jacob Astor,

> The field is immense, & would occupy a vast amount of capital. . . .
>
> You may be assured that in order to get the whole of this business passed into the hands of our own citizens . . . every reasonable patronage & facility in the power of the Executive will be afforded.[14]

A meeting was arranged with the enterprising merchant, John Astor. Later, the president had been observed crawling on hands and knees studying maps spread reverently on the office floor, thus enlarging his vision of the limitless possibilities of the Western continent. An exuberant Jefferson addressed Meriwether Lewis, governor of the Louisiana Territory,

> A powerful company is at length forming for taking up the Indian commerce on a large scale. . . . It will be under the direction of a most excellent man, a Mr. Astor, merch't of New York, long engaged in the business, & perfectly master of it.[15]

President Jefferson and the millionaire John Astor shared in the quest for American dominance of Pacific Trade. Astor's fur trading empire gave the Jefferson vision an infrastructure to build upon. The American Fur Company had well-established routes from New York through the Great Lakes, the Mississippi and Missouri Rivers, then various trails winding through the peaks of the Rocky Mountains.

The global ambition for Astor was to master a great international trade emporium, with his ships constantly circling the globe. From manufacturers in London, cheap trade goods—including knives, blankets, pots, and beads—would be shipped around Cape Horn to the Oregon Territory at his new outpost of Astoria, near the mouth of the Columbia River. This river would be the trade circuit for the inland Indians, exchanging their London trinkets for valuable beaver, bear, lynx, and sea otter furs gathered by the Indians. Full loads of furs would be shipped to China, Japan, and the Indies to exchange their fur packet cargoes for oriental goods of porcelain, silk, tea, and yellow Nankeen cloth. These laden ships would sail westward to the other side of the globe back to the London and New York markets.[16]

John Jacob Astor had attempted to create a virgin American settlement of a colony on the upper Pacific Coast. The Columbia River Basin was expected to provide the launch site of a global trading network eastward while linking with Asia and other global ports accessible by Pacific Ocean trade routes. Astor financed two expeditions: one by sea, involving navigating around the southern tip of South America, and then up the Pacific coastline to the Oregon Territory; the other overland, in which the party would trek through the mighty Rocky Mountains.

The Overland Route, headed by Wilson Price Hunt, included Ramsay Crooks. The seafaring team sailed aboard the ship *Tonquin,* commanded by Captain Jonathan Thorn. Both were focused on reaching their targeted site of what would become known as "Astoria."

The well-entrenched British merchant fleet network represented a formidable foe against the American plan, while amassing millions in payments to the British Crown and their favorite global agents. They shipped the same trinkets to their trading posts in the Oregon Territory and monopolized trade with the Blackfoot and Crow Indians, who were taught to hate the American fur traders. Their acquired Indian furs were exchanged for Oriental goods from the East Indies and China company cartels, or they were retained for European trade after returning to Liverpool.

Of the two parties sent out by Astor, the *Tonquin* arrived first, set anchor, and eagerly awaited the union with the overland team. The ship was attacked and sunk with its crew in the harbor. Hunt's overland party suffered terribly from various obstacles. They were attacked by Indians and nearly starved to death. But in November 1812, Ramsay Crooks discovered the secret access point through the Rocky Mountains. It would become known as South Pass.

A friend of Ramsay Crooks named Russell Farnham was also part of the initial Astoria settlement. While nearly starving and freezing to death after being dropped off in the Alaska Territory, he proved his loyalty to Astor, who employed him until his death.[17]

Anxious to capitalize on their secret, a small group formed a new fur enterprise. The "Missouri Fur Company" articles of association were signed February 1, 1812. Its express purpose being for "exploring in a commercial way, and hunting in that portion of country within the claim of the United States, and westwardly of a point, which shall be 500 miles from the United States present factories."[18] William Clark became president; other principals included Pierre and Auguste Chouteau and Pierre Menard. It lasted only two seasons.

Despite the failure of the Missouri Fur Company, Clark, the Chouteaus, and others continued to pursue the vision of a commercially connected continent. As the road extended to the Pacific, St. Louis would be transformed to the heart of commerce for the entire continent. Arteries already formed included the Great Mississippi to New Orleans, with the Missouri River merging from its Rocky Mountain headwaters to the north and westward. The New England seaboard accessed the Great Lakes through the Erie Canal. Plans to supplement this key artery included construction of the Ohio River and Lake Erie Canal and the Illinois River and Lake Michigan Canal to link with the Mississippi and south to St. Louis. Various entrepreneurs also anticipated connecting Lake Superior to the Great Mississippi. Other important arteries to be developed included the Des Moines River running westward toward Council Bluffs and the Arkansas River and its extensions. Under the domain of the Chouteau aristocracy, St. Louis had evolved as the "Gateway to the West."

The Rise of Thomas Benton

In October 1816, two adversaries opposed each other, representing clients in the courthouse at St. Louis. After Thomas Benton had argued his final pleas to the jury, he arrogantly asserted the jury must decide in his favor. Lucas, the US Attorney for the Missouri Territory, immediately arose, challenging that Benton had not presented adequate evidence. In brash retort, Benton railed, "I contradict you, sir." Lucas countered, "I contradict you, sir." Enraged, Benton accused his prim adversary, "If you deny that, you deny the truth." Likewise, Lucas defiantly responded, "If you assert that, you assert what is not true."[19] After the courtroom theatrics, the jury found in favor of Lucas. Within a month, Benton demanded satisfaction in the form of a duel. On that occasion, Lucas refused, but ill feelings continued. Benton went on to become a major player in the political and economical stage in Missouri, beginning with his involvement with the Bank of Missouri. The Bank of Missouri had been created by the legislature on December 17, 1816, with Auguste Chouteau as president and an enterprising young man, Lilburn Boggs, as cashier.[20] A youthful Boggs was introduced to the aristocracy of St. Louis, namely Auguste Chouteau, William Clark, and Thomas Benton. Initially, the Bank of Missouri was relatively stable due to conservative lending practices and because it had the benefit of being the Far Western depository for federal government funds. The following year, Benton was elected to the bank's Board of Directors.[21]

The Chouteaus, Benton, Boggs, and the other principals of the Bank of Missouri were committed to achieve what President Jefferson and Astor attempted in their noble national endeavor of a commercial transcontinental trade route across America. Benton's "Road to India" metaphor rose foremost in his lifetime pursuits carrying on the Jefferson vision of crossing through the American heartland to secure trade with China, Japan, and other Eastern trade centers.

Overland routes were also of extreme importance. The Santa Fe Trail was of particular interest to Benton and Boggs. Additionally, to these select few, the secret of South Pass had been fostered, providing a shortcut or concealed passage that shortened the "Road to India." It had been discovered by the earlier expedition to the Pacific Ocean.

During 1817, Benton reached out to a former friend and ally from Franklin, Tennessee, John Sappington, to come and develop a sizeable estate in the Missouri Territory. Benton loaned him 950 dollars, as Sappington, though heavily vested in Tennessee real estate, had little in liquid resources.

Sappington initially moved his family to Howard County, having purchased seven thousand acres. Two years later, he moved a few miles west of Arrow Rock, where he began building a massive commercial empire. As a frontier physician, he developed and marketed "Sappington's Anti-Fever Pills," being a quinine-based patented prescription for general fevers and malaria. He was also adept in diverse commercial ventures, including extensive agricultural pursuits. He became an effective exporter of cotton, tobacco, livestock, and lumber to New Orleans. He and his family developed a mercantile establishment in Jonesborough, in Saline County, and at Arrow Rock, and became active in the slave trade. He invested in real estate ventures and purchased thousands of acres in the Osage River Valley.

On election day, August 4, 1817, Benton entered the polling place, wherein Charles Lucas, his former nemesis, challenged his right to vote and queried Benton if he had paid his taxes. Benton ignored his previous adversary and addressed the voting clerks, "Gentlemen, if you have any questions to ask, I am prepared to answer, but I do not propose to answer charges made by any puppy who may happen to run across my path." Still agitated, a week later Lucas wrote to Benton and demanded for "that satisfaction which is due from one gentleman to another for such an indignity."[22] Benton, unwilling to recant, accepted the challenge for a duel.

On a narrow island on the Great Mississippi, two men, with thirty feet separating them, gripped smoothbore pistols, waiting anxiously for the command. Thomas Benton, the bullish Southern gentleman transplant, aimed steady. His bullet penetrated Charles Lucas's neck to the left of his windpipe. Benton, a much larger target, with his six-foot frame, was barely grazed below his right knee. Dr. Garrit Quarles, the attending surgeon, called off a second fire. Luke Lawless, Benton's second, questioned the dazed victim if he was satisfied. Lucas responded affirmatively and acknowledged he would not ask for a second meeting. Benton belligerently called out that he was not satisfied. Charles Lucas responded he would return when his wound had healed. His friends gathered to assist him back to the tethered boat, where he dropped motionless having fainted from loss of blood.[23]

The rematch was scheduled for September 27. Terms this time called for the two duelists to stand but ten feet apart. At the command to fire, both pistols discharged nearly simultaneously. Again, the fortuitous Benton was untouched. The discharged bullet coursed through Lucas's left arm and into his heart. "Colonel Benton, you have persecuted me and murdered me! I cannot forgive you." Momentarily, Lucas turned to address Benton again, "I can forgive you—I do forgive you." Shortly thereafter, Charles Lucas was dead at age twenty-five.[24] Henceforth, this island on the Great River became known as "Bloody Island."

Charles Lucas was expected to have a promising career advocating for his father's policies. At stake, who was to get the major share of the virgin lands of Missouri and surrounding areas?[25] In essence, Benton had just shot and killed a major challenger in the Spanish land grant wars.

Judge John Lucas vowed a personal vendetta against Benton for murdering his son, which plagued Benton for many years. Benton's reputation was further tarnished when a previous encounter with a well-respected war hero was publicized. Things went seriously awry for Benton in September 1813 at Clayton Talbot's Tavern in Nashville, Tennessee. Colonel Benton and his brother Jesse had been drawn into a barroom brawl with none other than General Jackson and his friend Billy Carroll. Carroll and Jesse Benton had faced each other in a duel just three months previously, resulting in both being wounded. In an all-out brawl at Talbot's Tavern, Colonel Benton shot General Jackson in the arm after Jackson had shot toward him. Benton left his residence at Leiper's Fork, Tennessee, knowing his confrontation with the popular Jackson had permanently stifled any hopes of future prominence in that region.

In St. Louis, the death of Lucas ignited further controversy surrounding Benton's motives in demanding a second duel. Joseph Charless, editor of the *St. Louis Gazette* for months, focused criticism of what he labeled the "little junto," which consisted of a group of French business leaders holding large Spanish land grants lead by Auguste and Pierre Chouteau. Political power of the alleged "little junto," or "St. Louis Junto," vested primarily in William Clark, Governor of the Missouri Territory, who, with Merriwether Lewis, had launched their famous Expedition of the West from the August Chouteau mansion and trading center. Charless had profiled Benton as catering his law practice to Spanish land grants favoring the Chouteaus. Charless himself advocated for the "anti-junto," consisting of American leaders and entrepreneurs having come to St. Louis after the Louisiana Purchase under the leadership of Judge Lucas and his son Charles.

Prior to the fateful duel, Benton had injected himself into various political controversies. In May, the *Western Emigrant* newspaper emerged to counter Charless's *Missouri Gazette*. From its inception, Benton became a frequent contributor to the politically biased periodical.

Less than six months after the controversies surrounding the dueling death of young Lucas, Benton again made St. Louis headlines. The rival Bank of St. Louis, which had begun in 1816, had succumbed to making excessive loans on real estate without maintaining sufficient specie (gold and silver) payments in reserve. Benton was a minor stockholder and had been asked by other stockholders to act as their agent to protect their investments in the bank. On February 11, 1818, an anxious crowd had gathered outside the bank concerned with rumors regarding its financial stability. Benton and a few others, including his friend Joshua Pilcher, brought some of the crowd members inside the bank for an impromptu shareholders meeting. A resolution was passed calling on the bank officers to turn over the keys to Benton. Benton and the other ringleaders padlocked the bank doors and commenced counting the bank assets. Two days later, Benton and his cohorts were brought before a grand jury to account for their coup against the bank. The bank was able to again open its doors, but within a year the Bank of St. Louis had failed leaving the Bank of Missouri to take the lead as Benton had connived.

During 1818, Benton's relationship with the Chouteaus intensified. The French group in St. Louis agreed to join John Jacob Astor's American Fur Company. Benton would find a way to reinforce his standing both with the local Junto and the millionaire industrialist John Astor. Benton was able to represent Astor and the American Fur Company in a few legal matters, which likewise elevated his standing in the Junto.

Seeking to add to his meteoric rise, Benton resolved to change his image to the St. Louis public and among the local elite. He presented himself as one of twelve candidates for a seat on the five-man Board of Trustees for the city. The election took place in January 1819. When the final votes were tallied, Benton was informed he had taken last place.[26] He knew he would have to find another means to elicit public affection and endorsement.

Benton's Thirteen-Point Agenda

For the previous few years, Benton had aligned with many of the leading merchants and political heads in St. Louis. He knew what causes to crusade to further enhance his standing in this dynamic and fast-paced community. In June 1819, he published his thirteen-point program, targeted to gain favor with the St. Louis Junto gentry, which called for the following:[27]

- Change of the Territorial for the state form of government
- Adjustment of land titles granted by the late Spanish government in upper Louisiana
- Protection of the Missouri frontier through the creation of more military outposts

- Protection for fur traders by building forts at St. Anthony Falls on the Mississippi River and at the Mandan villages on the Missouri River, as well as by abolishing the federally operated trading posts (factory system)
- Conversion of the principal salt springs granted back to the people or sold
- Conversion of lead mines to private "freehold title" for increased production
- Building a national road to Washington City (Washington, DC)
- Building a post road to New Orleans (this also for merchant operations)
- Building post routes throughout the territory
- Creating post routes between St. Louis and Louisville by way of Vincennes
- Having the federal government establish St. Louis as an official point of entry
- Building a canal between Lake Michigan and the Illinois River
- Building a canal to unite the Mississippi River and Lake Superior with its copper trade

With this bold and progressive agenda, Benton set the foundation to launch his political power base to unite and inspire an apathetic electorate to sustain his power quest for an entire political lifetime. These were to aid his overall quest for the "Road to India."

A few years later, Auguste Chouteau recognized the Bank of Missouri was having trouble. On May 1, 1820, a new board of directors was elected, which included Thomas H. Benton and Thomas F. Reddick. Reddick, a close friend of Joshua Pilcher, replaced Chouteau as president.

Besides their joint pursuit of the "Road to India," several of these partners were allied in another commercial endeavor. Benton had fought to help the Chouteaus in their legal pursuits of securing the critical Dubuque Spanish Land Claim and the Tesson Spanish Land Claim at the head of the strategic Des Moines Rapids on the Mississippi. Thomas Reddick had previously secured the Tesson Spanish grant from Joseph Robideaux. It was deemed essential for the future greatness of St. Louis to control the upper Mississippi and monopolize the lead trade from Dubuque and Galena. So committed was Benton to these pursuits that he had risked all at Bloody Island. But the Des Moines Rapids posed a unique and challenging natural foe.

Reddick was unable to reverse the course of the bank's plight. When the Bank of Missouri failed, Benton was personally charged a debt of nearly seven thousand dollars to the government due to the depository sums lost under their charge. Benton was not frugal in his lifestyle and enjoyed his political perks and appearance of wealth. It took most of his life to repay this debt.[28]

The Missouri State Assembly met late in 1820 to select its first two senators. Lucas made known his desires, as did both Benton and David Barton. After heated debate, Barton secured thirty-four votes, Benton twenty-seven votes, and John Lucas sixteen votes.[29] Barton and Benton were duly elected freshmen senators from Missouri. John Lucas extended his resolve to attack Benton publicly whenever given the chance. Animosity toward Benton, remained a serious unresolved matter.

Senator elect Benton immediately involved himself in issues pertaining to the Oregon Territory, while he awaited full senator status to be established after Missouri was declared officially a state. After meeting with Ramsay Crooks of New York and Russell Farnham of Massachusetts, both employed by the American Fur Company in the Northwest Territory, Benton wrote some essays regarding the need for a legislative committee to review the status of the Oregon Territory.

The uncle to Benton's wife, Elizabeth McDowell, was General John Floyd, a Congressman from Virginia who was selected as chairman of the Oregon Committee proposed by Benton in 1820. This committee suggested a bill be presented "to authorize the occupation of the Columbia River, and to regulate trade and intercourse with the Indian tribes thereon."[30] To secure, maintain, and expand the "Road to India," the British had to be evicted. Though unsuccessful by vote, it did alert the Congress to the critical issues involved.

Benton, as a leading advocate, identified critical considerations for a review of the American policy regarding the Oregon Territory:

- For the establishment of a port to shelter commercial and military vessels

- For the protection of the fur trade
- To secure aid to whaling vessels
- To realize the vision of Jefferson of commercial trade to Asia (this was according to Benton the legislative beginnings of the quest for a North American "Road to India")[31]

While meeting at Brown's Hotel on Pennsylvania Avenue, Washington, DC, the place of Benton's residence, Ramsay Crooks and Russell Farnham, representing Astor's American Fur Company, discussed the strategy wherein Benton would debate in Senate Hall the merits of closing the much abused and antiquated factory system with its twenty-two locations. Benton introduced the bill in March 1822 and was passed three months later. With gratitude, Crooks wrote to Benton, "You deserve the unqualified thanks of the community for destroying the pious monster."[32] As a reward, the American Fur Company again engaged Benton in another matter.

Knowledge of the secret in South Pass originated with Ramsay Crooks. After his perilous trek, his employer John Astor ordered the discovery silenced. Their unique knowledge could prove greatly fortuitous if it could be exploited before others happened on the same sojourn. Astor, Crooks, and the Chouteaus needed Benton's help and received it as planned.

Benton's bill, calling for the closure of the government-controlled Indian trading areas, also included a provision creating the new position of United States Superintendent for Indian Affairs. Naturally, Benton had flexed his political might to have his friend and fellow St. Louis Junto member William Clark appointed to fill the new position. The Chouteaus leading the St. Louis Junto were still under the domination of the American Fur Company. With the new appointment, Clark's scope of authority extended to all the Indian lands of the settled United States, which included thirty-six Indian nations. He reported only to the president and secretary of war and was charged with issuing trading licenses and entry permits for all traders and travelers in Indian settlements.

Clark was to work with the US Army in negotiating treaties, establishing tribal boundaries, arresting lawbreakers, and settling disputes regarding the various Indian tribes. Reporting to him were fifteen Indian agencies and ten sub-agencies, and included on the payroll were agents, interpreters, blacksmiths, and clerks.

After the law was passed, the US Indian office sent instructions to Governor Clark:

> In order to satisfy the Indians and to induce them to give assent freely to this measure, you are authorized to distribute among them, presents, in goods, to such amount as may be necessary . . . on as reasonable terms as possible.[33]

Few recognized the magnitude of what the junior senator from Missouri had accomplished with his Congressional peers. Benton had closed down the federal government trading post network while alleging mismanagement and replaced the national system with himself as the Senate Chairman of the Committee of Indian Affairs, William Clark, as the national Superintendent of Indian Affairs, and the Chouteaus and Pierre Menard paid by the government to assist in negotiating treaties with the Indian tribes and were granted many of the exclusive licenses for trading with the same Indian tribes.

This new structure allowed William Clark to negotiate treaties and set the amounts of annual annuities the government would fund the Indian tribes. Senator Benton was in the position to ensure Congressional acceptance of the treaties and annuities negotiated by Clark. When the annuity payments were made to the Indians, they usually had nowhere to spend it other than the many Chouteau-operated trading forts operating under the American Fur Company network. The entire system was being managed primarily by key leaders of the previously aligned members of the St. Louis Junto.

Under Benton's legislative arrangement, notice was given for the Osage chiefs to meet at Marais des Cygnes in Missouri to receive gifts in return for the closing of Fort Osage, established by treaty in 1808. Chief Cheveux Blancs, the younger, lead the Osage and accepted the sum of $2,329 in merchandise on August 31. Chouteau attended to support the transaction.[34]

Senator Benton was willing to flaunt his successes to his home constituency. In his newspaper, the *St. Louis Enquirer*, he triumphantly reported,

> Since the abolition of the United States factories, a great activity has prevailed in the operation of this trade. Those formerly engaged . . . increased their capital and extended their enterprises; new firms have engaged in it, and others are preparing to. . . . The Missouri Fur Company, which alone employs upwards of 300 men, has reached the mountains and will soon be on the Columbia River. Others have the same destination.[35]

As planned, George Sibley (previous factor), Lilburn Boggs (deputy factor), and Paul Baillio (subagent), all former management of the government-owned Fort Osage, signed an agreement to purchase the balance of the inventory of trade goods still remaining at the Fort. Sibley signed personally for the loan of approximately seven thousand dollars to the government for their partnership. Benton, the crafty politician, in this masterful stroke had managed to put Astor and his massive American Fur Company, George Sibley, and Lilburn Boggs in his debt.

This group of Sibley, Boggs, and Baillio were quite confident of a successful enterprise. They were well known to the Indians and many of the trappers and traders. While in St. Louis, Boggs had become familiar with George Sibley as a close neighbor. Seeking an opportunity to strike out on his own in 1819, Lilburn Boggs left employment with Chouteau, Benton, Reddick, and Pilcher of the Bank of Missouri to start a store in Franklin. While there, the opportunity to work with Sibley presented itself, and he became Sibley's deputy factor at Fort Osage.

Anxious to continue his legislative momentum and making the most of his initial years in the Senate, Benton introduced two other key bills. For the "junto," his bill called for the Federal District Court in Missouri to dispose of the old land claims and to settle them based on Spanish or French legal procedures and precedent rather than on English or American procedures.

In April, he presented before the Senate a statute calling for the private operation of the government-owned lead mines. Challenging the benefits of government control, Benton went directly on the attack against then Secretary of War John Calhoun, who had oversight responsibility on administering the lead mine-leasing policies. This bill, however, failed, but Benton had struck a damaging blow in favor of various Missouri constituents, especially the Chouteaus, who held a massive Spanish claim for the Dubuque mines.

He had sent a powerful message that his thirteen-point agenda was aggressively on track. Other hopeful beneficiaries were waiting their turn for Benton patronage.

Joshua Pilcher, anxious to move the upper Missouri plan forward, built on the original site of Manuel Lisa's Fort Raymond, of fifteen years earlier, a new wooden picket enclosed fort he named Fort Benton, after his friend and ally. They were determined to benefit from the secret South Pass access before others could secure it.

Having wintered at Fort Benton, Robert Jones, Michael Immell, and several others in their party, all employees of Joshua Pilcher's new Missouri Fur Company, were sent to the Blackfoot Nation with instructions "to obtain a friendly interview with the Blackfoot Indians . . . and to impress them with the friendly disposition of American citizens toward them."[36] They were attacked by a Blackfoot war party, killing Jones, Immell, and five others, with four more wounded. The wounded and others in the party narrowly escaped across the Yellowstone River into a Crow village, where they were given shelter. The Blackfeet stole their traps, horses, provisions, and pelts, valued at more than fifteen thousand dollars, which devastated this newer version of the Missouri Fur Company as well.

Expanding his reach and influence, in December 1824, Benton received a petition from "sundry inhabitants" of Missouri requesting aid in protecting the Santa Fe Trail caravans departing from and returning to Jackson County. He had the petition sent directly to him as Senate Committee Chairman over Indian Affairs. The real motive behind Benton's legislative intervention was to corner the silver and gold market coming from the New Mexican trade.

During the Congressional Christmas recess that year, he met with an ailing President Jefferson at Monticello. Jefferson disclosed to Benton the existence of an old map housed in the Library of Congress that would aid Benton in trade route negotiations for the Santa Fe Trail. They also engaged in various political discussions. It was a proud moment for Benton, who felt from that time on that he alone had been endowed with the Jefferson mantle for Western Expansion to the Pacific Coast and beyond to Asia and on to global commercial dominance.[37]

During 1825, the subject of the Oregon Territory again was voiced in the halls of Congress. Senator Benton summarized the basis for America's claim to that region:

- Discovery of the Columbia River by Captain Gray in 1790
- Purchase of the Louisiana Territory in 1803
- Discovery by Lewis and Clark of the entire length of the Columbia River
- Settlement of Astoria in 1811
- The Treaty with Spain in 1819
- Continuous possession of the region (Benton felt Britain had no valid Oregon claim)

Benton again reiterated the purposes in securing the Oregon Territory from the British:

- To keep out a foreign power
- To gain a seaport with a naval and military presence on the Pacific Ocean
- To save the fur trade and prevent British interference with the Indians against them
- For commercial trade between the Mississippi River and the Pacific
- To send the lights of science and religion to eastern Asia[38]

Benton was doing his best to resurrect the Astor global enterprise pursuit and Jefferson's similar "Road to India" vision. Astoria had previously been overrun by the British presence. Benton was looking to oust the British from what rightfully belonged to America and win the victory for Astor, the American Fur Company, and the St. Louis Junto. For the pompous and arrogant Benton, those coattails still were not long enough. Benton was focused on the other components of his previous thirteen-point agenda.

Upon returning to the Senate, Benton there presented a long letter answering twenty-two questions submitted by Augustus Storrs of his home state, advocating for Santa Fe merchant support. This letter was circulated by Hezekiah Niles in the respected *Niles Register* in Baltimore. From there, it continued circulation being picked up by other local newspapers.[39]

Benton allowing first for the Storrs's letter to gain traction, presented to the Senate a bill, to satisfy the inhabitants of Missouri, containing three key measures. First, it authorized commissioners to be appointed to mark a road from Missouri to the Mexican border and to treat with the Indians for peaceful passage. Second, it authorized the president to negotiate with the Mexican authorities to mark the road from the wild Mexican Territory to the New Mexico border. Third, it provided an appropriation of thirty thousand dollars to fund the provisions of the act.

In his Senate speech, Benton referred to his meeting with President Jefferson, and then he presented the map mentioned in their discussion. The map revealed a precedent for one nation marking a road in another nation's territory. Benton continued, "With this triumphant precedent, I leave the fate of the bill to the wisdom and to the justice of the Senate."[40] The Senate approved the bill with a vote of thirty to twelve, and the House likewise approved it. It was signed by President Monroe on March 3, 1825, as one of his last official acts before leaving office. Not missing another opportunity for Benton to extend his patronage, George Sibley was appointed one of the three Commissioners to mark the Santa Fe Trail.

Recognizing the role Fort Osage had played and the commercial potential going forward, Sibley convinced the newly appointed Santa Fe Commission to mark the distance of the Santa Fe Trail beginning at the site of Fort Osage.

Senator Benton was acutely interested in the activities and overall success of the trail marking expedition to Santa Fe. Benton was still focused on developing trade routes with Mexico for more gold and silver bullion. He was anxious to determine if the rivers could provide effective transportation means for merchant trade. He wrote to George Sibley on April 12:

> In executing the late act for marking a road to N. Mexico, you will have an opportunity to become intimately acquainted with the intervening country. . . . A problem yet to be solved, is to ascertain how

> much water transportation can be had between Missouri & Mexico. The trade carried on between them will not be in heavy and bulky articles, such as tobacco, flour, whiskey &c. which require large boats and deep rivers; but it will be in dry goods, and light articles, and small boats and shallow streams may be useful . . . it would be well to ascertain the character of the Kanzas, Osage, Arkansas, and of the Rio del Norte as far as the Passo; the periods of high and low water."[41]

America at the time was still restless for expansion westward. The government would again turn to the Osage to give up more land. Governor William Clark was tasked with reaching out again to the Osage chiefs to meet on June 2, 1825, this time at St. Louis. This treaty called for the Osage to give up all rights to their lands in Missouri and the Arkansas Territory. Sixty chiefs and warriors, of the Great and Little Osage Tribes, gathered for the signing. Terms of the treaty dictated that the Osage receive two thousand dollars for signing and four thousand dollars worth of merchandise to be delivered to their villages. Also, the Osage were to receive seven thousand dollars annually for the next twenty years, plus livestock, a blacksmith, and four homes built for their leading chiefs. The Osage Indian Nation was relocated to a strip of land fifty miles wide in the southern portion of Kansas Territory.

Governor Clark, long trusted by the Osage, claimed this was the hardest treaty he had participated in. He worried he had brought upon himself damnation in the hereafter for his role in this injustice to the proud Osage people. Pierre Chouteau and his son were at the treaty ceremonies to give support. Chouteau had also been a long trusted voice for the Osage.

Senator Benton was again anxious to enlighten George Sibley as to the extreme importance of his mission. He wrote to Sibley from St. Louis on June 30 regarding the Santa Fe road: "It is not a County or State Road, which they have to mark out, but a highway between Nations, and which when once fixed, cannot be altered for Ages & Centuries to come."[42]

Six weeks later, on August 10, the Santa Fe Commissioners signed another treaty with the Osage for rights of way for the Santa Fe Trail through their new territory.

The once noble and mighty Osage of the Missouri had been decimated. Their white allies, the trusted Chouteaus, had sold them out. They surrendered the treasured lands of their forefathers. Their ancient traditions spoke of this region from the days of Creation.

George Sibley would be engaged in the work of the survey commission, taking meticulous time in marking and mapping as they made their way the length of the Santa Fe Trail. He would be gone during 1825 and 1826. In Sibley's absence, Lilburn Boggs acted as his agent in Jackson County, Missouri.

It had been seventeen years since the first communication between Astor and President Jefferson regarding their joint transcontinental vision. During that time, the Erie Canal was being built as a crucial link to westward transportation and commerce and a vital component for the infrastructure to realize the Jefferson, Astor, and Benton quest.

At a quaint village named Palmyra in upstate New York, the famed Erie Canal had brought much excitement and dreams of renewed prosperity. While Thomas Benton was campaigning for the inaugural Senate seats for the new state of Missouri, a young fourteen-year-old lad beheld a divine vision that would prepare for the Restoration of the age of prophets. An angel had entrusted to his care an ancient sacred record of the former inhabitants of the region. A prophet would emerge who would lead his people in the building of a New Jerusalem. That quest for Zion was being aimed on a collision course destined to challenge the might of Senator Benton, Superintendent William Clark, Pierre Chouteau, the patriarch of the Chouteau family dynasty, and the entire hierarchy of the St. Louis Junto.

In 1820, exploration of Major Stephen Long from Pittsburgh to the Rocky Mountains likewise sparked entrepreneurial aspirations of the potential of transcontinental commerce from the East Coast. At Bloody Island, Benton showed he would use nearly any means to eliminate challengers that interfered with his self-proclaimed destiny and his thirteen-point agenda.

An emerging Lilburn Boggs was also coming to his own in power politics and mercantile pursuits. He had apprenticed under the tutelage of the Chouteau empire as bank cashier with seasoned merchants and government mentors such as William Clark and Senator Benton, who were perfecting a system of government preference and patronage.

The battle for Zion was coming.

2: The Upper Missouri Outfit and the Merchant Alliance

Securing the "Road to India"

For Senator Benton, Pierre Chouteau, Superintendent Clark, and others of the St. Louis Junto, the development of the Santa Fe Trail was proceeding well. However, expansion of the fur trade northward to connect with the Columbia River region was aggressively thwarted by other trading groups. In this, their greatest adversary and threat to the success of their quest for the "Road to India" was the Columbia Fur Company lead by Kenneth Mackenzie.

Mackenzie came from Canada after the War of 1812 had concluded against the Americans and bound himself to the North West Company of Montreal as a major fur trading company pursuing Canadian interests. After they merged with the Hudson Bay Company, he moved to St. Louis and joined the Columbia Fur Company. His aggressive skills lead him to leadership there within a few years, and they became a major threat to Astor's developing empire.

From his base at Fort Tecumseh, built in 1822 on the Missouri at the mouth of the Bad River, Mackenzie expanded his trading empire to include seven major fur trading posts and several small winter trading places. He dominated trade with most of the tribes of the Upper Missouri River region, including the Arikara, Mandan, Hidatsa, Teton, Yankton, Ponca, and Omaha Indians. Defiantly, Astor ordered his company to construct competing trading posts near every one of Mackenzie's Columbia trading outposts. Mackenzie was outraged and determined to fight back, but others recognized an alliance was a better alternative.[43]

Ramsay Crooks, representing Astor's interests, set an appointment to meet Mackenzie at Prairie du Chien to begin critical negotiations. As his party approached the Des Moines Rapids, his vessel was halted due to shallow waters. They transferred their provisions to keelboats and proceeded on to their scheduled rendezvous point. Crooks had observed some of Mackenzie's voyageurs and privately judged them as second rate. On August 13, 1826, they arrived at Prairie du Chien. Their initial talks failed to produce meaningful arrangements.

At the same time, Pierre Chouteau was determined to unite with the American Fur Company in a stronger alliance and engaged in conversations with Ramsay Crooks at New York City. On December 20, Chouteau and the firm of Bernard Pratte and Company became the western agents for Astor's massive enterprise. Through early 1831, their respective firms would share equally in profits on the trade of the Mississippi below Prairie du Chien and along the entire Missouri River regions. Bernard Pratte & Company, of which Chouteau was a major owner, assumed management of the new division known as the Western Department of the American Fur Company. Crooks was appointed general superintendent of affairs, and Pierre Chouteau was appointed to lead daily operations with a salary of two thousand dollars and a share of profits.

Pleased with the arrangements set with the Chouteaus, Crooks continued his pursuit of Mackenzie and the Columbia Fur Company. Initially, Mackenzie had sought too excessive a price and overplayed his hand. Patiently, Crooks countered. After various concessions, they came to an agreement by April 1827 for the purchase of the Columbia Fur Company. The recently formed Western Department assumed full control of Missouri River trade and portions of the Upper Mississippi trade, under the new title of the Upper Missouri Outfit (UMO).

Through his skillful negotiations, Ramsay Crooks, a friend of Senator Benton, had created for the Astor empire a great commercial colossus and trade emporium. This company dominated Indian trade from the Arkansas Territory on the south to the Canadian border on the north and from the Wabash River west to the Rocky Mountains. Also included was the prized Santa Fe Trail, engaging various Spanish towns in the New Mexico Territory. In the process, Chouteau and the St. Louis Junto had manipulated dominant control of local affairs for the vast region.

Jackson County: The Key to the Upper Missouri Outfit

To exploit their newfound gains, Pierre Chouteau and his allies sought to fortify their infrastructure extending along the Missouri River and from St. Louis up the Mississippi River to Prairie du Chien. Newly formed Jackson County, Missouri, at the far western border of the United States was to be a primary focus as the key site to provision the merchant trade northward to the upper Missouri River outposts, westward to the Indians of the Kansas and Oklahoma Territories, and southward along the Santa Fe Trail. Chouteau and other St. Louis Junto members recognized the need to better secure commercial traffic on the Mississippi below Prairie du Chien by enhancing their presence at the foot and head of the Des Moines Rapids to control steamboat lightening operations and thereby monopolize the lead trade from Dubuque and Galena.

Pierre Chouteau, nicknamed "Cadet," depended on his stepbrother Francois Chouteau to manage operations of the steamboat landing in Jackson County, Misssouri, in the geographic area known by the French as "Chez les Canses," to support the expanding UMO enterprise.

This site, built to support the loading and unloading of steamships, was named Chouteau's Landing. With merchant goods from St. Louis, this steamboat landing and warehousing center was intended to serve as a great *entrepôt* to service upper Missouri trading posts, Kansas and Oklahoma trading posts, and the Santa Fe Trail.

At this Company post, Francois, aided by brothers Frederick and Cyprien and local hired laborers, performed the tedious tasks of collecting, sorting, packing, and shipping furs brought in by Indians or trappers. In exchange for the furs received, they traded supplies and merchandise shipped from Philadelphia, New York, and London through Cadet's St. Louis operations. They also exchanged produce and other goods supplied from local farmers and merchants. The nearby Kansa and Shawnee Indians also traded for goods at this site using government annuities. The furs were of a common variety, including beaver, raccoon, otter, bear, and deer.

Francois also acted as primary overseer of other Company operations with other family members. Paul Liguest Chouteau's district secured trade with the Osage Indians from Neosho and the area aroung the Marais des Cygnes River in Kansas Territory. Across the Missouri border, their cousin Millicour Papin operated a Company outpost. August Aristide Chouteau monopolized the region near the Verdigris River in the Oklahoma Territory. Auguste Pierre Chouteau dominated the Oklahoma Territory region on the Canadian River near Camp Mason and Fort Holmes.[44] At best, competitors could squeeze some small amounts of trade with a few of the tribes, but the power of the Chouteau trading post empire was overwhelming and growing. All of this increased commercial activity with the Indians occurred with Senator Benton as Senate Chairman of the Committee on Indian Affairs and William Clark as Indian Superintendent. The Benton and Clark patronage network was again expanding.

Independence: The Key to Commerce and Western Trade

The town of Independence was created by the Missouri legislature on the former lands of the Great and Little Osage Indian Nations, which became available for settlement due to the efforts of William Clark and the Chouteaus by negotiating treaties in exchange for increased government annuities. These treaties were approved with the assistance of Senator Benton as the Senate Committee Chairman. From the beginning, this town was founded with the intent of developing a commercial base for international trade along the Santa Fe Trail and for trade with the Indians westward and northward along the Missouri River.

An alliance of several merchants gathered at the Jackson County Courthouse on July 9, 1827, to secure key strategic sites for new mercantile operations. Lilburn Boggs, Samuel Owens, and other merchants had come from the Six Mile Settlement region surrounding the old Fort Osage or directly from the town of Franklin. From these areas, Missouri trade merchants set up store operations to cater to Santa Fe merchants.

This new route lessened travel times for the various trading caravans, laden with merchandise to trade for Mexican gold and silver. This merchants' alliance was important as travel arrangements involving foreign officials and businessmen were complex and the threat of Indian and Mexican bandit attacks was intimidating.

The Jackson County Court conducted the first sale of lots, comprised of 147 parcels on 240 acres over 3 days, beginning July 9, 1827. Many initial inhabitants had gathered with friends from the area of Chouteau's Landing and the Six Mile area surrounding Fort Osage. Merchants engaged in the Santa Fe trade and the Kansas Territory and upper Missouri Indian trade purchased more than twenty-five of the seventy lots sold and in many cases acted collaboratively.

Samuel Owens and partner Ed Wilburn bought lot twenty-one for ten dollars, with Rowland Flournoy as surety. Flournoy family members, Jones, Lawrence, and Solomon (also merchants) purchased two lots each. Sureties for these purchases included other Flournoy family members or Samuel Owens. James Aull of Lexington, the employer of Samuel Owens, purchased lot eleven with County Court Judge Richard Fristoe as security. Gam Johnston and merchant Smallwood V. Noland both purchased lots and acted as security for each other. Thus, the initial land purchases in Independence were transacted as a collective effort by aligned merchants.

Samuel Owens was a visionary entrepreneur. He stood out from other local transplanted citizens, partly by his Southern aristocratic demeanor and partly from his disciplined economic focus. In his youth, he and his siblings had been tutored by scholars handpicked by their overbearing father, Nathaniel Owens. Samuel Owens could not forget his roots.

Lilburn Boggs, also engaged in mercantile pursuits with the nearby Indians and in the Santa Fe trade, with Samuel Owens became de facto leaders of the Jackson County merchants. For these Independence town merchants expectations of massive increases in trade along the Platte River and upper Missouri River routes was mounting as new developments were occurring in the Oregon Territory. They were counting on Senator Benton to clear the obstacles.

Linking Independence to the Oregon Territory

The Joint Occupation Treaty between America and Britain was set to expire during 1828. That treaty specified, "That any country claimed by either party on the northwest coast of America, together with its harbors, bays, and creeks, and the navigation of all rivers within the same, be free and open, for the term of ten years, to the subjects, citizens, and vessels of the two powers; without prejudice to any claim which either party might have to any part of the country."[45]

In Congress, Senators Benton and Floyd vigorously defended the exclusive right of America's claim for the Oregon Territory and sought an end to the Joint Occupation Treaty. In spite of Benton's spirited protestations, the Joint Occupation Treaty with Britain was extended.

For the last decade, Joshua Pilcher had been a close and trusted friend of Thomas Benton. Pilcher had supported Benton's aggressive stand against the Bank of St. Louis. With the aid of Senator Benton, Pilcher was appointed as United States consul to Chihuahua in March 1825.

With that position, he determined other commercial endeavors could be pursued. He envisioned a newly conceived realm extending from Chihuahua north to the Rocky Mountains. He was joined by his partners from the later Missouri Fur Company, including Lucien Fontenelle, William H. Vanderburgh, Andrew Drips, and Charles Bent. These five were licensed by the government to trade for one year at approximately a dozen locations between the mouth of Kansas River and the mouth of the Yellowstone. They put up capital of $7,200 in this make-or-break risky venture. Pilcher sent a letter to the State Department resigning as consul.

Unable to compete with the rejuvenated Western Department of the American Fur Company dominated by Pierre Chouteau, Pilcher sought to dominate trade from Chihuahua to the Rocky Mountains. Pilcher had reasoned why should anyone wear himself out "procuring fire wood, building houses, sawing plank, building boats, farming, and running from one post to another," while all the time losing money?[46]

After stocking up with whiskey in Liberty, Missouri, the group departed westward toward the Platte River. Their plan and perhaps only chance of business survival was to secure furs in the Rocky Mountains through South Pass and the Colorado River region, and then attend the great rendezvous scheduled at Bear Lake in the summer of 1828. During their various trips, the group secured a large quantity of furs, but when cached many of them were badly damaged. Their enterprise again failed, so they returned to Council Bluffs.

Charles Bent was convinced it was time to abandon the fur trade business and tried to secure the merchant trade of the upper Missouri area. Their experience in the Rocky Mountains and the Bear Lake area brought attention to the possibility of an overland route option to connect with the Pacific Ocean. Many still believed the Bonaventura River existed and could provide a river passageway from the Great Basin to the ocean. Others saw the route through South Pass as a viable alternative in case the Missouri River route could not provide access to the Columbia River region. To build a "Road to India," several options had to be considered.

Bent became intrigued with the previous successes of the merchants engaged in the Santa Fe trade. Others of his family and associates followed him. A group of traders met at Fayette, Missouri, to discuss forming a joint caravan for trade in New Mexico. Charles Bent from St. Louis and Samuel Craig Lamme of Independence joined with David Waldo. With Mexican authorities, Waldo negotiated transport and trade permits for Chihuahua and Sonora in September 1828 and followed up by investing in trade goods, mules, and specie.

For their new commercial venture, the group bought trading goods in St. Louis, and then gathered in Independence to launch their developing joint enterprise. Due to the political wrangling of their friend Senator Benton, they were met by a military escort with the approval of President Andrew Jackson. After other various merchants joined them, an informal election process concluded with Charles Bent to serve as captain and David Waldo as secretary of the assembled caravan, consisting of thirty eight wagons and seventy-eight men. The merchant Lilburn Boggs would join his brother-in-law Charles Bent on this landmark expedition.

Conspiracy at Carthage

After their military entourage separated from the caravan at the end of the United States border, a band of Indians attacked them. Samuel Lamme was killed in the ensuing battle. In spite of the tragic personal loss of his friend, David Waldo and company sold about two hundred thousand dollars of merchandise in trade that season.[47] The merchants of Independence were anxious to see the previous efforts of Joshua Pilcher and Charles Bent to expand the Santa Fe and Rocky Mountain trade efforts. These merchants controlled the strategic access point to the New Mexico and Rocky Mountain regions through their location.

The Rise of Lilburn Boggs and Samuel Owens

On the trail, they encountered Indians on the Cimarron River. It was observed by witnesses that traders on this wagon party had barbarously skinned some of the dead Indians.[48] The next season, the Indians of the Cimarron Plains were much more hostile to travelling parties.

Upon his return from New Mexico, Lilburn Boggs was confident there was ample money to be made in the lucrative Santa Fe trade, and he was desperate to counter losses from his previous partnership disaster with George Sibley and Paul Baillio. He was seeking to expand his mercantile pursuits to include trade with the Kansa Indians to redeem their annuity funds, trade to the fur merchants northward in upper Missouri, and trade southward to Santa Fe.

With the death of Samuel Lamme, there existed a void in leadership of the emerging merchant alliance at Independence. A select few were looking to pool their resources and leverage their relationships to seize control.

Lilburn Boggs was confident of his credentials earned spanning nearly twenty years in preparation. Boggs served eighteen months in the War of 1812 and fought in the Battle of Thames and the Battle of Tippecanoe.[49] After the war, he moved to St. Louis, where he was mentored by August Chouteau and Thomas Benton while serving as the cashier for the Bank of Missouri at Chouteau's home. With many others, he became an active proponent of the vision of President Jefferson and the Empire of Liberty. He witnessed the developing stages of the John Astor, Thomas Benton, and the Chouteau's "Road to India" pursuits, supported by the focused entrepreneurial disciplines of the astute members of the St. Louis Junto.

Boggs worked at Fort Osage in its glory years as an assistant factor under the tutelage of his friend George Sibley. When Fort Osage was closed due to Senator Benton's bill, Boggs partnered with Sibley and Paul Baillio, a former associate of Ceran St. Vrain in the merchant business. Over the years, he had become friends with several legendary traders and mountain men, such as William Sublette, Joe Walker, Peg Leg Smith, and Bill Williams.

Boggs had married well into two respected frontier families. He married, in 1813, Julia Bent, daughter of Judge Silas Bent, who would later serve on the Missouri Supreme Court, and sister to Charles and William Bent, adventurous traders and explorers. After her death in 1821, Boggs moved with his mother and family to Fort Osage. Two years later, he married Panthea Boone, daughter of Jesse Boone and granddaughter of the renowned Daniel Boone. With his new wife, Boggs and his two sons, Angus and Henry, moved to the Harmony Indian Agency.

The Harmony Mission had been formed with the full support of the Department of Indian Affairs in Washington in an effort to train the Great Osage in agricultural pursuits and to civilize the local natives with Christianity. George Sibley sent an invitation to Brothers Pixley, Austin, and Bright to establish the mission near a trading location on the Osage River. Soon after his arrival, Boggs was introduced to another missionary, Brother Samuel Newton, who was stationed at the Harmony Mission. Brother Newton successfully built a store at the Harmony Mission outpost.[50]

Lilburn Boggs felt well positioned to finally succeed and prosper in the highly competitive merchant trade in Jackson County, Missouri. He would need to support his family and his desired upper-class lifestyle. He was also committed to advancing his political aspirations and needed to be able to fund his campaigning. Locally, Boggs had developed key political relationships, having served as the first county clerk of Jackson County. He had rubbed shoulders with the local settlers as their postmaster, frontier doctor, and lawyer.[51] Boggs also served four years in the state House of Representatives and the state Senate in 1830. Also, with the aid of well-placed supporters within the ranks of the St. Louis Junto, he felt confident he was on a career path to the leading echelons of political power in the state.

Likewise, Samuel Owens catered to those of various interests and commercial pursuits. He performed legal services for the estate of Antonio Vasquez, an Indian agent. He worked with his partner, James Aull, in various transactions benefitting Francois and Pierre Chouteau.[52] Looking to bolster his commercial standing, Samuel Owens sought traders and trappers to furnish them with provisions, at a rather handsome profit. Owens had served as county treasurer, recorder of deeds, clerk of the county court, and special agent of land sales. He also served as a commissioner in Independence.

It soon became apparent to the increasing ranks of Independence merchants that a loose coalition, consisting of David Waldo, Samuel Owens with his Aull brothers partners, and the merchant politician Lilburn Boggs, were filling the previous void in local mercantile leadership and international trade.[53] At the same time, the regional and national infrastructure fostering their local alliance coupled with the Francois Chouteau lead Kansas, Oklahoma, and Missouri regional trading monopoly was advancing under the united forces mounted by the St. Louis Junto elite, including Pierre Chouteau, Senator Benton, and Superintendent William Clark.

In St. Louis, Cadet Chouteau continued to struggle with strengthening the Mississippi River region of the Upper Missouri Outfit. Access to the lead mines in Dubuque and Galena were important to Chouteau, Benton, Clark, and the other members of the Junto. Critical to this region was securing the Des Moines River Rapids.

Jackson County: The Key to Supplying the Indian Tribes after the Removal Act of 1830

With Benton's support and oversight in President Jackson's inner circle, the administration passed the Indian Removal Act in 1830. It was their intent to remove all the Indian tribes from their homelands to relocate in the Kansas and Oklahoma Territories. William Clark would participate in the treaty negotiations of all the new tribes reassigned. As the various Indian tribes relocated to the west of Missouri's border, they were provided with new yearly annuity payments, much of which would again be spent at Chouteau-controlled trading forts.

Once the Indians vacated their ancestral homelands, the lands they previously occupied were sold by the federal government to settlers under prior legislative acts while recognizing preemption right clauses. Benton relished his developing persona as the working man's politician and friend to the downtrodden farmer and settler. By opening up large new land for settlement, Senator Benton was able to secure voter loyalty from the new landowners and thus provided for himself an ever growing base to sustain him in power.

Besides the Chouteau's trading forts, various other merchants and trade groups were drawn to Jackson County in support of the Indian trade and fur trappers in the western country. Independence was also the last site where goods could be transported on the Missouri River destined for the Santa Fe Trail merchants and travelers. Warehouses were built and assorted businesses continued to gather, making Independence a major center for commerce; supplying merchant goods for the Santa Fe Trail, the Platte, and upper Missouri River trade; and the expanding base of Indian reservations brought about by the 1830 Removal Act.

Land purchases were filed at the Recorders Office in Lexington. In 1830, Senator Benton flexed his political might to appoint his close friend and campaign organizer, Reverend Finis Ewing, to the position of land recorder. Nationally, Benton was recognized as a leading advocate for the sale of government lands opened up by the departing Indian tribes for public sale with preemption rights. This area and the Boonslick Region of counties were the primary political strength geographic areas for Senator Benton and his fellow Democrats.

Mastering the Rivers

The maiden voyage of the steamboat, *Yellow Stone*, began in St. Louis on May 16, 1831, to extend westward to Jackson County and northward up the Missouri River toward the Rocky Mountains. The visionary for this bold project was Pierre Jr. (Cadet) Chouteau himself. This single engine side-wheeler steamship was expected to afford their company, the Upper Missouri Outfit (UMO), dominance in the fur trade. With its shallow six-foot draft, this steamship could navigate the treacherous Missouri currents, concealed sandbars, logs, snags, and roots. The route plan was to transport supplies in the spring for their fur trading partners for two thousand miles upriver from St. Louis, and then reload with stored tons of furs, hides, and pelts on the return voyage.

Francois Chouteau and his associates at Ches Les Canses were to provide ten cords of wood for the *Yellow Stone* to take on near the mouth of the Kansas River for fuel to continue upriver. While at this landing site, residents of Westport, Independence, and northward could engage in the lucrative benefits of the imports and exports handled.

Sail-powered keelboats had been the dominant means of transport along the Missouri River, but winds rarely blew in the right direction. Manpower generally propelled the keelboats, laden with up to twenty tons of furs or trade goods. These keelboats could travel up to fifteen miles a day. In contrast, steamboats could carry seventy-five tons of cargo and travel twenty miles a day upstream and a hundred miles a day downstream.

The *Yellow Stone* arrived at Fort Tecumseh on June 19, with Chouteau on board. He learned that during the spring the high water of the Missouri had endangered the fort. He knew that the success of his steamboat voyage would propel much more trade, necessitating the need for a larger and less risky site. Chouteau ordered construction of a new fort at a more secure site. Leaving Fort Tecumseh, the *Yellow Stone* was reloaded with buffalo robes, furs, and pelts and ten thousand pounds of buffalo tongues, destined for St. Louis. The experiment worked in a most promising fashion, and Cadet with his partners Bernard Pratte and Jean P. Cabanne dramatically broadened the prospects for the St. Louis Junto. John Astor wrote from France, "Your voyage in the *Yellow Stone* attracted much attention in Europe and had been noted in all the papers here."[54]

The second voyage of the *Yellow Stone* far surpassed the previous year's destination at Fort Tecumseh, continuing up the Yellowstone River to Fort Union, about eighty miles from the Canadian border. This fort, erected in 1829, served as a base for fur gathering by the Crees, Assiniboines, and other Missouri River tribes in the Rocky Mountains. Mackenzie moved his primary base of operations because this was the site of the richest beaver country in North America. It provided a critical source of revenues for the Chouteaus. For Senator Benton, he had hoped these new developments would further support

Fort Benton begun in 1822 by Joshua Pilcher, located more than two hundred miles further southwest on the Yellowstone River.

By the spring of 1832, the Chouteau family trading empire had grown to other locations to service the newly transplanted Indian tribes resulted from the Relocation Act. Frederick Chouteau had his own trading operations at Horseshoe Lake on the Kansas River, and his brother Cyprien was managing the Shawnee Reserve in Kansas Territory. The dominating Chouteau empire was comprised of Cadet in St. Louis, supported by Francois at Chouteau's Landing and kinsmen, Auguste Pierre, Liguest, Cyprien, Charles, Frederick, Auguste Aristide, Cerre, and cousin Millicour Papin, spread out in Kansas and the Oklahoma Territories—several of whom were also on the government payroll as Indian Agents. These were all under the direct administration of Superintendent Clark and his Indian agents, including Richard Cummins of Jackson County.

The American Fur Company (St. Louis Segment) Hires Mark Aldrich

Mark Aldrich and his young bride, Margaret Wilkinson, boarded the Steamboat *Red Rover*, heading north with great expectations for his new assignment with the American Fur Company. Her father was an army surgeon stationed at Jefferson Barracks, near St. Louis. They were married at that post in 1829. Aldrich had been employed by John Jacob Astor's Company in that region but was reassigned. At Keokuk, Aldrich took over the fur trading post set up by Russell Farnham, who was still managing the Fort Edwards site. With the closing of the factory system lead by Senator Benton after 1822, Fort Edwards was structurally and economically in decline.

To house the workers of the American Fur Company, a row of hewed log homes were constructed and referred to as "Rat Row." Distant neighbors included Dr. Isaac Galland and his family living near the Mississippi, seven miles to the north. When the opportunity arose, Aldrich brought his young wife across the Mississippi to Fort Edwards and worked directly with Russell Farnham. Aldrich built their new home just outside the fort. Farnham was a great mentor.

With the outbreak of the Black Hawk War that same year, Galland also moved to Fort Edwards with his then fourth wife, Elizabeth

Wilcox, sister to the commander of the fort, John Wilcox. During his stay, Galland was given the rank of Colonel in the 59th Regiment of the Illinois Militia[55] and had frequent contact with Aldrich.

During the late 1820s and early 1830s, the once-mighty Sauks and Fox Tribes were seemingly at war on two fronts. The Dakota Sioux were fighting to force them off the lands west of the Great Mississippi, which the American government had given by treaty. To the east of the Mississippi, settlers and miners were encroaching on the lands the government had given them.

Taking on the Des Moines Rapids

The St. Louis Junto leadership was attempting to restructure their Mississippi River Commerce monopoly around the ore and fur trading industries. While the fight to secure their claim on the Dubuque Spanish Mines continued, with Senator Benton leading the charge through the Legislative Branch, the local trading forts needed to be reinforced. Russell Farnham had risked his life to advance the global vision of the Astoria settlement, and it became his reassigned duty to secure the Keokuk region, as it represented the critical steamboat landing site at the foot of the Des Moines Rapids.

Thomas Reddick was to expand and secure the Montrose region at the head of the Des Moines Rapids. Joshua Pilcher was the interim Indian agent at Rock Island in charge of assisting the Junto develop that relay point. Rock Island was a strategic point on the Mississippi between Dubuque and the Des Moines Rapids. Senator Benton was using his clout to get Pilcher's position as Indian Agent at Rock Island made permanent.

The Junto wanted to control the massive output of the lead operations of Dubuque and Galena and supplement that with a connected network of fur trading operations along the Mississippi River down to the St. Louis main *entrepôt*. To complement these pursuits, Senator Benton was still focused on trying to secure legislation to fund and advance the Illinois and Michigan Canal to link with the Erie Canal system. The advancements of the fur trade, lead mining, and the Illinois Michigan Canal were all important components of his thirteen-point agenda of 1819. Another great challenge yet remained. The treacherous nature of the Des Moines Rapids limited steamboat traffic to just a few months each year. Engineering assistance would need to be solicited from the federal government through the Army Corps of Engineers.

Frustrated by the favoritism granted the American Fur Company, agent Thomas Forsyth plead to Superintendent Clark in regards to the cutthroat tactics of the American Fur Company: "It appears hard to me that the Indian property should be stolen, their huts torn down and burned down, and their persons insulted by Strangers." He further expressed his hopes to Clark that "our Government will render some justice to those Indians, and not encourage those intruders."[56]

Clark arranged for a council to be conducted at Prairie du Chien to settle with the Indians. He was fearful that the Sauks and Fox delegations would not attend. He noted that they "have more national character than any tribes we have within this Superintendency, . . . and a firm and decisive course is necessary with them."[57]

The Tribal Council was opened on July 7, 1830. After a week of negotiations, Chief Keokuk and 112 other chiefs and tribal leaders signed the treaty to cede a forty-mile section of land in Iowa Territory to the US government. In return, they were granted ten years of an annual annuity of $2,500 and blacksmith services. In response, a disappointed Chief Big Elk of the Omahas expressed that "ten winters" was not nearly enough for his people. "In that time I may be dead . . . and what am I to leave to my children?"[58] The American Fur Company with the St. Louis Junto had won again. Senator Benton and his cronies readily accepted the deal, and it was approved through Congress.

The near total monopoly of the Indian trade controlled by Senator Benton, William Clark, and the Chouteaus, along with various business enterprises in support, was about to be challenged by a new type of competitor. Likewise, the alliance of Independence merchants in Jackson County lead by Lilburn Boggs and Samuel Owens, who were dominating New Mexico trade by organizing caravans to Santa Fe, were soon to be competing with an unanticipated rival. The leader of this new emerging threat to the St. Louis Junto and the Independence merchants claimed to be a prophet sent by God to a place called the New Jerusalem in Jackson County, Missouri. The corruptions of Senator Benton, Superintendent Clark, and Pierre Chouteau—as well as the abusive and greedy practices of the entire vast Chouteau network and their allies in Jackson County—needed to be challenged and abated. A prophet, called of God, was being raised for that purpose.

3: The Mormons Are Expelled from Jackson County

Oliver Cowdery, Peter Whitmer Jr., Ziba Peterson, and Parley P. Pratt were huddled in an Indian lodge on the plains of Kansas Territory, waiting for their turn to speak. They were surrounded by forty tribal leaders of the Delaware Nation. The chief motioned for them to address the gathering. Elder Cowdery arose and testified from his heart,

> Thousands of moons ago, when the red men's forefathers dwelt in peace and possessed this whole land, the Great Spirit talked with them, and revealed His law and His will, and much knowledge to their wise men and prophets.[59]

Elder Cowdery continued his message to this captive audience, indicating that the Book of Mormon contained the history and prophecies of the "things which should befall their children in the latter days." He promised if they would follow the teachings of the Book of Mormon, the "Great Father" would assist them to prosperity and a return to their former greatness. Chief Anderson appreciated their heartfelt messages and said, "It makes us glad in here," while placing his hand over his heart. The concerned chief continued,

> It is now winter, we are new settlers in this place; the snow is deep, our cattle and horses are dying, our wigwams are poor; we have much to do in the spring—to build houses, and fence and make farms; but we will build a council house, and meet together, and you shall read to us and teach us more concerning the Book of our fathers and the will of the Great Spirit.[60]

The elders continued teaching, and several of the Indians were desirous to learn more. Copies of the Book of Mormon were distributed and gratefully received. Chief William Anderson, an elderly Indian chief of the Delaware Tribe, born of a Scandinavian father and Indian mother, listened to the message of the Mormon elders, and then he too spoke from his heart. Missouri Protestant ministers had earlier attempted to preach to Chief Anderson, but to no avail.

Oliver Cowdery Writes to Superintendent William Clark

The prescribed order of dealing with these Indians had been challenged by outsiders. Isaac McCoy had control of the nearby Harmony Mission. Lilburn Boggs was also allied with the Harmony Mission leaders. The locals felt they knew what was best for the Indians. Indian agents were notified the Mormon elders were preaching on Indian lands without permits. They were ordered to leave until they had permission from Superintendent Clark to return.

Heeding their instructions, Elder Cowdery wrote to Superintendent Clark on February 14, 1831. In the letter, Elder Cowdery reported it was their intent to establish schools for the Indians as others were, but they would not interfere with any other Mission established to teach the Indians. Promptly, the local Indian Agent, Richard Cummins of Jackson County, wrote to Superintendent Clark of the Mormon request:

> They say they are sent by god and must preach, they have a new Revelation with them, as [their] guide in teaching the Indians, which they say was shown to one of their sect in a miraculous way, and that an angel from heaven appeared to one of their men and two others of their sect, and showed them that the work was from God and much more etc. I have refused to let them stay, or, go among the Indians unless they first obtain permission from you.[61]

Superintendent William Clark apparently chose not to reply to their request.[62] A capable administrator, Clark simply filed the two letters he had received from Cowdery and Cummins. Another letter came from Agent Cummins the month earlier, reporting of the failure of the McCoy Harmony Mission for the Delaware and Shawnee Indians. Cummins observed, "I have not been able to find one that was willing to send his Child so far from home even if the schooling would come gratis."[63] Even so, the missionaries were unable to return to their Lamanite friends. Discouraged, they removed to nearby Independence to preach to the locals.

Preparing to Establish Zion

With much contemplation about Zion, and during great anticipation by the Saints, the Prophet Joseph received instructions to prepare for the call to build Zion on March 7, 1831:

> And with one heart and with one mind, gather up your riches that ye may purchase an inheritance which shall hereafter be appointed unto you.
>
> And it shall be called the New Jerusalem, a land of peace, a city of refuge, a place of safety for the saints of the Most High God;
>
> And the glory of the Lord shall be there, and the terror of the Lord also shall be there, insomuch that the wicked will not come unto it, and it shall be called Zion.
>
> And it shall come to pass among the wicked, that every man that will not take his sword against his neighbor must needs flee unto Zion for safety.
>
> And there shall be gathered unto it out of every nation under heaven; and it shall be the only people that shall not be at war one with another.
>
> And it shall be said among the wicked: Let us not go up to battle against Zion, for the inhabitants of Zion are terrible; wherefore we cannot stand.
>
> And it shall come to pass that the righteous shall be gathered out from among all nations, and shall come to Zion, singing with songs of everlasting joy. (D&C 45:65–71)

It became a matter of frequent and passionate discussion as to when and where the Lord would reveal the site of Zion. On July 20, 1831, Independence, Missouri, was revealed as the center place of Zion. The whole of the surrounding country, to the westward regions, was to be purchased as the lands of promise for their inheritance. Sidney Gilbert was appointed agent to receive monies for the Church and establish a store where profits would be dispensed to purchase additional lands. Bishop Partridge was to stand in this office and divide the inheritances. Then came a revelation and a voice of warning:

> Ye cannot behold with your natural eyes, for the present time, the design of your God concerning those things which shall come hereafter, and the glory which shall follow after much tribulation.
>
> For after much tribulation come the blessings. Wherefore the day cometh that ye shall be crowned with much glory; the hour is not yet, but is nigh at hand. (D&C 58:3–4)

They were called to lay the foundation of Zion, but before the New Jerusalem could be built, the Saints had to endure great tribulation to be worthy of such a noble cause. Not all the Saints were to come to this land right away, and not all would be found worthy. During this time, a small body of Saints left Thompson, Ohio, and settled in Kaw Township, just to the west of Independence. Here, they established the Colesville Branch. The law of consecration, also referred to as the United Order of Enoch, was given to apply to all who receive an inheritance in Zion. Each person would receive enough property to support his family. It was not a communal plan because the family owned the property privately.

The temple site, consisting of sixty-three acres, was purchased by Edward Partridge from Jones Hoy Flournoy, a merchant friend of Lilburn Boggs and Samuel Owens. To press forward with his divine mandate, the Prophet gathered the Saints for a solemn occasion on August 3. The dedication service proceeded with a reading from Psalm 87, extolling the glory and majesty of Zion. A single stone was situated in the southeast corner as a perimeter marker.

After the sacred services were completed and other preparations made, the leaders began their trek back to Kirtland. The Prophet's company, transported by canoes on the Missouri River, rested the first night at the old Fort Osage. On the third day, Elder Phelps reported a vision from which he witnessed "the destroyer in his most horrible power" riding upon the water (D&C 61:4–5). Joseph Smith later instructed that the waters of the Great Missouri River in this area held particular dangers for travelers. There was indeed an unsavory element of dangerous men patrolling along the river anxious to rob and molest wayward travelers. The current of the Missouri River was also dangerous, particularly to the infrequent traveler unaware of sandbars, floating logs, and cross currents. Storms could wreak havoc as well.

Prices for the various land parcels in Jackson County were set before their arrival. Late in December the previous year, the Missouri General Assembly passed an act providing for the sale of the secured seminary lands, at a price not less than two dollars per acre. Sales were made of these seminary lands, and other public lands in the fall of 1831 at Independence, Palmyra, and Benton. Lots sold at $1.25 an acre in blocks of eighty acres or more. The Mormons participated in the purchase of seminary lands, which later funded the University of Missouri. The seminary and government lands were cheap and often better than the land held by the old settlers who selected wooded hillsides as home sites. Saints were advised to buy improved lands from the old settlers.

The Enoch Prophecy Is Revealed

As the year continued, the old settlers of Jackson County continued to get more apprehensive at the rapid growth of the Mormon population and of their revelations. Also, the commercial network in the County were further aligning to dominate trade with the Indians, fur traders, and Santa Fe merchants, of which the Mormons were becoming a growing threat.

In the August 1832 issue of the *Evening and Morning Star*, William Phelps printed an article regarding "Excerpts from the Enoch Prophecy." The article began,

> Enoch continued, . . . Behold our father Adam taught these things, and many have believed and become the sons of God, and many have believed not and perished in their sins, and are looking forth with fear, in torment, for the fiery indignation of the wrath of God to be poured out upon them.—And from that time forth Enoch began to prophesy. . . .

> And it came to pass that Enoch continued to call upon all the people, save it were the people of Canaan, to repent: And so great was the faith of Enoch that he lead the people of God, and their enemies came to battle against them, and he spake the word of the Lord, and the earth trembled: and the mountains fled; . . . and the rivers of water were turned out of their course; and the roar of the lions was heard out of the wilderness; and all nations feared greatly, so powerful was the word of Enoch.

For the non-Mormon citizens, this publication was the only newspaper around. In print, the Mormons claimed God was on their side and that all others needed to fear God's wrath.

> And the Lord called his people Zion, because they were of one heart and one mind, and dwelt in righteousness; and there was no poor among them; and Enoch continued his preaching in righteousness unto the people of God. And it came to pass in his days, that he built a city that was called the city of holiness, even Zion. And it came to pass that Enoch talked with the Lord. . . .
>
> And he saw angels descending out of heaven; and he heard a loud voice, saying, Wo, wo, be unto the inhabitants of the earth! And he beheld Satan, and he had a great chain in his hand, and it veiled the whole face of the earth with darkness, and he looked up and laughed, and his angels rejoiced. And Enoch beheld angels descending out of heaven bearing testimony of the Father and Son; and the Holy Spirit fell on many, and they were caught up by the powers of heaven into Zion. . . .
>
> And he cried. . . . When shall the day of the Lord come? When shall the blood of the righteous be shed, that all they that mourn may be sanctified, and have eternal life? And the Lord said, It shall be in the meridian of time, in the days of wickedness and vengeance. . . . Enoch saw the day of the coming of the Son of man, even in the flesh. . . .
>
> And the Lord said unto Enoch, . . . I come in the last days, . . . to fulfill the oath . . . concerning the children of Noah; and the day shall come that the earth shall rest, but before that day the heavens shall be darkened, and a veil of darkness shall cover the earth; and the heavens shall shake, and also the earth; and great tribulations shall be among the children of men, but my people will I preserve . . . to gather out my own elect from the four quarters of the earth unto a place which

> I shall prepare; a holy city, that my people may gird up their loins, and be looking forth for the time of my coming; for there shall be my tabernacle, and it shall be called Zion, a New Jerusalem.[64]

The understanding of this prophecy had been revealed in Fayette, New York, during November and December 1830 and became Moses 7, which describes the City of Enoch being built, a city that was called the City of Holiness, even Zion (see Moses 7:19). This revelation provided the model and blueprint for the building of Zion. It proved most upsetting to many of the local Jackson County residents.

Mormon Life in Independence

David Pettegrew was a former Indiana resident. While visiting in Cincinnati, Ohio, in 1832, he was baptized into the Church by Isaac Higbee and was there given a letter of recommendation to the bishop of Missouri. He continued from Ohio with his family on a steamship destined for the place of Zion and the New Jerusalem in Jackson County. During the journey, several of the passengers contracted cholera, which had been sweeping through the entire region. Their voyage group was instructed to disembark when their steamboat became lodged on a sandbar at the mouth of the Ohio River.

While detained, two family members were likewise stricken: Pettegrew's wife and son Hiram contracted the deadly disease. Among the passengers were other Mormon families and, in particular, two Mormon elders: Solomon Hancock and Daniel Stanton.

> Through which means we found great blessing in the ordinance of the House of God, in laying on of hands upon the sick, though done in secret yet we believed that they were saved by that ordinance.[65]

By the time they arrived in St. Louis, both had regained strength. They continued on their journey to Franklin, where their passage was interrupted by ice on the river. After providing comfortable temporary lodging for his family, Pettegrew departed for Independence alone.

Pettegrew later recorded a particularly unique occurrence he had while on his way to Independence with one of the local ministers in the area:

> On the fourth day of my journey I arrived at a Mr. Ewing, a wealthy farmer, residing near Lexington County, and put up for the night. I was conducted to a room where there were several gentlemen . . . amongst whom was the Reverend Finas (Finis) Ewing, leader of the Cumberland Presbyterian Church, a man of great influence in this section of the country and also a receiver of public monies at Lexington. He spoke freely upon various subjects . . . then turned to me and said, "Sir, not that I wish to hurt a man's feelings or injure him in any way, but Sir, I would like to ask you a few questions." I told him certainly, any that I was able to answer I should do so with pleasure. "Well, Sir, I wish to know if you are a Mormon?" to which I answered that I had but lately joined that people and I was now on my way to see them, and my family was at old Franklin. . . . I replied that I had professed to be a convert many years ago, that I had been a member of the Methodist Church until I joined the Mormons, . . . and that I was now on my way to their place of meeting. . . . "Sir," said he, "you have gone far enough after those deluded people, you have given way to seducing spirits and believe doctrines of the Devil that you may be damned," and thus he went. . . . "But you have gone far enough, my advice to you, Sir, is to go back to your former church, and as for these deluded Mormons who are gathering in Jackson County, or Zion, as those deluded monsters talk about, I heard a Methodist minister yesterday morning say that he was at Independence the day before and heard the Mormons say that they had a revelation from God that they should possess that land by blood, if they could not get it otherwise, and we shall be under the necessity of going to Jackson County with our guns and bayonets and drive the Mormons from that county, before one year rolls around."[66]

Shortly thereafter, Pettegrew, ignoring the advice of Reverend Ewing, purchased a farm of 159 acres located six miles west of Independence, immediately upon the Big Blue River and on the main road leading to Fort Leavenworth and the Shawnee Indian Agency. Some of his neighbors in the "Big Blue Settlement" Branch included his friend Solomon Hancock, Horace Strong Rawson, Malin Johnson, David Dutton, David Bennett, George Burkett, Abraham Towner, David Frampton, John Carson Gates, Abel Sergeant, Isaac Sampson, John Brush, Isaac Higbee, and Orrin Porter Rockwell, who operated the ferry crossing on the Blue River.

While working his farm, Pettegrew, with his family, enjoyed the fellowship of the Saints as they practiced the priesthood in the "same order that was in ancient days." He accepted the great challenge given from the elders and consecrated his land to Bishop Partridge, who then laid it off into seven inheritances. These inheritances were at that time for himself, Elizabeth Alden Pettegrew (his wife), and Lucey Ann, Betsey Ann, Caroline Keziah, Lydia Louisa, David Alden, Hiram Ring Solomon, and James Phineas (his children). He recorded,

> We strove to live in harmony and righteousness. I hired labor and improved my farm; I purchased oxen, cows and farming utensils, and in a short time I had everything around in a flourishing condition. The Santa Fe and Rocky Mountain traders often passed by my house-large companies, well armed, wagons heavily loaded with merchandise, generally hauled by oxen and mules. . . . This trade is carried on to a great extent and very valuable, and the news from either places was . . . highly interesting.[67]

For the Pettegrew family, and their fellow Saints, they were about to go through the refiner's fire.

Seeds of Discord

The establishment of a central board, filled by General Authorities, was necessary for the evolution of the United Order of Enoch. It was intended for proper governance to have an Apostle preside with men qualified in different fields making up the balance of the boards.

In a short time, the entrepreneurial spirit of the Saints began to be felt in this frontier town of Independence. Mercantile establishments and warehousing facilities and such were escalating rapidly. The Mormons were focused on building Zion and laying the foundation for the New Jerusalem but also expanding pursuits to meet temporal needs. Church leaders praised the pursuits of commerce and agriculture to provide for the Saints there and make ready for many converts to follow. The fur business and Santa Fe trade drove a commercial boom. But the Mormon pursuits became strikingly different than those of their non-Mormon counterparts.

Sidney Gilbert put to provident use his mercantile expertise learned with his partner, Brother Newell Whitney, in Kirtland. Mormons were in great need of country produce, and Gilbert's general store was well stocked. As money was scarce, barter quickly became the common exchange. Farmers turned to the Mormons rather than to their non-Mormon neighbors. Further, as the Mormons began to heed the call from Sabbath sermons to engage in consecration, a constant source of new inventory was provided. Gentile merchants saw previous customers flocking to the Mormons. Gilbert and others expanded by directly marketing their wares to merchants of the Santa Fe trade. The independent local merchants couldn't compete. Great hostilities were mounting against the foreigners who were threatening their previous monopoly.

By year's end, there were eight hundred members involved in five branches in Jackson County. But there was severe discord amongst some of the Saints. Some chose to circumvent the actions of the ordained Church leaders. Some sought to obtain inheritances other than those provided according to the laws of consecration. Petty jealousies, covetousness, unbelief, and general neglect in obedience to commandments had been reported as serious matters, requiring intervention by the Prophet from Kirtland. He sent a copy of the "Olive Leaf" revelation to them. He also responded with a warning that "if Zion will not purify herself, he will seek another people. . . . Repent, repent, is the voice of God to Zion."[68] Temple construction still had not commenced.

In the northwest corner of Jackson County, another settlement was started by John Calvin McCoy, son of Baptist minister and Indian teacher Isaac McCoy. In 1833, McCoy built a log store near the mouth of the Kansas (Kaw) River, where it merges with the Missouri River. He sought a new access point to engage in trade with trappers and Indians away from the growing town of Independence. He too prospered from exchanging his goods for government annuity money, but he knew it could be threatened by the rapid growth of Mormon communities all around Jackson County. How could he compete with goods for sale that had come to Mormon storehouses from the charity of the Mormons? He paid dearly for his goods from the east and from other local farmers. McCoy's new settlement would be referred to as Westport.

After comfortably settling in to his new surroundings, Pettegrew was visited by a neighbor, who cried out at the top of his voice, "Mr. Pettegrew, you are at work as though you intended to remain here." Pettegrew explained he thought he had a right to stay upon his own land. The neighbor then expressed, "We are determined to drive you away from this country and we will stop you from emigrating here." Pettegrew defended that he had disturbed no one or interfered with any one's rights. The neighbor continued, "That is to no purpose. We will drive you from this place." Pettegrew challenged him, saying certainly the laws would not suffer him to commit such a crime. To that came the response, "The old laws and Constitution are all worn out and we are about to frame a new one." At that point, Pettegrew knew that "crime was written in their countenances."[69]

Less than a week later, Pettegrew and others gathered to call upon "the Almighty God for His assistance and protection." During prayers, two of the mob delegates appeared to explain to them:

> There is a great difficulty between us . . . a large body of men are already collected together at Independence and all are under arms, and now the proposals are these: If you will forsake your Mormon Prophet religion . . . we will become your brothers and will fight for you and we will protect you in any difficulties or troubles you may have. We will stand by you . . . but if you will not, why, we will fall upon you. Our men are now all under arms and it has been with great difficulty they have been kept back, and now you have some knowledge of your situations. We feel for, and beg of you to consider your situation and save yourselves from the calamity which will soon follow, should you fail to comply with our request. Forsake your Prophet religion, for we will not suffer Mormonism amongst us. We will now leave you to consider over what we have told you, and this is the message we were told to deliver to you. Farewell.[70]

The Mormon Problem

Having failed previously to exploit for personal gain his relationships with prominent Missouri families, Lieutenant Governor Boggs now hoped he could liaison with the Chouteaus to bring commercial opportunities to his fellow citizens of Jackson County from the fur trade. He also had maintained relations with key players in the Santa

Fe trade to likewise add additional entrepreneurial opportunities for his fellow Jackson County citizens. Finally, he was in a position to secure patronage and funding to occupy the governor's mansion, with its own perks and prestige. But then came the Mormons and talk of the New Jerusalem.

The old settlers gathered in April to develop a plan to deal with the Mormons. Several of the leaders had their own agendas. Four of them were local merchants unable to compete with Sydney Gilbert's store, which sold merchandise to Santa Fe merchants, fur trappers, and others at much lower prices. Mormons had no trouble buying goods from local farmers. Local merchants soon realized they couldn't compete with sales at the Church storehouse of goods, received by consecration from the Mormons to their bishop.

In mid-July, the old settlers again met to discuss the Mormon problem. One of the main issues regarded the claims associated with the Enoch Prophecy from the newspaper. Also, new revelations by Joseph Smith upset many residents. In their meeting draft, they raised,

> They [meaning the Saints] declare openly that their God hath given them this county of land, and that sooner or later they must and will have possession of lands for an inheritance; and, in fine, they have conducted themselves on many other occasions in such a manner that we owe it to ourselves, our wives, and children, and to the cause of public morals, to remove them from among us, as we are not prepared to give up our pleasant places and goodly possessions to them or to receive into the bosom of our families, as fit companions for our wives and daughters, the degraded and corrupted free Negroes and mulattoes that are now invited to settle among us.
>
> Under such a state of things, even our beautiful county would cease to be a desirable residence, and our situation intolerable. We, therefore agree (that after timely warning, and receiving an adequate compensation for what little property they cannot take with them), they refuse to leave us in peace, as they found us—we agree to use such means as may be sufficient to remove them, and to that end we each pledge to each other our bodily powers, our lives, fortunes and sacred honors.
>
> We will meet at the court house, at the town of Independence, on Saturday next, the 20th inst., to consult on subsequent movements.[71]

Meanwhile, in Kirtland, Joseph Smith was focused on the importance of advancing the Enoch Prophecy and the call to build Zion. Through inspiration, he laid out the town plat map for the city of Zion in Jackson County. The mile-square map was drawn with each block square representing ten-acre sections. It was sent to the leaders in Missouri on June 25, 1833.[72] At the same time, the enemies of the Church were in final preparations to force the Mormons out.

On July 30, 1833, the manifesto, including the drafts of mid-July, were presented to the Mormons of Jackson County, beginning with:

> We, the undersigned, citizens of Jackson County, believing that an important crisis is at hand, as regards our civil society, in consequence of a pretended religious sect of people that have settled, and are still settling in our county, styling themselves "Mormons"; and intending, as we do, to rid our society, peacefully if we can, forcibly if we must, and believing as we do, that the arm of the civil law does not afford us a guarantee, or at least a sufficient one, against the evils which are now inflicted upon us; and soon to be increasing, by the said religious sect, deem it expedient, and of the highest importance, to form ourselves into a company for the better and easier accomplishment of our purpose-a purpose which we deem it almost superfluous to say, is justified as well by the law of nature, as by the law of self-preservation.[73]

The leaders of this secret constitution included Samuel Owens,[74] county clerk and leading merchant in the area; Samuel Lucas, judge of the county court; John Smith, justice of the peace; Samuel Weston, justice of the peace; William Brown, constable; Thomas Pitcher, deputy constable; James Flournoy, postmaster; Moses and Thomas Wilson, merchants; R. W. Cummins, Indian agent; and Lilburn W. Boggs, lieutenant governor—who kept his involvement obscure.[75] Russell Hicks, Jones H. Flournoy, Judge Fristo, and Smallwood Noland also participated.[76] Smallwood Noland was a distant relative of Senator Benton. Many members were part of the Independence alliance of merchants, lead by Samuel Owens and Lieutenant Governor Boggs. Others were suppliers, farmers, and support providers for the merchant trade with the Santa Fe caravans, fur traders, or Indian tribes across the border.

It was the intent of this coalition group of city, county, state, and federal officers and administrators to govern themselves with a secret constitution that was alien to the laws of the land, for which some had sworn an oath to uphold. Of particular note, R. W. Cummins was a federally employed Indian agent reporting directly to Superintendent Clark, who reported to Senator Benton as committee chairman over Indian Affairs. Agent Cummins was a friend and associate of Francois Chouteau and Pierre Menard.[77] It was inappropriate for federal employees to collaborate against local citizens, and for Lieutenant Governor Boggs to aid a group who operated contrary to the laws of Missouri and to the United States.

With Boggs at their lead, the secret constitution apparently rationalized their illegal conduct under the banner of the state motto adopted in 1822: "salus populi suprema lex esto," meaning "let the welfare of the people be the supreme law." They believed the old settlers represented the majority of the people, whose welfare was supreme. But the old settlers were becoming outnumbered in population by the Mormons. Their rationale was about to reverse in favor of the growing majority Mormon.[78] This theme likewise became adopted by Senator Benton's supporters, though he himself preferred expressing the principle "demos krateo," meaning government by the people and majority rule.[79]

Taking Action

Local non-Mormon government officials were vested in several of the declining enterprises and determined to respond in force. Retaliation was organized through the dominant political structure—namely, the President Jackson–styled Democrat Party.[80] Their native son Lilburn Boggs took the lead, leveraging the strength of his position as lieutenant governor. Persecution was directed against the Mormons by those prominent in the government hierarchy.

Days later, the Pettegrew family at the Big Blue was visited by a large party of the mob, who began yelling, "Open, open, open this door," and then broke through the entrance. Brother Pettegrew and several others in the family were quite ill. Hugh Brazeale, after verifying their state of illness, told his fellow marauders to leave. Still, they threatened to destroy parts of the Pettegrew family home that day. The rabble force was armed with guns, swords, pistols, clubs, and butcher knives, while many were painted as savages.

As the mob departed, they assured the family of future destruction if they did not leave soon. The mob then proceeded to several of their neighbors and "threw down some houses and shot at Sister Shurwood and several other sisters as they were running in a cornfield."[81]

They continued on to Porter Rockwell's house and "threw his house down, or all they could, cut open feather beds, destroyed all of his furniture and all they could lay hands on." Leading the mob was the Reverend Finis Ewing. He was a close friend with Senator Benton, who had made him the local land registrar after Benton's first reelection campaign in 1826, when Reverend Ewing was actively "electioneering" for him. Many of these vigilante leaders were landowners west of the Blue who were engaged in merchant activities and were in competition with the trade of the Mormons near the intersection of the Blue River and the Santa Fe Road. These included Moses Wilson, Isaac McCoy, Robert Johnson, and Indian Agent Richard Cummins.[82]

Agent Cummins and Reverend Ewing were aggressively attempting to protect the established arrangement of the St. Louis Junto, including Benton, Clark, and the Chouteaus, with the Independence merchants and extended Chouteau family network extending into Kansas.

Nineteen members of the mob then proceeded to homes in the nearby Whitmer Branch of Saints to extend their reign of terror on those unsuspecting Saints. Three days later, the mob returned as Brother Pettegrew was visiting with a neighbor. "Their rage and looks showed but too plainly that they would carry their threats into execution if they could." The mob then proceeded to Pettegrew's house. By the time he was able to return home, he saw his family had been driven into the streets with others of the neighbors and threatened vulgarly.[83]

Mob members included brothers Moses and Thomas Wilson, a lawyer named Brazeale, Lewis Franklin, and Dr. Hedgepeth. The dominance of the evil opposition compelled the Saints of the four adjoining branches to combine and remove together as a group.

> Our company numbered eighty or ninety, and but seven men who were not sick. . . . We travelled south, nothing but the canopies of Heaven for our covering, the earth for our beds, and in a large open prairie we saw daily companies of armed men as we passed along. We had but little provisions, and how we lived to get through as well as we did is

> a miracle to me. . . . I shall always remember the suffering of my son, Hiram. I did not expect he would live. The cold was so intense; no bedding or covering or anything that we might make him comfortable during his illness. No, he had to lie and suffer. I shall also remember the privations and sufferings of the saints. . . . Our children, crying at every moment for something to satiate their appetites, and these little innocent ones were made to suffer by those blood-thirsty fiends of Jackson County.[84]

Pettegrew had remembered his discussion previously with Ewing and reported,

> Sure enough, his words were verified, for in little over one year he was at the head of two hundred men of Lafayette County, armed and equipped for the purpose of driving the Mormons from their home. I saw then what was in the hearts of the ministers and the people.[85]

The persistent raids drew a few casualties among the perpetrators. Hugh Brazeale, an attorney who had trespassed at the Pettegrew household, was among the dead. His grieving widow, Amanda King Brazeale, had sympathetic kinsmen in high places. Her brother was the circuit judge from Clay County, Judge Austin King.

Reverend Ewing had taken occasion previously to proclaim publicly, "The 'Mormons' are the common enemies of mankind and ought to be destroyed." During the persecutions, it was observed he went "from house to house, seeking to destroy the Church by spreading slanderous falsehoods, to incite the people to acts of violence against the saints."[86] Francois Chouteau and his siblings and other relatives, included in the local trade, were his brothers, Frederick, Cyprien, and Paul Liguest, as well as several other relations. (See the following historical map showing the effects of the 1830 Removal Act. The Chouteau family members dominated the trading forts of each relocated Indian tribe, where the Indians would pay them with annuity payments negotiated by Superintendent Clark and Pierre Chouteau and approved by Senator Benton as Senate Committee Chairman of Indian Affairs. Much of Jackson County is shown, but the town of Independence is covered by the top left corner of the chart.)

Reverend Ewing was performing well the handiwork of Senator Benton. The Mormons had interfered in Benton's grandiose plans far too well. Though unnoticed and from a distance, Benton was still plotting to realize his ambitions for the "Road to India." The trail through Fort Benton on the upper reaches of the Missouri River had to be sustained and the momentum advanced to the Northwest Territory.

Through the Senator's political shrewdness, he had closed the government factory system giving his allies of the American Fur Company access to secure the network of trading forts and to extend their reach to the Rocky Mountains. He had secured funding to enable Sibley to survey the Santa Fe Trail. He had pushed legislation for advancing trade on the upper Missouri. He and Superintendent Clark had coerced the massive annuity structures funding the displaced Indian tribes to patronize the Chouteau trade monopoly. Senator Benton felt entitled to the esteem of the masses for carrying on the mantle of the Jefferson Empire of Liberty campaign. Benton was not going to allow the Mormons to reap the spoils he had maneuvered for his partners.

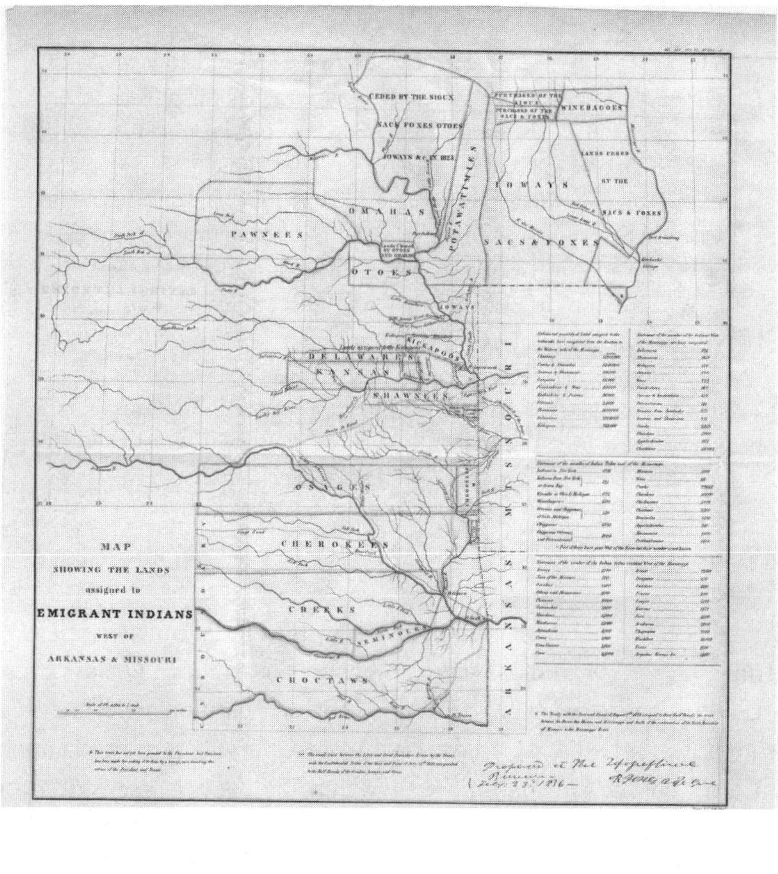

Lieutenant Governor Boggs serving as a colonel in the militia was directly involved in the violence in Independence. A faithful Saint, Horace Strong Rawson, reported of the incident,

> I saw Lyman Wight which was our captain deliver his sword to Colonel Boggs, exclaiming, "Take my sword or my head I do not care . . . which," and we were ordered to set our guns down on the Temple lot against the fence where the great Temple is to be built and dedicated unto the Lord in this generation and a cloud is to rest upon it by day and the shining of a flaming fire by night for upon all the glory shall be defense.[87]

The mob leader, Thomas Pitcher, at the time a lieutenant colonel in the local militia, was arrested but little came of the matter.[88] About twelve hundred members of the Church had been coerced to leave the county. Working with Alexander Doniphan, an attorney and politician and in conjunction with his colleagues, the Mormon leaders drafted a letter to Governor Dunklin on December 6, 1833:

> In behalf of our society, which is so scattered and suffering, we, your petitioners, ask aid and assistance of your Excellency, that we may be restored to our lands, houses, and property, and protected in them by the militia of the state, if legal, or by a detachment of the United States Rangers, which might be located at Independence, . . . till peace can be restored. . . . Also, we ask that our men may be organized into companies of Jackson Guards, and be furnished with arms by the state, to assist in maintaining their rights against the unhallowed power of the mob of Jackson County.
>
> And then, when arrangements are made to protect us in our persons and property (which cannot be done without an armed force, nor would it be prudent to risk our lives there without guards, till we receive strength from our friends to protect ourselves), we wish a court of inquiry instituted, to investigate the whole matter of the mob against the "Mormons."[89]

When the mobs attacked the Mormons in Independence, the two primary targets were the Gilbert storehouse and William Phelps's printing office. The mob felt most threatened by the Mormon merchandising enterprises and the issues of the *Evening and Morning Star*, proclaiming the depth of the Enoch Prophecy and the building of a New Jerusalem in their midst.

A great battle for Zion had commenced. The Mormons had been forced out, after threatening the commercial monopoly of the St. Louis Junto corrupt leadership and the alliance of Independence merchants lead by Lilburn Boggs and Samuel Owens. The landscape of the battleground for Zion was about to be greatly enlarged.

4: The St. Louis Junto Declares War on the Mormons

John Jacob Astor's involvement in his vision came to an end as he retired in the spring of 1834. The American Fur Company was divided. Ramsay Crooks purchased the Northern Department and retained the company title. Bernard Pratte and Company, with Cadet Chouteau as the dominant partner and in active daily management, purchased the Western Department. The Chouteau family network was focused on building their empire without interference from Astor in New York. Samuel Owens and the other merchants of Jackson County expected greater opportunities to develop more commercial opportunities for themselves under this new plan.

On February 24, 1834, Amos Rees, attorney for the state court, and Robert Wells, the state Attorney General, visited with the Mormons who were preparing to testify. Rees and Wells had decided "that all hope of criminal prosecution was at an end." They persuaded the Mormon leadership to drop their legal matter. They believed the grand jury would not indict the mob leaders nor would a trial jury of local peers indict any of the mob leaders if pursued.[90]

William Phelps, whose printing shop had been destroyed, had written Governor Dunklin. Sydney Gilbert had written to a recommended attorney, Abiel Leonard, in Fayette, Howard County. Gilbert was unaware of Leonard's client, John Sappington, who was a close friend of Senator Benton. Leonard did a great deal of collections legal work for the Sappington commercial empire, which fueled the power base of the emerging Central Clique.

On April 10, 1834, Mormon leaders appealed to President Andrew Jackson for relief. Jackson at the time was fighting the Nullification Battle regarding South Carolina. Jackson's Secretary of War Lewis Cass wrote back on May 2, stating, "The President cannot call out a military force to aid in the execution of the State laws, until the proper requisition is made upon him by the requisite authorities."[91]

On June 6, 1834, Governor Dunklin wrote to Colonel J. Thornton. The letter was published in the *Niles Register*, Baltimore, Maryland, on July 26, 1834. It addressed the following key issues:

> Our state constitution declares that the people's "right to bear arms, in defense of themselves, and of the state, cannot be questioned." Then it is their constitutional right to arm themselves. Indeed, our militia law makes it the duty of every man, not exempted by law, between the ages of 18 and 45, to arm himself . . . our constitution says, "That all men have a natural and indefeasible right to worship Almighty God according to the dictates of their own consciences." I am fully persuaded that the eccentricity of the religious opinions and practices of the Mormons, is at the bottom of the outrage . . . against them.
>
> They have their right . . . to believe and worship Jo Smith as a man, an angel, or even as the only true and living God, and to call their habitation Zion, the Holy Land, or even Heaven itself. Indeed, there is nothing so absurd or ridiculous, that they have not a right to adopt as their religion, so that . . . they do not interfere with the rights of others.
>
> I consider it the duty of every good citizen of Jackson and the adjoining counties to exert themselves to affect a compromise of these difficulties. . . .
>
> Rumor says that each party are preparing themselves with cannon. That would be illegal. It is not necessary to self defense, as guaranteed by the constitution. And as there are no artillery companies organized in this state, nor field pieces provided by the public, any preparations of that kind will be considered as without right; and, in the present state of things, would be understood to be with criminal intent. I

> am told that the people of Jackson county expect assistance from the adjoining counties, to oppose the Mormons in taking or keeping possession of their lands. I should regret it extremely if any should be so imprudent as to do so; it would give a different aspect to the affair.[92]

In the meeting called by Judge Ryland, Samuel Owens made "a flaming war speech," while General Doniphan replied on the side of peace. Owens, as an ally of the Chouteau network and a leading merchant in his own right, could not tolerate Mormon presence on the opposite side of the Missouri River in Clay County. They would continue to challenge—and then dominate—the trade commerce to the Rocky Mountains, the Santa Fe Trail, and the trading posts on the Kansas and Oklahoma plains.

It was believed that Joseph Smith was leading an army of Saints from Kirtland, Ohio, to aid their brethren in Zion and to restore them to their land, and they would arrive shortly. As their group known as "Zion's Camp" arrived in the area of Liberty, Clay County, mob members positioned themselves to ambush the unsuspecting Mormons. The enemy claimed to have nearly four hundred men in arms gathered from Ray, Lafayette, Clay, and Jackson Counties. In each attempted ambush scheme, they were unsuccessful. The Mormons arrived safely.

After a meeting, Samuel C. Owens and Thomas Campbell, as mob leaders, threatened to return to Independence and gather an army to destroy the Saints. It was later reported that Campbell in full rage swore, "The Eagles and Turkey buzzards shall eat my flesh if I do not fix Joe Smith and his army so that their skins will not hold shucks, before two days are passed."[93] After the avenging oath was uttered, Owens, Campbell, and thirteen others of the overconfident canaille got in a boat to cross the Missouri River. After rowing to the middle of the river, their boat began to sink as seven of the twelve conspirators were drowned. It was reported,

> Campbell was among the missing. He floated down the river some four or five miles, and lodged upon a pile of drift wood, where the Eagles, Buzzards, Ravens, Crows and wild animals ate his flesh from his bones, to fulfill his own words, and left him a horrible looking skeleton of God's vengeance. . . .

> Owens saved his life only, after floating four miles down the stream, where he lodged up an island, "swam off naked about day light, borrowed a mantle to hide his shame, and slipped home rather shy of the vengeance of God."[94]

On June 19, the Saints camped on a hill between two branches of Fishing River. In the distance, sounds of gunfire echoed, some anxiously positioned themselves for a fight. The Prophet promised the Lord would protect them and declared, "Stand still and see the salvation of God."[95]

Storm clouds rolled in, and a great storm came upon the mob as they were crossing by ferry. The Mormons sought refuge from the storm. So intense was the storm effects, the mob persecutors were broken up and deserted their cause. Joseph explained, "Boys, there is some meaning to this. God is in this storm."[96]

Following renewed assaults, Mormon leaders in Clay County sent the following to Samuel Owens and others of the Jackson Committee from Clay County, dated June 21, 1834:

> Gentlemen: Your propositions of Monday last have been generally made known to our people, and we are instructed to inform you that they cannot be acceded to. . . .
>
> We are happy to have it in our power to give you assurances that our brethren here, together with those who have arrived from the East, are anxiously disposed to make every sacrifice for an honorable adjustment of our differences that could be required of free citizens of the United States.
>
> Negotiations at the camp are now going on between some gentlemen of this county and our brethren which are calculated to allay the great excitement in your county. We are informed that the citizens of Jackson entertain fears that our people intend to invade their territory in a hostile manner. We assure you that their fears are groundless; such is not and never was our intentions.[97]

If the Saints could have pursued their Zion-building mandate in Jackson County, living the United Order of Enoch, goods consecrated for the storehouse in excess of what was needed for the destitute could have been sold to traders on the Santa Fe Trail or to traders engaged in the fur trade. And in New Mexico, the Zion trade merchants could exchange their surplus goods for silver or gold. By these means, the Saints could have secured specie reserves. Samuel Owens and Lilburn Boggs were committed to preserving the monopoly for the Independence merchants.

In regards to his previous conduct, the real character of Governor Dunklin was yet to be made manifest. Though in July he had written that the Church members had rights governed by the state constitution and those rights must be maintained, he also presented a twisted sense of justice in his letter to the Saints,

> Your neighbors accuse your people of holding illicit communication with the Indians, and of being opposed to slavery. You deny. . . . The fact exists, and your neighbors seem to believe it true; and whether true or false, the consequences will be the same, unless you can by your conduct and arguments, convince them of your innocence. If you cannot do this, all I can say to you is, that in this republic the vox populi is the vox Dei. [The voice of the people is the voice of God].[98]

Governor Dunklin, on August 15, also sounded a much different tone to Joel Haden:

> Upon the subject of the poor deluded Mormons & the infuriated Jacksonites, it is unnecessary now to say anything & I hope it will continue so. There can be no difficulty in ascertaining the correct course for me to pursue if I am compelled to act. I have no regard for the Mormons, as a separate people; & have an utter contempt for them as a religious sect, while on the other hand I have much regard for the people of Jackson county, both personally and politically; they are, many of them, my personal friends, and nearly all of them are very staunch democrats.[99]

The Saints importuned the local judiciary until their own attorneys admitted no jury would support them. They were lied to by Governor Dunklin and ignored by President Jackson's administration. The time the Lord would arise and in his fury vex the nation and cut off those wicked unjust stewards would come, but not until their enemies had ripened in their iniquities, and His judgments against the wicked would be borne by their posterity in future generations.

John Sappington and the Central Clique

In November 1835, John Sappington created Sappington and Sons. This partnership included his two sons, Erasmus and William, and his four sons-in-law: Miles Marmaduke, Claiborne Jackson, Layton S. Eddins, and William Price. Since Sappington first marketed his licorice-tasting "Sappington's Anti-Fever & Ague Pills" in 1833, demand for his quinine based medicine soared.

Sappington and Sons proved to be an immediate financial success. The primary sales areas included the Ohio River Valley, consisting of Illinois, Indiana, Kentucky, and Tennessee; the Mississippi River Valley from St. Louis to New Orleans; the White and Arkansas River Valleys of southern Missouri and Arkansas; and the Red River Valley in Texas. Many of the other states received distribution of the Sappington pills as well. Merchants, druggists, and others often wrote Sappington, eager to become one of his marketing agents for his miracle drugs.

Besides his growing practice and distribution network, he also worked in agriculture and money lending. He was heavily engaged in land acquisition owning thousands of acres. He was the largest slave owner and slave trader in the region. His empire was dominant in Howard and Saline Counties.

John Sappington was really active in promoting politicians who supported his causes. On holidays throughout the year, his residence would house gala affairs, attracting the leadership of his multiple businesses, as well as other local gentry and Democratic fat cats. Senator Benton was a frequent guest at these events and would deliver political orations.

Thomas Reynolds had been successful in Illinois politics. In 1829, he opted to move to Fayette in Howard County. He actively embraced the tenets of the Central Clique. In 1832, he won as the state representative from Howard County in the legislature. He was quickly chosen as Speaker of the House. After serving just one term, he was appointed judge of the second judicial district. He too became a friend and strong advocate for Senator Benton. The election profile in Missouri from 1835 to 1836 firmly embraced the Central Clique (also known as the "Boonslick Democracy") as the controlling force of most of the Democrat Party in the state. The founding members of the Clique established strong credentials for leadership and political patronage that dominated Party presence for decades.

Sappington and his sons-in-law Meredith Marmaduke and Claiborne Jackson were Clique top operatives. Other leaders included Thomas Reynolds, Joshua Redman, and Owen Rawlins. Other dominant leaders included Dr. George Penn of Saline County, William B. Napton of Cooper County, and Sterling Price of Chariton County.[100] All of the leadership followed Sappington's lead as committed advocates of Senator Benton. Their dominance at the convention ensured their approved candidates ran unopposed against Whig candidates and would not split the party.

The Central Clique found other ways to dominate elections and control all houses of Missouri state government. The state constitution provided each county shall have at least one representative but the whole number of representatives shall never exceed a hundred in representation. At the beginning of statehood in 1820, there were fifteen counties with forty-three members of the House of Representatives. In a deliberate move to counter growing Whig Party dominance in St. Louis and other areas around the Mississippi, the Democrats, backed by Senator Benton, promoted the establishment of many new counties by 1836, bringing the total to sixty and the number of representatives to the legislature at ninety-eight. With this maneuver, small rural county coalitions, beholding to Benton, had the same legislative aggregate power as the higher populated counties in the eastern areas in St. Louis and along the Mississippi.

The Supreme Court of the state, consisting of three members, would soon include key Central Clique leaders. The contest for the governor's chair was also of paramount importance to the Central Clique leadership and leaders of the St. Louis Junto. The Chouteaus and their junto partners typically promoted Whig causes and favored Whig leaders but continued support for Senator Benton. In the 1836 election, Lilburn Boggs was running against a strong competitor in William Ashley, formerly of the Rocky Mountain Fur Company, both as Jacksonian Democrats. Though he had left the daily activities of the fur business many years earlier, Ashley was aware of the commercial potential for South

Pass as a means of crossing the Rocky Mountains. It was feared he could jeopardize the plans of both the Central Clique and the St. Louis Junto. Ashley was also looking to dismantle some of the dominance of the Chouteau empire in the state.

Chez Les Canses Declares War against the Mormons

"Another Mormon Invasion" appeared as a headline in a St. Louis newspaper on May 3, 1836. In the article were details of various claims of an individual in St. Louis receiving letters from Kirtland, Ohio. According to the letters, residents had sent notice by mail that Mormons, numbering fifteen hundred to two thousand, were arming themselves and preparing to come to Jackson County, not as an army but in small groups. The leaders of the St. Louis Junto, east and west, were put on the alert.[101]

On May 12, Francois Chouteau, nephew of Auguste Chouteau, sent a letter to his father-in-law, Monsieur Pierre Menard of Kaskaskia, Illinois:

> *Cher oncle*. . . . Apparently we are going to wage war here very soon with the Mormons. They have a force of 2,000 men in Clay County who are organizing and making the arrangements necessary to attack us in Jackson County and we have to take measures in order to make serious resistance.
>
> It appears that they are disposed to retake possession of their land by force. We want to make the most advantageous propositions to them before taking up arms. And if they are unwilling to make any arrangements it is certain that we will have to fight them. The situation is alarming and upsetting in our area . . . we are determined to fight to the end rather than consent that the Mormons remain here, and really, if it were the case they would chase us from the country as they themselves were chased the first time. . . .
>
> Recently, by all the boats that come up the Missouri, the Mormons are coming from their satellites and all are armed, Jackson County is the Promised land where the New Jerusalem must be built.[102]

The message of the Enoch Prophecy had reached Francois Chouteau and the St. Louis Junto. The Mormons were intent on building the "New Jerusalem" on the same lands the Chouteau enterprises dominated.

Mormons were effective competitors, and the Indians were showing they might be receptive to their teachings. The high prices the Chouteaus charged their Indian clients put their relationships at risk in Jackson County, the Kansas Plains, and eventually all throughout the upper Missouri. Francois felt, for the sake of their enterprises, he had to make a stand. The Chouteau monopoly and their allies scattered in Jackson County and the Kansas and Oklahoma Territories would be threatened anew if the Mormons returned unopposed.

At the time the letters were written regarding the Mormons, Francois's wife, Berenice, returned to her father, Pierre Menard at the family home in Kaskaskia. Undoubtedly, the distant Chouteau and Menard family members in Peoria and elsewhere were aware of the tensions regarding the Mormon threat to their monopolistic enterprises. They would have shared similar resentments against the Mormons as missionary success expanded to their local neighborhoods.

Various Jackson County residents continued to stir the pot, driving the locals to a frenzied state in great anticipation and hostile dispositions against Mormons. Francois again wrote to Menard on June 6, 1836, "I have no other news to give to you presently. No one speaks of the war with the Mormons anymore, at least for the present."[103] In the next month, Francois mentioned increased financial dealings with Samuel Owens of Independence.

"Chez Les Canses" was the French name given to the area near the mouth of the Kansas River. Francois Chouteau was sent there by Pierre Chouteau in 1821. He was instructed to advance the fur trade and deal harshly with would-be-competitors. At this steamboat landing, Francois would have lumber cut for the steamships of the Chouteau Company working with the American Fur Company. Fur packs would come from the upper Missouri River, as far as the Rocky Mountain region, and from the several Chouteau trading posts, dealing with the Kansa, Shawnee, Wea, and Kickapoo Indian tribes, who had been relocated to Kansas and Oklahoma under the Indian Relocation Act of 1830. Chouteau family members manned those other trading posts and used Chouteau's Landing as a gathering site to repack the furs and forward them to St. Louis. Francois oversaw all the activity in the Kansas and Western Missouri regions.

Being responsible for such a large component of the Chouteau-Menard operations, Francois felt he needed to take the leading role with the locals to keep the Mormons from competing with merchants and Santa Fe traders. The Chouteau monopoly was expanding. The Chouteaus bought their Western Missouri Trade monopoly segment from John Astor's American Fur Company in 1834. With his new independence, Pierre Chouteau was driven to extend their Rocky Mountain operations and fortify their network of trading forts. They purchased Fort Laramie in 1836.[104] Francois clearly felt threatened by the Mormons' capabilities.

On June 29, 1836, Clay County residents gathered together to address the Mormon issue. A great many high-spirited speeches were made. Samuel Owens, James Campbell, Smallwood Noland, and a few other Jackson County residents attended this meeting in Liberty, Clay County, and were quite outspoken in their hatred of the Mormons. Colonel Alexander Doniphan had been in attendance, but he objected to some of the proceedings. Minutes of the meeting were kept:

> In November 1833, those people were expelled . . . in Jackson County, without money, without property, without means of subsistence for themselves. . . .
>
> They came to our county thus friendless and penniless, (seeking as they said) but a temporary asylum from the storm of persecution by which they were then buffeted. . . . They always declared that they looked not upon this county as their home, but as a temporary asylum; and that, whenever, a respectable portion of the citizens of this county should request it, they would promptly leave us in peace as they found us. . . .
>
> This period has now arrived. . . . Their rapid emigration, their large purchases, and offers to purchase lands, the remarks of the ignorant and imprudent portion of them, that this country is destined by heaven to be theirs are received and looked upon, by a large portion of this community, as strong and convincing proofs that they intend to make this county their permanent home, the centre and general rendezvous of their people. . . .
>
> They are charged . . . with keeping up a constant communication with our Indian tribes on our frontiers, with declaring even from the

> pulpit, that the Indians are a part of God's chosen people, and are destined by heaven to inherit this land, in common with themselves. . . . We earnestly urge them to seek some other abiding place.[105]

On July 18, 1836, Francois reported to Menard,

> I went to see Major Cummins a few days ago to speak to him concerning the debt of the Weas on behalf of William Marshall. . . . The major [Cummins] is a very good man, but very timid and fearful, and I believe he will say nothing, neither for nor against. . . . We will try to convince the Indians to pay the debt to us. We have no word yet of our annuities. The Indians are eager to receive their money. . . .
>
> Here from time to time, war with the Mormons is spoken of but I don't believe that will happen. They are not yet strong enough to take the Promised Land by force.[106]

The anti-Mormon leaders were still trying to keep alive the notion that the Mormons were attempting to mount another war on the innocent citizens of Jackson County.

On July 28, William W. Phelps received a letter from Governor Dunklin, which included a quote from Judge Luke Lawless, made previously to the grand jury of St. Louis:

> Public sentiment may become paramount law; and when one man or society of men become so obnoxious to that sentiment as to determine the people to be rid of him or them, it is useless to run counter to it.[107]

Apparently, Governor Dunklin was now looking to appease the Democratic Party political machinery by quoting from Judge Lawless. Lawless had a long history with Senator Benton, including the occasion of the duel between Benton and Lucas when Lawless acted as Benton's second. Judge Lawless was doubtless an advocate of Benton in these matters.

At this time, the issue of state-internal improvements was much debated. Railroads were a favorite topic for many of the merchants and farmers. Even Doniphan actively supported railroad development in key locations of the state. If they were to succeed in railroad projects, it was felt that the Mormons would have to be forced out. Otherwise they would likely attempt to use the railroads to continue to flood the various neighborhoods with more Mormons.

Formation of Caldwell and Daviess Counties for the Mormons

Throughout that summer, Doniphan worked with Mormon leaders to claim an area where the state would approve their relocation. Working with Atchison and Rees, Doniphan was able to secure unincorporated lands in northern Ray County.

The Mormon leadership purchased these lands and created the town of Far West on August 8. Due to the efforts of Doniphan, steps were put in motion for the creation of two new counties for the expanding Mormon population.

Lilburn Boggs was able to reach out to various entrenched groups beyond the Democratic faithful. His friend and former partner George Sibley was a prominent Whig and carried a large support base. Boggs's first marriage in the Bent family and his second marriage with Daniel Boone's granddaughter also broadened his base of support. These groups united against the threat perceived to exist if Ashley should succeed. With the active support of all his partisan supporters, Boggs won the election by a relatively wide margin. Unknown to many was the existence within many of Boggs's core political base groups of a pervasive anti-Mormon sentiment. As the newly elected governor, and having won by a large margin, Boggs felt he had a mandate to challenge the Mormon leadership again.

Soon after the creation of the two counties, settlers began pouring into the new fertile regions. Mormons and some non-Mormons had gone to the designated branch of the General Land Office (GLO) in Lexington and appeared before the Reverend Finis Ewing, the appointed registrar, and filed their applications to request their claims for preemption rights. Included were affidavits verifying that they were in fact improving and occupying their specified lands.

By December 17, formal steps were made by the House in regards to the creation of the proposed two new counties by appointing Doniphan to a special committee to study this project. Opposition in the form of a petition came from certain citizens of Ray County. During the process, Doniphan also contended with Smallwood Noland of Jackson County, a distant relative of Senator Benton, and Governor Boggs. Doniphan presented the bill to the legislature where both Houses approved it. Governor Boggs grudgingly signed it into law on December 29, 1836.

Early residents looked with anticipation to the growth of this region expected from the legislative act creating the county. As was predicted, the Mormons came to the county in large numbers, settling first in Colfax township in 1836. Lyman Wight settled in Daviess County the following year. These early inhabitants sought property in the timber lands rather than the prairie lands of the other neighboring counties.

In the act creating Daviess and Caldwell Counties, a commission was formed with Joseph Baxter of Clay County, Cornelius Gilliam of Clinton County, and William W. Mauzee of Ray County to select locations for the new county seats. Gallatin was selected for Daviess County.

The elections of 1836 were a decisive win for the Missouri Democrats statewide because of the concentrated effort by various leaders of the Central Clique after dominating the nomination convention the previous year. Sterling Price did win a seat in the state legislature that session. As a reward, the Speaker appointed Price to the Committee on Ways and Means and the Committee on Enrolled Bills on the part of the House.

Governor Boggs was quick to reward several of his favorites in the Central Clique. In January, he nominated his friend Thomas Reynolds to be the circuit judge for the second judicial district. He expected great things of Reynolds, including further loyalty.

On the basis of Benton's previous legislation, "An Act to Grant Pre-Emption Rights to Settlers on the Public Lands" (May 29, 1830), Daviess and Caldwell Counties in Missouri were about to go through the surveying and preemption process, as defined in Senator Benton's act.

By July 1837, non-Mormon residents were becoming concerned at the rate of growth of Mormon citizens in Daviess County. A few were bold enough to speak out specifically focusing on the Saints in the Grand River region. They warned them to leave the county or face consequences. The Saints felt they were following the will of God in their quest to build Zion. They believed that Doniphan had secured their rights and claims to this new homeland. Those recently gathered chose not to heed the threats of their neighbors, feeling God would provide for their safety. Mormon growth in the region continued to accelerate.[108]

Filling the Francois Chouteau Void in Jackson County

Meanwhile, back in Jackson County, the trade with the Indians, trappers, and Santa Fe travelers was booming. The American Fur Company was prospering there. During 1837, the Chouteaus were working with Moses Wilson and Samuel C. Owens. In Francois's letter to Menard on March 24, 1837, he indicated,

> As yet I have not collected the debt of Poole. Mr. Owens who was to receive the money, is at Philadelphia, and Wilson who was to pay, is not here either. Be assured that as soon as I can do that, I will advise you immediately.[109]

Several of the local citizens had been brought into the inner workings of the Chouteau commercial network. James Pool worked at the Delaware Shawnee Indian Reservation. Moses Wilson was to pay Samuel C. Owens, who was to pay Francois Chouteau for the Company. All three had shown rather strong hatred against the Mormons earlier.

Francois Chouteau again wrote to his uncle Pierre Menard on January 28, 1838, to notify him that their employee Labaume was to receive eight hundred dollars from Simpson and Owens from Westport. This was probably Samuel Owens and Richard "Duke" Simpson. Owens was still working with the Chouteau-Menard business group.[110]

Early in the spring, Francois Chouteau was told that wild horses had been caught by a tribe of Indians willing to sell the horses. Francois packed up, looking for a bargain to fill his stables. Chouteau bought nine of the horses. After leaving their camp, an Indian raiding party descended on Chouteau's small caravan. Francois's mount reared back and threw him. Other horses trampled him as they broke away from the commotion. Francois Chouteau died soon after on April 18, 1838. A void was created in the commercial power base in Jackson County.

James Hyatt McGee had been a resident in the same area for nearly a decade. He was one of the first to bring slaves to work his fields in his 320-acre section near Chouteau's Landing. For years, he had coveted the land around the natural rock landing that had been held by the family of Gabriel Prudhomme, a French Canadian and a friend of Francois Chouteau.

Prudhomme was killed as a result of a bar room brawl in 1831, putting an end to his dream of farming the area and running a ferry across the Missouri.

After the oldest daughter of Prudhomme requested the property sold, James McGee was appointed trustee for the estate sale. The court ordered McGee to auction off the valuable property that he desperately wanted. He placed notice of the auction in out of town newspapers to keep attendees absent. On the date of the auction, June 7, 1838, McGee acted as auctioneer and quickly sold the property to Abraham Fonda, a stranger in the area, for $1,800. The locals were outraged that they hadn't been given a fair chance to bid. The court set aside the sale and set November 14, 1838, as the date for the auction.

Some of the locals feared the Mormons would seek bidding on the Prudhomme lands at the rescheduled auction. This Missouri riverfront property of 271 acres, with its natural steamboat landing area in Jackson County on the border of the Kansas Indian Territory, represented a key strategic commercial trade site. Coincidence or not, the Mormon leaders were conveniently incarcerated under orders of Judge Austin King in the Liberty Jail nearby Clay County. Judge King was the brother of Hugh Brazeale's widow when he was killed in the raids against the Mormons five years earlier. Included in the crowd were bidders, several of whom had been mob leaders and friends of the deceased Brazeale.

The winning bid of $4,220 came from a collection of the old settlers of Jackson County, and they took the name "the Town of Kansas Company." This group included Judge Samuel C. Owens, his deputy clerk

Russell Hicks, Moses G. Wilson, John C. McCoy, William Sublette (a prominent Indian fur trader), William Gillis, Fry P. McGee, Abraham Fonda, William M. Chick, Oliver Caldwell, George W. Tate (auctioneer), Jacob Ragan, William Collins, James Smart, Robert Campbell, William Evans, and Henry Jobe. Many of these people had been active in forcing the Mormons out of Jackson County back in 1833.

Having built relationships with Francois Chouteau before his death, Moses Wilson and Samuel Owens felt that they were in a strong position to profit further from the Chouteau and Menard network with a part-ownership of the Prudhomme property. Moses Wilson, having secured a bridge across the Big Blue where Edward Partridge, David Pettegrew, Horace Rawson, and Porter Rockwell had lived, was also in a key position for trade with the Santa Fe merchants. Without fear of Mormon competition, Wilson used his Town of Kansas relationships to expand his mercantile pursuits.

Governor Boggs appointed his friend and ally William B. Napton to the state Supreme Court during 1838, after just two years as state attorney general. Boggs was focused on building a stronger coalition of Central Clique faithful and personal favorites in preparation for what was soon to rock the state morally and legally while targeting the Mormons.

The elections for 1838 lacked as much attention as in the previous polling process. Benton easily won reelection. Sterling Price, because of his involvement in the state militia, decided not to run for another term in the legislature, nor to participate in the party management process. But still, the Central Clique was firmly in control after the election. Their prior choices were still in place including Governor Boggs, Franklin Cannon as lieutenant governor, and Albert Harrison as Congressman. William Napton, a strong member of the Central Clique, was attorney general and John C. Edwards was one of three judges on the state Supreme Court. The Central Clique also had strong support in both houses of the state legislature.

Not long after their arrival in Far West, Joseph and other Church leaders felt prompted to visit the areas to the north. He recorded the intent of this quest: "To visit the north countries for the purpose of laying off stakes of Zion, making locations & laying claims for the gathering of the saints for the benefit of the poor."[111] The Prophet was focused on his divine mandate.

5: The Illinois Internal Improvement Act and Fiscal Crisis

News of the death of Russell Farnham spread along both shorelines of the Mississippi River, from Prairie du Chien to St. Louis. He died from cholera at Fort Edwards on October 23, 1832. Condolences were expressed in a letter sent by Ramsay Crooks to Pierre Chouteau.

> Poor Farnham; he has paid the debt of nature after a life of uncommon activity & endless exposure. . . . He was one of the best meaning, but the most sanguine men I almost ever met. . . . During all the ravages of the pestilence here, . . . I have never felt anything like the sensation I experienced upon hearing of my honest friend's death.[112]

Russell Farnham had been with Ramsay Crooks at Astoria and shared in the dream of finding an uninterrupted passage across the continent. He had embraced Benton's and Jefferson's "Road to India" vision and sought to exploit the secret access point through the Rocky Mountains at South Pass. He was mentor to Mark Aldrich and a friend to Isaac Galland.

A great stir throughout the state of Illinois had occurred from an article in the *Illinois Advocate* issued October 31, 1831. The paper reported that a Mr. Enoch C. March, an Alton merchant, had recently brought goods to St. Louis from New York by way of the Erie Canal and the lakes to Chicago. They were then transported in wagons to the Illinois rapids, and then loaded on to a steamboat on the Illinois River and onto the Mississippi, and taken to St. Louis. The transit time took twenty-five days, two-thirds of the time to convey them over the mountains or by way of New Orleans, which represented conventional transport.[113]

A new town was planned around the site of old Fort Edwards. An advertisement, listing the names of land speculators Mark Aldrich, John R. Wilcox, John Vineyard and John Montague, was released on New Year's Day, 1834. Various benefits were articulated: its river access, tillable soil, opportunity, and location in contrast to nearby Carthage and Macomb.[114]

The hopes of Aldrich, Wilcox, and the other land promoters peaked as news of a Democratic proposal in the legislature was made public. George Forquer from Sangamon County suggested in 1834 that a railroad line should be built from the Wabash River at Danville, through Decatur, Springfield, Beardstown, and Rushville to the Mississippi River at Quincy.[115] Access to this line could be extended by a state road from Rushville through Carthage and on to Warsaw and Commerce to cover the head and foot of the Des Moines Rapids.

Amended legislation passed February 9, 1835, to view, mark, and locate a state road from Rushville in Schuyler County proceeding to Hancock County at Carthage and thence to Commerce on the Mississippi River. The express purpose was presented "having in view its permanency and a due regard to the public convenience and private interest."[116] James Miller of Hancock County was called as commissioner. Three days earlier, the legislature approved a modification of the state road from Springfield to Alton. The legislature also approved the incorporation of the Winchester, Lynnville, and Jacksonville Railroad Company with Governor Joseph Duncan and John J. Hardin, both from Jacksonville, and several others as commissioners.

On February 10, the legislature launched their main state improvement project in "an act for the construction of the Illinois and Michigan Canal."[117]

A Memorial to Congress Requesting Aid to Fix the Des Moines Rapids Problem

For the citizens of Hancock County and surrounding areas, the peril of the Des Moines Rapids was a critical concern for their well being and plans for future development. Merchants were paying premium prices above the Rapids to cover the costs of transportation and lightening during times of low water on the river. Under the direction of Richard M. Young and several of the legal profession, a memorial was drafted for Congress to assist them in solving the perils and problems wrought by nature. It was submitted late in 1835. It read,

> The citizens of Hancock County . . . represent that the navigation of the Mississippi River and the Des Moines Rapids is greatly disturbed by rocks, which render it not only difficult but very dangerous. . . . Steamboats are often stuck on the rocks, their boilers have burst, several people's lives have been lost and many others jeopardized. . . . Above these Rapids, bordering on the Mississippi and its tributaries lies an extensive and fertile country, capable of supporting a dense population, much of it is yet beset by the general government and the value of which would be greatly enhanced by a free navigation. Add to this the lead in the country yet known. Immense quantities of lead annually pass over these rapids with a price levied upon it commensurate with the delays, difficulties and charges which have to be distributed. . . . We therefore pray . . . to grant a sum of money to be applied in removing the obstruction in the Steamboat Channel on the lower or Des Moines Rapids and your memorialists . . . shall be impressed with . . . gratitude.

The first signer was Richard Young, and then Cyrus Walker and O. H. Browning. Others included Wesley Williams, Walter Bagby, Hugh White, Onias Skinner, and Adolphus Allen.

The Warsaw Peoria Wabash Railroad Company Is Approved

In the adjoining state of Indiana, legislators made serious plans for extensive internal improvements of their own, as their General Assembly convened in December 1835. The chief engineer Jesse L. Williams voiced that the Wabash and Erie Canal should form the primary means as an outlet for trade of the greater part of Indiana and a portion of

Illinois. They were optimistic that, within the confines of the state of Indiana, they had valuable mineral resources to access and develop. By the completion of that term the legislature had approved a staggering list of approved projects aggregating $10.5 million.[118] Indianapolis had been targeted for the most opportunistic commercial development. An early favorite to complement the Wabash and Erie Canal was the Madison to Indianapolis Railroad to link at Lafayette.

Seeing the immediate benefits of such a development, Illinois politicians attempted to link with the Indiana proposals for the Wabash and Erie Canal and the railroad to connect at Lafayette. In Indiana, the three canal projects were allocated $6.2 million, and $1.3 million was allocated for this railroad project. Previously, in 1832, the state seriously considered building a railroad from Lake Michigan to Lafayette to add even more opportunity to Illinois plans.[119]

Expecting a new wave of economic prosperity emanating from the Illinois and Michigan Canal and the Wabash Erie Canal, the Illinois legislature approved several other railroad, canal, and highway projects. One of these endeavors with the most interest to Hancock County residents was the act authorizing the Warsaw, Peoria, and Wabash Rail Road Company, put in force effective January 14, 1836, which provided for several commissioners, including Mark Aldrich, James Montague, Walter Bagby, David Matthews, Joel Wright, Isaiah Stillman, and Cyrus Walker. The named commissioners were charged with the following:

> The duty of whom, . . . at some suitable place in Philadelphia, New York and Baltimore, and in the towns of Warsaw, Carthage, Macomb, Peoria, Chicago, Bloomington, in the state of Illinois, . . . to open books, to receive subscriptions to the capital stock of said corporation, . . . to get the said stock taken up.[120]

The act established the "Warsaw, Peoria and Wabash railroad from Warsaw, on the Mississippi, in Hancock county, by the way of Carthage, in said county, Macomb, in Macdonough county, to Peoria, on the Illinois river, in Peoria county; thence to Mackinawtown, in Tazewell county; Bloomington, in McLean county, to a suitable point on the line dividing the states of Illinois and Indiana, in a direction to the termination of the Erie and Wabash Canal."[121]

The intent of this railroad was to complement the two major internal projects of Illinois and Indiana. The Illinois and Michigan Canal would connect with Lake Michigan, where steamboats could travel through the Canal down the Illinois River and load and unload passengers and freight at Peoria. The Wabash and Erie Canal would connect with Lake Erie, where steamboats could travel through the Canal down the Wabash River and load and unload passengers and freight at some port or landing site near the town of Covington. The Warsaw and Peoria and Wabash Railroad would transfer freight to and from the Mississippi River from the canal intersecting sites at Peoria and Covington, Indiana. This railroad would benefit from the increased traffic accessing the Atlantic Ocean seaports in New England by way of the Erie Canal through the Great Lakes.

Unfortunately for the citizens of Hancock County and the rest of the state, the legislature had approved nearly nineteen million dollars in improvements. Whig and Democrat pet projects throughout the state were approved to get consensus for passing the bills through the legislature. None of the legislators were willing to give up their local projects.

There was no chance the state could fund all these projects, and yet costs were expended on each project so no one would feel slighted. These projects were approved with Joseph Duncan as governor. (The following map, printed in 1838, shows the planned canal, railroad, and highway improvement projects.)

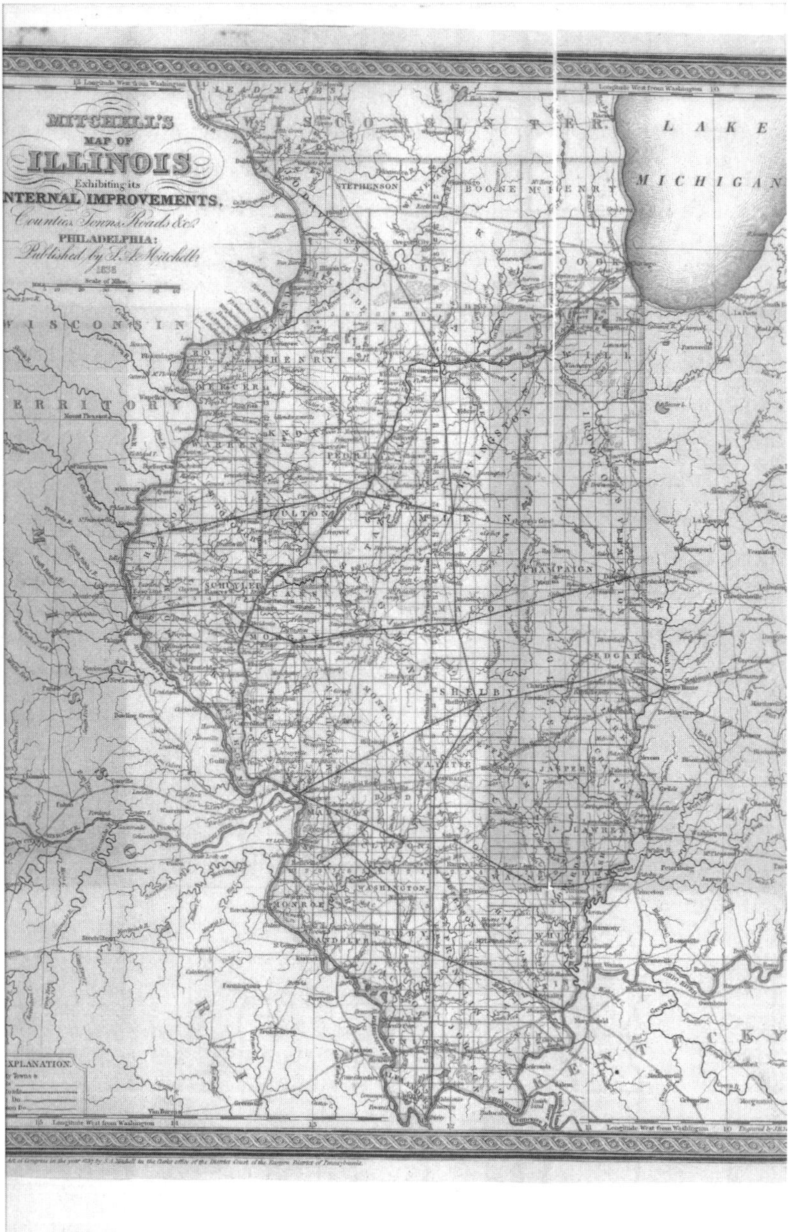

- River Improvements: $400,000
- Vincennes to St. Louis Railroad: $250,000
- Central RR (Galena to Cairo): $3,500,000
- Southern Cross (Alton to Mt. Carmel): $1,600,000

- Northern Cross Railroad (Quincy to Lafayette): $1,850,000
- Alton to Shelbyville Railroad: $650,000
- Warsaw to Peoria Railroad: $700,000
- Lower Alton to Central Railroad: $600,000
- Bellville and Lebanon Railroad connection: $150,000
- Bloomington to Mackinaw Railroad: $350,000
- Miscellaneous: $200,000
- Total Approved: $10,250,000[122]
- Illinois and Michigan Canal Estimate: $8,650,000
- Grand Total: $18,900,000

Residents of Hancock County in Commerce, Warren, and Warsaw still saw this development as providing a major boom in commerce, running through their steamboat landing sites at the head and base of the Des Moines Rapids. This increased volume was expected to spur more traffic on the Mississippi River from New Orleans, St. Louis, and Canada.

Mark Aldrich, active in the state legislature, played a significant role in garnering support in getting these statutes passed in the General Assembly. He had immensely powerful Whig political allies and some prominent Democrats in support of these internal improvement projects.

Various ceremonies and celebrations occurred on July 4, 1836, at Canalport on the Chicago River, to usher in the first day of actual construction on the Illinois and Michigan Canal.

Mark Aldrich sold Warsaw lands to Richard F. Barrett and Joseph Duncan on July 28, 1836. Previously, Barrett had purchased Warsaw lands from Calvin A. Warren and Mr. L. Allen Key of Philadelphia. In the Aldrich contract with Barrett and the governor was a provision:

> I, the said Aldrich also bind myself to all of the above land immediately divided into two lots on the place of those already laid off on the N. E. ¼ of Section 9, above mentioned; . . . I, the said Aldrich, am to pay and the said Barrett and Duncan have a plan by which they expect to sell the above divided lots and lands, but if their plans should fail and the lots and lands should not be sold as they expect, they have the full liberty of cancelling this contract and the said Aldrich binds himself to refund the $1,500 which is paid in hand and to the purchase money

> above mentioned, provided, the said Barrett and Duncan shall signify their disposition to cancel this contract and deliver up to me, the said Aldrich, this title bond between this date and January 1, next.[123]

Aggressive internal projects in Illinois and the neighboring states of Indiana and Michigan were adding greatly to the optimism of Hancock County leaders, anxious to create economic prosperity for themselves and constituents. By March 1837, Michigan was looking to develop their state with a series of internal improvements, which included railroads, canals, and improved river navigation with loan authorizations of five million dollars.[124] All of these massive state internal projects, however, relied on foreign investors. The major foreign player in providing financing for these extensive internal improvement projects was Baring Brothers of London.

An International Banking Crisis Is Developing

Across the Atlantic, events were transpiring that would have a serious impact on American commercial enterprises in the near future. On May 12, 1836, government officials in London had debated the merits and cautions pertaining to joint-stock banking. The *London Times* published articles of concern on the subject matter being aired in the Halls of Parliament. They reminded their readers of the previous collapse in 1825, which resulted in the end of the Bank of England's monopoly and created a series of business failures.

Discussions of British concerns over joint-stock banking extended fears of rampant American escalation of debt and investment. The *Times* referred to President Jackson's proposals and policies and reported the country is turned into a gambling-house for the benefit of legislative favourites. It contended that the American people were "delivered up, fettered and weaponless, to the tender mercies of a set of incorporated banks." They criticized the "paper mania" extant in the United States lacking the proper restraint of hard currency. A column made reference to a "currency distemper which rages so violently all over the United States." The paper advocated for President Jackson's calling for a return to the "constitutional metallic currency." In three years, American foreign indebtedness had risen from 110 to 220 million dollars.

Other British newspapers voiced alarm at the trend in which their species reserves were destined to America. The *Newcastle Courant* lamented that "a very considerable quantity of gold has been exported within the last three or four weeks, and the exportation is going on."[125] The *Brighton Patriot* wrote, "Gold continues to leave the country; the government of the United States . . . use our sovereigns as if it were their own."[126] Other British newspapers joined in warning of the British imbalance of trade with the United States. Their exports were declining when compared with the visible growth of American exports.

New York Congressman C. C. Cambreleng, a hard-money Democrat and friend of Senator Benton, voiced his concerns of the American financial system decline. He feared the "wild and uncalculating spirit of speculation" that produced a surplus could not continue. He presented statistics of "the vast and sudden expansion of the business of all the banks of the Union."[127]

By October 13, the Bank of England lost another million pounds sterling of gold from reserves. They felt compelled to act aggressively against American creditors, passing secret measures to retrieve their gold back from US banks. The policy was communicated abroad, "the extensive credits hitherto given to the Bankers of the United States & others . . . are objectionable so far as the Bank of England is concerned."[128] They further pressed the American banking houses support their new policy and agree to "checking that system, which they deem to be prejudicial to the currency of the country."

On American shores, the citizens knew little what economic storm was mounting against them. Their quality of life was in deep peril.

Samuel Hermann arrived home on December 2, 1836, to news that the Bank of England had issued significant policy changes and that Liverpool cotton prices had been drastically cut. The New Orleans *Commercial Bulletin* hinted that, based on reports coming from Liverpool, those merchants who were expecting profits on cotton sold at high profits were going to suffer drastically. They saw it as a temporary setback against their otherwise strong local economy.

Mr. Hermann got another devastating report. On December 8, his Mississippi River steamboat, destined for New Orleans, was lost in a violent storm. The insurance carrier found a way to avoid paying the claim. The mercantile firm of Hermann, Briggs & Company would have to absorb all losses. With other setbacks, they continued to drain their operating capital.

Hancock County and the State of Illinois Expand Projects Needing Funding

Development of Warsaw lands had not materialized as planned since the advertisement by Mark Aldrich, John R. Wilcox, John Vineyard, and John Montague was released. To further establish the beginning economic foundation for the town, John R. Wilcox conveyed land to David L. Witter for the exclusive purpose of building a steam mill, which would promote greater development in the new community. Wilcox, a West Point graduate, had served in the army at Fort Edwards, and then was hired on with the American Fur Company. John D. Mellen would later join David Witter in the steam mill enterprise. Wilcox secured and expanded his ferry operations.

James M. Wells was also associated with the early Warsaw land development. William H. Roosevelt, Thomas Morrison, and Malcolm McGregor were early residents of Warsaw, who had married sisters of James M. Wells.

Four days after Governor Duncan's transaction was completed with Aldrich, Duncan signed a new surety bond with others for his brother-in-law, William Linn. Linn was married to Duncan's sister, Polly Ann. The new surety bond was required for Linn's reappointment as the receiver of public monies at the Land Office of the District of Vandalia on February 12 of the previous year. In that capacity, millions of dollars transferred through his control each year.

Shortly after taking office as governor, Duncan nominated John H. Hardin as a commissioner and treasurer of the Illinois and Michigan Canal, but he failed to get legislature approval. Later, William Linn, the governor's brother-in-law, was approved as the commissioner and treasurer.[129] Early in 1836, when the Central Illinois Railroad Company was created, William Linn was a stockholder. The plan of the Central Illinois Railroad was to link the mineral rich areas of Galena and Dubuque and continue south to link with the Warsaw and Peoria and Wabash Railroad, continuing further south to link with lines connecting Springfield and Alton, and then further south to the Ohio and Mississippi Rivers.

In their joint capacities of governor and federal receiver of public monies, Duncan and Linn both became involved with the major players in the primary internal improvement projects of the state. The two were in strong positions to know the most valuable land projects.

Mark Aldrich recognized early the strength that Governor Duncan could bring to Warsaw and to Hancock County. Duncan went to Albany, New York, to place five hundred thousand dollars in bonds for the state to fund initial costs for the legislature-approved group of internal improvement projects. While there, he made many contacts with several banking executives in the state of New York.

Standing before the members of the Tenth General Assembly, Governor Duncan addressed the assembled legislators in session. On December 5, 1836, he recounted his efforts in the Illinois and Michigan Canal project, in which he had assisted in arranging financing. He again urged the creation of "a general and uniform system of internal improvement in the State" and further requested the state be authorized to purchase a certain amount of the capital stock of all canals and railroads. He updated those assembled as to the progress in construction of the canal and announced costs were going to exceed the previous estimates. He reiterated, "The work is of the highest importance both to this State and the United States and no ordinary difficulty or expense, should for a moment deter us from its vigorous prosecution."[130]

Within two weeks of Governor Duncan's earnest presentation to the state legislature, Mark Aldrich of Hancock County proposed that the House Committee on Internal Improvements be instructed to inquire into the expediency of the state in investing up to one-third of the capital stock.

With Duncan using his powers and access as governor and Aldrich leading the charge in the legislature, several roads were authorized in 1837. These were to connect with Peoria and link the Illinois River or integrate with the national highway, planned to come through the Southern portion of their state from Washington, DC. Also, specific roads were designated to link to Warsaw and Commerce in Hancock County as hub sites. These roads included the Warsaw and Quincy Road as far as Lima, the Warsaw and Carthage Road with an extension to become the Warsaw and Peoria Road, and the Warsaw Augusta Road.

Hancock County promoters also requested a road from Commerce to Farmington in Fulton County and a road from Rushville to Commerce. By linking to the Rushville Beardstown Road, residents in Hancock County would have access to the Illinois River, the Great Lakes, and the Atlantic Ocean via the new canal.

With the support of Governor Duncan, the state passed the Internal Improvement Act on February 27, 1837. This act created a board of commissioners of public works, consisting of seven members representing each of the seven judicial districts. These commissioners were to be elected biannually by the general assembly in joint session.

One of the commissioners of the Warsaw and Peoria and Wabash Railroad, Joel Wright, was appointed by the legislature to serve as one of the first seven newly organized commissioners of public works.[131] With the appointment of Joel Wright to the board of public works commissioners, Mark Aldrich, as a fellow Warsaw and Peoria Railroad commissioner, had access to inside information regarding the internal administrations of the various internal improvement programs in the state.

Governor Duncan was initially opposed to state funding of internal improvement projects, preferring instead private investment. Some of these he discretely participated in as an investor. Still, neither the governor nor the legislature had the courage to cut any of the planned projects.

From Hancock County, the quest for further improvements to attract commercial activity in the county was aggressively pursued by Mark Aldrich and others. The legislature approved in February 1837 "an act to incorporate the Mississippi Des Moines Rapids Bridge Company"[132] to establish a bridge across the Mississippi River at Des Moines City in Hancock County just north of Warsaw and Montebello and south of Commerce to a strategic point on the Iowa Territory north of Keokuk.

This was an ideal location, as both sides of the river were elevated so as not to obstruct steamboat traffic below. John Tilson Jr., Adolphus Allen, Sidney H. Little, David V. Matthews, E. D. Vandevert, and James Kent were appointed commissioners.

The International Banking Crisis Expands

March 4, 1837, was inauguration day for President Martin Van Buren. At the east portico of the White House, Chief Justice Roger Taney administered the oath of office. Across the Atlantic, the leading British investment banks were in crisis. The Liverpool cotton prices continued their downward trend. About 90 percent of their cotton came from US imports. Unable to sustain their losses the previously respected cotton brokerage firm of Hermann Briggs of New Orleans announced it was closing its doors. Of the total US cotton production, about 60 percent of it was shipped to Liverpool. Two weeks later, when news reached New York City that Hermann Briggs had collapsed, the firm of Joseph & Company, a major bill broker to whom Hermann Briggs owed a large sum of money, announced they were closing. The ripple effect swept through other commercial centers across the country. Some merchants committed suicide.

After the president of Mechanic's Bank in New York died suddenly, a false rumor emerged that he committed suicide. Four days later, Dry Dock Bank, which had been a federal depository bank, experienced a run as nervous customers exchanged bank notes for specie. By May 10, all the New York banks suspended redemption of their bank notes for specie. Within four months, gold and silver specie levels had dropped from six million to less than four million dollars. To maintain the peace, city leaders called out armed troops to quell violent protests.

The crisis reverberated back to London when in June, hearing that the New York banks suspended bank note redemptions, London bankers were hit with redemption demands. The Bank of England bullion reserve was losing half a million British pounds in value per month. In October, Irish banks needed to be propped up by the Bank of England reserves. By the end of the year, the Bank of England's bullion reserve had dropped from eight million to four million pounds. London banks raised discount rates as their sources of funds were drying up.

A wave of bank problems swept through America, compounding the problems for merchants and consumers. Local merchants couldn't find sources to borrow, so inventories were cut, which resulted in reductions in sales of manufactured goods. Many laborers lost jobs.

Governor Duncan Joins the Warsaw Land Company and Has His Own Financial Crisis

In the developing western region of Illinois, a few of Duncan's supporters became frustrated over his discrete connections to certain land deals. His partners wanted his involvement made public. Duncan, however, resisted, preferring anonymity. On one occasion, some of his land partners named a proposed town development project "Joe Duncan" as a hint for him to be more public. That stunt failed as the town plan for "Joe Duncan" never materialized.

Richard F. Barrett, Governor Joseph Duncan, and Mark Aldrich discretely formed a company under the name "the Warsaw Land Company" on May 15, 1837.[133] With concerns accelerating over the National Panic of 1837 and of the state's debt from failed internal improvement projects, Duncan called a special session of the legislature to convene July 10. In the governor's message, he called for legislators to repeal the internal improvements law to save the state from fiscal collapse. Abraham Lincoln sided with the majority that rejected the governor's plea. The legislature voted to legalize the bank's indefinite suspension of specie payments. A temporary fix was provided, which allowed construction of the canal to continue.

A supplemental large block of land in Warsaw was sold by Mark Aldrich to Governor Duncan on October 8, 1837, for the sum of six thousand dollars.[134] Again, the transaction avoided public attention and scrutiny, as these men continued to formulate plans for reaping the benefits of the expected windfall in land sales that was being experienced in Chicago from the canal construction and support industries. They were waiting to cash in on quick sales at inflated prices.

Dissention concerning the estimated costs of the canal increased. During 1837, a House Committee on Internal Improvements challenged the estimates put forward previously by the joint group of commissioners. They determined that the overall costs of the canal would amount to $13,253,875, nearly $4.6 million more than previously estimated. This House Committee pushed for the adoption of a "Shallow Cut Plan" instead. Arguments within the General Assembly resulted in the reorganization of the canal board and the appointment of Benjamin Wright of New York, as a special engineering consultant to reevaluate the feasibility of the two plans. Benjamin Wright made his report to the Illinois General Assembly, supporting the plan proposed by the commissioners. In a passionate plea he included in his report,

> The Illinois and Michigan Canal, as now projected, and under construction, may truly be considered as one of the greatest and most important in its consequences of any work of any age or nation. In looking over this connection between the Lakes and the Mississippi River, it is no doubt superior in its advantages to any other which can ever be formed. It is the shortest artificial work, with the least lockage. The climate, soil, and the capability of productions of the country which will be benefited by the construction of this work, will certainly equal, if they do not exceed, any other port of the United States; . . . I think it justly merits to be executed upon the best and most permanent plan, and will justify by its revenue any outlay which may be put upon it in reason.[135]

Wright's report was accepted by the Illinois General Assembly. Governor Duncan was in a panic as to how the canal was going to be financed. The General Assembly was not assuming responsibility for the economic crisis that was sure to follow and was thwarting his efforts to save the state from insolvency. To add to his worries, the State Bank of Illinois, which held $390,835 in canal funds, had suspended specie payments on May 24. The law demanded that after sixty days, if the State Bank still refused to make specie payments, the bank would be forced to forfeit its charter. That would tie up the canal funds in litigation for an indefinite period.

If the State Bank reversed its decision and made the specie payments, it would drain all their specie reserves, and they would be forced to pay its creditors in depreciated currency, causing serious damage to the state's credit worthiness and panic among its other creditors. Also with the depreciation of their currency, the state would be forced to pay higher costs on future construction costs for the canal or cause the contractors themselves into bankruptcy.

On November 22, the government made a demand for accounting aimed at William Linn, as the receiver of public funds. He was uncooperative and ignored their request. On April 2, 1838, the government renewed their demand for an accounting of the funds entrusted to Duncan's brother-in-law. Linn, caught up in the canal and railroad projects, spent the funds for personal investments and could not meet the requests for accounting or repay the funds. Duncan, with the eight other sureties, became liable unless Linn could rectify the problem.[136]

The International Banking Crisis Again Comes to America

During 1838, British banks again lost vast sums of wealth because of American borrowers' defaults, particularly those involved with internal improvement financing. That same year, the British harvest yields were greatly depressed, necessitating increased imports of agricultural commodities. With the balance of trade adversely affected, the British bullion reserves again retreated downward to three million pounds. Consequently, this forced a ripple affect back across America while the domestic cotton market was still impaired. Just as in the previous year, the American markets were savaged. President Van Buren blundered when he took the position that the financial panic was over and that the American economy would return strong. Van Buren lost all credibility in economic matters and disrespect in foreign diplomacy.

In New York, Wall Street business had come to a crushing halt, and the New York harbors were filled with ships with nowhere to sail as there was little cargo to transport. Prices continued falling, but consumers had no means to buy. The national economic crisis had caused thirty-three thousand business failures, leading to a half-billion dollars in losses. The values of real estate and stock holdings had dropped by over a billion dollars. The country was in a deep depression, and Van Buren, Benton, and the entire Loco Foco leadership were seen to be responsible.

Aldrich and others of the Hancock and Adams County delegations still pushed for their project's funding. Visible progress was made on this project, including prompt initial surveys and construction projects at Peoria and Warsaw. Railroad shanties were built. Grading efforts were made on the approach to Warsaw with culverts as far as Carthage. The projected railroad route ran parallel to the Warsaw and Carthage Roads to provide easy highway access to planned depots. William Grover was the railroad engineer overseeing funds that were spent in Hancock County.

The various project commissioners appointed envisioned Warsaw as an intermodal hub, leveraging its strategic location on the Mississippi for steamship access linked, with highway access through the various feeder roads and railroad access at Peoria. Peoria was itself a strategic location positioned to receive steamship traffic on the Illinois River when the canal would be completed.

Government officials and project commissioners from the sites most affected pushed as their highest priorities the Illinois and Michigan Canal and the Warsaw and Peoria and Wabash Railroad, which would then also link with Indiana's primary project of the Wabash and Erie Canal. Officials and leaders in other parts of the state also fought vigorously for funding. Canal construction during 1838 proceeded rapidly. By December, nearly the entire line of canal was under contract from the Chicago River to the termination at La Salle.

At the conclusion of his term of office, Governor Duncan addressed the legislature on December 4, 1838, and announced proudly that several sections of the western division of the canal were completed, and others were far advanced. Much of the state was complacent as to the disastrous fiscal condition the state was in. Matters would continue to get much worse. They were in desperate need of increased settlers who would bring greater development potential and tax revenues. They also needed more disciplined government leadership.

Seeds were being sown for a great migration of settlers to populate new regions of Hancock and Adams Counties in Illinois. It was hoped that this new group could advance development in the region through sweat equity, as all other attempts had failed and left the state, counties, and cities nearly bankrupt. Likewise, the land speculators and their victims who had paid dearly for their acquired lands at peak prices, captivated by greed, were in desperate need for outsiders to bring new life to the area so they could resell their lands and stop paying excessive property taxes and burdensome interest payments.

Nearly all were in bleak circumstances, waiting to be delivered from their extremely grievous plight and to restore their shattered hopes and dreams. But how would they treat their new guests, expected to liberate them from their self-inflicted woes?

6: Abraham Lincoln and the Springfield Junto

Bright autumn colors filled the leaves on the many trees surrounding Lashfield Plantation in Green County, Kentucky. Slaves in the field were clearing the last of the tobacco crop as Elizabeth Abell joined her husband, Bennett, and their four children, ages three to nine, wedged between furniture pieces in their loaded wagon. Her father, Nathaniel Owens, had built this 7,500-acre estate from cash and land grants provided by the government for his service in fighting the Indians during the Revolutionary War. This young Abell family enjoyed their lives together, but Bennett was far from providing the type of life that Elizabeth had been accustomed to at Lashfield. A change was in order.

By ox team, it took about three weeks to reach their home site in New Salem, Illinois. Upon their arrival, Rowan Herndon, one of her cousins, helped them to get settled in. With the help of some other cousins in the Herndon, Graham, and Green clans, the Abells cleared their lands of walnut trees and built a cabin overlooking the Sangamon River a mile distant. With Elizabeth's southern belle persona in this frontier community, the Abell home became a frequent social lure.

Elizabeth Abell likely first met young Abraham Lincoln while he was clerking at Denton Offutt's New Salem country store. Lincoln and the Abells became fast friends and spent a great deal of time together. They would often be found at the nearby home of Bowling Green, another cousin to Elizabeth.

When word that the steamer *Talisman* had left Cincinnati on a voyage to demonstrate that the Sangamon River was navigable, Lincoln and others from nearby New Salem joined with residents of Springfield to converge at Beardstown to cut back overhanging brush and remove debris to ensure a successful debut for the steamer. Lincoln had previously boasted he knew the Sangamon River better than anyone. When the opportunity presented itself, he embraced the challenge and took over as pilot of the steamer to Portland Landing to the cheers of the locals.[137]

Offutt's store failed a short time later. Unemployed, Lincoln volunteered to serve in the Black Hawk War. Joseph Duncan served as brigadier general and Enoch March as quartermaster. During his temporary military service, he met William F. Berry, a colonel in Lincoln's company. When the war ended, Berry determined to buy out the interest of James Herndon's general store at New Salem. Seeing an opportunity to advance his circumstances, Lincoln took over the interests in the store with Berry as a partner. The store failed, leaving Lincoln indebted to Herndon with little to show for their first business venture.

Choosing a new career path, Lincoln pursued surveying to provide more of an income. He also became the New Salem postmaster. Seriously short of funds, Lincoln often stayed at the Abell home, enjoying the sights and sounds of domesticated family life.

Lincoln Meets Mary Owens

In October, back at Lashfield, Mary Owens was anxious to visit her sister, Elizabeth Abell, whom she had not seen in three years. While visiting in New Salem, she was introduced to their guest, an eligible bachelor named Abraham Lincoln. In her brief visit of a few weeks, Lincoln became quite attracted to her while enjoying her grace, refinement, and intellectual prowess.

A favorite story circulated in the town of Lincoln's fondness for jam. As the story was told, while seated comfortably at the Abell dinner table, Lincoln helped himself to an extra portion of jam. Unable to get the lump out of the fruit preserves on his plate with his knife, he determined a dead mouse had succumbed previously to the sweetness of the jam, and the small carcass remained submerged on his plate. Lincoln, in a brief quandary, weighed the options. He clearly didn't want to embarrass the Abell's or alarm the visiting Miss Owens, nor did he dare leave the matter for someone else to discover. After a final look at the lump, he determined he must resolve the matter—he ate it.[138]

In the several weeks of her visit, Lincoln spent a lot of time with the welcomed guest. Yet their different pedigrees clarified his pecuniary dilemma. In a short time, she would be returning to her grand and stately plantation as he continued in humble and meager means.

It was at this same time, in 1833, that Elizabeth and Mary's brother, Samuel C. Owens, living hundreds of miles away in Independence, Missouri, had been utilizing his basic business skills learned from their same tutors at Brush Creek Academy. In Jackson County, Owens began working with the Aull brothers and expanded mercantile operations quickly. He was able to connect with the powerful Chouteau fur trading monopoly and worked under contracts with Francois and Pierre Chouteau from time to time.

As the Mormons began to respond to their call to Zion and gathered in Jackson County, Samuel Owens took an early dislike to the gathering Saints. The Gilbert Store began to compete with his mercantile pursuits. Within a short time, he developed a deep hatred of the Mormon people and actively participated in persecutions against them. He was one of the leading members of the secret constitution group who forced the Mormons out of the county. Owens continued to persecute the Mormons and traveled to join mobs in other counties in Missouri in open persecution of the Saints as they sought to build their New Jerusalem.

During that winter and next spring, Lincoln continued to live with the Abell family. Attempting to advance his surveying skills, Lincoln would often be gone on short out-of-town jaunts, earning but a basic living. Expanding his capabilities while there, Lincoln became the principal surveyor in locating a road from the Sangamon River through New Salem and on toward Jacksonville.[139] With Lincoln's frequent presence, the Abell home continued to be the neighborhood magnet, attracting many to listen to Lincoln's home-spun humor and antics. Beneficial for Lincoln, this arrangement allowed him to study a few books from the Abell personal library. While living with the Abells, and with their support and encouragement, Lincoln became motivated to run again for the state legislature in 1834. This time, he prevailed and was elected as part of the Ninth General Assembly, meeting at Vandalia, the state capital.

Lincoln Involved in Illinois Internal Improvements Legislation

Anxious to advance economic development in the state, Lincoln drafted a bill on January 12, 1835: "An Act of the Illinois Legislature to Lay Out a State Road from the Wabash to the Yellow Banks of the Mississippi River." His bill called for a state road to traverse the state from the Indiana border near Logansport to intersect the Illinois River at Allenton at the head of Lake Peoria, and then to travel through Knox and Warren Counties and continue to the Lower Yellow Banks on the Mississippi River.[140] Later, Sangamon's Democratic Senator George Forquer proposed a railroad from the Wabash River west to Springfield and Beardstown, intersecting the Illinois River, and then to Rushville and Quincy on the Mississippi River. Lincoln, as the Whig legislator from Sangamon County, wrote a letter that was printed in the *Sangamo Journal*:

> A railroad from Springfield to Alton would do ten times more toward building up the latter town, than the seat of government, the national road, the loan office and the state prison added together. If Alton could be made the depot of the productions of the Sangamon country, she would of necessity become an important town, and in our opinion she cannot be without it.[141]

As a result, in March 1835, a thousand citizens gathered to Springfield in support of Lincoln's proposal for a railroad from Springfield to Alton and the Mississippi River. Forquer's proposal for the Quincy Beardstown and Springfield and Wabash Railroad was relegated to secondary status, much to the dismay of the Hancock and Adams County supporters.

The issue of the Illinois and Michigan Canal came up frequently, of which Lincoln and other prominent Whig leaders were avid supporters. With the prospects of access from the East Coast through the Erie Canal via the Great Lakes, and connecting with the Illinois and Michigan Canal down the Illinois River, Lincoln was appointed with a five-member committee to incorporate the Beardstown and Sangamon Canal Company. In that capacity, Lincoln drew upon his brief experience as a steamer pilot and road surveyor to garner support for a canal to be built between New Salem and Beardstown.[142]

With attention being given to the possibility of that canal, renewed interest by Hancock and Adams County leaders, of expanding access to Beardstown through Rushville, was heightened. If the Beardstown Canal and the Springfield and Alton Railroad were built, the farmers and merchants in Hancock and Adams County would enjoy a rapid increase in prosperity by opening up greatly expanded commercial markets for their goods and increase land values.

Nancy Owens Moves to Warsaw, Illinois

Also, at this time, a stepsister to Elizabeth and Mary named Nancy Owens, with her husband, John W. Vineyard, moved to a site near Fort Edwards on the Mississippi River. Mr. Vineyard laid out this site to become the town of Warsaw, Illinois. He partnered with Mark Aldrich, John R. Wilcox, and John Montague in promoting this new area. In 1836, Richard F. Barrett, Mark Aldrich, John Vineyard, and the other promoters were partnered with Governor Duncan, who worked jointly in developing a plan to sell town lots and accelerate development in Hancock County and surrounding counties, including the Iowa Half-Breed Tract lands directly across the river. There was an agreement by Duncan and Barrett, made with Mark Aldrich, to the effect that "the said Barrett and Duncan have a plan by which they expect to sell the above divided lots and lands, but if their plans should fail and the lots and lands should not be sold as they expect, they have the full liberty of cancelling this contract."[143]

The dominant strength of the Illinois Whig party in 1836 was found in Sangamon County, with Springfield as the county seat. They were known as the "Long Nine." From the House of Representatives, they included Abraham Lincoln, John Dawson, Ninian Wirt Edwards,

William Elkin, Andrew McCormick, Daniel Stone, and Robert Wilson. From the Senate: Job Fletcher and Archer Herndon. They were effective because they worked together as a team in the General Assembly to get their measures approved. They were aptly named the "Long Nine" because of their aggregate sizes, which when added together totaled fifty-four feet. Lincoln was the most prominent and a natural leader.

Overall, the Whig Party was on the rise because of their strategy to recruit disaffected Democrats who were typically neglected by the established Democratic base or who found themselves with interests opposed to the Loco Foco leaders in the state. With their increased political strength, they became a target. A pro-Democratic newspapers began to refer to Lincoln and the other members of the Whig State Central Committee as the "Springfield Junto." They wielded substantial power and influence statewide. Junto members included Lincoln, Stuart, Ned Baker, Stephen Logan, Dr. Anson Henry, Simeon Francis, and Joshua Speed.

The Long Nine, and later the Springfield Junto, were quite effective due to the individual unions and coalitions they had formed with other Whig delegations, such as those in Alton, Quincy, and Warsaw. In time, as their strength expanded, the State Democratic leadership followed the same tactic of the Whigs to recruit as allies those prominent Whigs who found themselves disaffected by the Springfield Junto leadership.

In 1836, Elizabeth Abell came back to Lashfield after a six-year absence. She had a matchmaking agenda and convinced her sister, Mary, to return and court Lincoln, who seemed to have a promising political career. Meeting at the Abell homestead, Lincoln and Mary continued visits, enjoying poetry together and intellectual conversations. It was at this time that a simple incident offended Mary. Lincoln and Mary had been visiting mutual friends, and Mary decided to go up the hill to her sister's cabin. Nancy Green, holding their baby, Bowling Green Jr., had joined them but was fussing a bit during their stroll. Lincoln continued his pace with them, hands in his pocket, apparently oblivious to Nancy's discomfort.

Mary seemed upset with Lincoln's lack of chivalry and overall ignorance of Nancy's plight, showing no willingness to help. Her anger intensified as they continued, until she refused to speak to her lanky escort.

She expected Lincoln would apologize for their quarrel on the matter. That didn't happen. In December, Lincoln wrote to Mary Owens:

> I have very little even yet to write. And the longer I can avoid the mortification of looking in the Post Office for your letter and not finding it, the better. . . . You see I am mad about that old letter yet. I don't like very well to risk you again. . . .
>
> I feel that I would rather be any place in the world than here. . . . Write back soon as you get this, and if possible say something that will please me, for really I have not been pleased since I left you. This letter is so dry and stupid that I am ashamed to send it, but with my present feelings I can not do any better. Give my respects to Mr. and Mrs. Abell and family.[144]

In the afternoon of February 27, 1837, at the Vandalia state house, "An Act to amend an act for the construction of the Illinois and Michigan Canal, approved 9 January, 1836" was granted. This amendment changed the means of selecting officers for the canal project and authorized the Governor to borrow five hundred thousand dollars. A bond was made for the benefit of Charles Oakley, the fund commissioner. Lincoln was so committed to this Illinois and Michigan Canal that he joined with Warsaw legislator Mark Aldrich and many others consenting to be:

> Held and firmly bound unto Joseph Duncan Governor of the State of Illinois, and his successors in office, for the use of said state in the penal sum of Fifty thousand dollars . . . sealed with our seals and dated the Fourth day of March A.D. 1837.[145]

With the state capital relocating from Vandalia to Springfield, Lincoln determined to be closer to the power source for the Whig Party and therefore moved to Springfield in April 1837. In Springfield, he continued his close friendships with the Abells, Herndons, Grahams, and Greens, all with roots to Green County, Kentucky, and the Owens family.

Initially, he roomed with his fellow Whig Party compatriot and local storekeeper: Joshua F. Speed. The gregarious Lincoln naturally drew new close friends to his inner circle of bachelors. These included Joshua F. Speed, James H. Matheny, and Milton Hay.

On many occasions, huddled at the fireplace in the back room of Joshua Speed's store, these close friends swapped stories, debated politics and religion, and practiced various literary pursuits. Lincoln frequently took center stage, always with a new story to tell and to entertain.

While at Springfield, he joined his fellow state legislator John Todd Stuart in a soon-to-thrive law practice. They brought on Milton Hay, a promising law student, to clerk for them. Their extended legal practice would often take Lincoln into the various county courts in Tazewell, Macon, Morgan, and other nearby counties.

In May 1837, he again wrote to Miss Mary Owens, but this time conveying mixed signals:

> This thing of living in Springfield is a dull business after all, at least it is to me. I am quite as lonesome here as ever was anywhere in my life. . . .
>
> I am often thinking about what we said of your coming to live in Springfield. I am afraid you would not be satisfied. . . .
>
> Whatever woman may cast her lot with mine, should any ever do, it is my intention to do all in my power to make her happy and contented; and there is nothing I can imagine, that would make me more unhappy than to fail in the effort. I know I should be much happier with you than the way I am, provided I saw no sign of discontent in you.[146]

During the acceleration of Illinois internal improvements projects, John Vineyard determined other opportunities were more to his liking. He left with his wife, Nancy, in 1837 and settled in the newly partitioned Weston, Platte County, Missouri, much closer to their brother Samuel Owens, who was still in Independence.

Mary Owens Declines Lincoln's Marriage Proposal

From Springfield, Lincoln wrote his last letter to Mary Owens, dated August 16, 1837.

> You will no doubt, think it rather strange, that I should write you a letter on the same day on which we parted: and I can only account for it by supposing, that seeing you lately makes me think of you more than usual, while at our late meeting we had but few expressions of thoughts. . . .

> If it suits you best to not answer this farewell—a long life and a merry one attend you. But if you conclude to write back, speak as plainly as I do. There can be neither harm nor danger, in saying to me, any thing you think, just in the manner you think it. My respects to your sister. Your friend, Lincoln.[147]

Mary Owens returned home to Lashfield, the family estate in Kentucky. It was their last visit together. Their engagement was over.

On April 1, 1838, Lincoln wrote to Mrs. Orville Browning, describing his previous marriage proposal to Mary Owens:

> I mustered by resolution, and made the proposal to her direct: but shocking to relate, she answered, no. At first I supposed she did it through an affectation of modesty . . . but on my renewal of the charge, I found she repelled it with greater firmness than before. I tried again and again, but with the same success, or rather with the same want of success. I finally was forced to give it up . . . I was mortified, it seemed to me, in a hundred different ways. . . . I had so long been too stupid to discover her intentions, and at the same time never doubting that I understood them perfectly.[148]

Earlier in this letter, perhaps surprised and embittered by her rejection of his marriage proposal, Lincoln resorted to some rather unkind words toward Mary:

> I knew she was over-sized, but she now appeared a match for Falstaff. I knew she was called an "old maid" . . . and in short, I was not at all pleased with her. But what could I do? I had told her sister that I would take her for better or for worse; and I made a point of honor and conscience to stick to my word.[149]

He went on to pledge that he would "never again think of marrying; and for this reason; I can never be satisfied with any one who would be block-head enough to have me."

Several years later, at Lashfield estate in Kentucky, Mary Owens married Jesse Vineyard, the brother of her sister's husband, John W. Vineyard, who had worked closely with Mark Aldrich in promoting Warsaw land sales. Mary moved with her husband to Weston Township in Platte County, Missouri, to join John and Nancy, who had settled there after leaving Warsaw.

Lincoln Further Promotes the Illinois Internal Improvement Efforts

With the disastrous fiscal calamities from internal improvements devastating the Illinois state government budgets, leaders were looking for new citizens to sway voting for advancing their internal improvement projects ahead of others.

After winning reelection for the Eleventh General Assembly, Lincoln opposed General William Lee Davidson Ewing in competing for the position of the Illinois Speaker of the House. Ewing, a Democrat, prevailed as the legislature was predominantly Democratic. Graciously, Ewing reappointed Lincoln to the Committee on Finance and Counties.

Before the legislature, Mr. John Hardin of Morgan County asked for detailed information on all matters pertaining to the duties of the railroad and fund commissioners. Lincoln supported this investigation, acknowledging his was not an unfriendly view toward the internal improvement system. It was his desire that Hardin's resolution pass to enable the supporters of the system to detect any errors that might be found and to prevent their recurrence.[150]

On the finance committee, Lincoln reported to the House on January 19 that "we are now so far advanced in a general system of internal improvements that, if we would, we cannot retreat from it, without disgrace and great loss." He then proposed the state acquire the unsold public lands and sell them to generate a profit to be used to fund internal improvements.[151]

Lincoln wrote to his friend Congressman John T. Stuart for his assistance to secure federal support to help them in their fiscal crisis, but he was unsuccessful. During this time, Lincoln would become friends with another former Green County, Kentucky, transplant: Richard F. Barrett, who married the daughter of a prominent judge named Richard Aylette Buckner.

During 1839, Lincoln met Mary Todd, the daughter of a successful merchant and a banker in Lexington, Kentucky. Their off-and-on courtship would continue for three years.

During the 1838–39 legislative session, a select committee—including Senators Orville H. Browning and William A. Richardson and Representatives William F. Thornton, John J. Hardin, and William M. Roman, as well as a handful of others—was called to investigate fraud and incompetence, which had been brought against some of the internal improvement commissioners.

The Mormon Issue in Illinois

In Illinois, the partisan newspapers began using the Mormon issues in Missouri to affect the support of their respective parties locally. Following the August 1838 elections in Missouri, the *Quincy Whig* wrote,

> Caldwell County, Mo., is filled up most entirely with Mormons. They were worse upon the Whigs of Missouri than our canallers were upon us in this state. Thus the vote stood at the late election: Van Buren ticket 351, Whig 2. Delusion as well as ignorance have helped the Loco Focos over the river. Jo Smith, the high priest of the Mormons, deserves an office at the hand of the party.[152]

The *Sangamo Journal* reported, "In Missouri, those poor deluded creatures, the Mormons, voted for the Loco Focos to a man."[153]

Senator Richard Young Learns of His Anti-Mormon Relatives

Then, on February 23, the legislature authorized a loan of 4 million dollars, bearing 6 percent interest to be negotiated by agents. Governor Carlin appointed Senator Richard M. Young and former Governor John Reynolds to negotiate the loan. This was a particularly bad time to be placing loans as the European markets were accepting only highly discounted lending terms.

News reached Senator Young of the death of his Uncle Ambrose Young. He had kept his letter, explaining his ancestry, in his diary. It read:

> I will now agreeably to your request, . . . give you a short history of the genealogy of your relations. . . . Your great, great grandfather, Laurence Young, emigrated from England, and was the first white person who settled in Fredericksburgh. . . . He then had several children, . . . and his last son, your great grandfather, Richard Young, possessed the homestead and lived and died there at the age of 82 years. . . .
>
> Your Grandfather, John Young was born in Caroline County, Virginia . . . he married his first wife, Mary Martin, daughter of Robert Martin. . . . Your Grandfather had four children by this first wife, to wit: Nancy, Abner (your father), Ambrose, and Jane. . . .

> I Ambrose Young was born October 12, 1772, married Fanny Alcock of Virginia October 12. . . . Thus I have complied with your request. . . . Your affectionate uncle.

Through his Uncle Ambrose, he had been introduced to some of his more prominent children, who were Richard's cousins. These included Elizabeth Young, the wife of Thomas Reynolds, a prominent Democratic politician running for governor of Missouri, and Frances Maria (Fanny), who had married Samuel Owens, a prominent merchant in Jackson County, Missouri.

Lincoln and the Springfield Junto

Early in 1839, the Springfield Junto launched aggressive plans in preparation for the upcoming presidential elections. A meeting of the Whig Young Men of Springfield and Sangamon County was organized and met at the courthouse on Saturday, January 26, "for the purpose of organizing for future operations."[154] In support, the *Sangamo Journal* challenged,

> To the young Whigs, . . . we would say, that it is time you were up and doing. . . . At the last (election) more than 60,000 votes were thrown: and out of these our opponents claim less than 900 majority! One effort more and success will be ensured.[155]

Taking up the challenge, the enthusiastic Sangamon County Whigs issued an appeal to activate further support. They claimed that the current Van Buren administration sought to unite the president's control of:

> The sword and the purse. When these two are united in one and the same individual, despotism is not far distant. . . . Who can declare that at some future period some bold, ambitious aspirant, may not arise, who will stretch to the utmost his prerogative, and wield his powers with the most destructive energy for his own aggrandizement. . . .
>
> Assemble in your various neighborhoods. Appoint committees to confer with each other. Throw aside every jarring claim, and all discordant views. Let all, with united force and unity of sentiment, move on in one solid phalanx.[156]

A passionate and energized grass-roots movement to throw out the dominance of the Loco Foco and Van Buren aristocracy was emerging, with the Springfield Junto leading the charge. To further organize and improve their chances in coming elections, the Sangamon Committee of Vigilance was formed "to collect information from various parts of the county." Billy Herndon, at age twenty, was appointed to that committee. Other Whig Young Men activist members included James Conkling, Milton Hay (who at the time was a law student working for the Stuart and Lincoln Law Firm), James Matheny (Lincoln's friend and fellow poetry club member), and Allen and Josiah Francis (brothers of the editor of the *Sangamo Journal*).

Anxious to take initiative with his new appointment, Billy Herndon called a meeting for his committee for early April to select Whig candidates to run for county offices. After they had been operating a while, the Sangamon County group called for a statewide organization of Young Whigs. With that, the state Democratic Party took them more seriously.

At the state Whig Convention held at Springfield in October 1839, a Central Committee was selected to lead the party. The five men selected were Abraham Lincoln, Josh Speed, Dr. Anson Henry, Ned Baker, and Dr. Richard F. Barrett. Dr. Barrett already had a reputation for being one of the region's largest land speculators and a tough moneylender. It was not, however, well known that Barrett was partnered with former Governor Duncan and Mark Aldrich in the Warsaw Land Company. Though the convention was deemed a success by many, their greatest problem was that only half of the counties in the state sent delegates.

With the disastrous fiscal calamities from internal improvements devastating the Illinois government budgets, leaders were desperately hoping for large numbers of taxpaying immigrants to move in. In Hancock and Adams Counties, leaders were also looking for new citizens to sway voting for advancing their internal improvement projects ahead of others.

In nearby Sangamon County, the Long Nine—and particularly Abraham Lincoln—were gaining great public prominence. Lincoln's close circle of friends included several from Green County, Kentucky, including the family of Nathaniel Owens and the related Herndon,

Green, and Barrett families, several of whom were closely associated with Samuel Owens and other enemies of the Mormons in Jackson County, Missouri, and some who had lived in Warsaw, Illinois.

7: The St. Louis and New York Land Companies

The Building of Fort DesMoines Near the Rapids

In the aftermath of the Black Hawk War, Congress made provisions for a regiment of Dragoons to be situated in the frontier as a protection to settlers. Lieutenant Stephen W. Kearny was ordered to establish his regiment at the mouth of the Des Moines River with Captains Summer, Boone, and Browne, and with George H. Crosman as quartermaster.

Crosman went ahead early to oversee the construction of barracks and stables for his men. Crosman chose a site for Fort Des Moines on the Mississippi just north of an apple orchard planted by Louis Tesson years earlier. He made arrangements with Captain James White to take over this section of land that White claimed was his own. Unknown to Crosman was another claim emerging pertaining to an older series of transactions relating to a Spanish land grant during the Spanish occupation of the area. It was these types of claims that Senator Benton had focused his early law practice.

Superintendent William Clark appointed Jenifer T. Sprigg to survey the half-breed tract in the Iowa Territory, after Congress appropriated two thousand dollars for allocating lands to half-breed Indian claimants. Clark had been ordered that a town plot should be laid out at the junction of the Des Moines and Mississippi Rivers. Sprigg arrived during the middle of March 1832 to commence the survey by establishing section and township lines. Sprigg's crews stopped working after word of an Indian uprising under Chief Black Hawk was voiced about the various camps.

Sprigg's survey for the one-mile square town plot for Keokuk was completed in March 1833. John Johnson, the local government administrator, was surprised that more Indian claims had not been filed by the time the survey was done.

Johnson urged that each half-breed claimant be given title in fee simple for their portion of the 119,000 acres of Half-Breed Tract lands. Squatters had been seen in various areas in the tract as government enforcement was lax.

Isaac Galland Purchases Half-Breed Tract Lands and Joins the New York Land Company

In response to his letter, Superintendent Clark wrote Isaac Galland on January 7, 1834:

> Sir: Your letter of the 12th ult. On . . . the claim of Mary Tolman, formerly Mary Duque, and the accompanying deposition of Show-a-no-quoh, . . . in its support, have been received and shall be filed away for the necessary action at the proper time.
>
> The copy of a certificate from certain chiefs and principal men of the Sac and Fox Indians . . . stated by you to have been also forwarded with your letter has not reached this office nor has the deposition which you mention as having transmitted, proving the heirs of St. Jean to have been of Sac descent come to hand. Should it be the wish of those interested to these papers in this office let them be forwarded as early as practicable. And I would recommend that all claims forwarded be supported by the deposition of the claimants and by such other testimony as is available; the depositions should be taken before a justice of the peace, certified to be such by a clerk of some court of record. Mere unauthenticated copies of certificates or reference to individuals will most likely not be considered sufficient when the claims come to be decided on. . . .

> The object now in view is to give . . . all who consider themselves justly entitled to lands as half breeds under the Sac and Fox treaty of 4 August 1824, of presenting their claims with the evidence in their support. The time and mode of distribution of the lands, as well as the nature of the title to be conveyed, have not . . . been yet determined, but as the lands are surveyed the subject will . . . receive . . . attention at Washington.[157]

Isaac Galland, because of his many years in the area and his many dealings with the Indians, was successful in finding half-breed Indians, such as Mary Tolman, willing to sell their land claims. But the legal process had not been well established at the time of Clark's letter in 1834. Later, Congress passed "An Act to relinquish the reversionary interest of the United States in a certain Indian reservation lying between the rivers Mississippi and Desmoines."

> Sec. 1st. Be it enacted. . . . That all right, title and interest which might accrue or revert to the United States to the reservation of land lying between the rivers Desmoines and Mississippi which was reserved for the use of the half-breeds belonging to the Sacs and Fox nations now used by them . . . on the fourth day of August in the year one thousand eight hundred and twenty four, be and the same are hereby relinquished and vested in the said half breeds of the Sacs and Fox tribes or nations of Indians who at the passage of this act are under the reservations in the said treaty entitled by the Indian title to the same with full power and authority to transfer their portions thereof by sale, devise, or descent. . . . Approved June 30, 1834.[158]

With the change in the law, Galland moved forward in securing documentation for any half-breed families willing to sell their lands. Needing funding to finance his negotiations with various half-breed individuals willing to sell their interests, Galland joined with outside land speculators anxious to secure the half-breed lands in their strategic location in the Iowa Territory. The New York Land Company was formed with the specific purpose of securing the Indian lands along the Des Moines River and the Des Moines Rapids on the Mississippi River.

The partnership agreement, dated on October 22, 1836, provided that their agents Joshua Aikin, Robert Little, and Isaac Galland should transfer title to property previously purchased in the Half-Breed Tract amounting to about twenty thousand dollars to partnership members as joint tenants. At the time of their agreement, the titles for the previous purchased lands were still in the names of Aikin, Galland, and others. Also, the agents were to have the prior purchased lands and future purchased lands surveyed, improved, and laid out as towns and cities. Particular mention was made to focus attention on lands in reference to water power and hydraulic privileges. As the lands were resold, all costs were to be reimbursed, and remaining profits were to be distributed according to their partnership interests. The partnership agreement granted Isaac Galland a sixth of the total share of the partnership interests.

Isaac Campbell Forms the St. Louis Land Company

After the passing of Farnham and for economic reasons, the Chouteaus determined to withdraw from their Keokuk location on the Mississippi, and then resettled up the Des Moines River area. Isaac R. Campbell purchased the land and trading post improvements used by the American Fur Company in 1832 and began exploring opportunities to secure a promising return on his investment. Campbell was previously engaged in the Galena lead transport runs through the Rapids. This area had already been platted earlier that year by US government surveyors, hoping to use the site for a strategic presence in Indian Territory with easy access. The government was not aware initially they were trespassing on the site of a 640-acre Spanish land grant property held by the heirs of Thomas Reddick, who had recently died.

Isaac Campbell became well known for entertaining travelers and for his more lucrative enterprise of towing and lightening services for steamboats around the Mississippi Rapids. For much of the year, the Rapids between Keokuk and Commerce prevented loaded steamboats from continuing on. Workers would unload freight from the steamboats and transport them on shallow draft keelboats and simply tow them onward. Thus relieved, the steamboats continued their transport past the Rapids, and then docked as anxious passengers and crew waited for the previous contents to be reloaded before continuing to their destinations.

The St. Louis Chamber of Commerce began in 1836. Pierre Chouteau and other members of the St. Louis Junto took an early active role in this group of merchants. Other active St. Louis key merchants included Augustus Kerr, a leading dry goods wholesaler. Prudently these various commerce leaders sought to work with instead of against the dominant and extremely powerful St. Louis Junto leaders. Augustus Kerr and John P. Reilly were close friends with George T. M. Davis of Alton and referred legal work his way.[159]

With the change of the Half-Breed Tract legislation, a number of St. Louis merchants, some being half-breeds themselves, took a leading role to better organize and secure land opportunities. The St. Louis Land Company was created by Isaac Campbell, a local resident, with John and Edward Walsh, J. H. Overhall, and Colonel Crossman as partners. The St. Louis Land Company was successful early in securing the claim from Isaac Ataya, a recognized half-breed claimant.

John and Edward Walsh made their fortunes in milling enterprises and invested nearly a half million dollars in partial investments of twenty steamships. When the federal government opened the lead mines in Galena to leasing, they providentially secured three major leasing contracts. Though most business leaders in St. Louis and in the eastern Missouri counties were Whigs, some highly successful merchants were staunch Democrats, such as Edward Walsh, a close friend and chief supporter of Senator Thomas Benton.

By May 1836, Pierre Chouteau was well aware from his brother Francois Chouteau that the Missouri River trade was in jeopardy because of the growing merchant activities of the Mormons around the critical *entrepôt* in Independence and Chouteau's Landing in Jackson County. The interdependent coalition of merchants depending on the fur imports from the upper Missouri and the silver and gold from the Santa Fe trade, lead by Samuel Owens and Lilburn Boggs, were critical to the balance necessary for their export products to the Indians, fur traders, and outlying merchants. Various coalitions of St. Louis merchants were in agreement that the Mormons must not be allowed to upset their lucrative commercial arrangements in their regions.

It was of great relief that the Mormon threat spoken of by Francois Chouteau in Jackson County did not materialize as they had feared it would. But they were firm in their resolve that they would have fought them to the bitter end to prevent them from returning and interfering with them.

Edward Brooks and the Reddick Heirs File Suit for Montrose Lands

Various insurance companies were formed in St. Louis to protect and share the risk of steamboat accidents because of the many hazards found on the Missouri and Mississippi traffic routes. The dominant insurance companies formed included the St. Louis Insurance Company, with Edward Brooks as a director. He was also a stockholder in the planned St. Louis Hotel.

In various St. Louis merchant meetings and other encounters, the newspaper editors and their assistants (including George T. M. Davis, Adam B. Chambers, and John Bailhache) would be found engaged in many of the same commercial projects and ventures with the Chouteaus, Kerrs, Walshs, and others. George T. M. Davis found the St. Louis merchants, a prime source for securing additional legal work for his law practice.

In 1837, Isaac Galland recorded a map and platted the original city of Keokuk. While Galland was focused on Keokuk land sales and development, in that same year a new claimant was initiating legal process on other lands in the Half-Breed Tract. Edward Brooks, on behalf of his wife, Virginia—as daughter and heir to Thomas F. Reddick (also spelled Riddick)—made application to the commissioner of the General Land Office for an order of survey of a claim. Their records showed that, in 1799, Louis Tesson Honore obtained permission from the Spanish government of Louisiana to settle on 7,056 arpents of land, an area of about three miles.

In response to the Edward Brooks application, on October 11, 1837, the US commissioner directed William Willburn, as surveyor general, to have the claim surveyed. He ordered Isaac T. Woods, the deputy US surveyor, to do the survey. The parcel in question was located on the west side of the Mississippi River at a point referred to as "Head of the Rapids."

What was not readily apparent to many residents was that Edward Brooks and other Reddick heirs had close affiliations with the Chouteaus and their Indian agents. Joshua Pilcher was a close friend of Thomas Reddick. Edward Brooks was the son-in-law of Reddick and business agent for Joshua Pilcher, who was appointed through the efforts of Senator Benton as the replacement to William Clark as Superintendent of Indian Affairs.

Reddick and Pilcher had been associated with the original Bank of Missouri with Boggs and Benton. The site of Montrose was deemed important to the shipping of lead ore from the Dubuque and Galena mines down through the Des Moines Rapids, on to St. Louis, and then for export from New Orleans.

The regiment of Dragoons evacuated Fort Des Moines and were reassigned to Fort Leavenworth on the Missouri River in 1837. This lead to the opportunity of the Reddick heirs to take possession of the entire area claiming the 640-acre land tract and documenting their rights enhanced by actual occupancy. Isaac Woods arrived from St. Louis in April 1838. When doing the survey the only structures on the land were the remnant barracks of Fort Des Moines. When completed, Isaac Wood's field notes and data were sent to Washington.

David Kilbourne Becomes an Agent for the New York Land Company

David Kilbourne and Henry Austin replaced Aiken and Little as agents of the New York Land Company during September 1837. Kilbourne got caught up in the excitement of the commercial development and wanted a share of the coming wealth on the Illinois side. As a family enterprise, Kilbourne petitioned the Illinois legislature to authorize the "Illinois Beet Sugar Manufacturing Company" effective February 18, 1837, to be located at Galena, with David and Edward Kilbourne and brothers-in-law William Coleman and Alfred Buell as principals. Their charter authorized them to "carry on the business of cultivating and purchasing the sugar beet, and manufacturing sugar from the same, to export their products and manufactures, to erect mills, works, machines, and such other buildings . . . to carry on their business."[160]

Kilbourne was committed to profiting from the various competitors, seeking to link Galena and Dubuque for lead mining purposes. The same infrastructure and traffic routes would also benefit their beet sugar enterprise. He also supported a new church group settling near Galena.

Challenging the Des Moines Rapids

All of the land developers, merchants, and farmers of Hancock and Adams Counties were interested in the actions of Congress, with two major bills they were anticipating would have a major impact on their economic well-being. In need of federal financial assistance the political leaders of Illinois drafted a memorial in support of Senator Richard Young's proposed act in Congress on March 5, 1838, calling for:

> The improvement of the navigation of the great Wabash river, . . . over which the States of Indiana and Illinois have concurrent jurisdiction, for which improvement the sum of one hundred thousand dollars is hereby appropriated; which said appropriation the said board of public works are hereby authorized and required to expend . . . in conjunction with the State of Indiana, in equal amounts, and for like objects. . . .
>
> That it shall also be the duty of the board of commissioners to contract for the immediate construction, . . . of all the railroads or parts thereof contemplated between Quincy and the Wabash, as lies between Jacksonville, in Morgan county, Springfield, in Sangamon county, Decatur, in Macon county, and Danville, in Vermillion county; thence to the State line in Vermillion county in a direction to Lafayette, in Indiana, at such point as the commissioners of this State and of Indiana may agree to cross the same.[161]

A week later on March 12, another memorial from Illinois, under the name of Adolphus Allen, was submitted, calling for "Congress to construct a bridge over the Mississippi River at the town of Des Moines, in Illinois, and that the military road from Chicago to Fort Leavenworth may pass through said town."[162] The accompanying memorial was to provide reasons to justify building the bridge, approved by the Illinois legislature with federal funds. In the state bill, Adolphus Allen, Sidney Little, David W. Mathews, and E. D. Vandervoort were approved as commissioners and stockholders for the project. The memorial included as justification:

> That the defenseless situation of the frontier settlements on the west side of the Mississippi river, the numerous tribes of Indians that are concentrated there, the alarming aspect of our relations with Canada,

> (their former ally,) and the impassable state of the Mississippi river, call loudly for a more safe, sure, and expeditious mode of crossing . . . the river's surface is still covered with large cakes of floating ice, which cuts off all communication between the east and west side of the river. Should a war ensue, and the Indians at such a time fall simultaneously upon the unarmed and unprotected citizens of Wisconsin territory, a general massacre might ensue without a possibility of our crossing to their rescue . . . a charter has been granted for a bridge across the Mississippi river at the town of Des Moines, in Hancock county, and state of Illinois.[163]

Henry Clay presented the memorial to Congress. Unfortunately for the Hancock County residents, the project was not aggressively pursued or implemented by federal officials.

Lieutenant Robert E. Lee's Plan for the Des Moines Rapids

Lieutenant Robert E. Lee, with his wife, Mary Curtis, and two children, were sent by the US Army Corps of Engineers to find solutions to river channel issues on the Mississippi, which continued to cause navigation problems. Lee was transferred to St. Louis and found residence for his family in a cottage formerly occupied by Meriwether Lewis Clark and his wife, Abby. Superintendent Clark's Indian Agency Council Room in St. Louis had been converted into offices, leaving two upstairs rooms for rent. When Meriwether Lewis Clark and his wife moved to Fifth and Olive Street in St. Louis, the aging Superintendent moved in with them. This move left unoccupied the cottage, which the Lee family moved in.[164] It is probable that they had known each other at West Point, there being just a year's difference in their graduating classes.

Lieutenant Lee studied previous reports and proposals to alleviate the Des Moines Rapids challenge regarding the difficulty of steamboat passage during low water periods. He found that Captain Shreve's report in 1836 called for improvements to the Rapids by excavating a channel ninety feet wide and five feet deep along the Iowa shore, from Keokuk to Nashville and through the Upper Chain, near the foot of Montrose Island. Shreve reasoned in his report,

> By pursuing this plan the navigator will have the shore for his guide, and cannot miss the channel at any stage of water . . . it will not be necessary

> to excavate a channel more than 90 feet wide, . . . following the meanderings of the natural channel that now exists between the reefs.[165]

There was a secret regarding the Des Moines Rapids that but few were later made aware. From his examination and readings at *Lamalee's Chain*, Lieutenant Lee discovered a hidden natural channel in the Des Moines Rapids, which became known as the "Spanish Chute." Lee's plan was to follow the Spanish Chute and clear the jagged rocks causing obstructions near the river's surface. These efforts were confined initially to the Lower and English Chains.[166]

Under Lieutenant Lee's supervision, they would drill holes by means of iron tripods standing in the water, with platforms for workers to stand on and for drill guides. The holes were drilled about 1¾-inch in diameter through ⅔ of the stratum of stone. Tin tubes were filled with about a half pound of powder, and then sand was added. As the drill was removed, the filled tin tubes were inserted in the hole supported by the tripods and extending above the water's surface. The ensuing explosion served to simply split the rock. The challenge was removing the fragments. The tripods were again used in the extraction process. The tripods were repositioned, and workers would pry the rocks and fasten them. They were then hoisted out of the water by crane boats. Lee's fragmented rock removal teams were expected to keep up with the blasting teams.

Lieutenant Lee's crews were only able to work for twenty days in 1838 due to high water and early fall, but they cleared 318 cubic yards. They were able to work for three months in 1839 and cleared 1,027 cubic yards of stone weighing about two thousand tons. Steamship pilots claimed after Lee's efforts that they were able to pass through the Des Moines Rapids much longer in the season because the depths had increased draw from nine to twelve inches more water than before.

Continued affirmations by Lieutenant Lee, leaders within the US Army Corp of Engineers, and others disheartened the land promoters in Warsaw. Efforts were being directed to deepen the natural channel water levels on the Iowa side of the river from Keokuk to Nashville to Montrose and across to Commerce. Warsaw's landing site was beyond Lee's "Spanish Chute" passage and would consequently be seldom used if excavations continued in contrast to the steamboat landing sites at

Keokuk, Nashville, Montrose, and Commerce. Warsaw promoters were motivated to arrange and secure a better alternative for internal improvements to serve their purposes. However, they had no means of funding their ambitious projects.

Formation of the Des Moines Rapids Railroad Company

On February 19, 1839, the legislature established the Des Moines Rapids Railroad Company to be lead by eleven commissioners: Mark Aldrich, Joseph Duncan (the former governor), Richard F. Barrett, Calvin A. Warren, Isaac Galland, Daniel S. Witter, David W. Matthews, John Montague, William D. Abernathy, Joel Catlin, and Isaac N. Morris.[167]

Aldrich, Duncan, Barrett, and Warren were associated with the Warsaw Land Company, and Morris was the president of the Illinois and Michigan Canal. In addition, Mark Aldrich was associated with Joel Wright as a fellow Warsaw and Peoria Railroad commissioner and who also served as one of the seven commissioners of public works. The leadership of the Warsaw Land Company benefited from the inside information of the state's priorities and issues involved in all the improvement projects and in the details of the Illinois and Michigan Canal construction. This act authorized a hundred thousand dollars capital stock for the railroad company to build a railroad line:

> Commencing on the Mississippi river at the head of the Des Moines rapids, at or near the town of Commerce, in Hancock county, and from thence, in the direction to Warsaw, to intersect the Peoria and Warsaw railroad at such point as shall be determined upon after a survey shall have been made of the route by and between the Board of Commissioners of Public Works and the said company; . . . and for the purpose of cutting, embankment, stone, and gravel, may take as much more land as may be necessary for the proper construction and security of said railroad.[168]

This second railroad, planned from Warsaw to Commerce (Nauvoo), was to link with the Warsaw and Peoria and Wabash Railroad route already commenced within the initial construction phase eastward from Warsaw to Hamilton to proceed northward to Commerce. This segment was to provide an alternative means, during low-water levels, to avoid passage on the Des Moines Rapids through all the problematic lightening process. Cargo would be loaded on steamships directly at the landing sites. Railroad cargo destined north would be rerouted to Commerce from Warsaw, and then loaded on steamships bound for the lead mines of Dubuque and Galena. Cargo destined south would be unloaded at Commerce and routed to Warsaw. It was also intended that this rail line would intersect future rail lines and avoid further steamboat passage.

A supplemental act provided for a small Warsaw railroad with John Wilcox, instead of Isaac Galland, serving with the other commissioners. This short route was intended to pass through Warsaw to the vicinity of the Mississippi River near the steamboat landing site. The lands to be traversed by the Des Moines Rapids Railroad in or near Commerce had been owned by James White, sons Hugh and Alexander, and son-in-law Isaac Campbell. The White family had for years been engaged in running boats back and forth to Galena and the lead mines.

Hotchkiss and his investors purchased three hundred acres of land on the river and on the bluffs from George Atchison for eleven thousand dollars and also purchased a smaller parcel from Alexander White.

In May 1837, Hotchkiss and Gillett conducted a public sale of lots in Commerce City. The advertisement promoting the sale indicated that plans called for the erection of large warehouses. Contracts were to be drafted to quarry stone, dig foundations, and secure lumber for the various buildings and homes expected to be built in the immediate future.

With the frenzy created by the newspapers and local public officials in regards to the Illinois and Michigan Canal and all the railroad and turnpike roads planned for the immediate vicinity, interest in land purchases was heightened. Values on some of the lots had risen up to 1,000 percent in just the two years since they were purchased. Dr. Isaac Galland seeing a great potential investment purchased some of the land from Hotchkiss as did many others.

Joseph Teas sold land to Charles Munson and recorded the deed May 26, 1835, in a transaction that was clouded due to prior discussions to sell the lands to James Doyle. For this transaction, Charles Munson, living at the time in New Haven, Connecticut, had his sister Mary Ann Cutler make the purchase from Teas, who was then living in the Iowa Territory. Hiram Kimball, while living at the residence of

Alexander White, also acted as Munson's agent. Kimball worked as a clerk at the store of Mr. and Mrs. Cutler. Munson sold half of the Teas tract for six thousand dollars in 1836 to Benjamin Lee, Joshua Aikin, and Abijah Fisher—members and agents of the New York Land Company, who saw the potential in combining efforts of Half-Breed Tract land purchases with land purchases on the opposite shore with access to steamboat and ferry landings. They also needed to counter the growing strength of the St. Louis merchants.

After her husband, George Cutler, died, Mary Ann Munson Cutler married D. G. Whitney and moved to Adams County. Doyle moved from Adams County and in 1835 purchased three hundred acres of land two and a half miles south of Commerce City from James Miller for $1,200.

Hugh White and George Atchison were both steamboat pilots engaged in transport between St. Louis and Galena and Dubuque, loyal to the Chouteaus and the St. Louis merchants. They too resided in St. Louis and knew the best steamboat landing sites were on the Hotchkiss lands, just north of Commerce City. These were the most strategic sites due to the Des Moines Rapids. John Atchison, the brother of George, was a merchant at Galena at the time.[169]

Isaac Waggoner, also a steamboat pilot operating out of St. Louis, married another of the daughters of Captain White and had land in Montebello. Luther Whitney, a former county commissioner and Whig activist, with sons Edson and Horace, was also major landowners in Montebello Township. The local residents were all anxious to make large land profits due to the Des Moines Rapids and the Des Moines Rapids Railroad projects.

On February 20, the majority of the select committee previously appointed reported a list of charges determined from their investigations but made no official comment or requests for correction of the infractions or abuses. Nine days later, a minority of the select committee, including Browning, Roman, and Hardin, made a more lengthy report. In their report, they specifically called out one of the commissioners for selecting a longer route of improvements, contrary to the advice of the chief engineer. Charges were also brought against the engineer and commissioner in charge of the contract lettings for the Peoria and Warsaw Railroad on April 17, 1838, for improper conduct in not giving the work to the lowest bidder. Other charges were made for examples of incompetency and neglect of duty by some of the commissioners.[170]

Richard F. Barrett was appointed fund commissioner for Illinois on October 7, 1839, to clean up the work of the previous public service commissioners. The Warsaw Land Company had their partner well placed as an insider for all the efforts regarding state projects.

Isaac Galland conveyed his partnership interests in the New York Land Company to Franklin Wilcox on January 9, 1839, for the sum of twenty-one thousand dollars.[171] Galland, one of the Des Moines Rapids Railroad commissioners appointed in February, must have determined his best interests were to forsake his employer and join the other commissioners as St. Louis Land Company allies. He published notice of his withdrawal from the New York Land Company partnership in the *Iowa Territorial Gazette* at Burlington on April 27, 1839, and warned others to beware of dealings with the New York Land Company. He also claimed some of his prior partnership interest was conveyed in a fraudulent manner to Dr. William Channing of New York City.[172]

The great proliferation in internal improvement projects in Michigan and Indiana linked with the massive plans in Illinois for the Illinois and Michigan Canal, the Des Moines Rapids improvement, and the many railroad projects stimulated land speculation particularly when organized by prominent state political leaders as was the case of the Warsaw Land Company.

Across the river in Iowa Territory, the opening of land sales from the half-breed Indian owners to the ruthless land speculators, such as were involved with the St. Louis Land Company and the New York Land Company, brought out various levels of ambition, greed, and corruption.

The fiscal crisis that had swept the nation severely limited project construction plans. After all the hype and rhetoric passed in Hancock County, the leading citizen's optimisms were crushed—until an army of oppressed people would come to their lands with a call abroad to gather from the four quarters of the earth to build their Zion.

8: Governor Boggs's Extermination Order

A mass meeting of the people of Carroll County was held on July 30, 1838, at Carrollton, in which various resolutions were drafted and approved:

> Whereas the people called Mormons, about eight years since, located themselves in Jackson county, and for improper and dishonorable conduct, were driven from said county by the citizens thereof. . . . And whereas it was distinctly understood, and expressly agreed upon by said Mormons and the other citizens of the upper part of the State of Missouri, that they (the said Mormons) might select a tract of country uninhabited, and locate themselves in peace, but they should not intrude upon the citizens of any of the adjoining counties, agreeably to which contract the Mormons first settled that tract of country now known as Caldwell county, contrary to the express wishes of the citizens thereof: And whereas said Mormons and their abettors have threatened to assassinate some of our most valuable citizens.
>
> Therefore be it resolved by this meeting, That there be a committee of safety appointed . . . whose duty it shall be to correspond with the adjoining counties, and make known our distressed situation, and request aid to remove Mormons, abolitionists, and other disorderly persons, out of the limits of Carroll county.

> Resolved, that the committee of safety be authorized to adopt such measures as to them shall seem most expedient for the safety of the citizens of Carroll county.[173]

Dr. William Austin was chosen as a member of the Carroll County Committee of Safety. This was followed up by a similar meeting in Saline County on August 21: "Resolved in favor of helping expel Mormons from Carroll county if necessary"; and one in Howard County, August 30, also approved opposing the Mormons.

After the Carrollton Committee convened, some of the attendees approached George Hinkle, a local Church leader about voluntarily withdrawing from their homes. An enraged Hinkle "drew his sword and defiantly flourishing it, threatened the extermination of all those who should attempt to disturb the peace of himself and the Saints.[174]

During the summer and fall of 1838, Joseph Smith and Sidney Rigdon directed a group of Canadian converts to emigrate to Adam-ondi-Ahman. Three months later, due to rising hostilities in Ohio, more than five hundred Saints identified as "Kirtland Camp No. 1" arrived and settled in Far West. Hostilities continued to mount from the old citizens. The day for voting drew near, and politics became the frequent topic of discussion throughout the state.

On Independence Day, at a friendly gathering of the Saints, Sidney Rigdon's ill-advised speech whipped up a lot of emotion among the LDS faithful. Rigdon expounded,

> We have proved the world with kindness, we have suffered . . . and have endured without resentment, until this day. . . . But from this day and this hour, we will suffer it no more. . . . That mob that comes on us to disturb us; it shall be between us and them a war of extermination, for we will follow them, till the last drop of their blood is spilled, or else they will have to exterminate us; for we will carry the seat of war to their own houses, and their own families, and one party or the other shall be destroyed.[175]

That unfortunate speech by Rigdon fueled the Church's enemies with outrage and allowed the mob leaders to rally others in opposition. His words were exploited by foes claiming it was the Mormons who were advocating and escalating violent conflict.

Fighting the Mormons at Gallatin on Election Day

In mid-July, Judge Josiah Morin (from Millport, Daviess County) rode to Far West to warn the Mormons that trouble was brewing in the county, particularly after Sidney Rigdon's speech, with threats of extermination. He voiced concerns that Colonel William Penniston and others intended to prohibit Mormons from voting in Daviess County in the August election. Morin was a Democrat running for the state Senate and Penniston was running as a Whig for the state House of Representatives. Local Mormon leaders chose not to act on the warnings.[176]

Just as Judge Morin had warned, Colonel Penniston attempted to stop the Mormons from voting and incited a major confrontation in Gallatin, the county seat. Many were injured, but no one was killed. The next day, exaggerated accounts of the incident claimed that three Mormons had been killed. After this initial report reached Joseph Smith in Far West, the Prophet gathered a band of Mormons and rode to assist his fellow Saints. After he arrived, he quickly learned that previous communications had been exaggerated. He rode on with his band of followers to the home of Justice Black to appeal to him to assist in restoring order.

Previously, Black had sold land in the new town area of Adam-ondi-Ahman to Vinson Knight. He received the down payment from Knight, but Black considered a different agenda. If Vinson Knight were forced to vacate, he would likely then cease payments and Black could legally keep the down payment money and get the land and its improvements back. Others in the area were in similar hopes to secure improved lands from withdrawing Mormon families.

Joseph Smith wanted to confront Judge Black directly to know his intentions. The Prophet had brought an affidavit previously drafted and requested the judge voluntarily sign the document, pledging his neutrality in any coming conflicts. Judge Black preferred to draft his own statement, which satisfied the Mormons that he would act prudently if matters escalated.[177]

On the evening of August 8, Judge Joseph Morin (state Senator), John Williams (state Representative, having beaten Penniston), and William Slade (clerk of the circuit court) came to Adam-ondi-Ahman to settle the differences with the Mormons. The Saints were represented by Lyman Wight, John Smith, Vinson Knight, and Reynolds Cahoon. Their deliberations were successful. Joseph Smith later recounted what was agreed:

> The covenant of peace was to preserve each other's rights, and stand in their defense, that if men should do wrong then (sic), neither party should uphold them or endeavor to secret them from Justice but they shall be delivered up even all offenders to be dealt with according to law and justice. Upon these terms we parted in peace, and soon every man left the ground and returned to his habitation. We came home the same night arrived at home about 12 o'clock at night, and found all well in Far West.[178]

The expected goodwill was soon broken. The old citizens of Daviess rejected their committee's actions. Emotions were again heightened as Judge Black later claimed that he had been coerced by Joseph Smith and his oppressive band to sign his affidavit. Penniston authored an affidavit that Mormons threatened his life. The false affidavits were used to feed the frenzy of the old Richmond settlers at a citizens committee meeting held August 10, where a call was made for creation of a Committee on Vigilance to gather reports of Mormon actions and convey that information to Ray County citizens and to other counties. State representative Charles Morehead was called to this committee.

Encouraged by his newfound fame, and seeking his former agenda to compel Vinson Knight to default on his loan, Judge Adam Black gave his deposition to William Dryden on August 28, 1838. Dryden was another Justice of the Peace claiming Joseph Smith and a force of 150 Mormons threatened him if he did not sign a notice stating he would not molest the Mormons and also that they intended to make every citizen of said county sign such obligation.

The Political Rise of the Central Clique in Missouri

As the polling results for 1838 were released, the Democratic Party dominance was validated. The Whigs were successful in fifteen high population counties around the St. Louis area and bordering on the Mississippi. Democrats had won in forty-four counties in poorer and less populated regions. The Democratic Convention the previous year followed the precedent set in 1835 by Dr. Lowry, with the support of

Sterling Price in controlling the selection of delegates based on loyalty to Benton and his policies. With the Democratic win, Benton's prospects for reelection in November by the General Assembly seemed secure, but Benton had to be sure. His thirteen-point agenda had not been accomplished. His fame had not been manifested.

With the Central Clique carrying Benton's support in rural areas, Benton concentrated his personal campaigning efforts to make further roads in St. Louis. Montgomery Blair, son of Benton's Washington friend Francis Blair, opted to advance his political stock under the tutelage of Benton, both in the practice of law and in the political domain. The *St. Louis Argus* editor joined with Montgomery Blair in campaigning for Benton amongst the St. Louis power brokers.

Benton was keenly attentive to developments in Missouri through his federally backed land policy with preemption rights. He deemed success in Missouri for their homesteaders, as the flagship for the nation to profile and vindicate his beloved legislative cause.

On August 30—partially due to the skirmishes with Mormons at DeWitt, Carroll County, Gallatin, Daviess County, and Far West—Governor Boggs issued orders to his six standing state militia generals, warning, "Indications of Indian disturbances on our immediate frontier, and the recent civil disturbances in the Counties of Caldwell, Daviess and Carroll, render it necessary as a precautionary measure that an effective force of the Militia should be held in readiness to meet either contingency."[179] He then ordered each general to have five hundred armed men in readiness under their subordinate militia commissioned officers.

Then, on September 1, Senator Daniel Ashby, State Representative Sterling Price, and James Keyte sent a dispatch to Governor Boggs. It began,

> Dear Sir: Our Country is in a complete ferment, & our families are rendered daily unhappy, in consequence of the reports, which are constantly coming in concerning the hostile intentions of the Mormons and their allies as it is currently reported & believed that they have ingratiated themselves with the Indians (and indeed they say so) to assist them in their diabolical [career].[180]

They made reference to claims from a former Mormon and current resident of Chariton that Joseph Smith indicated he could raise fourteen thousand men (referring to Indians), with the aid of a "destroying

Angel," at a moment's warning to join him in attacking Missourians. They were referring to Nathan March, though not mentioning him by name in this notice.

That same day, an order by Boggs was issued to Major General David Atchison of the Third Division of the Missouri Militia to aid the civil officers of Daviess County to execute all writs and other legal process and to assist in the execution of the specific writ issued by William Dryden, within Daviess County.[181] This writ was issued in response to the deposition of Adam Black, taken just three days prior and on the same day of the David Ashby and Sterling Price request. Boggs was acting with the support of some of the leaders of the Central Clique.

On September 2, the Prophet contacted Doniphan and Atchison to assist with the hearing for which Judge King had issued his warrant. The attorneys arranged to have September 7 as the hearing date. When that legal proceeding was convened, a disorderly group of Daviess County residents made their presence known. At the hearing, William Penniston, representing the state, called Judge Black as his only witness. Judge King concluded sufficient evidence had been presented to bind the Mormon leaders over for trial on a misdemeanor and set bail for $250 each. When released, Doniphan, Atchison, and the Mormon leaders returned to Far West.

After returning to their homes in Far West, Church leaders met with a Chariton County commission investigating matters before committing volunteers requested by the mobs in Caldwell County. This commission was lead by Colonel Sterling Price, an active leader in the Central Clique who had been heavily involved in the Convention of 1835.

In the meetings, Generals Doniphan and Atchison presented a convincing case that the Mormons were victims of overzealous neighbors. It was suggested Colonel Price return to Chariton and calm down their citizens as to this matter. During the stay, Joseph Smith made an affidavit as to the real truth of the Judge Black allegations that he had been under duress when visited in August. The Prophet also provided assurance that the statements of Nathan Marsh regarding alleged negotiations between the Mormons and the Indians were false.[182]

Shortly after returning to Chariton, Colonel Price published in the *Columbia Patriot* his statement clarifying that the Mormons were acting on the defensive. Other papers picked up Colonel Price's letter and published it. In Baltimore, the *Niles Register* printed his comments.

> To the citizens of Chariton:
>
> The committee appointed for the purpose on the 3rd inst., have to-day returned from the neighborhood of the Mormon difficulties, and left the Mormons begging for peace. Joseph Smith and Lyman White came before judge King on Friday last for trial, and bound with security in the sum of $1,000 each, to appear at the next regular term of the court for further trial. The crime seems (from the evidence) only to have been the taking of an armed force into the county of Daviess, which the Mormons say they were led to do, from hearing that two of their church had been killed at the election, and that the citizens of Daviess had refused to suffer them to be buried . . . on their arrival in the county they learned that nobody had been killed. They then called at Adam Black's, to learn whether a mob would be raised, as had been reported; when Mr. Black assured them that he had not nor would not attach himself to any mob. Mr. Black was then requested to give up his statement in writing; he refused to sign the instrument presented . . . but drew an instrument himself and signed it, . . . that he was bound to support the constitution of this state and of the United States; and to that he was not nor would not attach himself to mob, nor would not molest the Mormons if they did not molest him. Mr. Black says, that Mr. Smith may have said that he would not be forced to sign any; and Mr. Smith proves that he assured Mr. Black that he should not be forced to sign any instrument of writing but that he requested it as a favor.[183]

The article, when it was published in the *Niles Register*, lead with the following introduction:

> The true secret of the excitement against the Mormons, it is shrewdly suspected, lies in the desire to keep them off some of the fine lands in Carroll, Daviess, and the counties adjoining Caldwell. They have settled some rich farms which are very tempting to the cupidity of some citizens, who think by raising an outcry against them and exciting them to violence they may be driven off and their lands be portioned out to other hands. Such we believe to be the very worthy purpose at the bottom of all this outcry, and to aid in carrying this laudable design into effect can but be the ultimate result, though perhaps, undersigned, of the movement of troops now against the Mormons.[184]

The *Niles Register* article concluded with a quote from the Missouri paper:

> The Mormon war ended—return of the volunteers. Before we had an opportunity to announce the departure of the volunteers of this county, for the seat of the Mormon war, we are greeted with their return. An express met them a few miles beyond Boonville, which caused this retrograde movement. The difficulty with the Mormons is amicably settled and quiet restored.

Colonel Price published the truth. The true secret of the Mormon enemies' plans had been exposed for all to see. Their joint hidden agenda was simply to take back the highly valued Mormon lands after they had improved and developed them. But another motive was concealed. The Chouteau, Benton, Clark, and Junto alliances were not going to let the Mormons gain a foothold at DeWitt for a steamboat landing on the banks of the Missouri River. Also, as time would later validate, the non-Mormons feared their commercial development, particularly in mercantile pursuits adjacent to the Central Clique base in nearby Saline and Howard Counties.

The anxieties, lies, and exaggerations promoted by non-Mormon citizens in Caldwell were put to rest temporarily. Joseph Smith later noted his conversations with Sterling Price had been worthwhile and that he appreciated the efforts of the Chariton Commission in their search for truth.

By September 20, Atchison notified Governor Boggs that all hostile civilian parties were returning to their homes. After returning to Richmond, Atchison and Doniphan reported to the governor that two armed troops still remained as hostilities were winding down. Boggs ordered Doniphan's troops discharged by September 23.

Hostilities with the Mormons Reignited

On October 1, renegade elements seeking to continue prosecuting their attacks engaged twenty-five mounted rangers from Saline County in patrolling areas east of DeWitt, looking for Mormons and turning back small groups trying to enter the town. Three days later, the anti-Mormons launched an artillery attack but found the settlement well fortified.[185]

On October 4, another Central Clique leader named D. R. Scott, traveled through the battle areas and spoke with General Lucas of further hostilities occurring elsewhere. The next day, a second commission was sent by a Chariton Committee, who reported the same observations as Colonel Price and his party earlier in the month. With the objective of keeping hostilities moderated, Doniphan told the Saints that Cornelius Gilliam was raising a mob to destroy their town.

On October 23, Captain Samuel Bogart was ordered to range the line between Caldwell and Ray Counties and prevent invasion. Instead, Captain Bogart violated orders, going house to house and capturing two Mormon prisoners. Seeing the frightening injustice, the Caldwell County judge sent Mormon militia leaders under David C. Patten for protection of the Mormon citizens. When Captain Bogart's troops approached Patten, he apparently perceived them as a lawless mob, as there was no initial indication they were acting as a sanctioned militia force. Patten was following orders from the Caldwell judge. Bogart was taking advantage of their ignorance to the coordinated evil forces arrayed against them.

Suspiciously, on October 23 Judge King, in a letter to Governor Boggs, asserted, "I have recently seen Col. Price, who made known to me the object of his mission to this part of the State."[186] Apparently, Colonel Price had been convinced to change his mind concerning his previous attitude toward the Mormons. Likely, pressure was coming from the Central Clique leaders and followers in nearby Carroll, Saline, and Howard Counties, fearful of the growing commercial efforts of the Mormon community. The Mormon-controlled steamboat landing at DeWitt on the Missouri was viewed with distrust and contempt. Boggs had discretely given Colonel Price a direct mission while he was under the command of higher-ranking senior officers in his regiment. Boggs sought to use the Central Clique network in conjunction with the state militia structure.

Amos Reese, a former attorney for the Mormons, turned enemy to the cause of Zion, and E. M. Ryland prepared an exaggerated report of the Battle of Crooked River on October 25. David Patten was killed, and a few of Bogart's troops became casualties. Reese and Ryland reported the entire militia company had been killed by the lawless Mormons. The following day, Governor Boggs gave General John Clark of Fayette total command of state militia operations and the authority to raise two thousand troops to march on the Mormon settlements.

Governor Boggs Issues the Extermination Order

As skirmishes between militia and the Mormons continued, Governor Boggs made no attempt to put hostilities to an orderly truce. Boggs simply made himself unavailable to both sides. As his officers pleaded for him to get engaged and stop the atrocities, it was clear Governor Boggs had different motives. He needed to orchestrate an incident to be charged against the Mormons to gain public support for what he was about to set in motion. His real objective was the assault and forced removal of an entire religious body, consisting of nearly fifteen thousand people, from his state under the approval and direction of the Central Clique based in Fayette, Howard County, and for the benefit of Boggs's allies in the St. Louis Junto.

After receiving the incoming letters of Reese and Ryland on October 27, 1838, Governor Boggs had what he hoped and planned for. He felt he had the justification to issue an extermination order against all Mormons in the state. He was confident that the infrastructure affecting all branches of Missouri state government was secure. He anticipated his order would be administered unopposed by either Party or by any government segment, including the state legislature and the state Supreme Court because they were nearly all aligned with the Central Clique.

With the Extermination Order issued, Captain William Durrett of Arrow Rock, a Central Clique stronghold, led a militia company from Saline County. In joining the confederation, Dr. William W. Austin, representing Carroll County, marched on DeWitt, threatening to kill every Mormon remaining in town. William Austin had been previously appointed one of the five members of the Carroll County Committee in July.

The First Brigade of the Missouri Militia from Howard County, having rendezvoused in Fayette, began their advance to Chariton County. There, Colonel Sterling Price was commanding the Chariton Militia and assisting General Robert Wilson prepare the Second Brigade for action. The entire division met at Keytesville on October 30 and marched to Far West.

Circumstances were tense as the Saints, under the command of Joseph Smith and various militia groups, were ready for war. At Far West, the local Mormon leader Colonel Hinkle informed Joseph and

Hyrum Smith, Sidney Rigdon, Parley P. Pratt, George Robinson, and Lyman White that General Lucas was willing to meet to secure peaceable arrangements. Under a flag of truce and a pledge of honor that they would be guaranteed safety, the Mormon leaders came voluntarily to the enemy camp to meet with General Lucas.

Colonel Hinkle had deceived the Prophet and the other Mormon leaders. They were immediately made prisoners of General Lucas. In the evening, the prisoners were tried in absentia by a military tribunal consisting of seventeen preachers and nineteen commissioned officers. General Lucas issued orders that the prisoners should be shot the next morning.

Lyman Wight reported a comment from Brigadier General Moses Wilson, their old Jackson County foe, "I regret to tell you your die is cast; your doom is fixed; you are sentenced to be shot tomorrow morning on the public square in Far West, at eight o'clock. Wight responded, 'Shoot and be damned.' "[187]

General Doniphan, after receiving the appalling orders, wrote to General Lucas: "It is cold blooded murder. I will not obey your order. My brigade shall march for Liberty tomorrow morning, at 8 o'clock; and if you execute these men, I will hold you responsible before an earthly tribunal, so help me God."[188]

Both Wilson and Lucas had been promoted in the Jackson County militia after their previous persecution efforts against the Mormons at Independence and the Big Blue settlement years earlier. At that time, Lucas was an active leader in the secret constitution. Lucas in particular was desirous to see Joseph Smith executed before a trial could be convened. Governor Boggs finally got involved and had the prisoners transferred for civil trial.

Governor Boggs and General John B. Clark attempted to rationalize their conduct in the Mormon war conflict. They discussed how to frame the image of guilt of Joseph Smith to provide themselves legal cover for their actions. Boggs was concerned about the prosecution standard for attempting to convict on a charge of treason. They needed this charge to keep Joseph and Hyrum in jail as it was a non-bailable offense. The governor wrote to Clark,

> Sir: You will not take immediate steps to discharge all the troops you have retained in service as a guard, and deliver the prisoners over to

> the civil authorities. You will not attempt to try them by court martial, the civil law must govern. . . . I am unable to furnish you with his (Attorney General) opinion on the points requested. One thing, . . . is certain, that so soon as an insurrection is quelled and peace restored, the military authority ceases; but the crime of treason, whether it can be tried out of the county where the act was committed, we have no precedent, only that of the case of Aaron Burr, who was charged with the commission of that offence against the United States.[189]

The trial of Aaron Burr, former vice president, set precedent for a high standard for prosecutors to convict for treason. In spite of Burr's conduct, he was still released. Joseph Smith would not have met the standard for a treason conviction, and Governor Boggs knew it.

Colonel Price, with his Chariton Militia, escorted Joseph Smith and the other Mormon prisoners from Independence to Keytesville and stood guard over them. This occurred in the bitter cold Missouri winter. The prisoners were quartered in empty warehouses under miserable circumstances. Parley P. Pratt, incarcerated with the Prophet and other Church leaders, recorded,

> While we had listened for hours to the obscene jests, the horrid oaths, the dreadful blasphemies and filthy language of our guards, Colonel Price at their head, as they recounted to each other their deeds of rapine, murder, robbery, etc., which they had committed among the "Mormons" while at Far West and vicinity. They even boasted of defiling by force wives, daughters and virgins, and of shooting or dashing out the brains of men, women and children.
>
> I had listened till I became so disgusted. . . . On a sudden he arose to his feet, and spoke in a voice of thunder, or as the roaring lion, uttering, as near as I can recollect, the following words: "*Silence, ye fiends of the infernal pit. In the name of Jesus Christ I rebuke you, and command you to be still; I will not live another minute and hear such language. Cease such talk, or you or I die this instant!*"[190]

The Preliminary Hearing with Judge Austin King

A preliminary hearing was scheduled for November 12–29 to determine if there was sufficient evidence to indict anyone. Amos Rees, concealed his treacherous involvement and supported General Doniphan, while serving as defense attorney for the Mormon leaders. James

S. Rollins of Columbia assisted the defense. Thomas C. Burch was called to prosecute for the state. Under Judge Austin King, the hearings proceeded in a circuslike atmosphere.[191] Judge King was still seeking revenge for the death of his brother-in-law, Hugh Brazeale when he raided the Mormon settlements in Jackson County five years earlier.

As the trial proceeded, the witness Sampson Avard referred to Daniel 7:27 and explained the passage foretold the destruction of all earthly kingdoms and would be replaced by God's kingdom. Judge King leaned over to his court clerk and said, "Write that down; it is a strong point for treason." In reply, Doniphan voiced, "Judge, you had better make the Bible treason."[192]

Senator Benton came to the state capital of Jefferson City to persuade state legislators to reelect him to the Senate in Washington, DC. Benton likely met with Boggs, who was also in town. During the senator's visit, Reverend Finis Ewing, as the registrar of the Land Office, was selling the improved Mormon lands to some of the mob participants and others. The Mormon landowners, who legally held the preemption rights, were standing trial in Richmond, prevented from attending the Land Office sale. Benton easily won reelection over Abiel Leonard of Fayette, Howard County. Meanwhile, the hearings in Richmond under Judge King dragged on. Their orchestrated scheme was working.

As the court of inquiry concluded, some were released, but the main Mormon leaders were again incarcerated. Judge King deemed the evidence sufficient to hold them for trial. That the actions against the leaders was a premeditated plan was evidenced by an occurrence witnessed by Hyrum Smith who indicated that one of the officers in charge confessed to him privately:

> The Judge declared his intention to keep us in jail until all the "Mormons" were driven from the state. He also said that the Judge had further declared that if he let us out before the "Mormons" had left the state, . . . there would be [a] . . . fuss kicked up.[193]
>
> The jailer [at liberty Jail], Samuel Tillery Esq., told us . . . that the whole plan was concocted by the governor down to the lowest judge in that upper country. . . . He told us that the governor was now ashamed of the whole transaction and would be glad to set us at liberty if he dared do it. "But," said he, "you need not be concerned, for the governor has laid a plan for your release." He also said that Squire Birch

> (sic) . . . was appointed to be circuit judge . . . and that he [Birch] was instructed to fix the papers, so that we would be sure to be clear from any incumbrance (sic) in a very short time.[194]

Judge King and Governor Boggs were clearly not in total control but were answering to other more powerful forces. Enemies of the Mormons could not risk a legitimate trial, where witnesses could be challenged and the actions of the real leaders exposed.

Legislative wrangling regarding the governor's conduct, the funding of the militia, and other matters continued into early December. A. B. Chambers, editor of the *Missouri Republican Daily*, went to observe the legislative proceedings regarding the Mormon war investigation. He noticed that many House members, though expressing verbally their support for a thorough investigation of the events leading up to and during the battles by the militia, in reality were opposed to the bill calling for the investigation. Chambers described their outward actions:

> [They] were no more than hollow pretenses. They talked about wanting an investigation—their constituents had nothing to fear, . . . and yet, they were opposed to the bill. They offered no amendment to it, . . . but whilst they urged the necessity of killing it, they professed that they wanted an investigation. Such running one way and looking another never was witnessed before in any deliberate body.[195]

As debate continued, a vote to table the proposed investigation bill was raised and carried. Atchison appeared thoroughly upset and made motion for reconsideration the same night. A heated exchange followed. In a surprise move, Atchison withdrew his motion so the previously voted motion to table was upheld. After observing these actions, Chambers then reported that Atchison's actions constituted a "complete surrender of the position he had maintained during the whole session on this subject."[196] Atchison later defended his actions, arguing that men who had constituents more deeply involved than his would never agree to an investigation; he merely wished to give them another chance to respond and felt his actions and proposal had accomplished that.[197] Chambers felt Atchison's abrupt change occurred after other legislators had reconsidered their positions and that had the bill been reintroduced, it might have passed.

On December 20, 1838, Boggs submitted an "Act to Amend an Act to regulate the Treasury Department." It included a "Memorial to the Congress of the United States on the subject of pre-emption rights."[198] Weeks earlier, the legislature tabled motions to discuss the Mormon war investigation, even while they were in discussions with various leaders of preemption administration in the courts who were themselves involved in the Mormon war.

Hearing of critical reports about the state directed at Boggs, the citizens of Keytesville held mass meetings during January 1839, in support of the governor and the Extermination Order. Colonel Price and three other residents drafted resolutions depicting the Mormons as "a set of lawless fanatics who had everything other than religious purposes in view."[199] They claimed that those who defended the Mormons had "some hidden purposes other than friendship to law and justice."[200] The governor's actions were said to be deserving of gratitude in avoiding more bloodshed and that his behavior reflected courage and honor. Colonel Price, as a leader in the Central Clique at the time, knew however the real hidden purpose of the scheme against the Mormon landowners. He had faithfully executed the specific mission issued by Governor Boggs.

While confined at Liberty Jail, Joseph filed notice, charging Judge King's prejudice against the Mormons emanating from Hugh Lawson Brazeale's death during the Jackson County conflicts. Brazeale was the husband of Amanda King, the judge's sister. Brazeale had been involved in the secret constitution efforts against the Saints and was a leader in the brutal raids against unsuspecting Mormon families in Independence and in the Big Blue Settlements of the Church. The Prophet also showed examples of bias during the court of inquiry.[201]

As the defendants were woefully neglected in Liberty Jail, Doniphan sought to break the stalemate. In early April, Judge King ordered the prisoners moved to Daviess County for a hearing before the grand jury as a preliminary to trial. On April 9, Joseph Smith and two others were taken to Gallatin in Daviess County. There they were indicted for alleged crimes previously charged with and bound over for trial. They had been granted a change in venue.

Governor Boggs, and his anti-Mormon patrons from the Central Clique and the St. Louis Junto could not advocate for a real trial. In a real trial, damaging testimony would have been elicited through cross examinations and defense witnesses. Testimony from Sampson Avard would have shown that he was responsible for the illegal conduct of the Danites. The affidavit of Judge Black should have been challenged. Contradictory statements of Colonel Price had been published. Others could have challenged Judge Black, but such was not the established agenda for Governor Boggs and his anti-Mormon constituency groups, including Judge King.

An issue that should have been raised was that the old settlers had assembled Vigilance Committee sin Carroll County in July 1838 and in Saline and Howard Counties in August, in violation of state statutes.[202]

According to the "Revised Statutes of the State of Missouri" compiled by Judge Austin A. King himself and passed by the legislature in 1834 and 1835, found under "Crimes and Punishments" Article 1 Section 5:

> If twelve or more persons shall combine to levy war against any part of the people of this state, or to remove forcibly out of the state, or from their habitations, evidenced by taking arms and assembling to accomplish such purpose, every person so offending shall be punished as declared in the previous section.[203]

The previous section, Article 1 Section 4, provided "for a period not exceeding five years, or by fine not exceeding five thousand dollars, and imprisonment in the county jail for a period not exceeding six months."[204]

The calling out of the militia and the immense cost to the state was primarily to benefit the commercial interests of Benton's and Boggs's political favorites. The use of federal employees Finis Ewing and fellow minister Sachel Woods—who benefited by getting Mormon lands by preemption claims provisions—was a problem if disclosed. The conduct of Agent Richard Cummins and his previous involvement in Jackson County could have been raised.

After Congress adjourned in March 1839, Benton discussed his planned departure back to Missouri to the former President Andrew Jackson "to see the faithful people who had stood so nobly by us and by their country." In May, he was shaking hands and delivering speeches in Cape Girardeau and elsewhere in Southeast Missouri. For Independence

Day, he had scheduled a special stop at Fayette, the Central Clique area of dominance. While there, he was toasted in praise by Party leaders. including Dr. John Lowry and Mayor H. H. Hughes. One toast was offered by Robert Hancock: "I am a pre-emptioner, and I am proud to see here today the pre-emptioner's friend, Thomas H. Benton."[205]

Later that same year, Senator Benton was discussing preemption rights with Senator John Davies of Massachusetts, giving his insights for the entire affair:

> Every inch of territory . . . now occupied by white people, was taken from the Indians by armed settlers, and that preemptions and donations of land have forever rewarded the bold settlers who rendered this service to the civilization of the world.[206]

They had won. The Mormons were gone from the state. The Benton and Central Clique power base was secured. Doniphan and Rees received nearly 1,080 acres of land in Jackson County to pay for their legal services. Joseph Smith had prophesied that Doniphan should not take the land because "God's wrath hangs over Jackson County."[207] Joseph Smith later accused Doniphan of cowardice in defending the Saints. "They have done us much harm from the beginning. They are coworkers with the mob."[208]

By February 1841, reports of consternation by the Missouri delegation in Congress were being published in national newspapers. Senator Linn in particular presented the legal testimony in the hearings against the Mormon leaders conducted by Judge Austin King in Richmond. The Missouri legislature had finally printed the documents in response to the request of Senator Linn. In a defensive posture, Senator Linn had presented to his Congressional colleagues this information, hoping to quell the backlash emanating from the Mormon memorials presented in the previous legislative session. Serious accusations were made of a lack of justice. Linn had expressed that he was aware "that the sympathies of the people were always on the weaker side, and that in this contest with the state the latter had been improperly reflected upon. He had the pleasure to present a statement of all the matters in dispute, which he asked might be printed."[209]

Senator Linn misled his peers in Congress; he was not truthful in his statement that he had the pleasure to present a statement of all the matters in dispute. He knew that Judge King's documentation was from a preliminary trial only and did not contain a complete, fair and impartial account of the events of the conflict.

In Illinois, Whig papers were anxious to expose all the illegal and immoral conduct demonstrated by the Democratic leaders of Missouri against the Mormons. They phrased the conflict as "the Mormons and Loco Foco War" to build resentment against the Democrats.

In Springfield, Illinois, the *Sangamo Journal* published on September 1, 1838: "It is stated that the Loco Focos of Caldwell County, Mo., have determined to drive the Mormons out of that county."[210]

The following year, as hostilities had concluded and Joseph Smith and others were in Liberty Jail, the *Sangamo Journal* again commented on bringing attention to the illegal conduct of Democratic leaders in the Mormon conflict. On March 23, 1839, the newspaper reported:

> Loco Focoism. It will be recollected that Governor Boggs, of Missouri, in the late disturbance, ordered General Clark, in the event of not being able to capture the Mormons, to "exterminate them." . . . They were then plundered of their property—many of them sent to prison, and the remainder compelled to sign an agreement to leave the state. . . . No wonder that the Van Buren legislature of Missouri refused to permit an investigation into the outrages committed upon the Mormons.[211]

A week later, the *Sangamo Journal* followed up with another article on the Mormons:

> The Van Buren paper here is displeased with our notice of the outrages committed by their party upon the Mormons in Missouri. That paper has beheld the murders—the robberies—the outrages upon women—committed upon the Mormons, under the direction of the Van Buren authorities of Missouri, and yet this (Springfield Illinois) Republican held its peace. And why? Because these outrages were committed by the Van Buren party.[212]

9: The Honeycomb Effect and the Nauvoo Charter

A **most unusual** militia unit was incorporated in February 1839 after it was introduced to the Illinois legislature by Edwin Webb, a representative from White County, three months earlier. The Invincible Dragoons, attached to the Second Division of the Illinois State Militia, were officially formed. Members of this militia from Edwards, White, and Wabash Counties elected Bennett brigadier general of the unit, and on April 25 his name was submitted to Governor Carlin for approval.

Early in March 1839, the *Quincy Whig* published, "a little knot of politicians denominated the 'Quincy Democratic Association' having been tampering with the Mormons now among us, for purposes which the reader can well imagine."[213] The Association decided to "bait a hook for this oppressed people, . . . offering relief conditionally. . . . How contemptible the object of this kind of third-rate politicians! The best sympathies of our nature were to be called into action—our benevolence was to be tested, our purses were to be opened—but it must only be done through the medium of the 'Democratic Association.' "[214]

Nehemiah Bushnell, Senator Orville Browning's law partner (who helped edit the *Quincy Whig*) voiced his objection to linking kindness to the Mormons with Democratic politics, saying he was willing to provide aid to Mormons as charity, but not to support the Democratic political party. Further, the *Quincy Whig* cautioned, "Mormons may be assured that this 'organization' party never move unless for some selfish purpose—and we do hope that they will stand aloof, and leave this party to work out its own objects with its own instruments."[215] The *Whig* further warned, "to treat all overtures from either political party as an intrusion upon their rights."[216]

Galland Sells Land to the Mormons and Admits a "Honey Comb" Scheme Is Planned

On May 1, 1839, Joseph Smith and associates purchased 135 acres from Hugh White for five thousand dollars, and lands west of White's from Isaac Galland. Improvements then included one stone house, three frame houses, and two block houses. These constituted the town of Commerce. Sidney Rigdon suspiciously persuaded the group that this purchase be done in the name of George Robinson, his son-in-law, to be deeded to the Church after the Church paid the debt.[217]

To initiate transactions in the Iowa Territory with the Mormons, Isaac Galland sold five shares of stock in the Half-Breed Land Company "for lands in the Sac and Fox Half-Breed Reservation." To Oliver Granger, Galland sold 1,998 acres for $5,000 on May 17, 1839, and 640 acres for $1,600 on May 29, 1839. Soon after, a sale was made to Vinson Knight of 12,745 acres for $32,342.22 on June 6, 1839, and 4,228 acres for $10,636 from June 26 to June 29, 1839.[218] Instructions were given by the Prophet to build a town on these lands to be named Zarahemla.

To assist the Saints, several leading citizens of Quincy, including Senator Richard M. Young and Isaac N. Morris, wrote letters of recommendation for John P. Greene and Sidney Rigdon to aid them as agents for the Church.[219] Additional lands were sold to the Mormons in Nashville, formerly the home site of Isaac Galland. After arriving in Chillicothe, Isaac Galland wrote Samuel B. Swasey in July 1839, commenting on his recent transactions with the Mormons:

> I feel greatly relieved in having got out of hearing of the half-breed lands. . . . I have disposed of my half-breed lands, for 50 thousand dollars, that is to say $2500, annually for 20 years, my home place, the

> same which I purchased of Capt. White, I also sold for 18 thousand dollars, to be paid likewise $900 annually for 20 years, the above sales were made to the people called Mormons who were last winter expelled from the state of Missouri. . . . The people have also bought out Hugh White and some others, and will probably continue to buy out the settlers of that neighborhood, until they again acquire a sufficient quantity of "honey comb" to induce the surrounding thieves to rob them again; at which time they will no doubt have to renounce their religion; or submit to a repetition of similar acts of violence, and outrage.[220]

Confidentially, Isaac Galland was explaining the pattern demonstrated at Missouri of "the honey comb scheme." After the Saints' initial land purchases, they would continue to buy lands of the old settlers, and then earnestly improve the sites with great zeal and determination. Enemies nearby including those that had sold them lands originally would rob them again. They would compel them to renounce their religion or escalate violence until they could force them out. They would then reclaim the lands with improvements while retaining the money paid for the land and prepare to resell it at higher prices. Such was the pattern in Missouri.

It was common for beekeepers to retrieve a full honeycomb from the hives, extract the honey, and replace it for the bees to replenish, which could then be reharvested and given to others. Galland knew the citizenry of Iowa, and those near Nauvoo to include lawless and greedy elements of society. He had been a partner of the New York Land Company and a commissioner for the Des Moines Railroad when writing to Mr. Swasey. Likely, his New York Land Company partners and fellow railroad commissioners, knew of "the honey comb scheme" from Missouri contacts. Galland was baptized and ordained an elder earlier that month.[221]

Governor Carlin Dismayed by Senator Young's Mishandling of Canal Funding

An agitated Governor Carlin wrote to Senator Young on July 11, 1839, expressing his dismay and anger toward the deals agreed to by Senator Young and Governor Reynolds for funding the Illinois and Michigan Canal. Carlin said in the letter that the state would suffer a loss of principal and interest of three hundred thousand dollars on just the preliminary deals they negotiated. Subsequent transactions agreed to by Young and Reynolds added to the state's fiscal woes. A large portion of the canal funding was placed with Wright & Company of London. Nearly five hundred thousand dollars was sold, and then Wright & Company went bankrupt.

The state's funding crisis continued to mount. Senator Young was serving as chairman of the Committee of Roads and Canals in Washington and was concerned his failed efforts to secure financing for his home state would demean him before his peers. A few months later, Governor Carlin again wrote Senator Young on February 3, 1840:

> A resolution passed, annulling all the negotiations for money made by the agents of the State during the past year, . . . but was reconsidered in the Senate. A resolution passed the House requiring the Secretary of State to transmit said resolution to Messrs. Wright & Co., in London, declaring that no law existed in Illinois authorizing the sale of bonds at 91 (British Pounds Sterling) to 100 (British Pounds Sterling), and requesting a return of the bond placed in the hands of your agent.[222]

Many in government leadership were still upset at Senator Young for binding the state to such a massive discount on the bonds for funding the Illinois and Michigan Canal. The legislature sought to cancel Senator Young's deal with Wright & Company, claiming Young lacked legal authority to commit the state to such a heavy discount. Governor Carlin was upset the Senate backed off. Senator Young was desperate to improve his image.

The Mormons Begin Developing Nauvoo

As the Mormons settled in to their new neighborhoods in Commerce and across the river in Iowa Territory, they were likely unaware of the high commercial expectations of their neighbors in Warsaw and Warren. They were also clearly unaware of the predatory ambitions of their surrounding enemy neighbors, known to Galland. The Mormons were focused on draining swamps and fighting the serious illnesses attributable to the conditions of their new homeland. Meanwhile, they were being watched by conspirators for the best time to harvest the honeycomb.

Within a few months, the Church leadership was approached by Mark Aldrich, Daniel Witter, and Calvin Warren, all fellow railroad project commissioners with Isaac Galland, anxious to sell more lands in the adjacent communities of Warsaw and Warren. John Vineyard was the former partner of Mark Aldrich and married to the sister of Samuel Owens. Richard F. Barrett was the new partner of Mark Aldrich and grew up near the Owens's plantation in Green County, Kentucky. Aldrich and Galland had lived as neighbors in Fort Edwards seven years earlier. Aldrich and his associates persisted in attempting to sell to the Mormons for the next two years. The "quantity of honey comb was growing . . . the surrounding thieves" were waiting.[223]

After Joseph Smith went to Washington and met with Democratic President Van Buren, he returned home ready to support the Whigs. In Illinois, the Whig Party leadership was anxious to gain the Mormon support of an estimated six thousand votes to offset the increased Democratic vote coming from alien canal workers. Joseph Smith was known to have spoken highly of Congressman Stuart, Lincoln's close friend and fellow Whig partisan.

On March 1, 1840, Lincoln wrote his friend and law partner Congressman John Stuart,

> Speed says he wrote you what Jo. Smith said about you as he passed here. . . . We will procure the names of some of his people here and send them to you before long.[224]

It was clear that Lincoln was interested in securing the names of the prominent Church leaders for his future campaigning and his Whig friends. His various relationships with the Owens family members, their cousins and neighbors that he was quite fond of, had not tainted or otherwise affected his attitude toward the Mormons or its leaders.

In the nearby town of Warsaw, in the debut issue of their local newspaper *Western World*, on May 13, 1840, a quaint article was written, entitled "Our Town and County." The piece was extolling the anticipated benefits the town citizens expected.

> Warsaw . . . commands a fine view of the river for several miles in each direction, and has one of the best Steam Boat landings on the river. It is about 3 miles below the foot of the Des Moines rapids, is thriving rapidly, and is destined to attain a high rank among the towns of the west. The advantages of its situation are obvious, being opposite

> the mouth of the Des Moines river, and the point of termination of the Peoria and Warsaw Rail Road. A company of gentlemen, in February 1839, obtained a charter from the Legislature of the State for a rail road around the Des Moines rapids, from Commerce to Warsaw, which is believed will be the most profitable Rail Road stock in the United States. The obstructions to Steam Boat navigation on the rapids are so great that the greatest part of the navigable season Steam Boats cannot ascend or descend with their cargoes with safety, and are under the necessity of lighting over the rapids in keel or flat boats drawn by team power. As the settlements on both sides of the river above this town increase, for a distance of some 5 or 600 miles above us, and as the resources of the upper country are brought into action, it is reasonable to suppose that trade and navigation on the upper Mississippi will increase in the same proportion. If so, the importance of the rail road from Warsaw to Commerce, round the rapids, must be evident to every reflecting mind. It is expected that all the stock will be taken and the road commenced before the end of the present year, which when completed, will add much to the business and prosperity of the towns of Warsaw and Commerce.[225]

Expectations were high that wealth was soon coming for the entire area from internal improvements. But what of the Mormons invading the area of the nearby town of Commerce?

John C. Bennett Contacts Joseph Smith

While in Springfield, John C. Bennett attended a Mormon Church service across from Lowry's hotel. On July 25, 1840, Bennett drafted a letter to the Prophet. On August 8, Joseph wrote to John C. Bennett, expressing,

> It would afford me much pleasure to see you at this place, and from the desire you express in your letter to move to this place, I hope I shall soon have that satisfaction. I have no doubt you would be of great service to this community in practicing your profession, as well as those other abilities of which you are in possession. . . .
>
> It is our intention to commence the erection of some public buildings next spring. We have purchased twenty thousand acres in the Iowa Territory opposite this place, which is fast filling up with our people. . . .
>
> A charter has been obtained from the legislature for a railroad from Warsaw, being immediately below the rapids of the Mississippi, to this place—a distance of about twenty miles, which if carried into operation

> will be of incalculable advantage to this place, as steamboats can only ascend the rapids at a high stage of water. The soil is good, and I think not inferior to any in the state. Crops are abundant in this section of country—and I think provisions will be reasonable.[226]

Bennett wrote the Prophet a week later, expressing his increased desire to move to Nauvoo and join him in building up this promising community. Unknown to Joseph was that dark forces from the region were already mounting in regards to the future of that previously chartered railroad. The former owners of the lands from Nauvoo to Warsaw, where the path of the railroad would follow, were anxious for the Mormons to clear the swamp areas and expand steamboat landings on the Nauvoo side of the river. Many of the surrounding neighbors were becoming alarmed at the rapid growth and dominance of the blossoming Mormon community.

For five months, John C. Bennett had promoted the development of improvements in Nauvoo related to the Mississippi River. Joseph Smith responded to Bennett with cautious support of his plans for Nauvoo's development. The Prophet was formulating his own vision of the future spiritual and commercial plans for the building of the city to accommodate the divine mandate to gather the Saints. He understood that Bennett could be of assistance perhaps, from some of his ideas, but especially through his political connections.

During the months of correspondence between the Prophet and Bennett, a few Church leaders purchased a steamship at auction from the government, being sold under the direction of Robert E. Lee, who had used the steamboat as an office for research and for surveying the Des Moines Rapids. Senator Young and D. G. Whitney, a Quincy merchant, wrote to Lee to vouch for the Church leaders as capable of paying a note when due.

D. G. Whitney was the husband of Mary Ann Cutler, sister of Charles Munson, who held lands near to the main section in Nauvoo from her deceased husband, George Cutler. Whitney was also anxious to see the lands of Charles Munson increase in value because of the expected efforts the Mormons would bring to the area. Both Whitney and Young hoped the Mormons would develop a steamboat landing after clearing the swamp areas and were lending their support.

Senator Young had other plans. On the Senate floor on January 25, 1838, he submitted a motion for the economic future of the state and particularly Hancock and Adams Counties.

> Resolved, that the Secretary of War be instructed to communicate to the Senate, . . . a copy of the recent report and survey of Lieutenant Lee, of the Corps of Engineers in relation to the removal of the obstructions in the channel of the Mississippi River at the Rock River and Des Moines Rapids, with appropriate drawings of the river at those points, indicating the course of the channel and the obstructions to be removed, with estimates of the expenses necessary to accomplish said objects.[227]

This report made by Lee in 1837 previously caused a dramatic impact on the commercial expectations for the area residents. He had discovered a previously unknown natural channel, the "Spanish Chute," within the Des Moines Rapids, which was hoped to be exploited.

But this new discovery had brought great concern to Warsaw town leaders. Lee's conclusions led to the need to secure the charter from the legislature to build a railroad from Warsaw to connect to Nauvoo. Otherwise, Warsaw would be excluded from commercial development with steamboats unable to dock much of the year at their landing, being outside the Spanish Chute route. On December 17, Senator Young submitted a follow-up motion on the Senate floor:

> Resolved, that the Committee on Commerce be instructed to inquire into the expediency of . . . appropriations for the improvement of the Rock River and Des Moines Rapids of the Mississippi River, so as to make said river navigable for steamboats at all seasons of the year, when the navigation of the same is not obstructed by ice.[228]

Senator Young had previously assisted the Mormon leadership by advising them in the preparation for formal submission of their Missouri redress petition to Congress in 1839. The assistance in securing the Corp of Engineers' steamboat, used by Lee, for the use of the Mormons was also intended to fortify the commercial potential for the Des Moines Rapids section on the Warsaw and Nauvoo riverfronts. Senator Young hoped to develop new measures to advance the internal improvement projects for which he had been tainted from funding blunders.

To purchase the steamboat "Des Moines," Peter Haws, Henry W. Miller, George Miller, Joseph Smith, and Hyrum Smith signed a note that was payable to the government for $4,866.38 on September 10, 1840. Charles B. Street and Marvin B. Street also purchased an interest in this steamship. They collectively signed as obligors to the note, with Robert F. Smith a listed surety.

Based on referrals that they were skillful and competent pilots with understanding of the steamboat channel, Benjamin and William Holladay were hired as steamboat pilots. These pilots proved incompetent or were guilty of sabotage, as they wrecked the steamboat by running aground upon rocks and sandbanks while outside the usual steamboat channel course. The Holladay brothers were arrested, but after being released on bond they fled the state.[229] Lawsuits were filed by the Church leaders, as the note debt was due in mid-1841. This unfortunate matter showed the resolve of the Saints to use the river for commercial expansion.

The Nauvoo Charter Is Accepted by the Legislature

Before the Illinois Legislative Assembly, Senator Sidney H. Little, a Whig leader representing McDonough and Hancock Counties, presented a bill authorizing the Nauvoo Charter. The bill consolidated requests for three charters, including the creation of the city of Nauvoo, a militia "as a body of independent military men," and a university as "an institution of learning. William A. Richardson, the Democrat from Schuyler County, called a motion to dispense normal Senate rules and had the bill read a second time.[230] Senator Little then made motion to send the bill to the judiciary committee for review. Little and Richardson were representing their Hancock, McDonough, and Schuyler County constituents, desperate to get needed tax revenues and votes to advance the railroad and other related improvement projects.

With a minor change the bill, authorizing the Nauvoo Charter was favorably reported back to the full Senate. After a third reading, the Senate passed the bill December 9, 1840. The next day, the bill was taken up by the ninety members of the House of Representatives. It was presented by Representative A. R. Dodge, and after two readings it was sent to the judiciary. They returned it unchanged back to the full House for another reading, where it passed with little opposition. After the vote, Whig House member Abraham Lincoln congratulated John C. Bennett on the charter's approval.[231]

Lincoln realized the potential the Mormon vote could add for him and Stuart in upcoming elections. Governor Carlin signed the Nauvoo Charter into law on December 16. City elections were scheduled to take place that same day.

With the severe state economic crisis and the diplomacy of Bennett, key provisions for protection of the Saints were accommodated in the approved charter articles. Fundamental to the design of the charter was that Nauvoo would be governed under the state Constitution and the US Constitution, not the subsequent laws of Illinois.[232] Two unique provisions were deemed critical for their welfare and protection. The charter authorized the municipal court to issue writs of habeas corpus in all cases of imprisonment or custody arising from city ordinances. When outside courts sought abusive privilege against Nauvoo citizens, the matter could be tried within the venue of the Nauvoo courts. The Charter also granted unique powers for their state militia.

According to Illinois law, the state militia was comprised of all the local military companies under the executive authority of the governor. Each military local unit elected its own officers, who were then commissioned by the governor. Arms were provided the militia members from the state through the quartermaster general, who reported directly to the governor. Some local units of the state militia were granted multi-county jurisdictions. The Nauvoo Charter establishing the Nauvoo Legion was unique in its provisions regarding the rank of lieutenant general. Only George Washington had held that rank previously in the national army. No one in the state militia could outrank Joseph Smith.

The Nauvoo Legion structure followed roughly the Roman pattern calling for two cohorts (brigades) to be commanded by brigadier generals. The first cohort was to consist of mounted cavalry, and the second was to include infantry units. During the year, the Legion would increase from six to fourteen companies, dominating all other state militia units in size and strength. Joseph Smith became its lieutenant general but left most of the administration to John C. Bennett. Wilson Law and Charles C. Rich were elected as the brigadier generals over the two cohorts. Besides his local leadership, Bennett had previously positioned himself well with the state as the quartermaster-general, amassing a significant power base in his own right.

Besides the Nauvoo Charter, the Nauvoo House Association and Nauvoo Agricultural and Manufacturing Association corporations were approved by the Illinois legislature. The Nauvoo House Association was created under divine direction as defined by revelation. (Doctrine and Covenants 124). These entities were expected to provide the means to expand critical services and functions in the development of Zion and the kingdom of God. They also represented different approaches to governance, based on their original charters.

While there was little opposition from the legislature to the approval of the founding of Nauvoo charter provisions, a few newspaper critics drew attention to their unique charter. George T. M. Davis with the *Alton Telegraph* was outspoken in opposing it. Davis was an attorney, having passed the New York bar before going to Alton. He served as the attorney for the Chouteaus and others of the Chouteau Company in 1839.[233] This legal matter concerned the steamboat *Pavilion* and the captain, T. H. Griffith, versus Mr. Tanner. The *Pavilion*, owned partly by the Chouteaus, was the first steamboat hauling lead from Dubuque and Galena to Keokuk. The Chouteaus were again fearful of Mormon interference.

The lawsuit between the New York Land Company and the Reddick heirs, of which the Chouteaus and Senator Benton had a great interest, was still in discovery phase. Benton had worked on many Spanish land claims as an attorney in 1817. He fought the dual with Lucas, who was with the opposition in challenging French and Spanish precedents. George Davis wanted to keep the Mormons away from the Montrose area, where the Reddick heirs, as Chouteau allies, were fighting for lands the Mormons occupied and developed.

Party leaders on both sides of the political spectrum hoped this influx of Mormons would sustain a renewed drive to advance their highly sought for but endangered improvement plans. All prior attempts of private investor and federally funded programs had failed. The state was in total fiscal ruin. The Mormon infusion was hoped to propel their former ambitions and dreams.

The Saints were optimistic as to the future potential of Nauvoo. The *Times and Seasons* published an article in June, listing the benefits, as the city was "situated on a beautiful point of land on the Mississippi . . . afforded good privileges for all kinds of machinery in consequence of the rapidity of the current."[234]

John C. Bennett had been earnest in securing the Nauvoo Charter through the Illinois legislature. He had successfully gained support from both sides of the political wings. For his efforts, Bennett was promoted to great heights within the Nauvoo leadership as mayor and second in command of the Nauvoo Legion.

Ten days after the governor signed the Nauvoo Charter legislation into law, Senator Young wrote from New York City to Governor Carlin, updating him on funding issues.

> I mentioned . . . that my subject in coming was to pay the January interest on our canal bonds, and to forward the 225,000 (British Pounds Sterling) bonds of the new denomination to Messrs. John Wright & Co. of London, to be substituted in place of the old ones deposited under the contract made with that house, by Gov. Reynolds and myself, on the 30th of October 1839. . . . At the request of Barrett, fund commissioner, with whose co-operation it was hoped that provision could be made for the whole of our interest, internal improvement and all, at the same time, so as not to make a difference in the price bonds until to-day.

Senator Young, still trying to salvage his reputation and remedy the funding problem for the state, was hopeful that Richard Barrett, the state fund commissioner, could help fix things. Meanwhile, for former Governor Duncan, Mark Aldrich, and others of the Warsaw Land Company and the Des Moines Rapids Railroad commissioners, the appointment of their fellow partner Richard Barrett to the state fund commissioner position was still perceived as a great opportunity to aid them in their financial pursuits. Isaac N. Morris, one of the Des Moines Rapids Railroad commissioners, was president of the Illinois and Michigan Canal. Morris was the brother-in-law to Calvin Warren, also one of the commissioners. Together, they were expected to reap great benefit in raising land prices so they could finally sell their lands profitably.

With their rights enumerated in the Nauvoo Charter and validated through the Illinois legislature and governor's office, the ecclesiastical vision of the Prophet was to be advanced by significant means. By revelation on January 19, 1841, the Prophet was instructed:

> I am well pleased with your offering and acknowledgments, which you have made; for unto this end have I raised you up, that I might show forth my wisdom through the weak things of the earth.

> Your prayers are acceptable before me; and in answer to them I say unto you, that you are now called immediately to make a solemn proclamation of my gospel, and of this stake which I have planted to be a cornerstone of Zion. (D&C 124:1–2)

The Prophet was instructed that this proclamation was to be made "to all the kings of the world, to the four corners thereof . . . and the high-minded governors of the nation" (D&C 124:3). The purpose of the proclamation was as a warning: "For, behold, I am about to call upon them to give heed to the light and glory of Zion, for the set time has come to favor her" (D&C 124:6). Also in this revelation was a mandate to build a temple and construct the Nauvoo House. These two construction projects were of the utmost importance to Joseph Smith and the Saints.

In his inaugural address, Mayor Bennett presented his plan for the construction of a wing dam to divert a portion of the flow of the Mississippi River through a canal. The canal was to run north and south down the middle of Main Street for a distance of two miles. The canal needed to be dug eighty-two feet wide to accommodate shipping, wharves, and mills. On the river, a partial dam was to be built diagonally from the Nauvoo shore to an island. In response, the city council formed a committee to evaluate the proposal, with Joseph Smith as chairman. Upon further scrutiny by Alanson Ripley, the city surveyor, it was found that Main Street in Nauvoo was built on top of a solid limestone formation, which made the canal project unworkable but still attracted attention as to a future potential for a dam project.[235]

Illinois in Financial Crisis

At the capital in Springfield, debate continued on the crucial issues affecting the state's economic crisis. Various measures were proffered to provide fiscal relief. It was still believed by many that the Illinois and Michigan Canal had to be completed to secure a new revenue stream to service the prior internal improvement debts.

On February 26, 1841, Democrat Wickliffe Kitchell took the floor to respond to Whig legislator Abraham Lincoln's proposal of new bonds backed by an immediate property tax for the key Illinois and Michigan Canal. The General Assembly had been debating the future of this project in view of the serious financial crisis of the state. The aggressive host of internal improvement projects, consisting of this canal project and several railroad and highway projects across the state, had encumbered the state to more than eleven million dollars in debt. Kitchell had been proposing that since the entire state internal improvement programs were significantly underfunded and they already had a crippling debt load, they should sell the depots, buildings, and railroad iron and materials inventories and stop the projects. It was reported:

> Mr. Kitchell was surprised at the course of the gentleman from Sangamon [Mr. Lincoln]. We were already prostrated by debt, and that gentleman thought it would be for the interest of the state to go still deeper. Mr. Kitchell said it reminded him of an anecdote, which he would relate. A drunkard in Arkansas took so much of the cretur that he lost his reason and remained for some time in a state of insensibility. His wife tried every experiment to cure him; but it was of no avail, until a neighbor came to the house and recommended some brandy toddy. The insensible man rose at the word toddy and said, "That is the stuff." It was so with the gentleman from Sangamon—more debt would be for the better.[236]

It was reported that Lincoln responded,

> Mr. Speaker, the attack of that member . . . reminds me of an old friend of mine. He's a peculiar looking old fellow, with shaggy, overhanging eyebrows, and a pair of spectacles under them. [Everybody turned to the member . . . and recognized a personal description.] One morning just after the old man got up, he imagined, on looking out of his door, that he saw rather a lively squirrel on a tree near his house. So he took down his rifle, and fired at the squirrel, but the squirrel paid no attention to the shot. He loaded and fired again, and again, until, at the thirteenth shot, he set down his gun impatiently, and said to his boy, who was looking on, "Boy, there's something wrong about this rifle." "Rifle's all right, I know 'tis," responded the boy, "but where's your squirrel?" "Don't you see him, humped up about half way up the tree?" inquired the old man, peering over his spectacles, and getting mystified. "No, I don't," responded the boy; and then turning and looking into his father's face, he exclaimed, "I see your squirrel! You've been firing at a louse on your eyebrow!"
>
> It is so with the gentleman from Montgomery. He imagined he could see squirrels every day, when they were nothing but lice.[237]

Of this political jarring, observers reported,

> It convulsed the whole House of Representatives with laughter. All business was at once suspended. . . . Members of all parties, without distinction, were involuntarily compelled to laugh. They not only laughed, but they screamed and yelled. . . . It was a scene of indescribable confusion. One paroxysm passed away, . . . another lull occurred, and still another paroxysm, until they seemed to be perfectly exhausted.[238]

Kitchell had earned the reputation of belittling the Whigs and pontificating for his favorite projects and overall becoming a legislative obstructionist. Fellow Whigs gave Lincoln the task of putting Kitchell in his place. After missing his mark, Mr. Kitchell, embarrassed, finished the remainder of that session in an inconspicuous manner.

On the same day as the entertaining exchange between Kitchell and Lincoln, the legislature with a strong coalition of Whigs and Southern Democrats were able to reinstate key railroad and turnpike projects back to active status as approved state internal improvement projects if funding could be secured. All previous improvement projects had been terminated by the legislature in February of the prior year.

On February 26, the Springfield to Jacksonville portion of the Northern Cross Railroad was reauthorized. On the next day, the Des Moines Rapids Railroad and the Mount Carmel Alton Railroads were again approved with specific instructions for the fund commissioner (Richard Barrett) to assume full charge of the Northern Cross Railroad line between Springfield and the Illinois River. Also, the Alton Springfield Turnpike, which was promoted by Lincoln as an intended supplemental railroad project, was added back. The turnpike road from Springfield to Beardstown and on to Quincy and Warsaw was likewise added to supplement the intent of the other railroads. Valentine Wilson was appointed a commissioner for this project.

With these projects reapproved, a major hub could have vested in Warsaw, Quincy, Carthage, Springfield, and Alton, if completed. If Nauvoo were added, a complete transportation system would be in place. Lead from Dubuque and Galena could be unloaded at Nauvoo, and then sent to Beardstown via rail with access to the Illinois and Michigan Canal. Or it could be routed to Springfield and on to Alton destined for St. Louis, or dispatched on the Alton Mount Carmel Line to connect with the Wabash and Erie Canal—or to connect with the Indianapolis to Madison Railroad, and then on the Ohio River to Pittsburgh. Produce and other supplies from Hancock merchants and farmers would have access to unlimited new commercial venues.

The crucial factor in getting funding for these projects was predicated on new funding for the Illinois and Michigan Canal. With the Des Moines Rapids Railroad plans renewed, the previous land owners, including three steamboat captains—Hugh White, George Atchison, and Isaac N. Waggoner with property along the route—were anxious for the Mormons to develop the area, and then clear out. D. G. Whitney, James Doyle, Luther Whitney, and others hoped the various internal improvement projects would continue and provide high returns in land sales.

During June 1841, Joseph Smith was arrested on a writ issued by Missouri. A writ hearing was held at Monmouth, with Judge Stephen A. Douglas presiding. The Prophet was defended by Charles A. Warren, O. H. Browning, and Cyrus Walker. During the hearing, Browning "gave a recitation of what he himself had seen at Quincy, and on the banks of the Mississippi River when the Saints were 'exterminated from Missouri.' "[239] Many in the court room were moved to tears, including Judge Douglas. After all the attorneys had finished, Judge Douglas ruled in favor of the Prophet.[240] Afterward, Joseph found Stephen Douglas to be a good friend to himself and the Church.

Monopolizing the Des Moines Rapids

Joseph Nicollet had been hired by the federal government to map key areas in the country, but his health had been in decline, leaving his report incomplete. Some of the upper rivers feeding into the Mississippi had not been adequately explored. Nicollet suggested his young protégé, John C. Fremont, be called in to survey the Des Moines River. Prior to his departure, Fremont had been introduced to the Benton family and quickly took attention to Benton's second daughter, Jessie. Much against Senator Benton's wishes, Jessie went to visit Fremont while he was conducting his surveying duties. In spite of parental protestations, Jessie Benton and John C. Fremont were married on October 19, 1841. Fremont had determined by his findings that the Des Moines River was navigable if improved. Many were hoping for such an improved route to quicken access to Council Bluffs, and then to continue west on the Platte to the Rocky Mountains.

Benton had, in the last several years, been promoting commercial projects on the Des Moines River at a site named Bentonsport. He was looking to unite projects of the upper Mississippi, involving the Des Moines Rapids with commercial benefits coming from the Des Moines River, both flowing south to St. Louis. Benton was also committed to the advancement of the Illinois and Michigan Canal, which would improve regional development.

Benton was also an early advocate for the National Cumberland Road from Washington, DC, which would cross Illinois and link to St. Louis. These projects were included in his thirteen-point agenda of 1817. They were again interrupting his plans for the "Road to India" and his various thirteen-point agenda initiatives. It was intolerable that his efforts to secure the Illinois and Michigan Canal, the national road, the lead trade from Dubuque, development of the Lake Superior access, and other projects should benefit his archenemies—the Mormons—to the detriment of the Chouteaus and his Central Clique loyalists.

Benton, the Chouteaus, the Reddick heirs, and others were anxious for the Corp of Engineers to finish the project laid out by Robert E. Lee. Securing uninterrupted passage through the Mississippi River was everyone's quest. A great battle was emerging as to who would succeed in securing the means of monopolizing the Des Moines Rapids with its four corners of Warsaw, Nauvoo, Montrose, and Keokuk.

Not to be outdone by their neighbors across the river, in the fall of 1841, Benjamin B. Gates and David Higby, two enterprising non-Mormons, hired Edward Worth to construct a wing dam on the Mississippi River between Nashville and Keokuk from the Iowa side. Their dam was completed the next year and was used to power a gristmill. While the Worth dam was in construction, the Prophet wrote to Edward Hunter, a recent convert in Pennsylvania, indicating that Nauvoo suffered due to a lack of steam engines and water mills.

By revelation, Joseph was instructed to move forward in building Zion in Nauvoo and to move on from the disappointments in Missouri. For their failure to establish Zion in Missouri, the Lord had forgiven them, but Joseph was given a stern warning for the Saints and oppressors:

> Therefore, for this cause have I accepted the offerings of those whom I commanded to build up a city and a house unto my name, in Jackson County, Missouri, and were hindered by their enemies, saith the Lord your God.
>
> And I will answer judgment, wrath, and indignation, wailing, and anguish, and gnashing of teeth upon their heads, unto the third and fourth generation, so long as they repent not, and hate me, saith the Lord your God.
>
> And this I make an example unto you, for your consolation concerning all those who have been commanded to do a work and have been hindered. (D&C 124:51–53)

With the new momentum in internal improvements in the Hancock area and heightened expectations toward the improvements of the Des Moines Rapids and the Des Moines Rapids Railroad, perhaps some sensed the need to start the movement to rid the area of the Mormons in anticipation of the need to exercise the honeycomb effect.

In June 1841, Thomas Sharp announced the creation of a new anti-Mormon Party in Warsaw and Carthage. Several of the internal improvement leaders and those with lands in affected areas eagerly participated, including Mark Aldrich, Joel Catlin, and Walter Bagby. The newly appointed Springfield, Beardstown, Carthage, Warsaw road commissioner Valentine Wilson would also take an active role in the anti-Mormon Party.

10: Francis Scott Key and the Half-Breed Tract

Francis Scott Key, author of the famous anthem—which had become a familiar song—wrote on July 9, 1838, from his Baltimore home to his client Samuel Marsh, a principal of the New York Land Company, acknowledging receipt of the fifty dollars they had sent him for services. The principals of the New York Land Company sought out Francis Key because of his well-entrenched political connections, his broad experience in the court room, and his significant reputation. It was likely felt that Key's close relationship with his brother-in-law Roger Taney, on the Supreme Court, was a significant plus for what they were planning to do. The political affiliations of these New York land promoters were both Whig and Democrat Party patrons.

This New York Land Company had been formed on October 22, 1836, with Isaac Galland as their local partner.[241] The focus of the company was to buy up parcels of the Half-Breed Tract located in Iowa Territory, from the inexperienced Half-Breed Indian occupants or their assignees. In legal matters, Samuel Marsh, William E. Lee, and Edward C. Delavan acted as trustees for the company and were the only names generally associated with this enterprise.

The General Land Office of the United States issued a formal patent, granting to the heirs of Thomas Riddick a patent for 640 acres on February 7, 1839. With that land certified, Edward Brooks filed for a hearing for the next session of the US District Court, to be convened at the Fort Madison Courthouse for Lee County. At this April 1839 court session, an action of right was commenced against William Coleman, David W. Kilbourne, Henry S. Austin, John Shaw, Thomas Gregg, George Stubbins, Isaac Williams, Elijah Fordham, Anson M. Bissell, Calvin Beebe, Wandle Mace, Joseph B. Noble, John Taylor, Brigham Young, Martin M. Kellogg, William Lewis, and Harmon Booth.[242]

After the Mormons were expelled from Missouri, a group of Saints, lead by Israel Barlow, moved south along the Mississippi and settled at the abandoned Fort Des Moines barracks. Barlow made the initial contact with Isaac Galland for Church members to buy the lands. They were followed by other leaders, including Brigham Young and John Taylor, who likewise agreed to rent space in the barracks to house their families temporarily.

With the filing of the lawsuit by the Reddick heirs, the Chouteaus made clear their intentions to renew their war with the Mormons, as they had done at Chez Les Cansas in Jackson County in 1836. Francois Chouteau had made clear to his father-in-law, Pierre Menard, that they were willing to fight to the end to keep the Mormons from interfering with them.

The Reddick heirs were specifically targeting the Mormon leaders, naming them as defendants. Left unabated, the Mormons were expected to disrupt the monopoly again, this time on the Mississippi. The St. Louis Junto had dominated trade on the Mississippi for more than fifty years. They had established their network of trading forts up to the British occupied lands in the northwest. Reddick and Pilcher had been loyal to the American Fur Company since before the days of the Bank of Missouri in 1817.

One of the early targets of the Reddick heirs' litigation efforts was against David Kilbourne, known to be an agent for the New York Land Company. Kilbourne and the New York Land Company, as defendants, determined to keep the matter concealed from Joseph Smith and the Saints. Early in the trial, David Kilbourne was replaced as defendant by Marsh, Lee, and Delavan, representing the New York Land Company.

Francis Scott Key Arrives in the Iowa Territory to Represent the New York Land Company

Hiram Barney, another agent for the New York Land Company, frantically wrote to Francis S. Key on July 30, 1839, "We deem it of the highest importance and it is our earnest desire that you should proceed to Iowa as soon as you possibly can."[243]

On January 7, 1841, President Van Buren reappointed Francis Key as district attorney, as his presidential term was near to expire. The Senate ratified his nomination quickly. Harrison was sworn in as the next American president during March 1841. With primarily a Whig administration under President Harrison, Francis Key's appointment as district attorney was revoked to make way for Whig loyalists to fill his spot. Key had enjoyed that position and worked in that capacity for eight years. Key turned more of his attentions to his legal practice.

Hiram Barney continued calling for Key to come to the Iowa Territory, as they were in serious need. Key responded that he couldn't come then because of sickness and that he was still heavily involved in other legal work, particularly regarding war reparations with the Mexican government. He was further delayed after the surprising death of President Harrison. In April, Key made final preparations to leave for the Iowa Territory with his son.

They arrived at Fort Madison on Wednesday, April 28, after traveling nearly a thousand miles. Francis Key arrived in the Half-Breed Tract area of the Iowa Territory early in May 1841 and toured the main sites of the holdings of his client for the trip, the New York Land Company.

The New York Land Company was in dire economic circumstances and were unable to sell land holdings without incurring costly litigation. The Iowa Territorial legislature was not supportive or helpful. The company was deeply in debt. Expectations were that if they lost in the courts, the company would be lost. Key, impressed with the area, wrote to Hiram Barney,

> I have never seen any thing like Montrose & the bluffs & prairies around it. It exceeds in beauty even what my imagination had painted. . . . Keokuk is to be the great place . . . lots could be sold there tomorrow, if the title is clear of doubt, for $100,000.[244]

Or at least he had been told as much by an excited local attorney, Hugh Reid. Reid and the others quickly upon his arrival filled him in on their local perspectives and prejudices. In the same letter, Key continued to Barney,

> The Mormons, if we don't soon adjust these matters, will over-run us . . . if they get fixed there, they will shut out all other settlers & greatly injure us. . . . If we settle with Reddick's heirs, we start a town at Montrose at once, & get ahead of them.[245]

Greatly concerned, Key wrote to Barney, "We are engaged in our Reddick cause. . . . I see that it is to be fought desperately and at great length" (referring to the Edward Brooks claims regarding the Thomas F. Reddick Spanish land claim). He had the day before been to the Fort Madison Federal District Courthouse, still under construction.[246]

The Reddick heirs were optimistic that the Chouteau's Dubuque lead mining claims would be settled favorably, and with Benton's political clout the Montrose steamboat landing would be the base for a valuable new commercial center. But the Mormons had possession of the Montrose site, based on their purchases from Isaac Galland. The Mormons still understood they were indebted to Galland individually for their lands in Iowa.

The Iowa Half-Breed Partition Plan Is Approved

Besides the Reddick cases, Key was updated on the complex activity regarding Josiah Spalding vs. Euphrosine Antaga legal matters. Employing his vast legal expertise and overall good sense, he sought a formula for the desired partition of the entire Half-Breed Tract properties. During a conference of shareholders that extended into the night, Key presented a plan to Judge Charles Mason. He explained this also to Barney back in New York:

> The Judge obliging us by continuing the Court for the purpose, I drew up a decree of partition. . . . Counsels are appointed, & very competent ones, to divide the reservation (excepting the lots of Montrose for the present at least) into 101 equal shares. . . . I think I may congratulate our clients upon a very favourable result of our labours. I do not mean as to the Reddick case.[247]

Judge Charles Mason had consented to Key's proposals and later issued a formal decree of partition based on his formula. It is likely that Judge Mason knew Key's brother-in-law was Chief Justice of the US Supreme Court and hoped not to have been overruled if these very hotly contested verdicts were appealed. Key recognized the primary problem for his client remained; the Reddick heirs were stubborn and unwilling to compromise.

What Key was unaware of was the circle of friends and associates surrounding Edward Brooks and the Reddick heirs. Thomas F. Reddick of St. Louis had been the president, succeeding August Chouteau, of the Bank of Missouri, while Benton was serving as a bank director. Thomas F. Reddick was a close friend of Joshua Pilcher, who was also associated with the Bank of Missouri with Reddick and Benton, while Lilburn Boggs was the bank cashier. It was Pilcher and Benton who stormed into the competing Bank of St. Louis, which lead to their closure. In 1821, Thomas Reddick and Benton were involved in the closure of the Bank of Missouri as well. Benton, at this time in 1841, was still paying off the debt he was allocated as a shareholder for the bank's demise. Edward Brooks was also well entrenched with the St. Louis Chamber of Commerce and was an officer in an insurance company in St. Louis.

The Chouteaus were expecting, through the support of Senator Benton, to finally secure the mining rights of the Dubuque Spanish Mines. Benton and the Chouteaus needed the Montrose site at the head of the Rapids and either Keokuk or Warsaw at the foot of the Rapids to avoid having to pay outsiders for all the transits by steamboat from Dubuque and Galena to St. Louis or New Orleans passing through the Rapids. Benton and the Chouteaus were also anxious for the completion of the Illinois and Michigan Canal and the railroads linking the Great Lakes to their enterprise distribution channels as well.

In 1839, Senator Benton had maneuvered to get Joshua Pilcher appointed superintendent of Indian Affairs to replace William Clark after his death. Pilcher was a close friend and ally of the Pierre Chouteau Jr. aristocracy in the fur trade. To secure their claims, Reddick heirs, closely allied with Benton and Pilcher, sued the New York Land Company for the rights of occupancy to the mile square lot occupied by David Kilbourne, who had been granted ferry rights, and the Mormons. The Mormon lands had been sold to them by Isaac Galland by June 1839.[248]

Key, as attorney for the trustees of the New York Land Company, agreed to join suit to the previous petition for partition, filed April term of 1840 to the District Court of Lee County in the Territory of Iowa. Hugh T. Reid and Edward Johnston made the earlier request to the court on behalf of Josiah Spalding, John and Edward Walsh, George Crossman, and several other St. Louis residents, claiming,

> They have a legal title to, and are seized in fee simple of twenty-three and one-third full shares, and five thousand one hundred and thirty-five acres of land, in that tract of land commonly called the Half-Breed Tract, situated in Lee county aforesaid, lying between the Mississippi and des Moines rivers, bounded on the north by a line drawn from the northwest corner of the State of Missouri east to the Mississippi river, and containing one hundred and nineteen thousand acres . . . together with one full share and one-sixth of a full share in Keokuk.[249]

Other local attorneys, representing petition claimants, agreed to join the 1840 petition of Spalding with Key, including William Henry Starr, Philip Viele, and Mr. Rich. Orville and Milton Browning were also involved in this suit. All these attorneys understood that by their actions they were disenfranchising all of the Mormon residents from their homes in the entire Half-Breed Tract. The lands purchased by Joseph Smith, Vinson Knight, Granger, and others of twenty thousand acres were being reallocated to the 101 claimants. Proper due process and notifications had not been provided the Mormons or their leaders.

As part of the required legal process, Key filed on behalf of his client on May 8, 1841, in the matter of "Spalding and others v. Antaya and others, for Partition":

> The answer of Samuel Marsh, William E. Lee, and Edward C. Delavan, trustees under articles of association, bearing date 22 October, 1836 . . . for the persons interested in said association, . . . to the petition filed by Spalding and others against Antaya and others in this court, for partition, . . . by their attorney, F. S. Key, respectfully showeth, that they, and the persons interested in said association, whom they represent, claim to be entitled to the shares and proportions of said half-breed tract, . . . are herewith filed and produced to the court, and

> the defendants are willing that their said claims, . . . should be decided and adjudged by the court, and partition decreed according to law.[250]

In the list of many half-breed titles claimed by Samuel Marsh, William E. Lee, and Edward C. Delavan—trustees of New York claimants—were two of particular note:

> Pa-pe-no-ah, Ganlette, one protion; Muk-e-ho, one portion; Se-pe-nah, one portion; Mary Tolman, formerly Mary Dugue (Duque), one portion . . . Christopher Antaya, one-third; Isaac Antaya, one and one-half acres in Keokuk.[251]

Before he departed the area, Key also advised Hugh Reid to erect public signs "at Montrose, Keokuk & other places stating the late decree of the Court establishing titles of the share holders & warning off all trespassers & intruders—also if necessary to sue some of them."

On May 13, Francis Key again updated Hiram Barney and further commented, "The Mormons have great additions coming to them daily." He also discussed Isaac Galland, another agent for his client who had converted to the Church, and Mayor Bennett:

> This man is now in N. York or Vermont collecting funds for their temple [Galland]. They have a Dr. Bonnet [John C. Bennett] with them. A man of no principle or character he is the Mayor of Nauvoo & commands their legion under Brigadier General Joe Smith the prophet of the Lord. I heard Bonnet preach at Montrose & attended one of their baptisms.[252]

Key, during his visit, had crossed the river on to the Illinois side and likely observed Nauvoo personally. He likely was told they had armed their Nauvoo Legion with "cannon & small arms." In another letter to Barney, Key referred to a revelation by Joseph Smith regarding the Half-Breed Tract of land, "that the Lord has given them the reservation," and "there is no limit to the knavery of the leaders & the folly of the led. They will believe any thing that Joe Smith gives out as a revelation & do any thing he commands them."[253]

Key had neither the time nor the inclination to meet with any of the Mormon leaders and understand their side of the story or anything of their religion. Key had an understandable bias because the Mormons were in opposition to his client. He saw the many opportunities for his client in developing this land into the great commercial center it could become. The Mormons were perceived as a threat because of their growing numbers.

The result of the partition plan had the New York Land Company holding 41.58 percent and the St. Louis Land Company holding about 15 percent of the entire 119,000 acres. Other claimants were allocated the remaining parcels. On his return trip home, Key still highly charged of what he had observed and accomplished wrote to his wife, Polly, "If I could . . . get $10,000 I would come back here & make a fortune at once. I am so sure of this that I should be almost tempted to sell Pipe Creek [their current home site]."[254]

The Mormons had in fact been aggressively buying lands earlier in Montrose and elsewhere but thought they were dealing only with Isaac Galland. Their deeds and other documents bore only his name, with no reference to the New York Land Company and with no indication of Reid's and Kilbourn's involvement. Isaac Galland had apparently not warned the Mormon leaders of the surrounding enemies to the Church and their "honeycomb" scheme.

For his two week stay, seeing the steamboat traffic on the river, hearing of all the railroad and highway road plans, and seeing Conestogas frequently brought in, Key was taken in by the lure of instant wealth for those fortunate investors, or so he thought at that time. Key wrote to his wife, Polly, on May 15, that while in New York, "I want to see my clients there, who I think will be much pleased with what I have done for them."[255]

The Mexican claims case that had occupied so much of his time prior to the Iowa trip was expected to finally pay out soon. Hiram Barney was getting concerned that Key was losing interest in the New York Land Company as his client. On August 31, 1841, Barney wrote,

> General Dodge has raised a great excitement against the Company by his representations, in political harangues, that the Company are a band of unprincipled speculators, whose interests are connected with the Whig party.[256]

Key received little in fees from his Iowa work because payment was contingent on future lot sales. Meanwhile, there arose a few challenges to his plan. Key wrote Barney in return: "I am Counsel for Mexican claimants to a very large amount. I have engaged to attend to these cases, & now, and for some time, my attention will be indispensable."[257]

An international arbitration board had recently set a fixed amount for the settlement from the Mexican government to the United States at $2.5 million. This was compensation for property damage against US citizens during the Texas War of Independence in 1835 and 1836 and for minor conflicts earlier. Key's clients were among those entitled to settlement. Key was to be paid in Mexican claim's certificates valued at fifty-seven thousand dollars, if paid at all.

After an exhausting engagement, he returned to his home on January 7, 1843, suffering from congestion and a sore throat. Three days later, a doctor diagnosed his condition as pleurisy or inflammation of the lungs, and proceeded to "bleed" his patient, which made him weaker. Key went to sleep that night, confident he was on the mend. The next morning, he awoke in a delirious, incoherent state. Key, sixty-three years old, died that night.

Key passed away with large amounts of outstanding debt. Many people owed Key large sums of money for his legal work that had not been paid. One of the worst clients to collect from was the New York Land Company. Many letters had been exchanged between Hiram Barney and Polly Key and their son Barton. It took until 1850 before the New York Land Company paid anything to the Key family. It was an offensive settlement of only $1,500 for his efforts in securing the massive Half-Breed Tract lands in Iowa. The Company required Polly and all their children to sign an agreement renouncing all claim to land or interest in the company.[258]

Iowa Vigilante Committee Formed against Anti-Decree Men and Mormons

In the summer of 1840, Laban Fleak purchased the new house built by Isaac Galland just south of the wharf at Keokuk. He had come from New York at thirty-two years of age a few months earlier. Fleak held a deep resentment against the Mormons. He had fought the Saints in the Battle of Crooked River in Missouri in 1838 and detested their religion and its leaders.[259]

With simple modifications, the building became a hotel and grocery for the transient river men. In a short time, Keokuk House became a social magnet and was often crowded to capacity. Fleak adapted well to the ruffian demeanor of his clientele. A friend, Abraham Chittenden, moving from Warsaw, also established a grocery store in Keokuk.

Within a week of his opening, William Price, leader of the Price gang, confronted Fleak that he was the "king" of the county. Fleak stood up to him and refused him service. Hawkins Taylor, the local sheriff, sought to recruit Fleak to rid the area of its worst undesirables. Fleak was quickly installed as a Justice of the Peace and "entered into a compact" with Sheriff Taylor and two other locals, Val Vanorsdal and Colonel Hillis, to consolidate efforts to eliminate the local gangs. Together, they brought a new and oppressive version of justice to Iowa.[260]

In the spring of 1841, Isaac Galland moved into Keokuk, unaware of the planned visit of Francis Scott Key. As Galland pursued land sales in competition with his former employer, Kilbourne brought suit against Galland. David Kilbourne, after replacing Isaac Galland as agent of the New York Land Company, established other agents and, in joint efforts with Fleak and his network of deputies, a Vigilante Committee for the Iowa Territory to oppose Galland and other "anti-decree" men. The Vigilante Committee became effective in maintaining relative peace and order in the area but held little regard for "due process."[261]

Like Kilbourne, Fleak expanded his hatred for the Mormon population. The Vigilante Committee formed by Kilbourne and Fleak, with the support of Sheriff Hawkins Taylor, relished in Mormon opposition within their self-imposed agenda of keeping the peace locally. They resented and distrusted the Mormons' growth on both sides of the Mississippi River.

Over the next few years, the Vigilante Committee coalition maintained a watchful eye over Mormon communities. Kilbourne, serving as postmaster, lead the opposition at Montrose and further north. Fleak, allied with Abraham Chittenden, lead the Mormon opposition in Keokuk. Through Chittenden's connection with his siblings and father in Warsaw, they kept the Vigilante Committee leadership updated on the dynamics of the Mormons on the Illinois side.

The Mormons, because they kept close to their own brothers and sisters of the faith, rarely mingled with the old settlers and were likely oblivious to the anti-Mormon organized opposition surrounding them.

Also, in spite of the best efforts of the Vigilante group, the "anti-decree" old settlers periodically waged their own form of opposition against the land grabbers.

After the partition plan's initial acceptance, Thomas Sharp gleefully announced the inauguration of the new "anti-Mormon Party." Their intent was to field opposition candidates and to counter the growing strength of the Nauvoo voting block. Several Chittenden family members supported Sharp's anti-Mormon efforts and had family ties with allies of Fleak and Kilbourne.

11: Fraud Perpetrated against the Saints in Iowa

On March 20, 1841, the Prophet received a revelation in answer to the interrogatory: "What is the will of the Lord concerning the Saints in the Territory of Iowa?" (D&C 125:1).

> Verily, thus saith the Lord, I say unto you, if those who call themselves by my name and are essaying to be my Saints, if they will do my will and keep my commandments concerning them, let them gather themselves together unto the places which I shall appoint unto them by my servant Joseph, and build up cities unto my name, that they may be prepared for that which is in store for a time to come.
>
> Let them build up a city unto my name upon the land opposite the city of Nauvoo, and let the name of Zarahemla be named upon it.
>
> And let all those who come from the east, and the west, and the north, and the south, that have desires to dwell therein, take up their inheritance in the same, as well as in the city of Nashville, or in the city of Nauvoo, and in all the stakes which I have appointed, saith the Lord.[262] (D&C 125:2–4)

Kilbourne Accuses Mormon Leaders of Fraudulent Iowa Land Deals

In hopes of showing the New York commercial marketplace that internal improvements and the land sales on the Half-Breed Tract were still commercially viable, Kilbourne sent an anonymous letter to the *New York Journal of Commerce Magazine*, which was published on June 19, 1841. It charged that Mormons were occupying lands on the Half-Breed Tract in the Iowa Territory without valid title. But he was premature, taking a dangerous risk, as the sinister deeds of the New York Land Company might be called out in public.

Isaac Galland was alerted to Kilbourne's allegations printed in the publication. Greatly incensed, Galland replied,

> The first fable . . . made its appearance in the *Journal of Commerce* of the 19th ult., and purports to be "an extract of a private letter from a highly respectable gentleman residing near the Mormon city [Nauvoo]" and reads thus: "Some months since the title being then unsettled, Joe Smith received a revelation from God to the effect, that the Latter-Day Saints should go in and possess this fair land and enjoy the fruits thereof, &c.—about 2000 of these people residing on said lands, who claim by the highest possible title—a title direct from the Creator; and they seem determined to set all human decrees at defiance, &c." It will be observed that the above quoted remark is in reference to the lands upon which the Mormons settled . . . in Lee County, Iowa Territory.[263]

Galland included a letter he had received in March 1839 from the governor of the Iowa Territory. Governor Lucas expressed, "They are citizens of the United States and are entitled to the same political rights and legal protection that other citizens are entitled to." He went on:

> The writer sold to the people called Mormons, a part of the city plot of Nauvoo [then called Commerce], in Illinois, as also the lands before alluded to, in Iowa Territory—these contracts were concluded in the months of May and June in 1839, and all the circumstances in connection with these events, together with the above letter from Governor Lucas were published in the public prints of the Western country about the time of their occurrence. The Mormons therefore set up no other title to their lands than that which has been obtained from the writer by purchase, and he has no claims to have any higher pretentions to title than that derived by purchase from the original reserves, . . . and vested the fee simple by a special enactment approved June 30, 1834. . . . The

concealment of the name of this "highly respectable gentleman" has not entirely answered his purpose. . . . We give the initials of his name as follows: D. W. K. [David Wells Kilbourne]. If we are correct in our suspicion, we will merely quote the concluding sentence of his own letter, "May justice be meted out to him for his villainy."[264]

On September 14, 1841, during a brief recess of military exercises, Kilbourne stood up in front of the great crowd and, with General Swazey, Joseph Smith, and others behind, read,

> Citizens of Iowa: The laws of Iowa do not require you to muster under, or be reviewed by Joe Smith or General Bennett, and should they have the impudence to attempt it, it is hoped that every person having a proper respect for himself, will at once leave the ranks.[265]

Joseph Smith later recorded his response to Kilbourne's disrespectful conduct:

> This however, had no effect whatever on the people. Myself and brother were not in uniform, but were treated with every respect that visiting officers of our rank could be, through the entire day. At the dismissal of the military, I went to Mr. Kilbourn's store, and desired to have some conversation with him, but was peremptorily ordered out of doors. This conduct greatly disgusted his few friends, who upbraided Kilbourn with his ungentlemanly conduct, and accompanied me to the ferry, where I left them, showing me every manifestation of friendship.[266]

Embittered, Kilbourne arranged to have the following printed in the Burlington *Hawk-Eye and Patriot* newspaper on October 7, 1841:

> In June 1834, Congress relinquished to the "Half-Breeds of the Sac and Fox Nation of Indians," this reversionary interest, and authorized them to transfer their portion thereof, by sale, devise, or descent. . . .
>
> In the summer and fall of 1836, a company of gentlemen from New York made extensive purchases of Half-Breed shares. On account of the intimate knowledge that Dr. Galland was supposed to have of the "Half-Breeds," he was admitted as a member of this company, and was constituted one of their five trustees. Their confidence however in his integrity was of short duration. . . .
>
> In the winter of 1837, a law was passed for the partition of the Half-Breed Tract; commissioners were appointed to receive testimony, &c.—the succeeding legislature, however, repealed the law, and left the matter,

> if possible, worse than before . . . and in 1839, he (Galland) matured the plan of a stupendous fraud. He wrote to Joe Smith, who was then most righteously imprisoned in Missouri, on charges of High Treason, Burglary, Arson, &c.—inviting him to purchase his land at Nauvoo [47 acres]. Smith, after making his escape, complied, and brought on his half-starved followers, a large number of whom settled on the "Half-Breed Reserve," in Iowa. Doctor G. then commenced selling half-breed lands, giving therefore, warrantee deeds, which of course, could convey no title while the lands remained undivided. . . .
>
> That he might the more successfully carry out the scheme of swindling thus commenced, . . . he deeded to Mormon Bishops and Prophets, . . . tens of thousands of acres of the reservation alluded to, and they are daily deeding by warrantee deeds the lands thus acquired, and receiving therefore a valuable consideration. . . .
>
> When it is known that one of these Prophets acts in the absence of Galland, as his Agent for the sale of these lands, what further evidence, we ask, is wanted, of the baseness and rascality of himself and his confederates?[267]

This article had been printed the day after the courts filed the final plat completing the partition of the Half-Breed Tract lands. Still not satisfied that he had humiliated the Mormon leadership enough, he had another article published on October 14, in which he claimed:

> In addition to the numerous difficulties surrounding the "Half-Breed title," an old "Spanish claim" was raked up . . . and a patent issued in 1839 to the claimants under it for a tract of land one mile square, including the town site of Montrose.
>
> The gentlemen in possession, however, having "nine points of the law" in their favor, could, of course, hold the premises against the world, till a final adjudication of the whole matter. This the "Spanish claimants" well knew, and recognized them as being in peaceable possession by instituting suit in our courts, which is still pending.
>
> The parties interested flattered themselves that when their conflicting claims should be settled, all obstacles to the improvement of the place . . . would be removed; but, alas! How vain and delusive are all human hopes and expectations. A third claimant appears in the person of Joe Smith, with a title purporting to be Heaven derived. Early one morning in March last, the quiet citizens of Montrose were surprised by a visit from some of Joe Smith's scullions from Nauvoo—who to

all appearance had but recently made their escape from a steel trap—headed by Alanson Ripley, a Mormon Bishop, who says that "as to the technical niceties of the law of the land, he does not intend to regard them; that the kingdom spoken of by the prophet Daniel has been set up and that it is necessary every kingdom should be governed by its own laws." . . .

A few days subsequently to these occurrences, it was ascertained that the exterior line of this "four mile" town had been run by order of Joe Smith, and a plot of it made and recorded, to which he gave the name of Zarahemla.

And who figures as proprietor of this renowned city? Joe Smith, to be sure, "the Agent of Doctor Galland"—a worthy agent for a worthy principal!

Having sold to his dupes a large portion of the Half-Breed tract, a happy thought strikes him that they can yet be "bled"; he orders them by "revelation" to leave their farms and move into the "city," sells them lots and conveys them by deeds. There would be some excuse for these proceedings had they taken place under any color of title, but he had not the shadow of a shade to found a right upon. . . .

On the 6th of April, at a conference held at Nauvoo, a Mormon leader publicly read a pretended "revelation" that the city of Zarahemla should be laid out and built up by the "Latter Day Saints"! Joe Smith then stated that, "in accordance with this revelation," a city had been surveyed, and the Saints desirous of purchasing lots could now do so. . . . "The people over there," said he, "are very much opposed to it, . . . we don't want their improvements without paying them for them; we expect to pay them a good price for their possessions, and if that don't satisfy them, *we'll have them any how.*"

Are the people of Iowa prepared to submit to such treatment from an Impostor as vile as ever disgraced humanity? Are we to be told that "if you choose to sell, we will buy your possessions, if not, we will have them any how"? Is the title to land hereafter to be settled by revelation through Joe Smith? Has the time indeed arrived when "the kingdom is to be set up by *forcible means* if necessary," and when the riches of the Gentiles are to be consecrated to the true Israel? Such were the teachings of the leaders of this society in Missouri, and the facts here stated show conclusively that such are their teachings and practices now.[268]

Kilbourne's article was reprinted by editor Thomas Sharp in *The Warsaw Signal* on October 27 to further embarrass Church leaders. Kilbourne and others were gleefully mocking Joseph Smith and his claims of revelation concerning the lands in Iowa.[269] They were attempting to stop the growth of the Church in their area. Kilbourne's statements of the transaction details between Isaac Galland and the Mormon leaders in May and June 1839 were wrong. It was his employers, the New York Land Company, who were the real scoundrels. Kilbourne was either being duped, or he was intentionally lying.

Galland had contacted William Clark in 1834 for Mary Tolman, as a valid half-breed Indian claimant. The law of June 1834 eventually clarified the process of claimant validations and submissions. The 1836 Association Articles of the New York Land Company acknowledged Galland was involved in previous transactions, which were referred to as the prior sales of twenty thousand dollars. Galland was to sign over the Tolman deeds and other prior half-breed conveyances to the New York Land Company. That apparently didn't occur.

Early in 1839, Galland disassociated himself from the New York Land Company and mentioned it publicly, which was published in the *Iowa Territorial Gazette*, printed at Burlington on April 27, 1839.[270] In February, he had been appointed a commissioner for the Des Moines Rapids Railroad and likely expected that the land values on both sides of the river would increase rapidly. He had substantial disagreements with the partnership management as well. The following month he sold approximately twenty thousand acres of Iowa land to the Mormon leadership.

In Galland's response to Kilbourne's June article in the New York paper, he clarified his legal authority in selling his lands to them. Galland asserted, "The Mormons therefore set up no other title to their lands than that which has been obtained from the writer by purchase, and he has no claims to have any higher pretentions to title than that derived by purchase from the original reserves."[271] He was stating that the lands he sold to the Mormons were lands he secured directly from the half-breed claimants. These were secured before his partnership arrangement and included, for example, the claims of Mary Tolman he had written to William Clark about.

Galland apparently had not felt obliged to transfer these claims made prior to the partnership formation and had not been compelled to assign them to the New York Land Company principals before he announced his withdrawal from the partnership in April 1839. It could well be argued that since Galland's name was on the original conveyance documents from the half-breeds and that he then drafted warranty deeds on these lands; conveyed to the Mormons, it was a valid transfer to them. As Kilbourne stated, the Wisconsin legislature in 1838 set up procedures regarding the Half-Breed lands when part of the Wisconsin Territory. When the new Iowa legislature first met, they repealed the prior act as of January 1839. The law regarding valid titles at the time of the sale to the Mormons in May and June 1839 was in question.[272]

The Half-Breed Tract Partition Plan Was Completed Amidst Fraudulent Conduct

Francis Scott Key, as a lawyer for the New York Land Company, developed a plan and drew up the decree that provided that the half-breed tract land should be divided into 101 shares and arranged so that each claimant should draw his portion by lot and accept the result whatever it might be. Prior to this, none of the Indian occupants knew which specific lots they owned. His plan was approved and signed in May 1841.

Key filed an "Answer of Samuel Marsh, William E. Lee, and Edward C. Delavan, Trustees," in the case of Spalding and others versus Antaya and others for Partition, stating,

> The persons interested in said association, whom they represent, claim to be entitled to the shares and proportions of said half-breed tract, the land mentioned in said petition, set forth in the annexed list or schedule of half breed claims, the proofs of their title to which, and authentic copies of the conveyances by which the same are held, are herewith filed and produced to the court, and the defendants are willing that their said claims, and the claims of the said petitioners, and of the other parties in this case, should be decided and adjudged by the court, and partition decreed according to law.[273]

Included in this schedule presented to the court was the claim for Mary Tolman, formerly Mary Dugue, among many others. A total of forty-one shares were claimed by the New York Land Company in their filings. This occurred while Isaac Galland was on a mission for the Church to the east coast. Fraudulently, the New York Land Company represented to Key and the court that they had claim to the half-breed conveyances secured by Isaac Galland before the partnership was formed, even though he had withdrawn from the partnership two years earlier and had not previously signed over these pre-partnership conveyances to them. The court was assuming that Galland, who had signed the half-breed conveyances submitted, was still entitled to his previous ownership of the partnership, not knowing he had withdrawn.

At the court house in Fort Madison, an order was made on October 6, 1841, "to make allotment of the shares mentioned in said order by first numbering the shares corresponding with the numbers mentioned in the report of the Commissioners . . . with the numbers marked on the map or plat of the land to be divided."[274]

Though Key was no longer associated with the Half-Breed Tract plan, local attorneys and government leaders in the Iowa Territory were perpetrating a great evil against the Iowa Mormon land owners. Secretly, their lands and improvements were being stolen from them, and Judge Charles Mason, attorneys Hugh T. Reid and Edward Johnston and Oliver Browning, and several others were complicit in this nefarious endeavor. All 119,000 acres of land of the Half-Breed Tract were reallocated to the 101 applicants without notice to the Mormon landowners, that the nearly twenty thousand acres of land they purchased from Isaac Galland was redistributed to the 101 claimants. Kilbourne claimed that Galland's share represented but a small portion, but the records showed he held a sixth's share in the partnership.

The St. Louis Land Company also committed fraud against the Mormons. Isaac Campbell sold all his lands pertaining to Isaac Antaya to the Mormons,[275] yet when the claims were filed for the St. Louis Land Company in the May 1841 partition petition, the Isaac Antaya claims were still listed. Joseph Smith and Vinson Knight still believed they were indebted for the Keokuk lands, even though the lands had been reallocated by the partition plan.

The court in October 1841 ruled that 101 claims were valid. Forty-one of those belonged to the New York Land Company. David Kilbourne held about ⅝ of one share, and Edward Kilbourne held about ½ of one share. John and Edward Walsh held 2⅛ shares, in right of Maria Hebert, Pierre Jeaudron, Francis Blondeau, and Isaac Antaya. Wilson Overall held one share "in right of Isaac Antaya," and George Crossman held just over ¼ of one share, in right of Christopher, Maria, and Isaac Antaya.[276] After October 1841, these land companies had to wait for court challenges to see if their treacherous practices could be upheld so they were committed to keep their foul deeds from being known by the Mormons.

Late in 1839, the Iowa Territorial legislature enacted a law for the benefit of settlers who had improved their lots and were later dispossessed of their lands. The act provided that any person who had color of title, settled upon the land, and made improvements before being dispossessed of such lands should be paid in full value for such improvements. In 1840, the legislature passed an act that provided that any settler on the half-breed tract, with some color of title, could select one section and hold such land until the title was finally settled.

During 1841, the legislature, to further protect the prior purchasers, passed another act, which indicated the settler could have a lien on the land for improvements that he had made.

Court Case: Edward Brooks and Reddick Heirs versus David Kilbourne (Marsh, Lee, Delavan)

Even as these legal manipulations were being orchestrated, the court case pitting the New York Land Company against the Reddick heirs was continuing. On May 9, 1840, the attorneys replaced Kilbourne as defendant with Marsh, Lee, and Delavan—trustees of the New York Land Company—and claimed to the court that the trustees represented the other owners at Montrose as their landlord. The attorneys agreed that the decision of this case would be binding on all other cases with Brooks and the other Reddick heirs as plaintiffs.[277] This arrangement was intended to include the Mormons, though no notice was provided the Mormons of these hearings.

Edward Brooks was closely involved with the merchants in St. Louis. He was anxious to assist the Chouteaus, who were becoming increasingly anxious as competitors were increasing. With the formation of the St. Louis and Keokuk Packet Company in January 1842 by John McCune and James Yateman, their monopoly was coming to an end. Other steamship companies, anxious to engage in the Dubuque and Galena mining exports and imports, were soon to follow.

This lawsuit was referred to by Kilbourne in his October 14, 1841, Burlington newspaper article, in which he ridiculed the Mormons for claiming rights to lands in Montrose. Again, Kilbourne was either duped by his employer, or he was lying. Isaac Galland held the Montrose lands prior to the partnership agreement with the New York Land Company from the half-breed conveyances to him. He sold these lands to the Mormons in 1839 after withdrawing from the partnership, having never signed the documents over to the principals of the New York Land Company. In this lawsuit, the New York Land Company was again deceiving the court.

In November, Kilbourne chose a different means to (again) focus attention on actions of the Mormons opposing him and his plans. He complained bitterly about the Mormons destroying his place of business in Nauvoo. He felt the Church leaders were mocking him when the editing staff in Nauvoo reported in the Mormon publication *Times and Seasons*:

> It is known to many of our patrons, that a certain young man very injudiciously, and contrary to the remonstrances of his friends, and in violation of the ordinances of this city, not long since erected a small building, near the Temple square avowedly for the purpose of transacting the business of a grocer . . . it was finally vacated, and stood some time, a lonely wreck of folly.
>
> In the meantime, the very sanctimonious and extremely unfortunate Mr. Kilbourn of Montrose, threw out to the public, ungentlemanly and slanderous imputations concerning the matter . . . the building having become a monument for every fool to write upon and exhibit his folly, to the annoyance of the citizens, the city council very judiciously ordered the building removed as a nuisance. . . . We suppose, however, that Kilbourn and his junto will bray worse than ever.[278]

The ire of Kilbourne escalated. He sought vengeance but was concerned they knew of his plans, hence their reference to "Kilbourn and his junto." How much did they know?

Joseph Smith's Warsaw Prophecy Told to Calvin Warren

On December 30, 1841, Mark Aldrich, Calvin A. Warren, and Daniel S. Witter visited the Prophet Joseph Smith in his office. These gentlemen had attempted to sell land to the Church in Warsaw and Warren since 1839. They finally sold some lands to the Mormons in 1841, but after prices were increased for various items, relations soured. These three were visiting Joseph Smith to try to smooth over the prior problems. The meeting ended cordially. That evening, Joseph found Calvin A. Warren alone and spoke to him abruptly,

> I prophesied in the name of the Lord, that the first thing toward building up Warsaw was to break it down, to break down them that are there, that it never would be built up till it was broken down, and after that keep them entirely in the dark concerning our movements; and it is best to let Sharp' publish what he pleases and go to the devil, and the more lies he prints the sooner he will get through; not buy him out or hinder him; and after they have been in the dark long enough, let a certain set of men go there who will do as I tell them, a certain kind of men, some of those capitalists from the Eastern States, say from Pennsylvania; wise men who will take the lead of business, and go ahead of those that are there before they know what we are about, and the place will prosper, and not till then.[279]

The message was timely. Warren wondered how much Joseph knew of their plans.

At the beginning of 1842, Joseph Smith was aware both parties were anxious to secure the Mormon vote. The *Times and Seasons* quoted the Prophet, "We care not a fig for Whig or Democrat. . . . We shall go for our friends, our *tried friends*, and the cause of human liberty, which is the cause of God."[280] The Prophet saw Democrat Stephen Douglas as "a master spirit."[281]

At a meeting of the St. Louis Chamber of Commerce during February 1842, Adam B. Chambers, the editor of the Whig newspaper the *Missouri Republican*, presented an extensive report to the members in regards to the critical need of improvements to navigation on the Mississippi and Missouri Rivers and how such improvements could impact the economics of the region. Chambers also had an associate from Alton, Illinois, who assisted him named George T. M. Davis, who likewise was active in Whig Party leadership. Copies of his report were sent to the president and members of Congress. In his presentation, he produced many statistics indicating the amounts and types of imports and exports passing through St. Louis, such as:

- Lead from the Galena mines amounting to nearly fifteen thousand tons annually, valued at a million dollars, traveling to New Orleans, "subject to the risks and increased charges created by the obstructions at the Des Moines Rapids, and . . . in other parts of the river."[282]

- "The trade carried on by the American Fur Company, . . . and by other independent trades, including the trade of nearly all the north and northwestern Indians within the jurisdictions of the United States, centers at this point. The importation of cloths, blankets, and other fabrics for this trade (exclusive of annuities, the pay of hands and the outfit of expeditions, boats, etc.)."[283] The exportation of furs, buffalo robes, and peltries exceeded five hundred thousand dollars annually. "The American Fur Company . . . several steam and other boats, and several thousand men. Their boats, at least once a year, ascend the Missouri to the mouth of the Yellow-stone, freighted exclusively with supplies for trade with the various Indian tribes between the State line and that river, and also, for the tribes extending from thence to the Rocky Mountains and the Pacific."[284]
- The Illinois River and the city of Alton combined sent out eight thousand tons of pork and hog products, valued at nearly $1.5 million annually.
- "The usual price of freight to that point is about $1.50, but the boats feared the low stage of the water, and expected that they would be unable to re-cross the Desmoine Rapids, on their return yet it is known that $100,000 judiciously applied, would enable boats to cross the Rapids at the lowest stage of water. . . . The obstructions by the Rapids operates as a charge upon the whole population on the Mississippi, above them."[285]

Chambers's assistant, George T. M. Davis, likely served as liaison between the St. Louis merchants, his friend Governor Duncan, and the local leaders in Iowa and Hancock County.

On March 3, Joseph Smith returned a letter to Hiram Barney from New York. Barney had written on January 24, offering to sell lands to the Church located between the Hotchkiss purchase and the Galland purchase in Nauvoo. Joseph likely did not know he was representing the New York Land Company, who had participated in the fraudulent partition plan that had disenfranchised the Church's lands across the river in the Half-Breed Tract.[286]

In the spring of 1842, the city council approved Newel Knight to construct a wing dam. On May 14, William and Wilson Law were approved to build piers for mills and shipping.

Church Leaders See the World in Decline and the Need for the Kingdom of God

Boldly, Parley P. Pratt wrote to Queen Victoria:

> The world in which we live is on the eve of a revolution, more wonderful in its beginning, more rapid in its progress, more powerful in its operations, more extensive in its effects, more lasting in its influence, and more important in its consequences than any which man has yet witnessed upon the earth.[287]

The Apostle Wilford Woodruff also concluded the world would see the collapse of the evil world governments, to be replaced by the coming kingdom of God. He wrote,

> It seems as though the Nations at the present time, were insane & their Kings, Presidents & Senators entirely destitute of all wisdom. But they will all Soon learn there is a God in Israel who is about to take peace from the Earth & cut off nations not a few for Great Babylon is about to come in remembrance before God.[288]

Parley P. Pratt saw the changing world events, leading to the prophetic fulfillment of the gathering of Israel. He believed the Ottoman Empire was about to allow the Jews to return to their Biblical home lands. Pratt published in the *Millennial Star*:

> Thus, all things seem preparing, in a political point of view, for the great restitution of Israel; and it is a matter of certainty that when the Jews gather home and rebuild Jerusalem, the second coming of Christ and the Millennium are just at the door . . . we feel that the Second Advent is near.[289]

In a quiet place, the Prophet recorded the sacred events of the day, May 4, 1842,

> I spent the day in the upper part of the store, that is in my private office . . . because in that room I keep my sacred writings, translate ancient records, and receive revelations . . . in council with General James Adams, of Springfield, Patriarch Hyrum Smith, Bishops Newel K. Whitney and George Miller, and President Brigham Young and Elders Heber C. Kimball and Willard Richards instructing them in the principles and order of the Priesthood, attending to washings, anointing, endowments and the communication of keys pertaining to the Aaronic Priesthood, and so on the highest order of the Melchisedek Priesthood,

> setting forth the order pertaining to the Ancient of Days, and all those plans and principles by which any one is enabled to secure the fullness of those blessings which have been prepared for the Church of the First Born, . . . in this council was instituted the ancient order of things for the first time in these last days. And the communications I made to this council were of things spiritual, and to be received only by the spiritual minded; and there was nothing made known to these men but what will be made known to all the Saints of the last days.[290]

The Chouteau's Extend Their Trade Monopoly Further Westward

Pierre Chouteau and his allies anxiously sought to expand western fur operations and penetrate the British-dominated Oregon Territory. David D. Mitchell, Superintendent of Indian Affairs and loyal to Senator Benton and the Chouteaus, issued a license on August 22, 1842:

> P. Chouteau Jr. & Company, having applied for a license to trade for one year at a point or points west of the Rocky Mountains, with the Eutas, Snakes, Flat Heads, and such other Indians. . . . P. Chouteau & Company having furnished an invoice of merchandise intended for trade and having given bond according to law . . . who are hereby authorized to take with them, James Bridger . . . as Traders.[291]

For the merchants of St. Louis, this was welcome news, hoping to finally break the British hold on Pacific trade. For Samuel Owens and his Independence merchant's alliance, optimism rebounded. They were positioned to expand trade to the Pacific Ocean as the last post within the United States border.

But Joseph Smith kept petitioning Congress for redress. Fraud had been committed against the Mormon landowners in Iowa. Kilbourne had drawn attention to his employer's previous dealings, which could have lead to the reversal of the Partition Agreement.

12: Governor Reynolds Duped

To the west, Missouri citizens were provoked to an uproar. Former Governor Lilburn W. Boggs had been shot at his home on May 6, 1842. An immediate search was engaged to identify the gunmen. Enemies pointed to leaders of the Church, particularly to Porter Rockwell and Joseph Smith, with suspicion, quick to use the event to entrap the Prophet.

David Kilbourne Seeks Aid from Governor Reynolds against the Mormons

David Kilbourne wrote Governor Reynolds of Missouri from Montrose on May 14, 1842:

> We have just rec'd via St. Louis information the Ex Govr Boggs of your State was murdered in his own house on the 9th last & that suspicion was that the awful deed had been committed by a follower of the wretched imposter *Joe* Smith.
>
> If it is true that Gov Boggs has been murdered . . . then I should not entertain a doubt that it was done by some of Joe's minions at his instigation. He has sworn Vengence publickly against Gov Boggs ever since he settled in this neighborhood. . . .

> Their city Nauvoo is directly opposite this. We look upon them as a *Banditti*; called together by their leaders for the purpose of forming a more perfect organization, to carry out their swindling & treasonable plans.[292]

Shortly thereafter, *Hawk-Eye and Iowa Patriot* published a letter, dated May 14, claiming that Missouri officials expected the murderer to be a Mormon. To make matters worse, *The Nauvoo Wasp* printed, "It yet remains to be known who did the noble deed!"[293]

Kilbourne was desperate. What if the Mormons were to find out about the lawsuit with the Reddick heirs? What would be the aftermath, should they lose to their St. Louis opponents? What if the Mormons realized the Iowa lands, bought from Isaac Galland, were claimed by his employer and had been stolen away in the finalized partition plans?

Kilbourne, signing as postmaster, appeared to be a concerned fellow public servant and mask the massive economic and political interests that he was trying to protect for himself and his employer. He was careful not to involve politics, as there was a wedge between them. He, an aspiring Whig from Iowa Territory, and the governor, a powerful and seasoned Democrat Party leader (backed by the Central Clique), were engaging in a common cause. Unknown to Kilbourne was that Reynolds had been a friend to Boggs. It was Boggs who appointed Reynolds in 1837 to the judgeship covering Boone County when he was reinforcing the state leadership hierarchy with Central Clique faithful and packing the judiciary at the district and Supreme Court levels in anticipation of his final plans to deal with the Mormons.

Mayor Bennett Becomes an Enemy to the Church

In Nauvoo, the Prophet had not forgotten Bennett's actions. A diabolical attempt had been made on his life. On May 7, a mock battle, as scheduled for the Legion's Programma Militaire, was scripted by Bennett to separate him from the commander of the guard, Captain Rockwood, making him an easy target for enemies. General Law commanded the First Cohort.[294]

Many reports were being circulated regarding various acts of immoral conduct by Mayor Bennett and claims he had abandoned his former wife and children. Sensing the futility of trying to regain favor, Bennett tendered his resignation as mayor and voluntarily left the Church on May 17. Two days later, Joseph Smith was elected mayor. Joseph Smith reported at council meeting: "On account of the reports in circulation in the city this day, concerning the ex-mayor, . . . I asked John C. Bennett if he had aught against me." Bennett stood and indicated he had "no difficulty with the heads of the Church" and publicly asserted that anyone suggesting that Joseph Smith had given him "authorization to hold illicit intercourse with women" was a "liar in the face of God."[295]

During this same meeting, the council passed a "vote of thanks" to Dr. Bennett: "Resolved, . . . that this Council tender a vote of thanks to general John C. Bennett, for his great zeal . . . and for the faithful discharge of his duty while Mayor."[296]

Rumblings of Bennett's embittered changed heart began to surface. Joseph Smith felt the need to confront Governor Carlin of the conduct of the former mayor of Nauvoo.

> Dear Sir, It becomes my duty to lay before you some facts relative to the conduct of our major-general, John C. Bennett, which have been proven beyond the possibility of a dispute, and which he himself has admitted to be true in my presence.
>
> It is evident that his general character is that of an adulterer of the worst kind, and although he has a wife and children living, circumstances . . . have proven . . . that he care not whose character is disgraced, whose honor is destroyed, nor who suffers, so that his lustful appetite may be gratified; and further, he cares not how many or how abominable the falsehoods he has to make use of to accomplish his wicked purposes, even should it be that he brings disgrace upon a whole community. . . .
>
> It is rumored, and strong evidence exists, that Dr. Bennett and David and Edward Kilbourn have posted bills in Galena, calling upon the people to hold meetings, and have themselves in readiness at a moment's warning to be assembled and come here to mob us out of the place, and try to kidnap me; we know not as to the truth of this report, but we have conversed with some transient persons who had the report from a gentleman who lately came from there, and had seen those hand bills posted in Galena.[297]

Angrily, Bennett wrote to James G. Edwards, editor of the *Hawk-Eye and Iowa Patriot* that the split between him and Joseph Smith was permanent and that his life was in peril. The next day, June 28, under the direction of the Prophet, Bishop George Miller wrote to Governor Reynolds, indicating that he had "learned from respectable sources that John Cook Bennett has entered into a conspiracy with some of the citizens of your state, to bring a mob upon us, and thereby disturb our peaceful vocations of life, and destroy and drive us from our homes."[298]

Bennett again wrote to the editor of the *Hawk-Eye and Iowa Patriot*, this time on July 7, and requested copies of the articles written by David Kilbourne that were published in October.

Four days later, Joseph took time to report on the appalling conduct of the former mayor. Brother Hyrum and Elder Kimball later expressed concern regarding Bennett's conduct from various reported activities. Joseph mentioned that he had heard that Edward Kilbourne of Montrose, the brother of David, had been engaged with Bennett to bring a mob on their city, from Galena, and mentioned that he had confronted Edward Kilbourn directly on the matter. On that occasion, Mr. Kilbourn denied the charges.[299] To himself, Kilbourne knew otherwise and cautiously wondered how much the Prophet knew of their mounting plans against the hated Mormons.

Laban Fleak Writes to Missouri Governor Reynolds

Bennett then contacted Laban Fleak from Keokuk and discussed his plans to contact Missouri's governor. Fleak determined to reach out to the governor to aid in Bennett's plans for revenge. Fleak sent a letter to Governor Reynolds of Missouri on July 12, 1842:

> General Bennet, late a Mormon leader, now a dissenter goes to you . . . for the purpose of giving information touching the attempted assassination of Ex Gov Boggs. . . . Bennet accuses a fellow by the name of Rockwood or Rockwell & from some circumstances I suspected him the very day the news reached & I wrote the Post Master of Independence, Missouri, for a description of the person, . . . immediately preceding the news reaching here of the attempted assassination, Smith stated that he had it revealed to him of God himself *that Boggs would not die* in his bed . . . we are compelled to believe him to be . . . the author of

> that most foul deed. Ever since he was compelled to leave your State he has denounced the Citizens with heaviest imprecations. . . . Nearly his whole conversation & thoughts are taken up by planning the destruction of Missouri.
>
> Now, Sir, it is in your power to break up this horde of villainy and murder by removing its head or leader. Is not Smith a refugee from your State? And does not justice to her citizens require you to demand from Illinois his immediate surrender? Rest assured your call would be rec'd with loudest cheers from this quarter & from the adjoining counties on the opposite side of the Mississippi.[300]

Laban B. Fleak was born in Hamilton County, Ohio. In 1836, he moved to Richmond, Missouri, and opened a jewelry store. The following year, he helped found Buffalo City on the Crooked River in Ray County. A Whig Party supporter and political enthusiast, Fleak, in 1838, attended the first territorial convention for Iowa at Burlington. On making his return trip home, he missed the intended passage and was waylaid at Keokuk, where me met Robert E. Lee. Returning home to Buffalo City, he learned of a recent fuss regarding the Mormons. In the Battle of Crooked River, Fleak was called out by the Ray County militia, in David Snowden's Company.

Tom Sharp, editor of the *Warsaw Signal*, included Bennett's "sworn statement" in an issue published July 23:

> Smith drew a pistol on me and said, "The peace of my family requires that you should sign an affidavit, and make a statement before the City Council . . . exonerating me from all participation whatsoever, . . . in the spiritual wife doctrine, or private intercourse with females in general; and if you do not do it with apparent cheerfulness; I will make cat-fish bait of you, or deliver you to the Danites for execution."[301]

The *Niles Register* in Baltimore also ran the following on the same date of July 23:

> In your paper of the 23 June, you allude to the "trouble among the Mormons," and express a desire or hope that "the schism is incurable" and I assure you it is really so. The holy Joe fears the consequences of my disclosures, and has threatened to take my life. . . . If he murders me, others will avenge my blood, few days until you see my expose in the *Sangamo Journal* of next week, or the week following.[302]

In the *Logansport Telegraph* of July 30, a similar article was printed with Bennet, claiming,"I am threatened with death by the holy Joe and his Danite band of murderers, in case I dare make any disclosures in relation to the conduct of that polluted mass of corruption, iniquity and fraud—that king of Imposters—the holy and immaculate Joe Smith."[303]

For three months, Bennett lectured along the East Coast while continuing correspondence with Samuel Owens of Independence, Missouri. Other newspapers picked up Bennet's claims and circulated them in their communities. One of Bennett's letters was published by the *Illinois Register*, containing Bennett's bold charge for Owens. He challenged him,

> [Get] up an indictment immediately against Smith, for the five or six year old treason of which he was accused several years ago . . . when the indictment shall have been found get a copy and go immediately to the Governor and never leave him until you get a demand on the Governor of Illinois for a warrant, and let him never leave the Governor until he gets it; and then let him never come back to Missouri without Smith.[304]

Bennett's defection and alignment with a group of conspirators was linked and secured.

In the state office elections, Thomas Sharp was running as a Whig candidate against the Prophet's brother William for the state legislature. Because of the strength of the Mormon vote, William Smith handily beat him. The loss added to Sharp's hostility against the Mormons, and particularly against Joseph Smith.

Fleak was anxious to renew contacts with Governor Reynolds. He wrote on August 8:

> Dear Sir, I have just this hour recd intelligence from Nauvoo that the Mormon Prophet Joseph Smith has this day been arrested on your requisition. . . . The amount of it will be this Smith will be rescued by those devils which surround him & there will be another war more bloody than those villains say theirs was in Mo.
>
> Nothing can save Smith this time, nine tenths of our Citizens will support the Sheriff although he belongs to another State. The news of his arrest had not been here an hour before every Mormon in Our

> Town had left for Nauvoo I shall be with the Sheriff this evening . . . you may expect a note from me every Mail.
>
> You could have done nothing else that would have given the people of this Country & of Illinois the satisfaction that this requisition has given them.

Kilbourne was anxious to be brought up to date by Fleak, who had already been in communications with John C.Bennett relative to the plan to work with Missouri's governor. Kilbounre addressed his letter to "Friend Fleak":

> The Sheriff returned from Quincy yesterday & demanded Joe of the Marshall of Nauvoo; . . . the Marshall Saint had let him go.
>
> The fact is the Mormons defy all the force that can be brought against them & swear in their strength that Joe Shall not be taken to Mo. Does not his conduct show the despot guilt (sic)? They are all in a great stew. Every old Rifle, Pistol, Cutlass, Knife etc. among them is being put in order.
>
> If Joe does not appear I suppose the next step will be to offer a reward for him as a fugitive from justice—as he has now escaped from an officer of justice. . . .
>
> Will Mo now give up the chase? Will Gov Boggs be willing to rest & let a man who would murder him any moment go "unwhipped of Justice"?—for the good of the country & the peace of Society I hope not.

Kilbourne's previous letter to Governor Reynolds was written before the development of Bennett's break with the Mormons. Kilbourne knew this definitely improved the chances of getting the governor to follow through. A new network of collaborators against the Mormons was evolving. Fleak again wrote to Governor Reynolds on August 14, 1842:

> Smith is now shulking around in this Territory and will probably stay here until a requisition on our Gov. drives him somewhere else. He was in our Town at 12 o'clock last night consulting one of our Attorneys. The Cause of his being given up to the Marshall of the City of Nauvoo was this, they have an ordinance in their City which prohibits any persons being taken away from theirs without a hearing, & the Sheriff who

> arrested him having no counsel was obliged to go to Quincy to procure it. In his absence Smith procured an examination, before a Mormon Mayor & of course was liberated.
>
> The Mormons say that Smith shall not be taken to Missouri, that they will fight & all this. We had a sample of that in your State. I will write as often as I can.

Fleak was definitely enjoying his entry into the intrigues of opposition to the Mormons. He was the self-appointed knowledge source for the Missouri governor. He saw no problem in the political differences between him, a loyal Whig, and the governor, a powerful leader of the Democrat Party and a high ranking leader in Sappington's Central Clique. Fleak again wrote Reynolds on September 6 from Keokuk:

> Nothing short of a reward or a regiment of Militia will get him from his hiding place. A reward will, I think make or find a "Judas" among them . . . in short they say that "Brother Joseph" shall never be taken to Missouri. . . . I am as well satisfied, as is this whole community, that Rockwell, by the order of Smith, is the person that attempted the assassination of Boggs as I am about there is such a place as Paris. . . .
>
> Should Smith make his appearance again in our Town he will be arrested, as every thing is in readiness to convey him across the Desmoines River & in the mean time should any thing occur that would be important to be known by you I will advise you of it immediately. Be good enough to command me at all times.

A plan had been set at Keokuk that if Joseph Smith would set foot again in the town, the local vigilante justice would be invoked to kidnap Joseph and immediately get him away from the Nauvoo area.

During September, John C. Bennett was finalizing his book for publication. Various portions had already been printed in the *Sangamo Journal*. Bennett included the three letters of David Kilbourne, two of which ridiculed the Mormons for selling lands in Iowa Territory for which they had no legal claim. His book, entitled *The History of the Saints; or an Expose of Joe Smith and Mormonism*, drew even more attention to the risks of the leaders of the New York Land Company being exposed for their treachery in both the Montrose lawsuit and in the partition proceedings pertaining to the Half-Breed Tract.

During the time of the book's initial release, a change had occurred in regards to the Montrose lawsuit. During the September 1842 court term, they agreed all suits regarding parties in the one-mile area under question would abide to the resolution determined in their proceeding.[305] They had already made claim to the court that the New York Land Company was the landlord for all parties living in that one-mile area. This was, of course, false in regards to the Mormon land owners. The plaintiff Edward Brooks doubted their claim as landlord, believing that Isaac Galland as an individual laid claim to the land.[306] The Mormons had purchased their lands from Isaac Galland after he withdrew from the New York Land Company and were not bound to them. No tenancy relationship was signed between the Mormon owners and the New York Land Company. If the Mormons pursued this matter after reading of it from Bennett's book, the principals of the New York Land Company could have been exposed. After this time, no other accusations or references to the Mormon's lack of title to Iowa lands was published by Kilbourne or the New York Land Company for many years following. They needed their secret maintained.

Duncan's Anti-Mormon Campaign and Joseph's Visits with Remmick

The election for Illinois governor was of critical importance to the Saints in Nauvoo. The leading Whig candidate was Joseph Duncan. He sought the editor from Alton, George T. M. Davis, who was influential in the state Whig party structure. On June 14, 1842, Duncan sent a biographical sketch for Davis to publish and a letter boasting recent successes.

> I met at Winchester Court yesterday and made a speech. . . . A. W. Cavarly Esq. spoke several hours in opposition to me and in defense of the legislature and the mormons, his attempt to produce a sympathy in favor of the mormons was a perfect failure producing disgust and contempt in every mind. His plan . . . was to produce the impression that I am persecuting them when I said not one word against them or there (their) religion. . . .
>
> Cavarly was course and vulgar in attacks upon me. . . . He gave me a fine opportunity by those attacks of referring to the many measures I had introduced and carried through Congress and the legislature. . . . The appropriations for the Harbor at Chicago, the lighthouse, the removal

> of the obstruction on the Rapids of the Mississippi at Des Moines and Rock River also of the Wabash and of the Ohio and Mississippi, the Cumberland Road. . . . Your friend, Joseph Duncan.[307]

Duncan was deliberate in confirming his mutual focus with Davis of discrete opposition to the Mormons and of promoting key internal improvements. Duncan knew of Davis's connections with the St. Louis merchants and their Chamber of Commerce group, who likewise were interested in most of the same internal improvement projects that would add further commerce to St. Louis enterprises. Particularly, Duncan was referring to his continued campaign focus on the Illinois and Michigan Canal and harbor improvements, the Des Moines Rapids improvements, connections to the Wabash Canal in Indiana and the Erie Canal through Ohio, links to the National Cumberland Road, and the crucial commerce of the Galena lead mines. These were perceived as election winning platforms that would link Illinois and St. Louis commerce through the upper Mississippi, the Great Lakes, and Washington, DC, to greatly improve the commerce of the merchants and the overall quality of life to all their citizens. Duncan was also motivated in the promotions of the various internal improvement programs to enhance the value of the Warsaw area lands and the opportunities he expected as president of the Warsaw Land Company with Mark Aldrich and Richard F. Barrett.

On the afternoon of Monday, July 11, 1842, Joseph Smith enjoyed a more leisurely time of reading the papers, and then decided upon buying a horse from a Mr. Harmon T. Wilson. He was amused to name his new horse "Joe Duncan."[308]

Back in Nauvoo, Joseph had been contemplating a most unusual visit from a stranger who had approached him in great need. The traveler was Jacob G. Remmick from St. Louis. He said to the Prophet that he was going to lose $1,400 of property at a sheriff's sale unless he could pay $300 in cash to his creditor. He insisted that he had the money and that he expected it to be sent to him from St. Louis within a few days. Joseph Smith noted,

> I thought on the subject over night, . . . I did not like the looks of the man; but thought I, he is a stranger. I then reflected upon the situation that I had been frequently placed in, and that I had often been a stranger

> in a strange land, and whenever I had asked for assistance I had obtained it, and it may be that he is an honest man; and if I sent him away, I shall be guilty of the sin of ingratitude. I therefore concluded to loan him $200 in good faith sooner than be guilty of ingratitude. He gave me his note for the same, and said, "Whenever you call on me, you shall have the money."[309]

On September 14, 1842, Joseph Smith made note of a follow-up conversation with the stranger. "Mr. Remmick gave me a deed of one half his landed property in Keokuk, though it will be a long time, if ever, before it will be of any benefit to me."[310] Remmick had purchased his lands from Galland in January, eight months earlier.

The Prophet later recalled and noted other details regarding Remmick's visits:

> He then said, "Since I saw you, a project has entered my mind, which I think may be profitable both for you and me. I will give you a quit claim deed for all the land you bought of Galland, which is twenty thousand acres. You paid Galland the notes, and ought to have them: they are in my hands as his agent, and I will give them up. I also propose seeding to you one-half of my right to all my land in the Iowa territory; and all I ask is for you to give your influence to help to build up Keokuk." I answered, "I have not asked for your property; I don't want it, and would not give a snap of my finger for it, I will use my influence to help to build up the place; but I won't give you anything for the land," and told him I wanted the $200 which was due me. He made out the deeds and gave them to me, and I got them recorded, and he gave up the notes, except a few.[311]

Because Joseph Smith had recorded the deeds regarding the Iowa lands, the leadership of the New York and St. Louis Land Companies knew that he had physical proof of the setup and that their evil designs could be exposed. Joseph had the former Galland deeds, which could have been traced back to the specific land transactions Galland secured directly from the half-breed owners and included as part of the twenty thousand dollars' worth mentioned in their partnership agreement.

With the recording of the deeds by the Iowa Territory recorder, two claims for the same lands were existent. The Iowa court held the documents signed by Galland submitted by the New York Land Company for the partition plan. At the same time the recorder's office held the warranty deeds for the same property with Galland's signature.

If researched and challenged, the claims filed by the New York Land Company would have exposed their treachery, having filed decree petitions the previous year on the same lands sold to Mormons by Galland two years earlier. Only the courts could resolve the matter. Because of the extensive nature of nearly twenty thousand acres being involved, the courts would probably have had no other choice than to throw out the October 1841 ruling and start again with the Mormon land claims represented separate from the New York Land claims conveyed during the time of the partnership. The deeds provided by Remmick apparently held no assignment to the New York Land Company, or they would not have been recorded.[312] If the New York Land Company's misdeeds were discovered, the treacherous actions of the St. Louis Land Company against the Mormons would likely also have been discovered.

Joseph Smith tried to give the titles to his Uncle John Smith in Iowa, but he refused. Joseph also gave Remmick cloth valued at between six and seven hundred dollars. Remmick, after the generosity displayed by Joseph, voiced to other leaders that the Prophet was under obligations from him instead of his owing the Prophet approximately $1,100. Because of his deceptive conduct, Joseph publicly warned others not to engage with Remmick and made clear, "I was not going to use any influence to have the brethren go to be swindled. My advice is, if they choose, that they come away from Keokuk, and not go there any more. It is not a good location."[313]

Keokuk at that time was dominated by ruffians and crude men engaged in the difficult tasks of lightening for the steamboats crossing the Des Moines Rapids. The area had a poor reputation for scandalous land deals. It was not a place yet to raise a family in the gospel. But Keokuk had great potential due to its strategic location at the foot of the Rapids. Joseph earlier agreed the land in Keokuk could provide lands for an inheritance for the Saints but the time was not right yet. He had also offered to promote the land in Keokuk but required full disclosure on valid ownership first. This again would have exposed the corruptions of the two land companies and undone the entire previous allocations of October 1841. The Church members should have participated as valid owners in the allocation process of the Half-Breed Tract lands.

At the Masonic Hall on February 9, 1843, Joseph met with Remmick, who was trying to make a settlement with the Mormon leadership.

Remmick promised to give him "notes on a paper maker in Louisville" to settle his debt. Instead, he "then went off contrary to promise."[314] But Joseph still held the Galland and Remick recorded deeds for lands in Keokuk. That same day, Joseph wrote the Honorable Richard M. Young, the former Senator of Illinois, regarding payment of a loan and a request to have another postmaster appointed for Nauvoo.

> Dear Sir: I have this day received your favor of the 7th ult., covering one from John C. Walsh, . . . I shall dispatch a messenger immediately to Quincy, to deposit the $500 in the hands of General Leach. . . .
>
> I shall not be able to obtain George Miller's name as security. . . . I can, however, obtain the signature of Mr. Edward Hunter . . . which I presume will be entirely satisfactory to Mr. Walsh, instead of Mr. Miller. Judge Higbee's name will be on the obligations.[315]

This favor asked by Senator Young may have been a ruse to get the Nauvoo House land and building as collateral for the security to John Walsh because George Miller was the president of the Nauvoo House Association, which owned the Nauvoo House under construction.[316] In this letter, the Prophet was asking for the status for Rigdon's replacement as postmaster.

Fleak Continues Letters to Governor Reynolds Regarding Joseph Smith's Kidnap Plot

Perhaps feeling the risks of exposure of their fraudulent acts, Kilbourne may have further encouraged Fleak to increase efforts to involve Governor Reynolds to get Joseph Smith extradited. Fleak continued his communications with Governor Reynolds on October 5, 1842:

> Since writing the above another respectable man has arrived at my house with the same report that my brother sends me—he obtained his information from one of the leaders of the Church. In fact he told me that he had seen a letter from Jo. stating that there would be no chance for him longer to escape, that the officers were there in Nauvoo & c. In this same package I send you another letter that I had written before I was in receipt of either yours or my brothers' letters. It is a fact that Smith ordered the Mormons back to Nauvoo. . . . Success to the enterprise. . . .[317]

Fleak sent another letter to the governor, dated October 5:

> Your reward for Smith & Rockwell is making a great stir among the "brethren" at the "City of Nauvoo." . . . I am informed that the Gov of Illinois has added $400 more to your reward and I at this time know of no less than three persons that are on the alert determined to arrest him if possible. . . . Yesterday was a day that was set for about 50 of them to come down to our Town to select lots, but by an order from the Prophet they all remained at home. This information I have from one of the Mormons & I have no doubt but it is correct. The intention of the three persons above alluded to, is to seize Smith some night in his own house perhaps, gag him, & carry him on board a small boat and bring him down to my house & keep him securely in a room in the 3rd story until the arrival of our regular St. Louis Packets, one of which leaves here every night in the week except Monday night. I am the agent for all those Packets & when once on board there will be no difficulty. If the enterprise succeeds I am entitled to one fourth of the Reward which I will take pleasure in bestowing on the State of Missouri.
>
> Thus I have given you the Outlines of the plan & it is needless to say to you that it is in confidence. In the course of two months our Town will be overrun with those cutthroats as one of the principal owners in the Town has sold his interest to them.
>
> I shall leave here with my effects in the Month of March for Missouri. . . . I have now on hand about 70 head of Cattle that I shall send off this fall to Van Buren County.[318]

He concluded this second letter, "Success to the enterprise." Fleak felt quite passionate about his role as an integral player in the scheme to kidnap and extradite the Prophet. Their previous plan of kidnapping Joseph Smith had been abandoned based on the message received from his brother in Montrose that Smith had already been taken.

From the contents of the first letter dated October 5, Fleak was frustrated that the Mormons were going to overrun his town. Fleak affirmed that with his position, performing lightening services at the Des Moines rapids for a major steamship packet company, he could secure any of several steamboats anchored at Keokuk to transport the kidnapped Prophet and elude Mormon supporters unnoticed. Fleak was also quite appreciative of the efforts of the governor to provide a reward and pleased that Illinois was adding to the reward incentive. Fleak received from his brother, or perhaps brother-in-law, a letter, dated October 5, written from Montrose:

> Dr. Brother, I heard that Jo Smith is taken again. Some say the Mormons have themselves taken him for the purpose of getting the reward but others that the Officers from Quincy have taken him. He has gone to Carthage to day & is to have a trial tomorrow. The Mormons think the Judge will set him at liberty I shall go to Carthage this evening if I can get over the River In haste, H. B. Whetset.

Fleak, disapppointed and embarrassed, soon after wrote Governor Reynolds on October 7 from Keokuk, attempting to reinstate the previous plan against the Prophet:

> I hasten to correct the information which I gave you per last nights Boat respecting the supposed arrest of Jo Smith.
>
> Smith is not arrested as was reported. This I have heard from my brother. . . . The note before me from him is dated at Nauvoo & was written the morning after the other was written. What can be the object of the Mormons in reporting his arrest I cannot conjecture, they must have something in view. . . . In the meantime the plan proposed in my note of the 5th Ins will be vigorously prosecuted.

Two months later, on December 4, an immensely frustrated Fleak again wrote Reynolds:

> All of our efforts to seize the renegade Smith, have proved fruitless and we have been compelled though with reluctance to abandon the project. He keeps constantly around him as body guard of some 12 to 14 enthusiastic fanaticks which renders a secret approach impossible, and with the River frozen over as it now is, even if we were to get him it would be impossible to get away with him, for one haloo from him (sic) call a thousand men to his rescue.
>
> The only possible way to get him is through the newly elected Governor. He may do something but Carlin never would if he were to continue Gov 20 years. . . .
>
> Depend upon it, those fanaticks will one day give your State a great deal of trouble, their whole thought is how they shall injure or destroy Missouri & the first thing taught their new members is to despise Missouri. They have now purchased the principal part of Keokuk & are

> coming into it very fast, which puts a body of them within 3 miles of the Missouri line. I shall leave here in March for Missouri.

Fleak was dejected. The Mormons were expected soon to be overrunning Keokuk. Fleak cautioned the governor that the Mormons were going to be a bigger threat, as they were then only three miles from the Des Moines River separating Missouri from the Iowa Territory. Fleak's letter played the governor to get him to take a more aggressive stance.

Governor Ford Defeats Former Governor Duncan

The 1842 election for a new governor was a serious matter. Adam Snyder was expected to represent the Democrats but died as Duncan began voicing negative attacks on Mormons. Caught unprepared, the Democrats nominated Thomas Ford to run against Duncan, who was blamed for the financial chaos the state was in. Duncan had focused on a policy of internal improvements that would help himself and his partners in the Warsaw Land Company.

Thomas Ford knew he was not a strong leader. Ford had been one of the judges of the state Supreme Court. He had never run as a candidate for any elective office. Ford knew his limitations as a viable candidate for such a lofty office:

> [He was nominated] not because I was a leader, for I was not, but because I was believed to have no more than a very ordinary share of ambition; because it was doubtful whether any of the leaders could be elected, and because it was thought I would stand more in need of support from leaders, than an actual leader would. To this cause, and perhaps there were others, I trace the fact which will hereafter appear, that I was never able to command the support of the entire party which elected me.[319]

As the two-party convention structure was taking hold in Illinois, a shift in the powerbase of the state was moving from individual leadership and strength of character to a shared collective of party faithful who held the real power. Ford explained on a later occasion:

> The State leaders, whether democrat or whig makes no difference, they give the word to the little cliques of leaders in each county; these county leaders convey it to the little big men in each neighborhood, and they do the talking to the rank-and-file of the people. In this way principles and men are put up and put down with amazing celerity. . . .

> The organization of men into political parties under the control of leaders . . . necessarily destroys individuality of character and freedom of opinion. . . . It is therefore a very common thing for men of all parties to make very great sacrifices of opinion, so as to bring themselves into conformity with the bulk of their party. . . .
>
> Either moral or physical force must be used for purposes of government. When a people are so gross that moral power cannot operate on them, physical force must be resorted to. Also, when the officers of government lack talents and moral power, physical force may thereby be made necessary.[320]

Governor Ford saw himself as a puppet serving the Party elite. In spite of the law, he felt it appropriate to concede a resort to physical force. Sadly, he would govern that way.

The attorney Justin Butterfield addressed Joseph Smith on December 17, 1842:

> I have heard the letter read which Governor Ford has written . . . and his statements are correct in relation to the opinion of the judges of the Supreme Court. The judges were unanimously of the opinion that you would be entitled to your discharge under a habeas corpus to be issued by the Supreme Court, but felt some delicacy in advising Governor Ford to revoke the order issued by Governor Carlin. My advice is, that you come here . . . and you do not run the least risk of not being protected . . . and of being discharged by the Supreme Court by habeas corpus. I have also the right to bring the case before the U.S. Court, . . . and there you are certain of obtaining your discharge. I will stand by you, and see you safely delivered from your arrest. . . . J. Butterfield.[321]

When Governor Ford took office, an old arrest warrant for Joseph Smith by Governor Carlin had not been executed. Missouri claimed that Joseph Smith was involved in the attempted murder of Governor Boggs, and his living in Illinois made him a Missouri fugitive from justice.

With Governor Ford preferring to clear the matter from him, the old warrant was executed against Joseph Smith, who selected Justin Butterfield of Chicago to represent him. This was a fortunate and providential choice. At the time, Justin Butterfield was the hero of the state regarding all hope for progress with the Illinois and Michigan Canal and other key internal improvement programs. It was Justin Butterfield who promoted a plan to move construction of the Illinois and Michigan Canal forward. He met with capitalists Bronson, Ryan, and Leavitt, who then met with Baring Brothers in London, to consider Butterfield's plan. Governor Ford, though a Democrat, fully supported Butterfield, a prominent Whig, in this essential plan to save the Illinois and Michigan Canal project.

As Joseph Smith's hearing commenced, Butterfield addressed the court and remarked that he appeared on behalf of the Prophet, with the attendance of Apostles before the Pope (Judge Nathaniel Pope) and in the presence of angels (women, including Mary Todd Lincoln, were in the court room gallery observing the proceedings).

In March 1843, Colonel Charles Oakley and Senator Michael Ryan were appointed agents to negotiate the Illinois and Michigan Canal loan. They departed for England, carrying letters to Magniac, Jardine, & Company and Baring, Brothers & Company of London and Hope & Company of Amsterdam, who had loaned vast sums previously to the state and represented some of the wealthiest capitalists in Europe. These lenders were looking to the value of the entire Illinois and Michigan Canal properties deeded by the US government to Illinois as collateral for their consolidated five million in loans.[322]

Fleak Resumes His Letters to Missouri's Governor Reynolds

After a brief respite, on March 1, Fleak again wrote to Governor Reynolds:

> It is currently reported here that another requisition has been sent to Illinois for the delivery of Joe Smith to the authority of your State. The requisition is said to be founded on the indictment of 1838. . . . I know Smith fears it for I am informed that he has ordered the Mormons to leave our County and concentrate at Nauvoo, at any rate they are all (sic) about leaving our Town. . . . They are becoming very numerous, hundreds of new recruits are weekly arriving & this same Temple that they are now building is in my opinion intended for a fortress. The strength of the place is proof of the fact. . . .
>
> I shall be ready to leave this accursed Mormon Country by the Middle of May or the first of June next. . . . I shall take with me from 100 to 120 head of Good Cattle. . . .
>
> P. S. Rockwell, Smith's tool is in Wisconsin Territory in the pine country near the Falls of St. Croix.

Persistent and driven, Fleak once again wrote Governor Reynolds on March 20:

> I have read with pleasure of the arrest of that notorious Rockwell. . . . I am now more than ever satisfied of the guilt of Joe & I know he fears that Rockwell will turn traitor. . . . Those villains at Nauvoo have ascertained by some means that I was watching them closely and they deceived me egregiously in regard to the location of Rockwell. What I wrote you a short time ago respecting his being in the Pinery in Wisconsin was told me in a very careless manner by one of the leaders & I supposed it to be true, but I am now convinced that it was done purposely to deceive me.

Fleak was again humiliated, leading the governor astray. His information had not been vetted ,and he had speculated and lost. His joint conspiracy plan of Missouri and Illinois participants to kidnap Joseph Smith had failed.

Meanwhile, the master of the *Maid of Iowa* steamship, Dan Jones, had been expanding his scope of services. He was in direct competition with Mark Aldrich and Thomas Sharp for ferrying services across the Mississippi.

13: The Corrupt Conspiracy Exposed

Immediately after his election, Governor Ford was thrown into the crisis of the state's fiscal woes and dormant internal improvement projects. With more than thirteen million in debt, the state was nearly bankrupt; the loans were in default. Though the project added greatly to the state debt, priority was given the Illinois and Michigan Canal venture, which was then in gridlock for lack of additional funding. Ford knew the only option to salvage the state's dismal condition was to finish the canal to provide revenues to the state to debt service their prior loans.

Ford immediately began meeting with investors in pursuit of the plan presented by Justin Butterfield, a Chicago lawyer, retained previously by Joseph Smith. Butterfield was closely involved in drafting the Canal Bill of 1842–43, which was approved by the state legislature. The canal properties granted to the state by the federal government were to be conveyed in trust to previous investors who would advance an additional $1,600,000 in funding for the project. As a condition to the plan, Governor Ford had to institute a stronger taxation system to guarantee the means of debt servicing for the former and future funds borrowed.[323]

Meanwhile, financial pressures were constantly being thrust upon the Prophet. In the early spring of 1843, various letters were received from Horace Hotchkiss, wanting to be paid on the debt servicing for the parcels the Church had bought years earlier. This land included the two steamboat landing sites. The enemies of the Church put pressure on Hotchkiss to pay for high property taxes on the lands, and Hotchkiss earnestly requested payment from Joseph Smith to stop Joel Catlin from pressuring him for the tax money.[324] The Church's enemies hoped to find a way to repossess the extremely valuable Hotchkiss property, with its steamboat sites, which were critical for the success of the proposed Des Moines Rapids Railroad. George W. Robinson was also having land problems, probably based on tax assessments as his name was on the deed for the Church properties from Hugh White and Isaac Galland purchased in 1839. Robinson at some point left the Church and cooperated with the anti-Mormon Party leaders.[325]

Joseph Smith Recognizes a "Corrupt Conspiracy" Forming

Samuel Owens wrote from Independence, Missouri, on June 10, 1843, to Governor Ford:

> Sir: For the last three months I have been corresponding with Dr. John C. Bennett relative to one certain Joe Smith, Mormon Prophet, etc. of your state. In several of Dr. Bennett's letters to me, he informs me that my name is known to you. . . .
>
> At the last term of the Circuit court of Daviess county, an indictment was found by the grand jury of said county against Joseph Smith for treason against this state. The necessary papers are now on their way to Governor Reynolds, who, on the receipt thereof, I have no doubt, will make a requisition on you for the apprehension and delivery of said Smith to the bearer, Mr. Joseph Reynolds, who goes as a special agent. . . .
>
> Dr. Bennett further writes me that he has made an arrangement with Harmon T. Wilson, of Hancock county (Carthage, seat of justice) in whose hands he wishes the writ that shall be issued by you to be put. . . . I am induced to believe that he has made the same suggestions to you. The only wish of the people of this state is, that this man, Joseph Smith, may be brought to that justice which the magnitude of his crime merits.

The conspiracy was expanding. First, Kilbourne in May 1842 wrote Governor Reynolds, attempting to get the Missouri governor engaged to pursue Joseph Smith in Illinois. Shortly thereafter, Laban Fleak, a friend of Kilbourne continued, his series of letters engaging Governor Reynolds in their plot to kidnap and extradite the Prophet. These letters continued after July 1842. Before Fleak's first letter, he had met with the defecting mayor of Nauvoo, John C. Bennett, who planned to contact Governor Reynolds with supposedly new information that would implicate Joseph Smith in the former Governor Boggs's attack and near murder.

Upon learning of the letter from Samuel Owens, who a leader in the secret constitution band that had forced out the Mormons in 1833, the Prophet recorded, "To show the wickedness and rascality of John C. Bennett and the corrupt conspiracy formed against me in Missouri and Illinois, I insert the following under date of the letter June 10, 1843."[326]

Joseph Smith recognized that a corrupt conspiracy had been formed. Samuel Owens represented the desires of the merchants of Independence to continue their trade domination on the Santa Fe Trail and the commerce with the Indians and trappers on the Platte and Missouri Rivers to the Rocky Mountains without Mormon interference. They feared Joseph could prevail in his Missouri redress petition hearings. Owens and the Independence merchants depended on the Chouteau and St. Louis commerce leaders to supply them. Intentions of war with the Mormons had been validated by Francois Chouteau in 1836 and continued when the Mormons resettled in Iowa and Nauvoo and jeopardized the Chouteau upper Mississippi commerce.

Governor Reynolds, named in the letter, represented the desires of the Central Clique to keep the Mormons from returning to Missouri because of the redress petitions. Reynolds was married to Samuel Owens's sister-in-law. Harmon T. Wilson of Carthage represented the Carthage and Warsaw local conspirators committed to the various improvement projects. These included the railroad and highway project commissioners, land speculators such as the Warsaw Land Company leaders, land owners (particularly those settled on or near the railroad and highway routes), and the many farmers and merchants wanting access to coastal markets.

For more than a year, Joseph was suspicious that the Kilbournes had allied with John C. Bennett. The Mormon expose attempt written by Bennett included the three letters drafted by Kilbourne. Kilbourne and his employer needed the Mormons to vacate the area.

All five groups were compelled by greed and ambition. After the economy collapsed, they were driven by desperation. The Independence merchants and Chouteau family network and allies forced the Mormons out of Jackson County to sustain the trade monopoly formed by Senator Benton, Superintendent Clark, and the Chouteaus after the Mormons began trading with the local farmers and Santa Fe traders at lower prices. The Mormons, who were friendly to the Indians, created fears that they would interfere in that trade monopoly enhanced by the Relocation Act. Central Clique leaders were concerned at their steamboat operations at DeWitt.

Each of the groups had secrets to conceal. Some of the Missouri mobs forced the Mormons out of Missouri under the Extermination Order to prevent them from exercising preemption rights to reclaim their lands and improvements. The New York and St. Louis Land Companies had to keep secret their fraudulent means of stealing the Half-Breed Tract lands from Mormon owners. Mark Aldrich and his fellow land speculators and railroad commissioners had to keep secret their activities to control the various internal improvement projects needing access to land and steamboat sites controlled by Mormons.

Five persecution groups, with common interests and secrets to conceal, began working with each other to kidnap Joseph Smith in hopes of forcing the Mormons out of their areas. Many were anxious to join efforts to plan the murder of Joseph. Family links were leveraged to enhance contacts and solicit outside aid. Samuel Owens's wife was a cousin to Senator Young of Illinois, and his sister was married to John Vineyard, a former partner with Mark Aldrich. Owens had many contacts with the Springfield Junto members and others with roots near his Green County, Kentucky, plantation. John C. Bennett was working with David Kilbourne and Laban Fleak and arranged to bring on Harmon T. Wilson of Carthage.

In the letter of Isaac Galland to Mr. Swasey immediately after the sale to the Mormons in July 1839 of the Iowa and Nauvoo parcels, Galland presented an alarming omen to occur after "a sufficient quantity of honey comb" had been achieved. That occurrence would "induce surrounding thieves to rob them again." According to that scenario, the Saints would then be given a choice to deny the faith "or submit to a repetition of similar acts of violence, and outrage."[327] It was common to extract the honey from the honeycombs, and then return it to the hive to be filled again and served to someone else. It was planned that after the Mormons had improved the site, mobs would rob them again. If they failed to renounce their religion, they would be forced out as that had occurred in Missouri. This "honey comb" scheme was near ripe for harvest.

The Reynolds and Wilson Failed Attempt

When news reached Nauvoo that Reynolds and Wilson were trying to arrest the Prophet while with his family about two hundred miles away in Dixon, Stephen Markham and William Clayton were dispatched to warn him. Though riding frantically, they arrived after Joseph had been seized. Either by coincidence or as many suspected a Whig plot, Cyrus Walker, an attorney who claimed to be in nearby Dixon by happenstance, offered to defend Joseph if he could secure the Mormon leader's vote in the upcoming Congressional election. Joseph agreed he would vote for him but did not commit other Mormons to pledge their votes for him.

Reynolds and Wilson were brutal in the mistreatment of their captive. After Markham joined them, they also threatened Markham's life. Markham and Clayton had Reynolds and Wilson arrested for their misconduct. They did not have money for bail, so they too sought for a writ of habeas corpus. The hearings for Joseph Smith, Reynolds, and Wilson were to be resolved by the judge at Ottawa, Illinois. Finding the judge out of town, Markham fortunately had the new writs issued with wording that they could be heard before any judge in the fifth district.

Along the way, Markham overheard Reynolds, Wilson, and a landlord discussing plans for a company of men to overtake their party by force then to take Joseph Smith to the mouth of Rock River on the Mississippi and cross there to a band of allies, who would kidnap the Prophet on the Iowa side. If caught, it was doubtful the Prophet would live long enough for trial. Markham told Sheriff Campbell what he overheard, who then ordered a guard placed on the house to guarantee no couriers could come or go to warn their enemies.

The following night, Peter W. Conover overheard Reynolds and Wilson meeting with the son of the landlord. They were planning at night to take the carriage horses, go to Monmouth, raise a mob, come back to the farmhouse, seize Joseph, and take him to a steamboat waiting at the mouth of Rock River. Again, Sheriff Campbell was notified, who locked Wilson and Reynolds up to prevent their escape. The full plans of the conspiracy to kidnap the Prophet and take him to a steamboat were revealed. It was clear this plot had been carefully planned and funded by several conspirators in advance.[328]

While they were making their way back to Hancock County, they came upon a Mormon group who insisted they be taken to Nauvoo, not Carthage, to satisfy the writ issued. At Nauvoo, the court released Joseph on a writ of habeas corpus. Anti-Mormons in Missouri and Hancock County were again foiled in their evil designs but became more resolute to find a way to remove Joseph Smith permanently to pursue their many economic ambitions.

Fleak again wrote the governor on August 3, 1843, from Keokuk, with a concocted story:

> Dear Sir, Herewith I send you a copy of an affidavit that is now in my office, although there is nothing definite in it, yet you may rely upon it that if those Mormons do not give you trouble on your Western & northern line this Fall, it will be because they cannot get enough of the Indians to fall in with their diabolical schemes.

Fleak inserted the affidavit of Emanuel Hitchcock of July 27, 1843, and commented,

> I do fully believe that there will be an attempt made on the frontiers of Missouri. . . . That the Mormons have a fixed hatred against Missouri you are well aware. One of the principal articles of their creed is the destruction of Missouri. No Mormon has prayed yet I expect without calling for the vengeance of Heaven on Missouri. Well I claim to be a Missourian & glory in the name & I hope the Mormons will make their intended invasion, then the extermination of their (sic) would take place beyond a doubt.

Fleak expressed his despicable hopes that Mormons would invade Missouri, with Indians at their side, and all would be killed in battle. Anxious to be relevant in the capture of the Mormon leader, Fleak was reaching for any grounds to advance their sinister plot.

The Anti-Mormon Party and the Hancock County Vigilance Committee of Safety Meeting

The anti-Mormon Party again met at Carthage on September 6, 1843. The Whig Party was outraged that Cyrus Walker was not elected in August. From their trap, they assumed he was certain to capture the Mormon vote. The matter was exposed by Democrat Party leaders just before the election. For those in leadership in the anti-Mormon Party, Cyrus Walker was seen as a critical candidate for Congress to carry forward the railroad and various internal improvement projects in cooperation with other supporting states. Walker had previously been appointed a commissioner for the Warsaw and Peoria and Wabash Railroad Company with Mark Aldrich and was to rally other states involved in the integrated improvement plans to pass critical legislation for the entire region and secure more funding. At their Hancock County Vigilance Committee of Safety meeting, the irate attendees drafted and unanimously approved a preamble:

> This meeting having convened for the purpose of taking under advisement a subject of vital importance not only to this county, but to all the surrounding counties, . . . that a certain class of people have obtruded themselves upon us, calling themselves Mormons, or latter-day Saints and under the sacred garb of Christianity, assumed, as we honestly believe, that they may . . . perpetrate the most lawless and diabolical deeds that have ever, in any age of the world, disgraced the human species.[329]

They needed a cover to conceal their real intentions. To advance their true cause, they also defined certain dangerous and unlawful resolutions in this meeting, targeting the Mormons:

> Resolved, that while we would deprecate anything like lawless violence, without justifiable cause, yet we pledge ourselves in the most solemn manner to resist all the wrongs which may be hereafter attempted to be imposed on this community by the Mormons, to the utmost of our ability, -peaceably, if we can, but forcibly, if we must.
>
> Resolved, that we pledge in the most determined manner that if the authorities of the State of Missouri shall make another demand for the body of Joseph Smith, and our Governor shall issue another warrant to stand ready at all times to serve the officer into whose hands such warrant may come . . . in order that it may not be said of us, in future, that the most outrageous culprits have been suffered, "to go unwhipped of justice."

> Resolved, that when the Government ceases to afford protection, the citizens of course fall back upon their original inherent right of self-defense.
>
> Resolved, that a corresponding committee be appointed to communicate with the different parts of this county, and also with other counties; and we would also recommend to all surrounding counties to appoint like committees for the purpose of a mutual interchange of views in regard to the subjects embraced in these proceedings. . . . The following gentlemen were appointed to act as a central corresponding committee at Carthage-namely, Captain Robert A. Smith, major T. J. Bartlet, Harmon T. Wilson, Frank A. Worrell, and Walter Bagby.[330]

These anti-Mormon leaders were using the same methods as those in Missouri by the previous mobs and invoked the same language: "peaceably, if we can, but forcibly, if we must."[331] They were inviting a coalition of Missouri leaders to assist them. Their corresponding committee was designed to engage local militia leaders and sheriffs under the direction of this anti-Mormon group without consent of the governor. This new structure was a prelude to circumvent federal and state laws, to be invoked when they felt "the Government ceases to afford protection, the citizens of course fall back upon their original inherent right of self-defense"; a familiar sentiment to the feelings of the Jackson County members of the secret constitution.[332]

The battle for Zion had been elevating in intensity. Joseph Smith was valiantly disarming the political forces aligned against him. He was able to escape another attempt by Missouri to arrest him. The parties were in stalemate. In the prior year, Joseph took to the pulpit to highlight the battle that was indeed coming and to exhort the faithful to be valiant in the cause. He referred to Matthew 16:19: "I will give unto thee the keys of the kingdom of heaven: and whatsoever thou shalt bind on earth shall be bound in heaven: and whatsoever thou shalt loose on earth shall be loosed in heaven." He elaborated on its importance:

> Now the great and grand secret of the whole matter, and the *summum bonum* of the whole subject . . . consists in obtaining the powers of the Holy Priesthood . . . to whom these keys are given there is no difficulty in obtaining a knowledge of facts in relation to the salvation of the children of men, both as well for the dead as for the living. . . .

> Brethren, shall we not go on in so great a cause? Go forward and not backward. Courage, brethren; and on, on to the victory! Let your hearts rejoice, and be exceedingly glad. Let the earth break forth into singing. Let the dead speak forth anthems of eternal praise to the King Immanuel, who hath ordained, before the world was, that which would enable us to redeem them out of their prison; for the prisoners shall go free. . . .
>
> Behold, the great day of the Lord is at hand; and who can abide the day of his coming, and who can stand when he appeareth? (D&C 128:11, 22, 24)

Joseph, in preparing the Saints to give their all in the battle for Zion and the kingdom of God, used the term *summum bonum*, meaning that which is of ultimate importance—the great and grand secret for this dispensation, to assume its rightful crown, was based on receiving and magnifying the keys of the priesthood. The prophets of previous dispensations held their keys for the Prophet in Kirtland at the temple dedication, in recognition that this was to be the final dispensation preparatory to the return of the Savior. Here, he admonished the Saints to search their hearts and muster their courage and consider if they were worthy and pronounced clean and thus worthy to stand and welcome Christ to His rightful throne.

The keys of the priesthood differentiated the Saints from all others upon the earth. The admonition and mandate was going forth; the faithful had to stay focused on completing the temple and receiving their full temple ordinances. With the holy temple completed, they then would be empowered from on high to defeat Babylon, which was persecuting and menacing the fold in all their efforts to bring to pass the long-awaited Zion.

Ruling on Trial of Brooks and Reddick Heirs versus Marsh, Lee, and Delavan

As the district court in Henry County, Iowa, convened on the matter of Edward Brooks and the Reddick heirs versus Samuel Marsh, William E. Lee, and Edward C. Delavan, as trustees for the New York Land Company, the judge ruled that the Reddick patent of 1839 for the Montrose Spanish land claim was superior to the Half-Breed Tract general land claim.[333] The Reddick heirs and Chouteau coalition won this ruling, which occurred in September 1843, but the New York Land Company, with Kilbourne as their agent, appealed to the Iowa Supreme Court. Neither side wanted to alert the Mormons as to the status of the Montrose land disputes.

In spite of the appeal, this was a significant victory for the Reddick heirs and their allies. Edward Brooks, representing the Reddick heirs, was a prominent member of the St. Louis Chamber of Commerce and aligned with the insurance industry there. Isaac Campbell, the founder of the St. Louis Land Company, had been a brother-in-law to the steamboat captain Hugh White, who held the mortgage on a large portion of Mormon Nauvoo lands. Campbell himself had previously owned lands in Nauvoo occupied by the Mormons. These lands were on the proposed train route of the Des Moines Rapids Railroad. If the Mormons were forced out, they expected windfall profits on their lands, as did Mark Aldrich, his fellow Warsaw Land Company partners, and their clients as well as his fellow Railroad commissioners.

For the New York Land Company and David Kilbourne, the loss of this case would have major consequences against their overall plans. The New York Land Company officers, who took over some of the Doyle and Teas lands in the undeveloped lands adjoining Nauvoo, were anxious for the Des Moines Rapids Railroad to increase their land values. They had been disappointed to learn from the Doyle legal hearings that their lands could not provide an adequate steamboat landing site to compete with the successful two Nauvoo landing sites.

During this time, Governor Ford was focused on his own pressing crisis with the advancement of the canal to speed up tax revenues and rescue the state from insolvency. A provisional arrangement for funding the Illinois and Michigan Canal was made by the lenders during the summer of 1843 that their representatives in Boston appoint new appraisers. Ford and other Illinois leaders were relieved and optimistic that canal construction would be resumed with the $1.6 million infusion, as promoted by Justin Butterfield.[334]

On November 23, 1843, Joseph Smith gave renewed support to a dam project on the Mississippi. In his proposal, the Prophet suggested a petition be sent to Congress calling for a large dam to be built on the River to supply Nauvoo with adequate water power to support plans for Nauvoo as a rising industrial center. Also in the proposal was a call for Congress to authorize construction of a canal for steamships to be able to bypass the treacherous Des Moines Rapids.

By the end of 1843, Joseph had a strong resolve to move forward on the proposed Dam project. The New Year's Day 1844 issue of the *Times and Seasons* reported, "A charter [had] been granted . . . for the erection of a dam upwards of a mile long . . . [to] afford the best mill privileges in the western country."[335] The dam was to be constructed below the Nauvoo House to intersect with the island near Montrose. The city council approved further that "a dam, pier, or breakwater" was to angle north for a short distance from the island where the main dam would terminate. It was designed to create a large harbor on the river for boats. Joseph Smith and his successors were authorized to manage the waterworks with Nauvoo, receiving toll revenues. The public proposals of Joseph Smith's dam and canal projects heightened concerns of the anti-Mormon leaders promoting other competing alternatives to the Prophet's plans.

Anti-Mormons Kidnap the Averys to Lure Joseph Smith

Late in 1843, Colonel Levi Williams had hatched another sinister scheme to trap the Prophet. Williams, a legislature appointed road commissioner, was a leader among the internal improvement project advocates in Hancock County. Williams and other close allies from Illinois and Missouri sought to kidnap a Mormon and force him across the border into Missouri. It was then planned that Joseph Smith, in retaliation, would lead a Mormon team to rescue him, which would be defeated, with the Mormon leader captured. With the Central Clique in firm control of that state, Senator Benton's support and oversight, and as a backup the powerful influence of the St. Louis Junto members, prosecution against Joseph seemed guaranteed.

To aid in the execution of his plan, Colonel Williams was joined by his son John Reid Williams and John C. Elliot, a deputy US Marshall, and about a dozen well-armed local Illinois residents.[336] Two residents from Clark County, Missouri, allied with them.

Daniel Avery was a forty-five year old Mormon farmer who witnessed firsthand the bitter persecutions of Missouri mobs. As a victim, he filed petitions with fellow Mormon friends and leaders in 1840. Leaving Missouri, he settled for a time in Montrose, Iowa Territory and was called to preside over the elders quorum. After two years, he took his wife and son Philander across the Mississippi and secured his family in the small settlement of Bear Creek near Warsaw.

On Saturday evening, December 2, the criminally motivated gang converged on Vernon Doty's mill and abducted Daniel Avery. They forced him across the river into Iowa Territory, and then to Waterloo, Clark County, Missouri, where a local sheriff took him before their magistrate. A coerced affidavit, signed under duress by his son Philander, was presented. Holding the youthful Philander Avery at knifepoint, the lawless perpetrators forced him to claim his father had stolen a horse and colt from Joseph McCoy when living in Missouri. Bail was a thousand dollars.[337]

Outraged by the extreme abuse of power and the unrelenting evil forces at hand, Joseph wrote to Governor Ford to get involved and perform his duty on behalf of the Averys. Philander Avery had escaped his captors and returned to Nauvoo on December 14. That same day, the Prophet received the governor's response. Ford replied he was powerless to call out Illinois militia unless Missouri's governor would authorize it. Ford knew Governor Reynolds was a leader in the Central Clique that dominated in Missouri, and it would be politically dangerous for him as a fellow Democrat to interfere with the strength of their political machine. Ford showed no resolve to rescue a kidnapped citizen for whom he was duty bound to protect.

On December 18, Constable King Follett arrested John Elliott for his part in the Avery kidnapping and taken to Nauvoo for trial. Based on his testimony, a writ was issued for the arrest of Colonel Williams. General Law, commanding the Nauvoo Legion, ordered Colonel Markham to take one hundred troops to serve the writ upon Colonel Williams. A showdown between two Illinois militia units ensued. Ford, by his cowardly failure to act, had taken himself out of control of his own state militia units. When word was received that a warlike assemblage of militia was forming at Warsaw, the Nauvoo Legion withdrew to avoid serious conflict.[338]

Meanwhile, Daniel Avery had been taken to Palmyra, Missouri, and put in jail for two weeks. Avery filed for a writ of habeas corpus. On Christmas Day, he was released by the Clark County Court and made his way back home.[339] The whole sordid affair launched by Colonel

Williams failed. Colonel Williams and his fellow conspirators concocted a more sinister plan.

As the year 1843 was coming to an end, the Prophet became more determined to heed the admonition of the parable for Zion as to the importunate widow. The matter of seeking redress for the Missouri atrocities was foremost in the Prophet's mind as evil forces were mounting. With the earlier letter to Governor Ford, Joseph was forewarned the "corrupt conspiracy" was afoot. Samuel Owens had already teamed with John C. Bennett, Laban Fleak, David Kilbourne, and the members of the New York Land Company in dealings with Governor Reynolds.

The Reddick heirs were anxious to secure the Montrose steamboat landing site to benefit from the lead trade to and from the Dubuque and Galena mines to Chouteau headquarters in St. Louis. Samuel Owens and the Independence merchants wanted to ensure the Mormons would fail in their redress petition efforts. Owens was also familiar with Mark Aldrich, Richard F. Barrett, and former Governor Duncan (with the Warsaw Land Company) through his brother-in-law, John Vineyard. It is likely that after John Vineyard moved to Weston in Platte County, he kept contact with his Warsaw partners. A Congressional investigation, as repeatedly called for by Joseph Smith, could have also linked Samuel Owens to the Springfield Junto. In addition, Charles Hay was an active member of the anti-Mormon Party in Warsaw. His brother was Milton Hay, who had apprenticed in the law firm with Abraham Lincoln and who was a leader in the Vigilance Committee of Springfield. Milton Hay partnered with E. D. Baker of the Springfield Junto and state Whig Party.

The entanglements of the corrupt conspiracy, identified by Joseph Smith through Samuel Owens with several clusters of Mormon haters, were ominous. With the Illinois and Michigan Canal back on track, the commissioners of the Des Moines Rapids Railroads were also optimistic; their ambitions were back in play. But the Mormons were still entrenched in Nauvoo. The Dubuque and Galena export and import trade was soaring. The most promising means of exploiting that venture was from Dubuque down the Mississippi and diverted from the Rapids to Nauvoo. There, it could be loaded on the Des Moines Railroad and rerouted by way of the Illinois River through the new canal and the Great Lakes. Freight and passengers at Nauvoo could also be transported to Warsaw at the foot of the Des Moines Rapids on the Des Moines Rapids Railroad and reloaded on to steamships for St. Louis or on to New Orleans. All the conspirators were united in one resolve. The Mormons had to leave Iowa and Nauvoo.

Missouri Governor Reynolds Commits Suicide

On October 24, 1843, Shadrach Penn, the editor of *The Missouri Reporter*, published a series of eight letters to Senator Benton, drawing attention to Benton's connections to the Central Clique and the St. Louis group. He challenged Benton on key issues, such as the hard currency debate which broke the Democratic Party into two factions: the "Hards" and "Softs." Collateral damage included drawing attention to Governor Reynolds while alleging that he was the head of the Central Clique.[340] A barrage of accusations followed causing great worries for the governor.

After Senator Linn passed away in November 1843, the selection of his replacement to finish his term fell to the governor. To placate those who were targeting him, he chose David R. Atchison of Clinton County, a "Soft" and "anti-Benton" advocate, to take Senator Linn's seat. Later, Senator Benton gave his support of the governor's action, not expecting Atcheson would dare support the Mormons in their redress petition efforts, though he knew of their guilt.

At the December 1843 term of the state Supreme Court, the matter of Patrick Doyle versus Joseph B. Teas was settled in regards to the unincorporated lands formerly belonging to Joseph Teas just below the main part of the City of Nauvoo. What was at stake was whether the lands were properly sold to Doyle, who in turn sold the land to the New York Land Company.[341]

In the governor's mansion, Governor Thomas Reynolds altered his normal daily routine as he offered a blessing on his morning meal. When finished, he arose from the table went to his office, seeking privacy and locking the door behind him and closing the shutters. That morning of February 9, 1844, a passerby was alarmed to hear a rifle discharge coming from the mansion. Inside, the governor's lifeless body was grotesquely positioned, slumped at his desk. A string had been attached to the rifle trigger. A sealed message addressed to G. Minor was left on the writing table. The note read, "I have labored and discharged my duties faithfully to the public, but this has not protected me from the slanders and abuse which has rendered my life a burden to me. . . . I pray to God to forgive them and teach them more charity."[342]

Speculation ran rampant as to the reasons for his untimely demise by his own hand, with ten months remaining in his first term. Was it mental illness, or had he been racked with the burden of a guilty conscience? He had for so long kept many secrets as to his dealings in the leadership of the Central Clique. Some speculated that his failed efforts in securing Joseph Smith had resulted in intense criticisms from his political associates and that had been a factor.[343] He had been in direct communications with the opposition Whig party operatives, namely David Kilbourne and Laban Fleak. He had been working with his wife's brother-in-law, Samuel C. Owens, all working to extradite the Prophet. Had he been duped by the Whigs, using family relationships to put him at odds with his own Democrat Party leadership partners? In the prior few months, he had been rigorously targeted in the press, exposing his inner workings with the Central Clique political machine. If the printed smears continued, the public outcry would demand investigations of his conduct and that of his friends and associates in both the local and national political networks.

Perhaps to avoid further probing, Reynolds's associates launched a crusade against mental illness. The governor's widow soon moved to Weston in Platte County, near other kinsmen of Samuel Owens, including Nancy and Mary Vineyard.

Since October 1842, when the "enterprise" plot was first presented from Laban Fleak to Governor Reynolds—which included plans to seize Joseph Smith from his home, take him to Fleak's house, and then force him aboard a steamboat—various extensions to the plan were developed that expanded the coalition of conspirators beyond Fleak, Kilbourne, and their local allies.

The next phase involved Samuel Owens manipulating a new Missouri grand jury indictment in coordination with his brother-in-law, Governor Reynolds, and the Mormon apostate John C. Bennett. Governor Ford went along with the plan, which included "special agent" Joseph Reynolds, representing the Jackson County merchant group, and Sheriff Harmon Wilson, aiding the Hancock County anti-Mormon group. All worked together to kidnap the Prophet.

After securing their prisoner, they were to take him to the mouth of the Rock River on the Mississippi to be secured on one of various steamboats, likely owned and operated by the Chouteaus or from the fleet of Edward Walsh or from any other available steamboats aligned with the St. Louis merchant interests.

That plot being defeated, Colonel Levi Williams, representing the Warsaw and Carthage anti-Mormon Party and various internal improvement authorities' interests, sought to lure Joseph Smith to be hijacked after kidnapping another Mormon as bait. Included in his group was Deputy Federal Marshall John Elliott.

Each new iteration of the plan further aligned the five main groups of persecutors of the Mormons, which included the Jackson County merchants alliance headed by Sam Owens, the Central Clique, the Chouteau St. Louis Junto, and allied merchants; these merchants included Edward Brooks and Isaac Campbell's St. Louis Land Company, the Warsaw Land Company principals, and improvements commissioners (headed by Mark Aldrich, Governor Joe Duncan, and Levi Williams), and the New York Land Company, lead by their local agent David Kilbourne and friend Laban Fleak. With the death of Governor Reynolds, the Central Clique appeared to have become less involved in direct actions against the Mormons.

Four previous kidnapping attempts to capture Joseph had failed. Fleak's plans at Keokuk, Kilbourne's attempts in Galena, Reynolds's and Wilson's efforts, and Colonel Williams's Avery kidnapping all had gone for naught. The various conspiracy leaders instead began organizing a plot to murder Joseph Smith.

14: "The Voice of Truth" Compiled

On the national scene, the inner circle members of the Democratic Party at Washington were diligently focused on their return to power. Their plans had been upended by the sudden rise of support and momentum achieved by William Harrison in the 1840 election, which had a ripple effect of adding strength to the Whig power base at all levels. Benton and his allies were determined that their party must unify under the banner of Martin Van Buren and not become fragmented because of the threatening field of contenders from within.

In Illinois, activities were escalating in preparation for the 1844 elections. Amongst the Whig party leadership, a sense of optimism was spreading. They were expecting that Joseph Smith would unite the Mormon vote and direct it their way. As preparations were being made for their upcoming state convention in December, one of its most visible leaders, Congressman John J. Hardin, was settling in at Washington, DC. Hardin was quite anxious to hear that his party was generating momentum to carry Illinois for his kinsman, Henry Clay. On December 4, Quincy attorney Orville Browning sent a message to his longtime friend, Congressman Hardin:

> We are nothing daunted by the disasters of the past year, and do not despair of being able to give even this State to the Great Kentuckian. . . . Van Buren can never get the strength of the Democratic party in this state and that there are certain courses operating which I think will certainly give Clay more than the strength of the Whig party.[344]

In the early stages of the convention, another one of Hardin's close friends, and likewise Clay's political operatives, Anson G. Henry was elected to chair the state Central Committee tasked with prescreening candidates in each congressional district in their state. Archibald Williams, cousin to the mob leader Colonel Levi Williams of Green Plains, was elected chairman of the fifth district, assisted by Abraham Jonas. Also in attendance at the convention was George T. M. Davis, another committed Clay supporter. After the state Whig Convention at Springfield, another close friend of Hardin and passionate Clay supporter George T. M. Davis sent off this passionate update of their convention to the Congressman:

> It is admitted upon all hands, to have been the best ever held by the Whigs in Illinois. We have gone into a thorough systematic organization, and every Whig that had been here this winter has left determined to conquer in 1844 or perish in the effort. . . .
>
> We have instructed our congressional central committees that they must raise at least twenty five dollars in each of their districts to be transmitted to you for Junius tracts. . . . If a life of Mr. Clay with the leading views of his public policy gotten up in a succinct form is printed in German, we will order and pay for at least a thousand copies.[345]

Surprisingly, Davis concluded his communication with Hardin with the statement, "Another source of excitement has grown out of the kidnapping of two Mormons by the Missourians from the neighborhood of Nauvoo."[346] Davis had deliberately disassociated the kidnapping of the Averys by Illinois Whig members. As a dominant Party leader, Davis would have known that Colonel Williams lead the raiding party of more than a dozen Illinois residents with a few Missourians. For the sake of the Whig movement, it was deemed imperative that the Mormons not know it was the Whig leadership behind the kidnapping plot. In the wings, Davis was advancing plans in support of his client: the Chouteaus.[347]

The convention had agreed to sponsor the publication of a German campaign paper, targeting the large immigrant population vote. Davis was seeking approval to publish the Junius tracts or other publications approved by Hardin in German to fulfill the convention request.

The Junius tracts were an influential series of campaign propaganda published by Horace Greeley, the editor of the *New York Tribune*, and a Party loyalist committed to getting Henry Clay elected as president. Newspaper articles and letters to the editor were sent to the newspaper by Calvin Colton through his pen name "Junius," which originated during the Revolutionary War. Earlier, it was used by an anonymous English Whig who attacked King George III for not allowing a Whig compatriot to take his elected seat in the British Parliament.[348]

During the 1844 campaign, Horace Greeley continued efforts to counter Francis Blair's promotion of Martin Van Buren in the *Globe*. Because of his success in defending the Whig cause, the unknown author of the Junius tracts sent his propaganda to Greeley to print.

Shortly after Joseph Smith announced his candidacy for president, playing on the publicity of Greeley's publications, a disgruntled local Whig supporter sent a grievance against the Mormons referencing it as the "deadly coils of Mormon mobocracy" under the name "Junius Secondus" to the anti-Mormon Thomas Sharp, editor of the *Warsaw Signal*. The comments referred to a complaint against Joseph Smith for autocratic rule and alleged the Prophet had plans to establish a new political kingdom of God on the ruins of the current government.[349]

As Joseph Smith was the only lieutenant general in Illinois, Brigadier General Hardin was anxious to have his competition eliminated. Local militias in Carthage and Warsaw felt threatened by the massive dominance of the Nauvoo Legion and envious of their superior arms and more disciplined recruits. The local non-Mormon residents of the county, both Whig and Democrat, hated the political control the Mormons wielded in county elections. Open conflict was inevitable; the clear sentiment unifying them was that the Mormons must be stopped.

The coming of the new year of 1844 brought upon the Prophet deep reflections in matters of politics. It was an election year, and with it political discourse was rampant. Joseph had taken time to ponder his response to a communication received by Senator Calhoun a month earlier. Joseph initiated the dialogue when he had written Calhoun in

November, as a candidate for president, asking his stand regarding the petition for redress against Missouri. In a brief reply, Calhoun affirmed his position that their case regarding the Missouri matter "does not come within the jurisdictions of the federal government, which is one of limited and specific powers."[350]

On January 2, 1844, Joseph again responded to the South Carolina senator, but this time in a clear rebuke for his cowardly reply. Joseph sarcastically commented,

> Go on, then Missouri, after another set of inhabitants, (as the Latter-day Saints did) have entered some two or three hundred thousand dollars worth of land, and made extensive improvements theron: go on, then I say, banish the occupants or owners, or kill them, as the mobbers did many of the Latter-day Saints, and take their lands and property spoil: and let the legislature, as in the case of the Mormons, appropriate a couple of hundred thousand dollars to pay the mob for doing the job.[351]

The Prophet was clearly upset that not only had the Missourians stolen their lands, they also used their power in the legislature to pay the mobbers as militia to force them from their homes.

On January 19, Joseph took occasion to lecture on the Constitution and render various comments on the candidates in the national limelight. Frequent news accounts of political misdeeds and controversies stirred greater concerns as he performed his various duties.

It was determined that the Nauvoo newspaper take a more active and investigative approach to political events and rebuttals of national campaign rhetoric. It was intended also that the Quorum of the Twelve take a more commanding role and assume oversight for the messaging emanating from Nauvoo. The following week, the transfer of the printing office was completed. Ebenezer Robinson had agreed to sell the various printing equipment, including the press, bindery, foundry, office, and building lot. John Taylor would take over operations of the newspaper and printing orders.

Joseph Smith's "Views on Government" Pamphlet Is Published

On Friday, the 26, Joseph tasked Phelps to draft a piece on the situation of the nation. On Monday, he followed up with a meeting of the Twelve in the mayor's office. A motion was made by Willard Richards that Joseph become a candidate for president, to which the Quorum unanimously approved. Strategically, it was determined that the campaign would be launched by means of independent electors, faithful to the cause of Zion, to engage in missionary and electioneering activities. A few were immediately assigned locations to serve as advocates of the Prophet's candidacy. Joseph instructed, "Tell the people we have had Whig and Democrats [as] Presidents long enough. We want a President of the United States. . . . The Whigs are striving for a king under the garb of Democracy."[352] Joseph then gave advice on content for Phelps to begin a draft of views on the powers and policy of the US government.[353]

The following Monday, the requested first draft of the "Views on the Government" was read to the Prophet for his editing. On Thursday, at a meeting in the assembly room, Phelps read the revised treatise for the first time publicly. Elders Hyde and Taylor then gave speeches at this political gathering. Joseph concluded with his speech.

During a Nauvoo city council meeting on February 12, members signed the "Memorial to Congress" petition of December 21. Their intent was the pursuit of the divine admonition from the parable of the importunate widow. Also during the meeting, Orson Pratt was assigned to take the document to Washington to follow it through and report regarding the legislative process on the matter. Dr. Richards read Joseph's correspondence with Calhoun, and Phelps then reread the treatise of views on the government. Later, the document went through further revisions, based on recommendations of Joseph's dear friend Dr. Bernhisel. Thomas Bullock had also provided assistance in the drafting of this poignant document.

In its finished form, the pamphlet drew attention to the sterling qualities of leadership and integrity in the Founding Fathers. Washington, Adams, and Jefferson were extolled for their principled and selfless characters. Then, Joseph departed from his historical narrative and introduced key economic principles referred to as "the four main pillars of prosperity."

> When the people are secure and their rights properly respected, then the four main pillars of prosperity, viz: agriculture, manufactures, navigation, and commerce, need the fostering care of government, and in so goodly a country as ours, where the soil, the climate, the rivers, the lakes, and the sea coast; the productions, the timber, the minerals, and

> the inhabitants are so diversified, that a pleasing variety accommodates all tastes, trades, and calculations.[354]

Here, Joseph prophetically presented the economic principles he had fostered and tested in Missouri, Ohio, and Nauvoo. It was based on these economic principles for which the inspired Saints toiled diligently to secure Zion and the kingdom of God. In each major attempt, power-hungry government factions had solicited local citizens, who selfishly sought self-aggrandizement from these same economic principles, and fought the Saints. Had Joseph succeeded, the Mormons could have created an unrivaled economic model with Enoch-like liberations of the poor and downtrodden.

Continuing in the pamphlet, Joseph praised Presidents Madison, Monroe, and John Quincy Adams. He was also praiseworthy of President Jackson for his efforts to rid the nation of the federal debt. Then, Joseph lashed out at the administration of President Van Buren:

> At the age, then, of sixty years our blooming republic began to decline under the withering touch of Martin Van Buren! Disappointed ambition; thirst for power, pride, corruption, party spirit, faction, patronage; perquisites, fame, tangling alliances; priest-craft and spiritual wickedness in high places, struck hands, and reveled in midnight splendor. Trouble, vexation, perplexity and contention mingled with hope, fear and murmuring, rumbled through the union and agitated the whole nation. . . .
>
> No honest man can doubt for a moment, but the glory of American liberty is on the wane; and, that calamity and confusion will sooner or later, destroy the peace of the people. . . . Democracy, Whiggery and Cliquery, will attract their elements and foment divisions among the people, to accomplish fancied schemes and accumulate power.[355]

In his scathing rebuke against the Van Buren administration, Joseph was attempting to reach out to the American people with a warning and a call to unite and return to the original Constitutional principles. The people needed to return honorable leaders to seats of government, which Van Buren, Benton, and others had so tarnished.

The "Views on Government" continued,

> Then why? Oh! Why! Will a once flourishing people not arise, phoenix like, over the cinders of Martin Van Buren's power; and over the sinking

> fragments and smoking ruins of other catamount politicians; and over the wind-falls of Benton, Calhoun, Clay, Wright, and a caravan of other equally unfortunate law doctors, and cheerfully help to spread a plaster and bind up the burnt, bleeding wounds of a sore but blessed country?[356]

Joseph Smith had thrown down the gauntlet from the distant land of Illinois. He had openly challenged the integrity of the leaders of both parties, and taken direct aim at the corrupt political cliques in each state, which were subversive to the Constitutional principles and the will of the people.

The Prophet and the Saints had been victimized by the cliques he was calling out. The Saints had been abused by the leaders of the secret constitution and the St. Louis Junto, supported by then Lieutenant Governor Boggs in Jackson County. The Mormon war, which gave rise to Governor Boggs's Extermination Order, was fomented by the workings behind the scenes of the Central Clique of the Boonslick region. Nationally, the Loco Foco leadership of Van Buren, Benton, Blair, and others was mounting an attack on the Prophet as he had injected himself squarely in their course of a return to victory and dominance. The opposition was preparing to fight back, in sinister plots.

In the publication, Joseph spelled out various key platform issues. A solution to the slavery issue by having the government buy out the slaves and set them free, the creation of a national bank with branches in each state, prison reform, militia reform, and a clear policy regarding Texas and Oregon and others that might be brought into the United States. These matters resonated with the people and appealed to many, as instinctively aimed in the right direction but were in conflict with the platforms of the two leading parties and their candidates.

Joseph had previously determined the need to relocate the main body of the Saints, as persecution and hostilities continued to mount. On February 20, he instructed the Twelve to send a delegation to investigate the frontier regions of California and Oregon to find a location "where we can remove after the Temple is completed and build a city in a day and have a government of our own in a healthy climate."[357] The next day, the Twelve named eight men to fulfill the call for an exploring expedition to the West. Also, a new piece, identified as " A Pacific Inuendo," and a letter from Governor Ford were published in *Nauvoo Neighbor*.[358] In the governor's letter, Ford recounted the attempts of the legislature to repeal the Nauvoo Charter:

> If there is anything wrong in the Nauvoo charters, or in the mode of administering them, you will see that nothing short of legislative or judicial power is capable of enforcing a remedy. I myself had the honor of calling the attention of the legislature to this subject at the last session; but a large majority of both political parties in the body, either did not see the evil which you complain of, or if they did, they repeatedly refused to correct it. And yet a call is made upon me to do that which all parties refused to do at the last session.[359]

On Friday, the meeting with the Apostles and others resumed. The Prophet provided new details regarding the expedition to the West. The group was to consist of twenty-five who could raise five hundred dollars and who would preach the gospel, as occasion presented. It was also announced in the meeting that 1,500 copies of Joseph's "Views of the Powers and Policy of the Government of the United States" had just come off the press at the printing office.

On the Sabbath, Joseph and Hyrum commenced preaching near the site of the temple. Later, Joseph noted that he had prayed that the "Views on Government" pamphlet "might be spread far and wide and be the means of opening the hearts of the people."[360] Indeed, a great movement was about to commence. On Tuesday, February 27, a mass mailing of two hundred pamphlets were sent out. Addressees included the president, Cabinet members, Supreme Court judges, senators, representatives, principal newspapers, governors, and many postmasters and individuals. The seats of government were about to be challenged.

By March, the Temple Committee and others felt a need to change the priorities of their construction projects and put a hold on building the Nauvoo House and concentrate their time and energies on the temple alone. Brother Woodworth was reassigned to return to Wisconsin to the lumber mill sites and lead the next delivery of the processed lumber for the temple.

On Monday, March 4, Joseph instructed a letter be written to his friend and ally General James Arlington Bennett of New York. This letter was to inform the popular general that he had been selected to serve as Joseph's vice presidential running mate.

By this time, conflicts within some of the leaders of Nauvoo were starting to challenge the progress of Zion building. Some misunderstood Joseph's intentions in running for the White House. On one such occasion, Joseph responded,

> I do not care one half so much about the Presidential election as I do the office I have got. We have as good a right to make [a] political party to gain power to defend ourselves as for demagogues to make use of our religion to get power to destroy ourselves. We will whip the mob by getting up a President. When I look into the Eastern papers and see how popular I am, I am afraid I shall be President.[361]

Joseph Smith Issues "A Friendly Hint to Missouri"

Contemplating the events as they were unfolding, Joseph lamented that "the Mormon Zion has endured all animus."[362] On the morning of March 8, Bishop Miller arrived from the Pineries, carrying a letter drafted by leaders of the Pinery Group. Lyman Wight was still in Wisconsin. During that same day, Willard Richards reported to the Prophet that General James Bennett, their proposed vice presidential nominee, had been born in Ireland and hence would not qualify as a candidate. Joseph called a special council to meet with Bishop Miller and the Twelve later that evening. During the council meeting, Brother Phelps read the piece entitled "A Friendly Hint to Missouri," which was intended to be sent to the US government and had been previously written under direction from the Prophet. The contents of this writing began with a cordial call for peace and the blessed roles of peacemakers, and then continued:

> So much to preface this friendly hint to the State of Missouri, . . . some of her private citizens and public officers, have committed violence, robbery, and even murder, upon the rights and persons of the Church of Jesus Christ of Latter-day Saints; yet, compassion, dignity, and a sense of the principles of religion, among all classes; and honor and benevolence, mingled with charity by high minded patriots, lead me to suppose, that there are many worthy people in that state, who will use their influence and energies to bring about a settlement of all those old difficulties; and use all consistent means, to urge the state . . . to restore every person, she or her citizens have expelled from her limits, to their rights, and pay them all damage!
>
> The voice of reason, the voice of humanity, the voice of the nation, and the voice of heaven, seem to say to the honest and virtuous, throughout the State of Missouri, wash yourselves, make you clean, lest your negligence should be taken by the world, from the mass of facts before it, that you are guilty!

Also in this poignant missive, Joseph warned the people of Missouri of the state statute:

> If twelve or more persons shall combine to levy war against any part of the people of this state, or to remove forcibly out of the state, or from their habitations, evidenced by taking arms and assembling to accomplish such purpose, every person so offending shall be punished by imprisonment in the penitentiary for a period not exceeding five years, or by a fine not exceeding five thousand dollar; and imprisonment in the county jail not exceeding six months.[363]

Judge Austin King had redrafted this statute in 1835 as part of his revision of the Missouri state code. Joseph was putting those responsible for crimes against the Saints on notice. This communication was to be presented at the national level, and then to filter down to the offending communities. It would apply to all those who formed ad hoc community committees, designated as Vigilance Committees or otherwise, to plan and execute illegal actions against the Mormon citizens of the state. Governor Boggs and many of the leading legislators, county officials, and merchants of the region had violated this statute. If the Mormons prevailed in calling for a Congressional investigation, charges could be brought against those other citizens involved. The hierarchy of the Central Clique and the St. Louis Junto likewise took notice as some of them could be implicated as well. A heightened resolve by national and state leaders to thwart the Prophet's attentions to the crimes committed ensued.

Because this statute was prefaced with the description "of offenses against the government and the supremacy of the laws," enforcement was not subject to limitations imposed on individuals. The fines from enforcement would increase the state treasury. With the limits as high as five thousand dollars per individual, the aggregate sums could be of great interest to the state.

Church leaders were seeking the assistance of the federal government to ensure the state statutes were to be enforced both in regards to this statute and to the many civil suit claims available to Church members individually. These revised statutes also defined the time periods in which plaintiffs could file actions. Passed in March 1835, the limitations included twenty years for grievances regarding real property and ten years for trespass on real property. Personal property matters were allowed five-year filing limitations.

For the Mormon leadership focused on the filings of the redress petitions, those actions involving the conduct of mob members in 1833 and 1834 in Jackson County seemed secure with twenty-year limitations. For the actions against mob members in 1838, which included the events leading up to the Extermination Order by Governor Boggs in late October of that year, the limitation period appeared to be subject to the twenty-year limitation for real property matters and the ten-year limitation for issues regarding trespass on real property.

Irony was evident in these statutes. Judge King, who took the lead in researching and preparing the revised statutes of 1835, was himself directly involved in the hearings in 1835 against Joseph Smith and more than forty others. Lilburn Boggs, who was involved in the 1833 and 1838 mob violence, agreed to the 1835 statutes, serving as the state lieutenant governor, which held the dual role as president of the state Senate of Missouri to affirm the provisions of the revised statutes.

The Apostles and various members of the Temple Committee met in the Nauvoo Mansion on March 10. The letter of February 15 from Lyman Wight, George Miller, and others was read, advocating that the members of the Black River Falls Pinery group depart from Wisconsin and remove to the Republic of Texas to engage in the building up of the kingdom of God.

> We have in our minds to go to the table-lands of Texas, to a point we may find to be the most eligible, there locate, and let it be a place of gathering for all the South . . . and for us to employ our time and talents in gathering together means to build according to the commandments of our God, and spread the Gospel to the nations according to the will of our Heavenly Father.[364]

Actions of the Council of Fifty

After this, Joseph organized the Council of Fifty to oversee the settlement of Texas and eventually to rule over the political kingdom of God on the earth. It was understood that the approval of the Nauvoo House Association subgroup, known as the Black River Falls Pinery, was authorized through Joseph Smith and the newly constituted Council of Fifty to establish the settlement and building up of the kingdom of God in the Republic of Texas. This was considered a key but initial step in the building up of the global political kingdom of

God, in which the Council of Fifty would preside politically.[365] A select committee was charged with the task of drafting a new constitution for the Council of Fifty, with the US Constitution as a guide.

In the *Washington Globe* of March 14, Francis Blair published an intended demeaning commentary directed at Joseph's pamphlet known as the "Views on the Power and Policy of Our Government." Blair and his fellow Loco Foco Party bosses pursued their objective to ridicule the Mormon leader and stifle momentum of the Prophet's incessant attempts to get the federal government to provide an investigation. Blair's focus was directed at challenging Joseph's defense of a realigned National Bank. Joseph would deliberate on how to respond.

Also on March 14, Lucien Woodworth, the Prophet Joseph's ambassador to Mexico, left Nauvoo bound for Austin to meet with the Texas Republic President Sam Houston.

A memorial to Congress was drafted and approved by Joseph, and it asserted,

> Whereas, many of the citizens of these United States have migrated, and are migrating, to Texas, Oregon, and other lands contiguous to this nation; and whereas, Texas has declared herself free and independent, without the necessary power to protect her rights and liberties. . . . Be it ordained . . . that Joseph Smith, of the city of Nauvoo, in the State of Illinois, is hereby authorized and empowered to raise a company of one hundred thousand armed volunteers, in the United States and Territories.[366]

St. Louis was disseminating the word of warning as to the intentions of Joseph's election bid and sounding the alarm. "If Joe Smith is elected President, he will raise the devil with Missouri; and if he is not elected, he will raise the devil anyhow."[367]

Many were fearful of prosecution, based on Joseph's "A Friendly Hint to Missouri," and citing the Missouri statute calling for large fines and jail terms. Missouri residents took the warning that Joseph would "raise the devil with Missouri" seriously.[368] Leaders of the Central Clique and St. Louis Junto were concerned about more unpleasant and unwanted attention to their past acts and misdeeds. Senator Benton had been threatened again by his nemesis Joseph Smith in the halls of Congress because of the Mormon memorial. Benton's "Road to India" was to be hijacked by the Prophet leading troops to the

Oregon Territory. The Mormons continued to implement barriers and impediments to Benton's ambitions and his thirteen-point agenda. The enraged senator had again been challenged to a duel, but not on Bloody Island. Benton was calculating, methodical, and vengeful. Allies were summoned. The Mormon leader was in his sights.

News of a secret meeting with the Laws, Higbees, and Fosters, "red hot for a conspiracy" to endanger the lives of Joseph and Hyrum, was voiced to the Church leadership in Nauvoo.[369]

On April 8, Joseph made a new proclamation: "I have another great and grand Revelation." He proceeded to explain that the whole of America is Zion.[370]

The April 17 issue of *Nauvoo Neighbor* carried Joseph's scathing reply to the *Washington Globe*:

> Without reference to men, parties, or precedents, the plan of banking, suggested in my "Views" is assumed upon the all-commanding, and worthily considered, omnipotent petition of the people, and whether, as a "fiscal agent, great financier, prophet, priest, or king," I act wisely and righteously, so as to answer their virtuous prayers, without fear, favor, or partiality; and produce union; give satisfaction to twenty millions of freemen, rather than sport with their holy supplications to boost a few hungry, crafty, hypocritical demagogues into office . . . or whether I raise the honor and credit of the nation above the little, picayune, cramped, narrow minded schemes of the dominant, undominant and would be dominant parties, cliques, knots and factions, or whether, like the venerable fathers, I launch my new ship into the great ocean of existence, and, like them, luckily bring relief to the oppressed, is all the same, so long as the people are honored as noble in their patriotism; and almighty in their majesty; vox populi; vox Dei![371]

Joseph used this occasion initiated by Blair and the national Democratic Party aristocracy to draw national attention to the illegal actions and unpunished violence against the Saints. Blair had sought to diminish Joseph and bury the Missouri Mormon issue. Instead, Joseph hoped to make it a national point of discussion if other papers would print his rebuttal. With literary flair, "vox populi; vox Dei!" was added, meaning "the voice of the people is the voice of God," which was the phrase used against the Church leaders from Governor Dunklin's letter in 1834 and later used against the Church's enemies. Again, Joseph targeted the puppet masters, Senator Benton and President Van Buren, and continued:

> The United States is the boasted land of "Liberty," where "these truths are held self-evident—that *all* men are created equal; and endowed by their Creator with certain unalienable rights, that among these are life, *liberty*, and the pursuit of happiness:" but at the same time, . . . slavery is tolerated by law; and even fifteen thousand free citizens are exiled from one state to another—and the General Government has no power (according to the opinions of Van Buren and Benton) to redress the wrong.
>
> Party spirit, cuts the cords of union; patronage veils the face of justice, and bribery closes the lips of honor, and when the wicked rule the people mourn.
>
> The only suggestion worthy of commendation relative to a National Bank, in Mr. Blair's remarks, is that the mother bank should be located at Nauvoo.
>
> As the "world is governed too much," and as there is not a nation or dynasty, now occupying the earth, which acknowledges Almighty God as their law giver, and as "crowns won by blood, by blood must be 'maintained,'" I go emphatically, virtuously, and humanely, for a *theodemocracy*, where God and the people hold the power to conduct the affairs of men in righteousness. And, where liberty, free trade, and sailor's rights, and the protection of life and property shall be maintained inviolate, for the benefit of *all*. To exalt mankind is nobly acting the part of a God; to degrade them, in meanly doing the drudgery of the devil. . . . With the highest sentiments of regard for all men, I am an advocate of unadulterated freedom."[372]

Intended for national awareness, Joseph also commented to *The Globe*, "And when great men, in high places, see a Governor Reynolds shoot out his own brains with a rifle; . . . then know ye, the *hour of his judgment has come!*"

On April 27, Joseph called a meeting to instruct the elders departing on electioneering missions and proclaiming the gospel. They were also addressed by Sydney Rigdon and William Smith. George Miller returned from the Pineries the following Thursday, and the Council of Fifty was then convened to hear Miller's report. It was understood that Wentworth and Houston agreed in preliminary negotiations that the Mormons were invited to settle in Texas as a buffer appendage and would provide opposition to aggression from Santa Anna. It was expected the Saints would organize in Nauvoo Legion fashion to repel attacks from Mexican troops.

The Reddick Heirs Prevail in Their Montrose Lawsuit against Marsh, Lee, and Delavan

From Washington, DC, a critical ruling was made on the first day of May regarding the status of the 640-acre plot in Montrose, which had been the subject of litigation between Marsh, Lee, and Delavan—as trustees for the New York Land Company—versus the Thomas F. Reddick heirs. Commissioner Thomas H. Blake, of the US General Land Office, determined,

> In answer to your letter of the 30th ultimo, . . . I have the honor to inform you that the "Reddick" claim, for 640 acres, (in township 66 north, or range 5 west) situated within the limits of the half-breed Sac and Fox reservation, has been recognized as a confirmed claim, and that a patent was issued for it under the date 7 February, 1839.[373]

With this confirmation, the Reddick heirs and their St. Louis merchant allies felt confident they would win the appeal filed by the New York Land Company trustees after the September 1843 ruling in favor of the Reddick heirs. This land represented an important commercial site, in which the Montrose steamboat landing site was important to the Chouteaus upper Mississippi commerce. The Chouteaus had dominated the area below Prairie du Chien after the negotiations in 1827 created the upper Missouri outfit division of the American Fur Company, which was managed by Chouteau. Then the foot of the Des Moines Rapids was secured by Russell Farnham at Fort Edwards (Warsaw) and Mark Aldrich at Keokuk. The Fort Des Moines barracks had been built on this land that was used by Mormons after fleeing Missouri.

Edward Brooks took the lead of the Reddick heirs for litigation for the Montrose lands. He had been a business agent for Joshua Pilcher, Superintendent of Indian Affairs, with the aid of Senator Benton, after William Clark died. Eliza Reddick, the wife of Thomas F. Reddick, was a listed defendant as guardian for their unmarried children. Joshua

Pilcher died in June 1843, and in his will assigned a note for $3,800 from Senator Benton to his daughter Susan, and a portion of his estate to Eliza. Pilcher appointed Edward Brooks to administer his estate.[374]

With the Reddick heirs closely aligned to Senator Benton and the Chouteau commercial empire, Pierre Chouteau was anxious to again strengthen his hold on the Des Moines Rapids. With access to the Montrose landing afforded by the Reddick heirs, and with Mark Aldrich their former employee at Warsaw, the Chouteaus would again control access at the head and foot of the Rapids. The Mormons, however represented a major impediment to their plans.

David Kilbourne and the New York Land Company controlled a lot of the Half-Breed Tract, and especially the key steamboat landing site in Keokuk. There, Kilbourne's friend and fellow Mormon hater Laban Fleak was employed by the steamship lines. The litigation against the Reddick heirs was to allow the New York Land Company control of the head and foot of the Des Moines Rapids, both at Montrose and Keokuk. They too were anxious to rid the area of the Mormons because of their growing commercial dominance and to cover up their prior fraud.

The Mormons dominated the region from Nauvoo. The *Maid of Iowa* steamship was a successful enterprise, which piloted passengers and freight throughout the region. The Nauvoo steamboat landing was in high use. Enemies also feared Joseph Smith's interest in developing a canal and dam would conflict with their plans for this critical site.

Mark Aldrich had other concerns regarding the Mormons. His friend and partner, Joseph Duncan, had passed away earlier that year. His estate was seized by the US government to pay the debts of his brother-in-law, for which Duncan served as surety. The appointment of an administrator of Duncan's estate by the government to settle Duncan's interests in the Warsaw Land Company could draw attention to the involvement of Duncan, a known enemy to the Mormons. Mormons would be outraged that Duncan was the former president of the Warsaw Company in partnership with Aldrich and the former Illinois Fund Commissioner Richard F. Barrett, at the time when Aldrich and Calvin Warren were selling their Warsaw lands to them.

With the implementation of Justin Butterfield's plan and the efforts of Governor Ford in 1843 and 1844 to get the Illinois and Michigan Canal moving forward again, many commercial leaders expected a surge in commercial trade expansion. They understood the canal would add more traffic to the Mississippi River commerce, which was affected by the Des Moines Rapids. Land company developers in Illinois and in the Iowa Territory were expecting large growth because of the canal construction, which would enable them to finally sell their lands profitably.

The commercial interests of the Chouteaus, Mark Aldrich, his fellow commissioners—aided with their allies of the anti-Mormon Party—and Kilbourne, with the members of the New York Land Company, were all contingent on ridding the area of the Mormons. The corrupt conspiracy identified the previous year by Joseph Smith was expanding to include an alliance amongst the Mormons' greatest enemies. Their collective aim was, in essence, the working of the honeycomb scheme, as mentioned by Isaac Galland, the former agent for the New York Land Company and railroad commissioner with Aldrich, Duncan, Barrett, Warren, and others.

Francis Higbee, an apostate who had styled himself with the others as "Reformers," purchased a printing press from one of the Whig leaders, Abraham Jonas, formerly an admirer of Joseph Smith and one who had initiated the Freemason Lodge in Nauvoo.[375] In a letter from Francis Higbee to Thomas Gregg, former editor of the *Warsaw Signal*, plans were laid out:

> Above all, it shall be the organ through which we will herald his Mormon ribaldry. It shall also contain a full and complete expose of his Mormon seraglio, or Nauvoo Harem; and his unparalleled and unheard of attempts at seduction.[376]

On May 10, the "Prospectus" of the *Nauvoo Expositor* was published by William Law, Wilson Law, Charles Ivins, Francis M. Higbee, Robert D. Foster, and Charles A. Foster. The express purpose of the publication was announced as supporting:

> The Unconditional Repeal of the Nauvoo City Charter . . . to restrain and correct the abuses of the unit power—to ward off the Iron Rod which is held over the devoted heads of the citizens of Nauvoo and the

> surrounding country—to advocate unmitigated disobedience to political revelations . . . [by a] *self-constituted monarch* . . . to oppose, with uncompromising hostility any union of church and state or any preliminary step tending to the same.[377]

Two days after this was released, William Law conducted services in his home for his new reformed church, adopting many of the teachings of the Prophet, but declaring Joseph as having departed the true faith.[378]

William Law had indeed fallen from his former high station. He had repudiated the instructions and warnings given by way of revelation just three years previously and abandoned the call and high honor he had been offered. "And he shall be led in paths where the poisonous serpent cannot lay hold upon his heel, and he shall mount up in the imagination of his thoughts as upon eagles' wings" (D&C 124:99). William Law wanted prosperity from the internal improvements coming. He felt threatened by the Prophet's proposed dam and canal projects, which would interfere with his plans that he purchased two islands on the Mississippi River for. He, with his associates, were in the land business and expected their own version of the honeycomb effect. They expected that lands they sold by notes to fellow Mormons would return to them with improvements after all the Saints were forced to leave by the mobs.

Robert Foster too had repudiated the offer extended by revelation if he would "repent of all his folly, and clothe himself with charity; and cease to do evil" (D&C 124:116). He had, in 1842, transferred his interests in the stone house he purchased from Hyrum Smith in exchange for seventy seven shares of stock in the Nauvoo House. His actions promoting the *Nauvoo Expositor* were an abomination to the counsel given him. His conduct would deny himself and his future generations in contrast to the challenge he was given to purchase stock in the Nauvoo House "for himself and for his generation after him, from generation to generation" (D&C 124:117).

On May 12, the Prophet presented his convictions pertaining to his prophetic calling:

> It has always been my province to dig up hidden mysteries—new things—for my hearers. . . . All the testimony is that the Lord in the last days would commit the keys of the priesthood to a witness over all people. Has the Gospel of the kingdom commenced in the last days? And will God

> take it from the man until He takes him Himself? I have read it precisely as the words flowed from the lips of Jesus Christ. John the Revelator saw an angel flying through the midst of heaven, having the everlasting gospel to preach unto them that dwell on the earth. . . .
>
> In relation to the kingdom of God, the devil always set up his kingdom at the very same time in opposition to God. Every man who has a calling to minister to the inhabitants of the world was ordained to that very purpose in the Grand Council of heaven before this world was. . . . It is the testimony that I want that I am God's servant, and this people His people. The ancient prophets declared that in the last days the God of heaven should set up a kingdom which should never be destroyed, . . . and the very time that was calculated on, this people were struggling to bring it out.
>
> I calculate to be one of the instruments of setting up the kingdom of Daniel by the word of the Lord, and I intend to lay a foundation that will revolutionize the whole world.[379]

A divine economic plan was underway to revolutionize the world, but it was predicated on the obedience and fortitude of the Saints to abide the covenant to build Zion. The following day, the Prophet finally responded to Henry Clay, the leading Whig candidate for president:

> For the glory of America has departed, and God will set a flaming sword to guard the tree of liberty, while such mint-tithing Herods as Van Buren, Boggs, Benton, Calhoun and Clay, are thrust out of the realms of virtue as fit subjects for the kingdom of fallen greatness; *vox reprobi, vox diaboli!* . . .
>
> And ask the people of this enlightened Republic, what they think of your powers and policy as a statesman; for verily it would seem, from all past remains of parties, politics, projects and pictures; that you are the *Clay*, and the people the *potter*; and as some vessels are marred in the hands of the potter, the natural conclusion is that *you are a vessel of dishonor.*[380]

So it seemed that "The Voice of Truth" was yet to expose the "Voice of Reprobates" and the "Voice of Devils." Further in the letter, Joseph stated with plainness:

> Benton and Van Buren, who make no secret to say, if they get into power, they will carry on Boggs' exterminating plan to rid the country of Latter Day Saints.[381]

Eloquently, the Prophet of the final dispensation declared to the world his divine mission and mandate. He knew his earthly battle to bring about Zion and the kingdom of God was about to conclude. He had fought the battle for Zion in Jackson County, in the northern counties of Missouri, in Kirtland, and later in Nauvoo and Iowa.

Arrayed against Babylon, Joseph valiantly fought those corrupted in their pursuits of power and vanity under the subversive elements of "Democracy, Whiggery and Cliquery." The Prophet declared, the devil had been setting up his kingdom simultaneously in opposition to God. Hence, the battle for Zion and the kingdom of God was waged with both divine and diabolic intervention by proxies in vigorous combat. As was his "province," he would leave a hidden mystery for his hearers by which he would expose those in political cliques acting in opposition to the kingdom of God. In the end, he would do as he declared: "to lay a foundation that will revolutionize the whole world."[382]

15: The Martyrdom

On Tuesday, May 21, Apostles Brigham Young, Heber C. Kimball, and Lyman Wight, with about a hundred elders, boarded the steamship *Osprey*, bound for St. Louis. Departing the steamboat launch site from the shore, a voice rang out for three cheers, "Joseph Smith, the next president of the United States."[383] This was the launching point for the electioneering Church leaders and missionaries, armed with Joseph's "Views on Government" pamphlets.

Upon arriving in St. Louis the next day, Apostles Brigham Young and Heber C. Kimball called the Saints together and instructed the members on spiritual and political matters. The St. Louis Church membership consisted of some seven hundred Saints.

Thomas Sharp again rallied anti-Mormon supporters. The *Warsaw Signal* reported on May 29 that he "would not be surprised to hear of his [Joseph Smith's] death by violent means in a short time."[384] He had inside information regarding their violent plans afoot to murder the Mormon leader. A new trap had already been set. Several apostate Church leaders secured a printing press from Abraham Jonas, a dominant Whig from Adams County. Francis Higbee and William Law had warned John Birney that they planned to use the newspaper to expose Joseph Smith and would continue, law or no law. Francis Higbee revealed their true intentions when he threatened Stephen Markham: "the interest of this city is done, the moment a hand is laid on their press."[385] These apostates knew they had the support of Sharp, the anti-Mormon party, and other various Mormon opposition groups in Missouri, Iowa, and Illinois. They were confident, if damage was brought against their press, the backlash would take the Prophet down.

For Sharp and his commissioner associates—anxious to advance the various internal improvement projects in the region and increase land values—the deadline to be rid of the Mormon opposition was near. Even with the advancements in the Illinois and Michigan Canal project, major investors were wary in committing to fund the projects until the Saints were gone. Sharp had high expectations that the lands and ferry operations to Alexandria, which he received by his marriage to the widow of Major Wilcox, would add greatly to his personal wealth and status.

On June 7, the first issue of the *Nauvoo Expositor* was circulated. The Nauvoo city council met three days later and determined the paper was libelous and slandered the city. Markham's and Birney's concerns were voiced, but the decision was made to go forward. The Nauvoo council issued an order to destroy the paper as a public nuisance. Based on the council order, Joseph Smith issued an order to the city marshall to have the press destroyed. Those dispatched consisted of nearly a hundred orderly individuals, including Colonel Stephen Markham.

David Kilbourne Writes to Reverend Dent in England

An anti-Mormon Party mass meeting was held in Warsaw on June 13. Attending it were George Robinson, C. L. Higbee, and Francis Higbee. Perhaps Robinson was there because his name was on the deed involved in the Church purchase from Hugh White and Isaac Galland in 1839. With the Saints gone, he likely had hopes of taking over that valuable property.

At Fort Madison, Kilbourne had a different account of what had transpired and indicated his role. In a letter to Reverend Dent at Billington, England on June 15, Kilbourne discussed his views of the actions of the Mormons and that the city council declared the *Nauvoo Expositor* a nuisance. He indicated that three hundred men marched in and destroyed the press:

> They then proceeded to Joe's residence & gave him three cheers, They then went to the resident (sic) of Law & also his brother & several others who had dissented & gave them notice that they must not be found in Nauvoo the next day at 4 O clock P.M. at the risk of their lives.
>
> The next morning the 12th Inst a messenger came up here to get a steam boat to go & bring them off—accordingly a boat started from here with some 50 of our citizens to assist removing those families whose lives were threatened.
>
> About dark the boat return[ed] here laden with men, women & children. With horses, wagons, furniture & c. The boat proceeded to Burlington about 20 miles above this where Mr. Law told me they intended to secure quarters for the women and children & return to Nauvoo to fight if necessary.
>
> Law told me that he would just as soon live in hell as in Nauvoo—that Joe would have no scruples to cause any man's life to be taken to carry out his plans. . . .
>
> Joe & his men were arrested the day after the press was destroyed—but he immediately cleared himself & the others by the exercise of his writ of Habeas Corpus authority.
>
> Another writ is out for him & . . . in the surrounding counties to raise sufficient force to arrest him & take him out of the City.
>
> I anticipate . . . then sooner or later bloodshed must take place. Nauvoo has become the receptacle of outlaws & robbers for the whole country, & the people it seems to me will be oblige[d] to resolve themselves into the original elements of society & rise in their majesty & disperse the banditti. . . .
>
> The night after Law left, two attempts were made to fire his mill & house.[386]

With exaggerations and embellishments, he revealed his intended plan. He implied in this account his actions were spontaneous. But to accomplish all that was done in that day would have required substantial prior planning and cooperation from others. His plan to solve the crisis for him and his employer was that after blood was shed, the people would see Nauvoo was the receptacle for criminals for the whole country. Then the people would feel compelled to "resolve themselves into the original elements of society" (in other words, ignore the lawful approach) and rise spontaneously "in their majesty" and force the Mormons out. This was his version of the "honey comb" scheme.

Joseph, Hyrum, Stephen Markham, and others were arrested June 17 by Constable Joel Miles on a writ from Justice Daniel Wells, based on a complaint filed by Mr. Ware for the riot on June 10, when the *Nauvoo Expositor* press was destroyed. That same day, they were tried by Justice Wells and discharged as they were acting by order of the city council.

Also on that day, Henry Clay, presidential candidate, wrote to his Illinois party operative:

> I am rejoiced to hear of your flattering prospects. . . . You will have heard that they have given you Polk to combat, who is opposed to every interest and stands counter to every prejudice of Illinois. You certainly will not allow the State to go for him.[387]

Henry Clay was still offended at Joseph Smith's public rebuke of him. Earlier in the year, he was quite optimistic he had secured the Mormon vote, which would make him the clear winner in carrying the state of Illinois. Joseph Smith's aggressive campaigning as a third party contender and the sheer size of the ever-growing Mormon population could conceivably cost him the election. He had witnessed how his friend and ally Thomas Corbin had lost with but 2 percent of the event secured by the Liberty Party, which robbed him of a victory.

This same day, a committee lead by Onias Skinner, selected at the previous Hancock County Vigilance Committee meeting in Carthage, met with Governor Ford and requested the militia "be ordered out to assist in executing process in the city of Nauvoo." Ford declined their request and determined to visit Carthage himself. "No order for the militia was made" by him.[388]

On June 20, Dr. Southwick arrived from Louisiana to meet with Joseph Smith and reported a cannon from Quincy had just arrived in Warsaw. Hostilities were escalating rapidly.

Governor Ford at Carthage

Governor Ford arrived at Carthage the next day and found armed militia units assembled under the direction of the constables of the county to serve as a *posse comitatus* to assist in the execution of process. The general of the state brigade called for militia units from McDonough and Schuyler Counties to supplement the Hancock County units. Colonel Williams assembled a large number of troops from Warsaw.[389] After the governor had declined their request for the state militia, the Hancock County Vigilance Committee took the initiative themselves to gather various militia units.

This process was prearranged at the anti-Mormon Meeting held in September the previous year by resolution that if they felt the established government didn't meet their needs, they would call out various militia units on their own.[390] Congressman John Hardin, a relative of Henry Clay, was a brigadier general of the state militia. It was known that Lieutenant General Joseph Smith was the highest ranking militia leader in the state.

Governor Ford, pretending to be in command, ordered the militia to organize in normal ranks. It was a farce that all these militia gathered because of a perceived violation of freedom of the press having occurred against a few citizens in Nauvoo. Ford was also secretly developing his own plot to rid the state of Mormons. Committed to the success of the Illinois and Michigan Canal, Ford had concerns that the Mormons would attempt to use his pet project for their own benefit. He hoped their leaders could be put in jail and escape, similar to the previous experience in Missouri. The Mormons would follow their leaders out of his state en masse.[391]

Ford noted the shocking conduct of Hancock County officials after arriving at Carthage:

> These also were active men in blowing up the fury of the people, in hopes that a popular movement might be set on foot, which would result in the expulsion or extermination of the Mormon voters.
>
> For this purpose, public meetings had been called; inflammatory speeches had been made; exaggerated reports had been extensively circulated; committees had been appointed, who rode night and day to

> spread the reports, and solicit the aid of neighboring counties. . . . A system of excitement and agitation was artfully planned and executed with tact.

Ford had learned that, at a public meeting earlier in Warsaw resolutions, were approved to expel Mormons from their area.[392] After additional militia units arrived from McDonough and Schuyler Counties, a "Council of Officers" assumed charge over the group. They, not the governor, were in charge. Schuyler County leaders, particularly in Rushville as well as McDonough County, were supportive of the planned improvement projects under Commissioner Valentine Wilson of the Hancock anti-Mormon Party leadership. They would all benefit from the Illinois and Michigan Canal driving commercial traffic down the Illinois River to Beardstown, Rushville, Quincy, Warsaw, Carthage, and Nauvoo and other key sites on the Mississippi River. Macomb, in McDonough County, would also benefit greatly.

In an early session of the Council of Officers, Governor Ford suggested he lead a small militia group to Nauvoo. Ford observed, however, that the constable feared the Mormons might submit to the governor and end their chance for an assault on the Nauvoo residents. The Council of Officers rejected the governor's suggestion. The officers instead insisted upon the necessity of marching to Nauvoo "to search for apparatus to make counterfeit money, and more particularly to terrify the Mormons from attempting any open or secret measures of vengeance against the citizens of the county, who had taken a part against them or their leaders."[393]

When the resolution was put to a vote by the Council of Officers, most officers of the Schuyler and McDonough militia voted against the measure, while officers of Hancock County pushed for its passage. Hancock County militia officers included (from Warsaw) Colonel Levi Williams, Major Mark Aldrich, and Captains William Grover and Jacob Davis. Captain Robert F. Smith represented the Carthage Greys. They were driving the plan to march on Nauvoo and incite a war to result in the extermination of all Mormons from the region. In the end, a small majority of the militia officers prevailed in securing the resolution to march against Nauvoo.

Governor Ford agreed to this arrangement, and June 27 was predetermined to rendezvous at Golden's Point, near the Mississippi River and half way between Nauvoo and Warsaw.

Hancock anti-Mormon leaders hoped chaos and confusion would make the Mormons look guilty for causing a war. Originating with either anti-Mormon Party members or apostate Mormons, it was expected their shots would be directed at Ford's troops, and then Mormons would be blamed. Some of the mob hoped Governor Ford himself would be assassinated while laying it on the Mormons as a people committed to lawlessness and anarchy.[394]

During the Council of Officers meeting, to try and placate the leaders, Governor Ford volunteered to lead the militia troops to Nauvoo "and deliver an address to the Mormons, and tell them plainly what degree of excitement and hatred prevailed against them in the minds of the whole people, and that if any open or secret violence should be committed on the persons or property of those who had taken part against them, that no one would doubt but that it had been perpetrated by them, and that it would be the sure and certain means of the destruction of their city and the extermination of their people."[395] Governor Ford went to General Wilson Law for information on the extent of arms possessed by the Nauvoo Legion. The apostate Wilson Law assisted Ford in pursuing attempts to force Mormon leaders to surrender their arms under the governor's orders.

On June 25, Joseph and Hyrum Smith and the accused participants in the destruction of the *Nauvoo Expositor* surrendered to Constable Bettisworth on the charge of riot. Soon after, the others were released (pending trial) and Joseph and Hyrum were charged with treason for having declared martial law in Nauvoo. For the next few days, Southwick met with the Prophet to convince him to purchase massive lands in the new nation of the Republic of Texas.

The Secret Meeting of the Hancock County Vigilance Committee

The next day, delegates and interested parties gathered from most of the states involved in various internal improvement projects and met at the Hamilton Hotel at Carthage. They were attending the secret meeting of the Hancock County Vigilance Committee of Safety.[396]

Governor Ford had been requested to attend. Also, Robert Smith, captain of the local Carthage Greys, was invited. Dr. Wall Southwick also attended the meeting.

Joseph and Hyrum Smith, John Taylor, and Willard Richards were incarcerated in the nearby Carthage Jail, awaiting trial, unaware of the extent of evil plotted against them. As the secret meeting continued, it was pledged that any volunteers from Missouri or Illinois who participated in the executions of Joseph and Hyrum would not be punished for their crimes.

During these intense discussions, Colonel Markham, oblivious to the treachery being concocted at that precise moment, was coming down the stairs after leaving the Prophet at Carthage Jail. Upon seeing him approach, a posted sentinel inside Hamilton's Inn sounded the alarm to those in the secret council. The meeting dismissed abruptly, with the attendees fleeing in panic, helter-skelter. In the chaos, their discussion minutes were left on the table. Southwick seized the abandoned minutes and, after finding Markham alone, confronted him and offered to share the minutes with him. He warned Markham of what had just transpired.

> The purport of said meeting was to take into consideration the best way to stop Joseph and Hyrum's career, as Joseph's "Views on Government" was widely circulated and took like wild fire. He said that if he did not get into the Presidential chair this election, he would be sure to next, and if Illinois and Missouri would join together to kill them, they would not be brought to justice for it.[397]

Markham did not secure the meeting minutes from Dr. Southwick, but notes were taken by another attendee, George T. M. Davis, who worked for the Whig newspaper in Alton and was one of the main Whig Party activists throughout the state. Davis was there for their paper to feature eyewitness accounts of the events leading up to the murders. He was to take the role of the apologist and defend the actions of the mobs in print form. Davis was also there to represent the interests of his client, the Chouteaus, who were leading other merchants of the St. Louis Chamber of Commerce engaged in commercial enterprises related to the Des Moines Rapids and St. Louis. There was no doubt in Davis' mind that the Smiths deserved execution.[398]

Four years earlier, Davis represented the Chouteaus as their attorney regarding the steamship *Pavilion*, which sailed between Dubuque and Galena to Montrose and Keokuk.[399] After the Reddick heirs won their case against the New York Land Company in September 1843, Davis knew the Chouteaus were anxious to clear the Mormons from the Montrose site and take over the Mormon improvements and the landing site. This was necessary to validate all their legal claims as to physical possession. George T. M. Davis later recorded,

> There existed a secret tribunal in the county of Hancock, known as "The Vigilance Committee of Safety," all of whose members were old citizens of that county of the highest repute. They had determined that one of two results must occur. Either that immediately after the governor had taken up his line of march upon Nauvoo with the State Militia, the two Smiths must be shot by a detail from the Quincy Guards; or that, on the arrival of the State forces at "the City of the Beautiful," it must be laid in ashes, and its men, women, and children left to the disposal of the soldiers. This Committee decided that justice and mercy demanded that the lives of the two Smiths should be the penalty for the transgressions of their own dupes, and the people of Nauvoo should be shielded from bodily harm, and their property saved from infamy or destruction, upon condition that within a given period of time they would leave the State in a body, taking with them all their movable effects.[400]

The corrupt conspiracy was exposed. David Kilbourne, agent for the New York Land Company, was assisting the Law brothers and others associated with the *Nauvoo Expositor* to provoke an incident leading to the arrests of Joseph and Hyrum. George T. M. Davis, as attorney to Pierre Chouteau and others of the St. Louis Junto, was at the Vigilance Committee Meeting, with the backing of various St. Louis merchants, supporting the plan to integrate the Des Moines Rapids, Northern Cross, and the Alton Springfield Railroad projects.

These plans also incorporated the turnpike project of connecting Warsaw, Nauvoo, Carthage, and Quincy to the Rushville Beardstown Road for access to the Illinois River as well as the Illinois and Michigan Canal, of which Valentine Wilson, an anti-Mormon Party leader, was commissioner. Sharp, Aldrich, and others of the anti-Mormon

Party were also at this meeting, formulating their final plans in the plot to murder Joseph Smith.

Previously, the St. Louis and New York Land Company leaders had been enemies. Such was the case in the ongoing lawsuit at Montrose and the competition for key land allocations from the Iowa partition plan. On the Illinois side, the New York Land Company claimed ownership from the Doyle sale of the Teas' land in Nauvoo. Nearby, their' land was the former lands of various White family members, including Hugh White and his brothers-in-law, Isaac Campbell and Isaac Waggoner. Finding a common interest in wanting the Mormons vacated from Nauvoo and the Half-Breed lands, these former enemies joined the other conspirators.

The Martyrdom of Joseph and Hyrum Smith

On June 27, George T. M. Davis and Colonel Enoch March rode with Governor Ford to Nauvoo in the pre-planned expedition that the governor had earlier agreed to support and the Council of Officers—lead by Williams, Aldrich, and Grover—had insisted on. March had served as quartermaster to General Joseph Duncan during the Black Hawk Wars. Soon after, he helped plan and lay out the city of Beardstown and became a major landowner there, anxious for further development. With the opening of the Illinois and Michigan Canal, the link with the Illinois River and the Great Lakes would have generated a major boom for Beardstown. Beardstown was also the crossing point of the road from Springfield to Warsaw. Enoch March was likely welcomed at the Carthage meeting as an original promoter of the Illinois and Michigan Canal in 1832 and as an aggressive enthusiast of the canal for Beardstown and Alton's commercial development plans. While in town, they met Johnathan C. Wright and had a lively discussion as to his impressions of the fate of the Prophet. In a serious and dramatic tone,

> Col. March replied, "Mr. Wright, you are mistaken, and I know it; you do not know what I know; I tell you they will kill Joe Smith before he leaves Carthage, and I know it, and you never will see him alive again." Said I, "Enoch, I do not believe it, he is in the hands of God, and God will deliver him." Says he, "I know better; when you hear of him again,

> you will hear he is dead, and I know it. The people at Carthage wanted permission from the Governor to kill you all and burn up your city, and Ford (the Governor) asked me if I thought it was best to suffer it. I replied, "No, no, for God's sake, Ford, don't suffer it, that will never do, no never. Just see for a moment, Ford, what that would do; it would be the means of murdering thousands of innocent men, women and children, and destroying thousands of dollars' worth of property, and that would never do, it would not be sanctioned, it would disgrace the nation. You have now got the principle men here under your own control, they are all you want, what more do you want? When they are out of the way the thing is settled, and the people will be satisfied, and that is the easiest way you can dispose of it; and Governor Ford concluded upon the whole that was the best policy, and I know it will be done."[401]

The Warsaw militia gathered at the railroad shanties. The ranks were formed into different units under the direct commands of Colonel Levi Williams, Major Mark Aldrich, and Captain William Grover. While there, the governor's order to disband was read. Aldrich and Williams called for volunteers to continue to Carthage in spite of the governor's order. Thomas Sharp spoke of "the necessity of killing the Smiths."[402] Grover was the first to volunteer. About one hundred agreed to continue their march to Carthage lead by Williams, Aldrich, and Grover.

About four miles west of Carthage, a man in a Carthage Grey uniform met the mob and delivered a message, which was read by Aldrich. It indicated this was a good time to murder the Smiths; everything was arranged, and the guards would not resist. Aldrich, Williams, Grover, and Sharp were observed in Carthage at about three o'clock. Two hours later, the mob attacked, and the Carthage Greys made little effort to protect the captives, as was previously arranged.

Joseph's fatal bullet was fired by US Deputy Marshall John C. Elliott, from Hamilton, Ohio.[403] While living in Warsaw under cover as a school teacher, he had participated with Colonel Levi Williams in the Avery kidnapping. Later that night, Captain Grover was reported to have boasted that he had killed Joseph Smith. At the Warsaw House, Eliza Graham heard Thomas Sharp proclaim, "We have finished the leading men of the Mormon Church."[404]

The conspiracy to murder Joseph Smith, presented at the previous meetings of the Hancock County Vigilance Committee, had been executed as instructed by Aldrich, Williams, Grover, and Sharp. The Warsaw and Carthage militia members had performed as directed by the Hancock County leaders and in opposition to orders known to have been issued by the governor. It was expected that the Missouri conspirators representing Jackson County, the Central Clique, and St. Louis Junto would do their part in hiding the murderers and preventing their convictions.

Four persecution groups united in the execution of their joint plot, finalized at the Vigilance Committee meeting at Carthage the night before. George T. M. Davis, previous attorney for the Chouteaus, aided the extension of the war declared by the St. Louis Junto and their merchant alliance against Mormons eight years earlier. Kilbourne, while agent of the New York Land Company, aided the apostate leaders involved in the *Nauvoo Expositor* publication. Colonel Levi Williams, Major Mark Aldrich, and Captains Grover and Davis, with the assistance of Thomas Sharp, lead their militia mob to the jailed prisoners. The concentrated efforts of Samuel Owens from Jackson County had been achieved. Their secrets had been preserved.

Involved in this plot to murder Joseph Smith were nine individuals directly associated with the planned railroads for Hancock County. Seven of these were state approved commissioners for the Des Moines Rapids Railroad or Peoria and Warsaw and Wabash Railroad, including Mark Aldrich, David Matthews, John Montague, William Abernathy, Joel Catlin, Calvin Warren, and Walter Bagby. Thomas Sharp, by marriage to the widow of John Wilcox, took over for his association with the Warsaw Railroad. William Grover was the railroad engineer who had worked on the Warsaw to Carthage railroad line in grading and shanty construction.

Three other individuals approved by the state for main turnpike or state roads were also directly involved in the murder. Colonel Levi Williams was the county road commissioner tasked with oversight as commissioner on the Warsaw to Meredosia road, which would have connected to the only actual railroad line built at the time, from Jacksonville to Meredosia. Valentine Wilson was the commissioner for the

Beardstown to Warsaw turnpike road, and John Atherton was also a road commissioner.

Legislatures had approved Mississippi River ferry rights for Mark Aldrich, David Matthews, Thomas Sharp, and David Kilbourne on the Iowa side. David Matthews was also an approved commissioner for the planned bridge. Most of these were active in anti-Mormon Party leadership and all participated in the Martyrdom.

George T. M. Davis and Enoch March of Alton were anxious that the planned Hancock County improvements would proceed to link to Alton's and Beardstown's railroad plans. They were working with Quincy, Jacksonville, and Springfield promoters to advance the Northern Cross Railroad linkage as well. Governor Duncan and Richard Barrett had been strong supporters of these efforts.[405] Other leaders, including William Richardson, were working on the linkage with Indiana railroads and the National Cumberland Road.

The railroad shanties where the militia rendezvoused represented to Aldrich, Grover, and many others the failed previous attempts to secure the hopes of the commercial development of Warsaw, in particular from the Des Moines Rapids and the previous Warsaw and Peoria and Wabash Railroad plans. Aldrich, and later Jacob C. Davis while in the legislature, had promoted the internal improvements craze, which had put the state in financial crisis. Aldrich had been selected by the general assembly as a commissioner for both the Warsaw and Peoria and Wabash and the Des Moines Rapids Railroads and held state approved ferry rights. Since his days with the American Fur Company and the Chouteaus, he was anxious for his turn to prosper. All they had to show for their efforts were weed-infested graded roads and deserted railroad shanties.

With the Illinois and Michigan Canal construction back in place, it was hoped the railroad and other road projects in Hancock County would again be funded. The canal linkage to the Illinois River was far less effective during the frequent times the water level below Peoria was inadequate for steamboat traffic. The Warsaw and Peoria Railroad was hoped to fill that need. It was likewise perceived as a critical need to proceed with the Des Moines Rapids Railroad in order to avoid the Des Moines Rapids' similar problems for steamboat traffic. That railroad line would provide commerce to transfer to Nauvoo for shipments on the Mississippi northward or to Warsaw for shipments on the Mississippi southward.

If Robert E. Lee's plan were achieved, the main steamboat traffic would be diverted to Keokuk, Nashville, Montrose, and Nauvoo, and away from Warsaw because of the Spanish Chute natural channels. It was believed the Des Moines Rapids Railroad could have placed Warsaw back as a main commercial center.

Previously, the Mormon domination of Nauvoo, and especially their steamboat landings at Nauvoo, Montrose, and Nashville, served as a deterrent to proceed with the railroad. None of these avid supporters wanted to pursue any developments that would further benefit the Mormons.

After the assassinations were confirmed, George T. M. Davis and Enoch Marsh fled to Warsaw "just in time to take the St. Louis steam-packet for our homes."[406] The leadership of the murderous mob escaped to Churchville, Missouri, near Alexandria, where they were afforded concealment and protection aided by Thomas Sharp's ferry run from Warsaw. Sharp could maintain a lookout and provide advanced warning regarding any efforts to secure the perpetrators of the Mormon murders.[407]

Pilcher sent a letter to Augustus Dodge, claiming these Sac and Fox lands south of the Des Moines River were clear of legal entanglements. That communication created a public uproar. The escaping mob leaders were seeking refuge in these same lands. Benton and his allies would also provide a watchful eye in support of the assassins. Pilcher and Benton had an interest in seeing that section of their state developed and along the Des Moines River to Council Bluffs.

The well-planned conspiracy at Carthage had begun.

David Kilbourne was quick to communicate about these recent developments. From Fort Madison, he again wrote the Reverend Dent in Billington, England, on June 29, 1844:

> My dear Sir, I hasten to inform you of the wonderful events which have taken place at Nauvoo since my letter to you a few days since. The work of death has commenced. The Mormon Prophet Joe Smith & his

brother Hyrum are no more. I have just returned from Nauvoo & I this day looked upon the lifeless remains of these two men—the great heads & leaders of Mormonism. Their work of infamy is finished their dupes about two hours since committed their remains to the silent grave. But I will hasten to give you the particulars as full as I am able in a single letter. . . .

On Thursday morning 27 Inst the order for all the troops to march to Nauvoo were (sic) for some cause countermanded. Most of the troops at Carthage some 800 in number were discharged. One company of some 50 men were left at Carthage to protect the prisoners, only eight of this Company were stationed at the Jail as guards while the remainder of the Company were (sic) in Camp a quarter of a mile distant.

The Gov with some 60 horsemen marched to Nauvoo where he made a speech to the Mormons telling them of the excitement that was abroad against them & the dangerous ground on which they stood.

In the absence of the Gov. & about 4 O Clock P.M. of this Thursday 27th day of June, an armed and disguished (sic) band of men, about two hundred in number attacked the Jail—overpowered the guard of eight men, entered the Jail and shot both the Smiths. Hyram received a ball in the head, and mearly (sic) had time to exclaim " I am a dead man," and expired; Joe received a number of balls which pierced his body, some while still in the Jail, some while he was in the act of leaping from the window of the Jail, and others after he reached the ground, he exclaimed " O God"—and expired.

Elder (John) Taylor who was also in the jail received several flesh wounds, is considered dangerous. The disguished (sic) band immediately escaped to the woods & were not pursued for want of force sufficient to take them. They were all disguised (sic) with paint, & of course not known.

There is but one feeling throughout this country in regard to this last tragedy, & that is, that merited vengeance had fallen on the right men, at the same time all regret that it happened while he was a prisoner & had a right to expect protection. It is regretted because his followers will now claim that he died a martyr when if he could have been tried on the charges & convicted he would have died a felon.[408]

Kilboune was well informed as to the particulars of the Prophet's murder as he was part of the coalition of conspirators. Kilbourne decided again to update his British minister friend. Again, from Fort Madison on July 29, 1844, he wrote to Reverend T. Dent:

> My dear Mr. Dent, I wrote you under date 29 ultimo giving you an account of the death of Joe & Hiram Smith. As my brother leaves tomorrow for New York I will improve the opportunity to send a few lines by him, believing that you will feel some solicitude to know what has become of the "Saints."
>
> There have been no further hostilities since I last wrote you. They are perfectly quiet in Nauvoo & in the surrounding country. The Mormons are much more decent in their deportment—not insolent as formerly.
>
> They have been taught a lesson which I think they will not soon forget. They will hereafter be afraid to interfere at all with the rights of the people.
>
> All the Elders abroad have been sent for to return to Nauvoo—also the 12 Apostles—who are I understand to appoint a successor to Joe. They continue to work on the Temple & matters go on there about as usual. There is however great distress there for the want of the necessaries of life. It is also very sickly there this Season.
>
> It is impossible to say what will be the result there—but my opinion is that there will be great trouble among the ambitious leaders & that hereafter the doctrine will not prosper. I think very likely they may open papers purporting to be sealed up by Joe—saying who shall be the Prophet & giving other instructions in regard to their future course.[409]

Because of serious injuries, John Taylor remained in Carthage until well enough to travel home. After a brief respite, Taylor, though emotionally distraught, returned to some of his duties in the *Times and Seasons* printing office. There, in the stock room was their shared publication of "The Voice of Truth," which had been intended to promote the Prophet's national campaign.

George T. M. Davis, as the apologist, published what he deemed an unbiased rendition of the killing of Joseph and Hyrum in his pamphlet entitled, "An Authentic Account of the Massacre of Joseph Smith, the Mormon Prophet, and Hyrum Smith, His Brother: Together with a Brief History of the Rise and Progress of Mormonism and All the Circumstances Which Led to Their Death." This pamphlet was published in St. Louis by A. B. Chambers, who was closely allied with the many merchants and leaders in the St. Louis Chamber of Commerce. Davis was attempting to justify the murders and divert attention from all the conspirators, including associates seeking the benefits of the internal improvements available if they could force the Mormons out.

Davis was in the final meeting of the Hancock Vigilance Committee where the orders to the militias were given for the Prophet's murder. He had accompanied Governor Ford on the prearranged march to Nauvoo to attempt to minimize Mormon retaliation against his comrades. In his preface to the account in which he described the gathering of the Mormons to Jackson County, Missouri, he demonstrated his strong bias:

> About this time, the Prophet, as he asserted, was favored with a revelation from the Almighty, in which the western part of the State of Missouri was designated as the promised land for the chosen people of God, upon which Zion was to be built, and they to await the second advent. Selecting a location upon unentered lands in one of the most fertile and desirable portions of that State, there Joe Smith and his deluded followers took up their abode, and a second time commenced erecting their Zion. . . .
>
> All the circumstances surrounding the expulsion of the Mormons from Missouri, and the reasons offered in justification of their course, has by the Legislature of that State, been long since spread before the public in the shape of a report. . . . It may not, however, be improper to mention that the Prophet was subsequently indicted in that State for the crimes of theft, arson, murder and treason.[410]

As an attorney admitted to the New York Bar and practiced law in Illinois, Davis knew he was lying. He knew the entire legal accounts held by the legislature were based solely on the preliminary trial held by the biased Judge Austin King. No cross examinations of their witnesses, or even the most basic of legal rights, were provided for their defense. There was never a trial, and yet Davis claimed the legislature had all the information and knew "all the circumstances" regarding the Mormon view. Davis knew from his connections that the indictments from Missouri were based on the efforts of Samuel Owens and the Chouteaus, who were trying to lure Joseph Smith back to Missouri under the groundless claims that Joseph ordered the assassination attempt on former Governor Boggs.

Davis concluded with an account of an anti-Mormon meeting held before the murders:

> Subsequently, a mass meeting was convened at Carthage on the 13 of June, 1844, at which the body of the most intelligent, influential, substantial citizens of the county, gave their attendance. At this mass meeting, the preamble and resolutions adopted at the Warsaw meeting, were read and unanimously adopted. From them we select the following, as embracing all that is material to inform the reader of the threats made against the life and property of Sharpe. . . .
>
> And whereas, Hyrum Smith did, in presence of the City Council, and the citizens of Nauvoo, offer a reward for the destruction of the printing press and the materials of the Warsaw Signal—a newspaper also opposed to his interest. . . .
>
> And whereas, Hyrum Smith has, within the last week, publicly threatened the life of one of our valuable citizens. Thos. C. Sharpe, the editor of the *Signal*, therefore, be it solemnly
>
> Resolved, by the citizens of Warsaw, in public meeting assembled, that we view the recent ordinance of the city of Nauvoo, and the proceedings thereunder, as an outrage of an alarming character, revolutionary and tyrannical in its tendency, and, being under color of law, as calculated to subvert and destroy, in the minds of the community, all reliance on law.
>
> Resolved, that as a community, we feel anxious, when possible, to redress our grievances by legal remedies, but the time has now arrived, when the law has ceased to be a protection to our lives and property; a mob at Nauvoo, under a city ordinance, has violated the highest privilege in our government, and to seek redress in the ordinary mode, would be utterly ineffectual.
>
> Resolved, that the public threat made in the Council of the city, not only to destroy our printing press, but to take the life of its editor, is sufficient . . . to command the effort and the services of every good citizen, to put an immediate stop to the career of the mad Prophet and his demoniac coadjutors. We must not only defend ourselves from danger, but we must resolutely carry the war into the enemy's camp. We do therefore declare, that we will sustain our press and the editor, at all hazards—that we will take full vengeance—terrible vengeance,

> should the lives of any of our citizens be lost in the effort—that we hold ourselves, at all times, in readiness to cooperate with our fellow-citizens in this State, Missouri and Iowa, to exterminate, utterly exterminate, the wicked and abominable Mormon leaders, the authors of all our troubles.[411]

Somehow in his twisted logic, Davis attempted to justify the assault of up to 150 armed men against Joseph and Hyrum, locked up in jail awaiting trial, and murdering them in cold blood because they had allegedly threatened Sharp and committed property damage. Davis, when writing this fabled account, knew that Thomas Sharpe lead the mob that killed Joseph and Hyrum, and yet he tried to paint Sharpe as the only real victim and that all others were innocent, just like the Missourians were innocent and victims of the Mormons, which led to the Extermination Order.

George T. M. Davis was himself a part of the corrupt conspiracy in the plot to murder the Prophet, which Joseph Smith warned of in 1843. He with his friend Enoch Marsh could have stopped the murders. They knew in advance what was going to happen and explained as much to Jonathan Wright. They did not interfere or stop the murders because they were supportive of their plans. They had been invited to attend the Carthage meetings because they were known to be supportive, and they had key connections with other influential supporters. They were from distant Alton, far from being affected by day-to-day activities in Hancock County. Davis also put in print that the citizens of Missouri and Iowa were also part of the conspiracy against Joseph Smith and the Mormons.

For Samuel Owens of Independence, Missouri, news of the death of his archenemy, Joseph Smith, was received as he was coping with the news of his own father's recent passing. The patriarch of Lashfield, Nathaniel Owens, died on June 1, 1844. His epitaph read:

> He was a farmer of good education of the times, and a high order of native intellect. He was a man of untiring perseverance and industry . . . was thought by many to be selfish in his disposition. . . . He was a close, economical, money-making man, but punctiliously honest in all his dealings. He dispensed but little, if any, of his property to his children

in his life-time, but they and their descendants received it all after his death.[412]

The estate sale regarding the holdings of Nathaniel Owens occurred that August, which brought Samuel Owens, his sisters, and brothers-in-law together in Kentucky to mourn and help settle estate matters. It was estimated that the Nathaniel Owen's estate totaled some thirty thousand dollars in value, including seventeen slaves valued at more than five thousand.

Senator Benton again sought reelection by the General Assembly in late 1844. The August elections greatly increased Whig seats in the Missouri legislature. Benton's views against Texas annexation were troublesome for many in the General Assembly and Central Clique. But Benton had other problems; his pompous vanity compelled him to buy a new home two years earlier, but his lifestyle had not moderated. Deep in debt, he reached out again to his friend and Junto leader, Pierre Chouteau, and secured another thousand-dollar loan from him and a thousand-dollar loan from his Congressional ally John Miller.[413] He still owed Pierre Chouteau more than five thousand dollars and balances from the failed Bank of Missouri burden he was allocated.

When the thirteenth General Assembly of Missouri met in late November, the Central Clique, still in control of their state powerbase, again came to the aid of Senator Benton. To enhance their chances, the Central Clique leadership divided the state into single member Congressional districts, with a series of resolutions that they wanted statewide. Under pressure to support Benton, he prevailed seventy-one to fifty-seven over a coalition of "Soft Currency" Democrats, Whigs, and Independents. Atchison was selected to complete the term of Lewis Linn.[414]

In August, the *Times and Seasons* called upon Church members for support in expanding the Nauvoo industrialization base, expressing, "Nauvoo must be built up," and it must be "supported by the gathering of those who have capital, who are willing to lay it out for the erection of every branch of industry and manufacture."[415] By late 1844, Church leaders were willing to consider moving forward on the dam project initiated by the Prophet. It soon became apparent that to move the project forward, it had to be advanced other than through the name of Joseph Smith, as his assets were still tied up in legal matters. It was determined to use the entity known as the Nauvoo Agricultural and Manufacturing Association to advance the project, but that too became problematic after the state legislature repealed the Nauvoo Charter and corporations.

Hugh T. Reid brought suit against Joseph Webster on October 1, alleging,

> Hugh T. Reid claims against Joseph Webster a tract of land, with the appurtenances, . . . containing 160 acres, more or less; and thereupon the said Hugh T. Reid says that he has right to the immediate possession of said property, and to the ownership thereof in fee simple, . . . and offers to prove that such is his right.[416]

In a discrete sheriff's sale held by Sheriff Hawkins Taylor on January 1, 1842, Hugh T. Reid purchased the entire 119,000 acres of the Half-Breed Tract for a mere sum of $2,884.66, to cover back property taxes. Reid waited for the right time to test his claim in court and singled out Joseph Webster. He wanted to keep the matter from the Mormons and had waited until after the murders of Joseph and Hyrum. Joseph Smith—as trustee for the Church properties in the Half-Breed Tract purchased by Vinson Knight—Israel Barlow, and others from Isaac Galland in 1839 were part of the lands claimed by Hugh Reid from the sheriff's sale then being tested.

Reid was the Prophet's attorney of record while in jail at Carthage awaiting trial when the mob broke in and murdered Joseph and Hyrum. It would not look well for him if his scheme were discovered. Reid had been the attorney for the New York Land Company, of which David Kilbourne and previously Isaac Galland had been employed. Reid was actively involved in the Half-Breed Tract partition plan. David Kilbourne had acted to promptly rescue the Law brothers and other apostates and remove them from Nauvoo a few days before the Martyrdom.

During the course of the Reid trial, it was determined that Richard F. Barrett, associated with the Warsaw Land Company (with Duncan and Aldrich, who was appointed as one of the commissioners of the Des Moines Rapids Railroad), had also purchased lands from a sheriff sale by Hawkins Taylor. It would take ten months before the judge would rule on this lawsuit.[417]

On December 3, Governor Ford addressed the General Assembly, demanding immediate action on the taxation question of concern by the London lenders. Michael Ryan wrote Ford that the bondholders would not complete the subscription of the $1.6 million until the legislature approved an increased tax mill levy to provide state revenues to make interest payments. The house finance committee proposed to levy a one mill tax, which met with opposition from the legislators serving the south and eastern sections of the state. On March 1, 1845, the legislature passed the levy of one mill on each dollar valuation of property transferred from the county to the state tax. A new canal law was passed by the legislature, updating the various changes. In the canal regions of the state, public meetings passed resolutions praising and thanking Oakley, Ryan, Leavitt, and Governor Ford for their exceptional efforts in advancing the canal project.[418]

The *Joliet Signal* editorialized that the people of northern Illinois would not forget the steady and unfaltering support that Governor Ford had dedicated to the canal project. By May 1845, the European bondholders had formally agreed with the actions of the governor and legislature and ratified the contract for the $1.6 million loan. Construction efforts were accelerated and optimism returned to the various internal improvement commissioners and those who previously had made plans and commitments predicated on the canal construction.

To the Saints in Nauvoo, their focus also was directed to advancing significant improvement projects. The Nauvoo Water Power Company was formed on February 26, 1845, with John E. Page as president. The *Times and Seasons* for March 5 and 12 published progress reports and calls for support from the members and for "wheelbarrows, picks, shovels, and crowbars"—and especially for cash.[419] In an article in the *Nauvoo Neighbor*, the editor noted,

> Here is the proud and gallant Mississippi, with her rapid current, rumbling to the broad Atlantic, seeming to say (as she quickens her pace over the rugged rocks of the lower rapids . . .), only improve my shores and banks, ye saints . . . and I will propel your mills, cottons and woolen manufacturies, by which your laborers can find employ, and your poor can be adorned after the similitude of a palace.[420]

The promotion of the Nauvoo projects intensified the worries of the opposition in the anti-Mormon Party, who had invested a lot of time and finances on their projects and watched as they felt their investments were being further threatened by a rejuvenated adversary. Further plans were being prepared to extend the plot beyond the murders to the forced exodus of all the Mormons from the region.

16: Judge Young, the Trial, and the Aftermath

Various skirmishes and vicious attacks were being perpetrated against the Mormons in the City of Joseph. The anti-Mormons were intent on provoking the Nauvoo Legion to take up arms to give provocation for the state government to disband the state's largest militia. After this failed, the enemies of the Saints sent notices in newspapers in Hancock and surrounding counties, calling for a "wolf hunt," meaning raiding (by mobs riding in the night), burning, and looting Mormon homes.

Governor Ford was becoming concerned that all the violence in Hancock County directed against the Mormons could shed unfavorable attention on that area, just as interest was rising on his pet Illinois and Michigan Canal project. Seeing matters could escalate out of control, Governor Ford called up General Hardin to lead a militia force of five hundred men to restore order in Carthage. The force arrived on October 25, armed with writs for the arrests of the leaders of the mob responsible for the murders of Joseph and Hyrum. Learning such a show of force was on its way, Colonel Williams and fellow Warsaw officers, as well as others in the contingent of the Carthage Greys, sought refuge in Missouri.

Conspiracy at Carthage

At the delegate meeting in Carthage prior to the Martyrdom, the message was clear. No one would be brought to justice for their involvement in the murders. Nearly the entire leadership of Missouri was under the control of the Central Clique. John C. Edwards, a stalwart member of the Clique, was elected governor in 1844. Sterling Price, who had turned on Joseph Smith, was Speaker of the House. Claiborne Fox, another son-in-law of John Sappington, was next in leadership in the House. William B. Napton of the Clique was on the state Supreme Court. Several members of the state legislature served in militia units who attacked the Mormons in the Missouri attacks. So dominant was the Central Clique's control that General Hardin's men were unwilling to execute the writs for arresting the conspirators.

Meanwhile, in Jackson County, Missouri, the commercial focus was again expanding. The town of Independence housed twelve merchandise stores catering to a broader clientele base. Independence had risen from a backwoods frontier town to a major thoroughfare for international commerce and communication. After years of legal entanglements regarding their acquisition of the Gabriel Prudhomme estate lands in 1838, the members of the Kansas Group, with Samuel C. Owens leading, were looking to profit much from the increased trade to the upper Missouri and the Santa Fe regions without fear that the Mormons would return.

The Trial of the Conspirators Who Murdered Joseph Smith

In a crowded and rowdy courtroom, the clerk announced that court was in session and presented Judge Richard M. Young as presiding. Judge Young was known throughout the state of Illinois. On Monday morning, May 19, 1845, the citizens of Carthage and surrounding areas came fully armed to witness the proceedings.

As a Democrat, Young had been elected Senator, representing Illinois, in 1836. He had frequently joined with Senator Benton in voting for legislation favoring western state issues. Also, he was assigned a critical task to secure loans from British financiers to build the Illinois and Michigan Canal. Illinois lost more than five hundred thousand dollars because of mismanagement on his assignment. Governor Carlin had tried to cancel the negotiations of Senator Young with the London lenders after he had committed the state to a discount of ninety-one points per hundred of bonds.

After losing support for a second Senate term, he withdrew and was appointed to the state Supreme Court. As a consequence, former Senator Young was presiding at the hearing against the murderers of Joseph and Hyrum Smith. Driven by ego, Judge Young was contemplating a run for the Illinois governorship soon and needed all the support he could muster from his colleagues. He also wanted to cover his former political missteps and his ties to Samuel Owens.

The clerk officially announced the case on the docket for that day as the people versus Levi Williams. To many of the Mormons back in Nauvoo, the trial was a sham. Hundreds had been involved in leadership roles in the murders. Why were only five faced with charges?

Across the river in Iowa, Judge Charles Mason had ruled on the case of Hugh T. Reid versus Joseph Webster a week earlier. The jury verdict was for the plaintiff, Hugh Reid.[421] Fortunately for Reid and the New York Land Company, the results of that trial were overshadowed by the commotion of the trial for the five defendants for the murders of Joseph and Hyrum. Reid's secretive purchase of the entire Half-Breed Tract, which directly involved many of the Mormons, was again successfully concealed. Hugh T. Reid had been the defense attorney for Joseph Smith while he was incarcerated at the Carthage Jail.

On trial for the murders of Joseph and Hyrum Smith were five defendants:

- Colonel Levi Williams—commanding officer of the Illinois 59th Regiment, farmer, cooper, and Baptist minister from Green Plains near Warsaw. Williams lead the mob that forcibly kidnapped Daniel Avery and his son in December. He had been appointed Hancock County Commissioner over Highways and was mentioned as having charge over specific roads in the county linking Rushville and Beardstown lanes to the Illinois River and Illinois and Michigan Canal.
- Major Mark Aldrich served as leader of the "Warsaw Independent Battalion," consisting of the Warsaw cadets and the Warsaw militia company under the command of Colonel Williams. Aldrich had served two terms as a Whig representative in the Illinois legislature from 1836 to 1840 and actively promoted internal improvements legislation while there. Aldrich, a land speculator, formed the Warsaw Land Company with Governor

Duncan. Earlier, he was awarded valuable ferry rights across the Mississippi. He had been appointed as a commissioner for the Warsaw and Peoria and Wabash Railroad and the Des Moines Rapids Railroad. Aldrich had been a former employee of the American Fur Company under tutelage from Russell Farnham, who had been part of the famed Astoria Expedition and who was a close friend to Senator Benton. Pierre Chouteau, years earlier, secured control of the head and foot of the Des Moines Rapids commercial traffic with Farnham at Keokuk, Aldrich at Fort Edwards (Warsaw), and Thomas Reddick, at Montrose. Across from Montrose, Captain James White with his sons and Isaac Campbell, a son-in-law, engaged in the lead traffic from Galena and Dubuque.

- William N. Grover was militia captain over the Warsaw cadets with forty-two men. He was an attorney and served as Justice of the Peace for Warsaw in 1843. He was a supervisor and engineer for the railroad projects in Hancock County and built the railroad shanties near Carthage. He boasted as being the one who shot Joseph Smith.
- Jacob Cunningham Davis, a militia captain over the Warsaw Rifle Company and a staunch Democrat, was serving as state Senator at the time he was indicted. He also served as a circuit court clerk. Whig conspirators needed a voice of support within the Democratic Party.
- Thomas Coke Sharp, editor of the anti-Mormon newspaper *The Warsaw Signal*, had recently gained a financial windfall in his marriage to the widow of John Wilcox, an original member with Aldrich of the Warsaw Land group. He was a commissioner for the Warsaw railroad and a holder of ferry rights from Warsaw to Alexandria, Missouri. The ferry operations were successful.

For the proceedings, it was important to Judge Richard Young that his agenda while Senator on the Committee on Roads and Bridges and his frequent involvement with the Illinois and Michigan Canal and the National Cumberland Road efforts not be publicized. As Senator, he secured the reports of Robert E. Lee and solicited federal funding for the Des Moines Rapids improvement project.

The Mormons had gotten in the way of the several commissioners engaged in their internal improvement projects planned to make Warsaw and Nauvoo major commercial centers. Initially, Young had been a great ally to the Mormons in 1839, by assisting them in purchasing the steamboat used in improving the Des Moines Rapids from Robert E. Lee. He helped push the Missouri redress petitions before Congress for Joseph Smith and the victimized Mormons.

During the trial, Judge Young also had to be scrupulous in keeping his family relationships a secret, as cousin to the wife of Samuel C. Owens, an enemy of the Mormons from Missouri, and cousin to the wife of Governor Reynolds, who committed suicide after being brought in to the extradition attempts of Missouri mob leaders. Young also wanted to avoid attention being focused on Governor Reynolds's Central Clique leadership involvement.

There were six defense attorneys: William A. Richardson, Orville H. Browning, Archibald Williams, Onias Skinner, Thomas Morrison, and Calvin A. Warren.[422]

William A. Richardson had helped get the Nauvoo Charter passed through the legislature. Three months before this trial, Richardson, as Speaker of the House, helped submit to the US Twenty-Eighth Congress the state resolution, calling for the Illinois Congressional delegation to "use their best exertions to procure a grant of land from the contiguous land districts, to improve the navigation of the Great Wabash river, so far as the same forms the boundary between this State and the State of Indiana."[423] Richardson was active in support of this key project to improve access to the Erie and Wabash Canal project, linking Lake Erie to the Wabash River and aiding Illinois and Indiana.

Richardson was from Rushville, the key connection site on the roads from Nauvoo, Warsaw, Carthage, and Quincy to connect at Beardstown on the Illinois River, and then Springfield. The Rushville and Beardstown Road was to be the key access point with the completed Illinois and Michigan Canal and the Illinois River for the merchants and farmers in Hancock and Adams Counties. The anti-Mormon Party leader Valentine Wilson had earlier been charged to oversee the Rushville turnpike project, with the hopes that the routes would convert to railroad lines.

Orville H. Browning was one of the very first to sign the Hancock County memorial petition with Richard M. Young, to request Congress to fund the improvement of the Des Moines Rapids. Browning was also involved in the Iowa Half-Breed Tract partition agreement initiative. Browning had previously served as Joseph Smith's attorney but was at this trial to defend those who had murdered the Prophet. Browning also sought to protect the Whig Party.

Previously, Richardson and Browning, while in the state Senate, were given oversight and appointed to investigate the conduct of various state internal improvement project commissioners for fraud and mismanagement. They were knowledgeable of the Illinois and Michigan Canal project, the Des Moines Rapids Railroad, and Warsaw and Peoria and Wabash Railroad. They knew the various commissioners well, including the ten members associated with these various internal improvement projects who were active participants in the Hancock County Vigilance Committee for Safety and the associated anti-Mormon Party. Browning was assisted as defense council by Archibald Williams, a cousin of the defendant, Colonel Levi Williams.[424]

Onias Skinner had been active in Hancock County's anti- Mormon Party and attended the meetings when the murder and extermination plans were being discussed. He, with Walter Bagby, was on assignment from the Vigilance Committee to meet with Governor Ford, update him on the meeting, and request the militia call out request, which Ford refused. Skinner was chosen to make the request to the governor because of a previous relationship as Ford's aide de camp during the hostilities.[425] He had also been appointed Joseph Smith prosecutor for treason.

Orville Browning, Senator Young, Archibald Williams, and Onias Skinner were all from Quincy, the key western terminus site for the Northern Cross Railroad on the Mississippi to connect at Lafayette, Indiana, to the east.

Thomas Morrison was added to the defense counsel team and was also an active member in the anti-Mormon party, serving on the Vigilance Committee in the central corresponding group. He was subpoenaed as a witness as he was highly suspected of having incriminating knowledge, but he was never called to testify. He married a sister of James Wells, a former partner with Aldrich involved with Warsaw land sales. Morrison was from Carthage.

Calvin A. Warren was a partner with Aldrich in Warsaw land speculation. They helped in each other's bankruptcy proceedings. They sought to sell lands on various occasions to the Mormons while partnered with Governor Duncan. Warren was a brother-in-law to the former president of the Illinois and Michigan Canal, Isaac N. Morris. He wanted to expand steamship operations from Cincinnati, Ohio. Joseph Smith had, "in the name of the lord," given Warren the "prophecy of Warsaw" on December 30, 1841: to withdraw from his partners and join him in developing Warsaw. Joseph told him the town of Warsaw would not prosper without the support of the Mormons.

The prosecuting attorney was Josiah Lamborn. He had been state attorney general from 1840 to 1843, while a good majority of the internal improvement funding issues were being promoted. He was aware of the controversies between the Whigs and Democrats and the funding problems associated with these highly volatile projects. Earlier, Lamborn was an outspoken advocate for the Northern Cross Railroad and knew the background of Judge Young in his mishandling of the Illinois and Michigan Canal loans. He was also aware of the fine line he was walking to not implicate the key players and improvement project commissioners.

After normal courtroom formalities, Defense Attorney Richardson asked Judge Young to discharge all the jurors for the case, legally chosen by the duly elected county commissioners. He asked the judge to disqualify the county commissioners and sheriff from their statutory duties in selection of jury panels and had the judge appoint successors to call a new jury panel after submitting defendants' affidavits that the commissioners and sheriff were biased against them.

Surprised, Lamborn replied that Illinois statutes contained no provision for quashing entire juries, and there were no laws authorizing a judge to disavow the efforts of legally elected county commissioners and sheriff from their duties. Lamborn charged if there were claims of prejudice against the elected officials, they should be addressed in a separate setting, where evidence could be presented rather than to just accept the word of the defendants. Lamborn then challenged the defense to provide a single precedent "in all the experience in this state or any other, in criminal cases." Browning voiced, "There had not been a precedent, in the United States, for such a proceeding." He added, "There had never been a case like this in the United States."[426]

To these initial unorthodox requests, Judge Young ruled, "I believe it is my duty to quash the array, and to appoint persons as elisors, to select another jury."[427] Young then responded to the jurors, "There was no charge against them, but the charge was predicated against the officers of the county only."[428] However, the officers of the county had acted according to law.

Judge Young then had two elisors selected from the masses of those attending the court proceedings, knowing that only non-Mormons were there. Mormons had stayed in Nauvoo, knowing their lives would be at risk in Carthage. One of the elisors chosen by Young was William Abernathy, a Warsaw and Peoria and Wabash Railroad commissioner and an active anti-Mormon Party loyalist. The other elisor appointed was Thomas H. Owen, a contractor on the Carthage to Beardstown state road. Both were expected to select jurors who already knew the background of the internal improvement projects and the impediments the Mormon landowners exhibited. It was important jurors understood the background of the issues without them brought in open court.

The fix was on. Browning hoped to steer proceedings away from the Springfield Junto. Charles, brother to Milton Hay, was an active participant with the mob and was closely linked to several Junto members. He was the brother-in-law of the defendant William Grover. Hay had been employed in the law firm of Stuart and Lincoln, and then joined as partner with E. D. Baker, a member of Ford's expedition that persuaded the defendants to surrender. Baker held more sway over the militia in pursuit of the assailants than the governor.

Richardson, a leading Democrat, was careful to avoid attention to the defendant Jacob C. Davis, also a prominent Democrat serving in the legislature. Richardson likewise did not want matters brought up that could draw attention to Judge Young's activities while as the Democrat Senator from Illinois and chairman on the national Senate Committee on Roads and Canals. These defendants were heavily involved in the internal improvement projects and some feared evidence could draw unwanted attention and scrutiny.

Governor Ford, by his own admission, was a puppet to the Party leadership[429] and had not been honest in disclosing his real actions or intentions. Ford had been the leading advocate for pushing completion of the Illinois and Michigan Canal. He attended the Hancock Vigilance Committee meeting just before the murders and worked with Williams, Aldrich, and Grover as they directed the Council of Officers. Though subpoenaed, Ford's testimony was never given.

As the proceedings continued, Lamborn called George Walker and John Peyton of the Warsaw militia as witnesses to establish critical testimony as to the conspiracy to murder the Mormon leaders. He established that after Joseph and Hyrum had been jailed, Ford ordered the Warsaw militia disband. At "the railroad shanties," about six miles from Warsaw, Colonel Williams disbanded the militia. Next, Williams and Major Aldrich vigorously sought to encourage militia members to accompany them to Carthage Jail. It was testified that Aldrich "spoke of the grievances of the people, and that the Mormons had the power themselves and they must do something to stop it."[430]

These witnesses claimed Sharp also made a speech to encourage the militia's support. After their pleadings, more than a hundred militia men joined officers, Williams, Aldrich, and Grover on a march to execute orders by the Hancock County Vigilance Committee, countermanding the orders of Ford. Captain Davis chose to return home.

Lamborn then skillfully probed deeper as he questioned Walker as to why Captain Davis did not join his compatriots. Much to the dismay of many, Walker testified Davis commented at the time: "He would be damned if he would go to kill a man that was confined in prison."[431]

Feeding on that momentum, he called Frank Worrell, a lieutenant of the Carthage Greys who had been ordered to defend the jail, to take the stand. Again, Lamborn skillfully got the witness to admit critical testimony. Worrell testified, "They came up on front of the jail, and when they had got formed there, they made a rush for the door." Worrell explained that the mob had pushed him and the other guards away and stated, "There was a great crowd, as thick as in this courtroom, Their pieces were going off all the time and [there was] so much noise and smoke that I could not see or hear anything what was said or done."[432]

In a surprise move at this critical juncture, Lamborn changed the questioning. Instead of getting definitive details about the actions of the Carthage Greys from Worrell, who was primed and "talking," Lamborn sacrificed his own momentum and avoided implicating the conduct of the Carthage Greys and their leaders. It had been widely supposed that the Carthage Greys and the Warsaw militia had been in collusion in the murders.[433] Meetings of the Vigilance Committee of Safety had ordered that conduct. Onias Skinner and Morrison on the defense team likely attended the secret meeting at Hamilton's Inn with Ford and the Carthage Grey's Captain Robert Smith, which had been broken up upon the arrival of Colonel Markham. Lamborn, the previous attorney general, was greatly concerned about his future in politics. He was inclined to guard against disclosures that could harm foes and allies.

The conspiracy against the Mormons at Carthage could have been admitted to by Worrell. By responding to orders to assume formation before breaching the jail, as Worrell testified, mob members were conducting their jail raid according to military protocol, as befitting a trained militia. Lamborn had the opportunity handed him to extend the reach to leaders who masterminded and directed the conspiracy; instead, he capitulated.

Before the trial, Lamborn had subpoenaed Ford and Captain Robert Smith, leader of the Carthage Greys, to testify. Both had participated in the secret meeting conducted at Hamilton's Inn, which included delegates and Dr. Southwick.[434] Collusion between the Carthage Greys and Warsaw militia should have been noted. Captain Smith earlier posted bond with a few others to release Colonel Williams from custody.[435] In another surprise move, Lamborn declined to call Governor Ford or Captain Smith to testify. Had he been willing, Lamborn, a Democrat, should have pursued the ringleaders, which could have implicated higher authorities of both parties.

Lamborn knew that Governor Ford had ordered the Warsaw militia to disband. Yet they continued to act as a militia body in defiance of the governor's direct orders. Lamborn also knew that Ford distrusted the Carthage Greys after they had showed mob sympathies and openly threatened harm to the Mormon leaders in his presence. Why didn't Lamborn call Ford to ask why he ordered the Carthage Greys to defend the prisoners knowing they couldn't be trusted?

Knowing of the complicity in the murders of the two militia groups, why hadn't Lamborn subpoenaed General Hardin, commanding officer over both militia bodies at the time. Hardin was the step nephew of Henry Clay, the Whig candidate for president, and a member of Henry

Clay's "secret committee."[436] Joseph Smith's stand against "Democrats, Whiggery and Cliquery" had been widely circulated in local newspapers. Joseph Smith, during his campaign for the presidency, was known to have voiced public condemnation against Henry Clay and the Loco Foco Democrat national and state leaders. Lamborn was unwilling to expose the national and state party machines and associated clique groups in open court at the sacrifice of justice.

The oppressed Mormons and their leaders felt dejected because of the obvious lack of justice against the murderers of the Prophet. Originally, writs had been called for against William Law and the Fosters, who were behind the publication of the *Nauvoo Expositor* that was at the heart of the events leading to the arrests of Joseph Smith and others. They were never charged, but Lamborn should have pursued them at least as witnesses. They could have revealed that the press and equipment used to print the *Nauvoo Expositor* had been provided by the Whig leader Jonas. In addition, writs had been initially intended against Captain Robert Smith and the other guards of the Carthage Greys.[437] These writs were likewise never pursued.

Calvin A. Warren, Onias Skinner, and Orville Browning gave closing arguments. They knew their clients were guilty and had acted under the orders of many of Hancock's leading citizens. They knew many others were likewise guilty of the murders. They had been involved themselves to varying degrees. The travesty of justice played on.

In the end, the makeshift jury acquitted all five defendants. An observer named John Hay later remarked, "There was not a man on the jury, in the court, [or] in the county, that did not know the defendants had done the murder. But it was not proven, and the verdict of not guilty was right in law."[438] His father, Charles Hay, had been involved as well, but he was never prosecuted. The local conspirators had been set free, as secretly promised at Hamilton's Inn. The identities of the local and national ringleaders and their close involvement was sheltered from national attention. The blood of Joseph and Hyrum had not been redeemed nor their murders vindicated.

The less-than-honorable Judge Richard Young, overseeing the trial of the conspirators, had succumbed to the multiple political pressures of the Democrats and Whigs. By his dismissing the legitimate jurors and replacing them with prejudiced trial attendees, the release of the guilty defendants was virtually guaranteed.

The Anti-Mormon Leaders Push for a Mormon Exodus from the State

Due to intense persecutions and a strict focus on completing the temple, the dam project had to be forsaken. Lots held for the purpose of the dam and use of the Nauvoo Water Power Company were made available for sale in mid July.

On the anniversary of the Martyrdom in 1845, the capstone had been secured on the temple, and workers were finishing up the roof and tower. During October, in Warsaw, just south of Nauvoo, Mark Aldrich was intent on keeping quiet news that William Thomas, the court-appointed administrator for the estate of the deceased Joseph Duncan, was the new president of the Warsaw Land Company.

After the trial, the anti-Mormons were waiting for some Mormon event they could spin to sanction driving them from the state.[439] The various canal and railroad projects were moving forward, and their commissioners were anxious to be rid of the Mormons so they could advance their plans. Kilbourne and the New York Land Company leaders needed to test their legal claims to the Half-Breed Tract by making their previous actions public but would invite the new Mormon leadership to contest the fraudulent agreement. They needed the Mormons gone.

Brigham Young, though not yet formally recognized as the leader of the Church, convened a gathering of the Council of Fifty. On September 9, this group called for a preliminary party of fifteen hundred men to go to the area of the Great Salt Lake Valley "to gather information relative to emigration, and report the same to the council."[440] Two days later, the Twelve met and selected members of the council to start westward the next spring. In prayer, they sought "that the Lord would give us wisdom to manage affairs with the mob so as to keep them off till we can accomplish what he requires at our hands in completing the Temple and Nauvoo House, also for wisdom to manage affairs in regard to the western migration."[441]

With General Hardin and Stephen Douglas sent by the governor, these two officials were notified of Mormon plans to evacuate to the Oregon Territory and offered their enthusiastic support of such a plan. They were not aware that, privately, the leadership was intending the

Great Salt Lake area as their new Zion. Hardin and Douglas established commissioners from surrounding areas to assist in policing against anti-Mormon violence as long as the Mormons were acting in good faith in preparing to leave to the West.

Of great frustration to the peace loving and law-abiding Saints was that the nation they loved showed no interest in affording them their Constitutional rights. That state leaders, using the state militia. could force the exodus of law-abiding citizens from their lands, which was difficult to accept. These same leaders, who had warranted the safety of their Prophet while incarcerated, further violated their most basic rights to life, liberty, and the pursuit of happiness.

By September 15, residents had reported that forty-five homes had been destroyed by arsonists. Theft, shooting attempts, and other types of mayhem continued against the Mormons, hoping again to provoke them to react in force. The "honey comb" scheme was maturing. The Mormons, unable to legally call out the Nauvoo Legion—though not formally disbanded—established a quasi-youth police force known as the "Whistling and Whittling Brigade" to draw attention to antagonistic travelers through their city. Also, in an attempt to restore order, Sheriff Backenstos organized small posses to patrol the area. When General Hardin arrived in Nauvoo in September, he ordered them to immediately disband. It was ordered that no Mormon or anti-Mormon groups could organize with more than four members.[442]

A nine county commission cooperated with the Hancock County anti-Mormons in September and October 1845. Isaac N. Morris—a railroad commissioner, Secretary of State nominee, and former president of the Illinois and Michigan Canal—joined the group calling for the prompt withdrawal of the Mormons.[443] They were in negotiations with Brigham Young to coordinate their exodus plans. Both the Illinois and Michigan and the Wabash and Erie Canal projects were progressing. The various railroad and other commissioners were anxious to get the Mormons to vacate so they could take over their ferry and steamboat operations.

On the Iowa side of the Mississippi, Mormon persecutors were also being organized and indoctrinated in the fall of 1845. The "Lee County anti-Mormon Meeting" was promoted and posted in Lee County. The meeting was conducted on the evening of Thursday, October 16, at the

Fort Madison Court House. Minutes were kept. A preamble was unanimously adopted:

> Whereas the late difficulties between the old settlers in Illinois and the Mormons, and the numerous offences committed in this county by persons professing to belong to the "Church of the Latter Day Saints" has caused great excitement among our citizens, and whereas it is firmly believed that the Mormons and others who do not belong to their peculiar faith cannot reside together in peace, and whereas for the purpose of preventing further violence it is thought advisable that the Mormons and the citizens of Lee County should no longer remain together, therefore,
>
> Resolved, that it is the opinion of this meeting that the public welfare requires that the Mormons should depart from this county at as early a day as practicable. . . .
>
> Resolved, that this meeting deprecates all acts of violence, but stamps with contempt the conduct of those sympathizing individuals who prate about the "cruelties of anti-Mormonism."
>
> Resolved, that two anti-Mormon candidates to represent Lee county in the next legislature be nominated by this meeting, whose election may fully ascertain and express public sentiment on the subject of the Mormons leaving this county.

In the evening, the meeting was addressed by Hugh Reid, Edward Johnstone, and Hawkins Taylor. On motion of Ed. Johnstone Esq., it was unanimously:

> Resolved, that the members of this meeting hereby pledge themselves to use all honorable means to secure the election of the candidates nominated this evening.
>
> Resolved, that the proceedings of this meeting be published in the newspapers at Burlington, and the *Warsaw Signal.*

An address was drafted and published:

> A very large and respectable meeting of citizens, favorable to the departure of the Mormons from Lee county, was held at the Court House in Fort Madison on Thursday evening the 16th inst. Two anti-Mormon candidates for the legislature were nominated at that time, and the undersigned were appointed a committee to address you in furtherance of the objects of said meeting.[444]

On December 16, 1845, Kilbourne again penned a letter to his British minister friend, Reverend Dent, but this time to Grindleton, Clitheroe, England:

> Respected Friend. . . . There have been exciting times at Nauvoo for six months past. Several dens of Mormon thieves [and] murders have been broken up. . . .
>
> These things so excited and exasperated the people in all this region of Country that publick (sic) meeting were held during the summer & resolutions passed giving the Mormons formal notice that they must leave Nauvoo. All those [Mormons] living out were compelled to flee to the city—such was the indignation of the old citizens. Under this state of things the Mormons made up their minds that they could not remain here. They accordingly decided to leave the country & they are now getting ready to leave for California in Mexico on the 1st of April next. . . . The head men are also negotiating a sale of their Temple & other public buildings together with the town site. I believe they have had some offers from the Catholics.
>
> [Sidney] Rigdon left them more than a year ago & settled in Pittsburgh Pennsylvania & is publishing a paper there. He denounced all the present leaders at Nauvoo—says that Joe Smith was a fallen Prophet—that he Rigdon is now the true & only Prophet of the church. Brigham Young one of the twelve is the leader. He exercises as absolute power over them as ever Joe did—he equals him in depravity & all evil practices. He pretends to have revelations. . . . I made the Mormons an offer for their temple & other buildings—having a large flock of sheep—I thought I could use their homes for sheep pens & the Temple to shear the sheep in, by which means the original design of the building would be carried out viz Fleecing the Flock.[445]

A month later, David Kilbourne was disappointed to learn that the trustees of the New York Land Company had lost their appeal in the Iowa Supreme Court. Edward Brooks and the other Thomas Reddick heirs had secured another legal victory, based on the court's ruling of January 26, 1846.[446] This lawsuit had started as a suit by the Reddick heirs against David Kilbourne. Further suits were expected earlier against Brigham Young, John Taylor, and other Mormons who had occupied the old Fort Des Moines barracks early in 1839. The attorneys for the New York Land Company had persuaded the court to change the defendant David Kilbourne to Samuel Marsh, William E.

Lee, and Edward C. Delavan—trustees for the New York Land Company. They were also able to get the parties to agree that they represented all residents of the Montrose square mile as their landlord. Their case would be binding on all residents, including the previous listed Mormons. The defense attorneys were also successful in changing the original court venue far away from earshot of the expanding Mormon community.

The matter involved the 640 acres near the shore line of Montrose, including the lands of the Mormon-controlled steamship and ferry landing across from Nauvoo. The court ruled the Spanish land claim given to Honore Tesson and to Thomas Reddick was made secure by the US land patent issued to Thomas F. Reddick in 1839. This patent was deemed a confirmed claim by Thomas H. Blake, commissioner of the General Land Office on May 1, 1844.

Thomas Benton had in his early legal practice assisted the Chouteaus and their friends in filing various Spanish land grant claims. Many of these were subsequently rejected. In this ruling, however, the Spanish land grant claim was upheld. Thomas Reddick had worked with Benton and Chouteau as the president of the Bank of Missouri in 1820. Reddick was also a close friend with Benton's friend and advisor Joshua Pilcher. The ruling by the Iowa court against the New York Land Company provided the Reddick heirs and their Chouteau, Benton, and Pilcher allies dominance of the steamboat landing at Montrose, but they had to get the Mormons to vacate. The Chouteaus had known Mark Aldrich since 1832, when he worked for them under the supervision of Russell Farnham at Fort Edwards.

With the Illinois and Michigan Canal construction proceeding well, there were expectations by some that the Des Moines Rapids Railroad, the Northern Cross Railroad, and the Alton Springfield Railroad projects could continue. These projects would need the steamship landings at the head and foot of the Des Moines Rapids secured. Aldrich and his friends and allies held possession of the Warsaw landing areas, and the Reddick heirs were expected to secure the Montrose Landing site based on the Iowa Supreme Court ruling. By forcing the Mormons out, they could secure Montrose and the Nauvoo steamboat landing sites, which were still critical to their commercial plans to dominate commerce on the upper Mississippi River. They also needed to keep their previous fraudulent conduct against the Mormons secret.

The various leaders of the Warsaw, New York, and St. Louis Land Companies were anticipating that the sheer news of the progress of the massive improvement projects would escalate land prices so that they could finally unload their land inventories they had purchased before the 1837 financial crash. Many had suffered bankruptcy or were still fighting it. Annual taxes on their large land holdings were oppressive, and they had to sell their lands to pay off stifling debt. If the Mormons were gone, they expected the lands would be easily sold.

The Nauvoo Temple was dedicated, with sessions conducted constantly. Over five thousand Saints received their endowments, and six hundred received their second anointings before they left.

Kilbourne Finally Posts Notice in Iowa

Finally finding it safe to proceed in making public the land claims of the New York Land Company—and his direct relationship to that organization—David Kilbourne posted a handbill on May 16, 1846. He no longer feared reprisals from the Mormons, whom they had deceived as to the real mortgage holders of the lands they had occupied in Montrose, Zarahemla, Nashville, Keokuk, and other parts of the Half-Breed Tract. It read in part:

> Whereas we are the owners in fee simple, of about 800 Lots, in the town of Keokuk, and about 50,000 acres of land in the Half Breed Sac and Fox Reservation, in Lee County, Iowa Territory; and having the legal and equitable possessory right to a large number of said lots—having purchased the improvements on the same, previous to the decree of partition of said lands (wherein Josiah Spalding and others were plaintiffs, and Euphrasine Antay, defendant), at great cost. We hereby give notice to all persons who have "Squatted"... and hold the possession in opposition to our title and rights, that we will claim rents from the date of said partition, and we warn all persons against cutting timber, enclosing or erecting Buildings on any of said lots or lands; as no improvements made subsequent to this notice, on any of our lots or lands, will be regarded.
>
> We offer to sell part of our lots, at prices we consider reasonable. Together with thirty or forty thousand acres of the above Farming lands, situated in different parts of the reservation, in lots and parcels to suit purchasers. Marsh, Lee & Delavan, Trustees. By D. W. Kilbourne, their Attorney in fact.[447]

With that statement, their share of the corrupt conspiracy was presented in full view. They were claiming the lands and improvements of all the Mormons who had purchased lots though Isaac Galland in 1839 and afterward and offered them for sale again. This included the lands purchased by Vinson Knight, Israel Barlow, Joseph Smith, and others. The land company's ownership claims were based on the plan initiated by Francis Scott Key, their attorney, who proposed the "decree of partition" plan during his visit in May 1841. Leaders of the company had lied to Francis Scott Key regarding the validity of the claims from Isaac Galland purchased before the partnership agreement. They also failed to disclose to Key that Galland had publicly announced his withdrawal from the partnership. Key warned they had to post their claims publicly. Because of their fears of Mormons, they waited until five years later.

Earlier, Kilbourne had been anxious to embarrass Mormon leaders by exposing to the public that they held no defensible legal standing in Iowa lands. Kilbourne wrote anonymously a letter to the *New York Journal of Commerce Magazine*, which was published June 19, 1841, as a formal challenge to the Mormons that they were occupying lands on the Half-Breed Tract in the Iowa Territory without valid title. He wrote two other articles published in a Burlington paper regarding their lack of valid title. Perhaps under persuasion from his employer, he let the matter drop until the Mormons could not retaliate. Their scheme under the decree of partition plan had been to discretely take the lands back from them and not to have to pay for their improvements.

With the Mormons vacating the lands and being in no position to continue to make mortgage payments, the lands and improvements were reclaimed by the New York and St. Louis Land Companies without opposition. Ownership of these lands was further supported by the legal suit of Hugh T. Reid, still pending in the Supreme Court.

With the publishing of this notice, the honeycomb effect, referred to by Isaac Galland in 1839 after he sold nearly twenty thousand acres to the Mormons, was being concluded through the patient, earnest efforts of Kilbourne, the partners of the New York Land Company, the members of the St. Louis Land Company and their merchant associates, Aldrich and his land company and railroad commissioner allies, and their many other supporters. Kilbourne had actively participated in aiding Wilson Law and other Mormon apostates involved in the printing of the *Nauvoo Expositor* and arranging their immediate departure from Nauvoo after the press was destroyed. The members of the coalition of conspirators were becoming more and more confident.

The many Mormon victims had been forced to leave with the Saints westward and were thus unaware of the schemes and treachery mounted against them during the previous years.

At Carthage, a group gathered during June 1846 to plan for upcoming Independence Day festivities. At the meeting, Thomas Sharp and his fellow conspirator Levi Williams determined that Hancock County could not celebrate Independence Day as long as Mormons still lived in the county. Another mob army of several hundred, under the direction of Sharp, rode toward Nauvoo to demand the immediate surrender and evacuation from the city.

Upon hearing the news of an invading party, Colonel Markham and Sheriff Backenstoss organized a resistance force to counter their illegal conduct. Sharp's forces aggressively escalated the conflict by capturing, whipping, and holding hostage several Mormons. Governor Ford was notified and, after learning that Sharp and the Hancock anti-Mormons had again defied his orders, made a token effort to respond with diplomacy by requesting two citizens from Quincy to arbitrate. Hostilities continued. Mormon defenders were lead by Daniel H. Wells, a long-time Mormon friend. After a few Mormons were killed, Wells queried the defenders,

> What interests have the Saints to expect from its defense? Our interests are not identified with it, but in getting away from it. Who would urge the propriety of exposing life to defend a place for the purpose of vacating it?[448]

Losing life to defend the near vacant city seemed a foolish quest. The defenders surrendered. Soon after, the few remaining faithful Saints left the near deserted City of Joseph. The honeycomb scheme, identified by Isaac Galland in July 1839, had succeeded in Iowa and Hancock County, Illinois. The corrupt conspiracy against the Mormons had concluded.

The Warsaw and Peoria and Wabash and the Des Moines Rapids Railroads were never completed as planned. The former defendant William Grover made several unsuccessful attempts in 1847, 1849, and later to get the Nauvoo Railroad built. In 1849, the former elisor Thomas

H. Owen was granted ferry rights from Nauvoo across the Mississippi River. William Roosevelt, also an active anti-Mormon Party member, with Grover became active in railroad management.

In 1845, George T. M. Davis provided early support for the Alton Springfield Railroad. The attempts to rejuvenate the Northern Cross Railroad were commenced and continued the next four years. Calvin Warren and Isaac N. Morris purchased the land originally intended for the Northern Cross Railroad. Calvin Warren, Isaac N. Morris, and Onias Skinner were among the reconstituted Northern Cross Railroad's first thirteen incorporators. Orville Browning and Abraham Jonas later joined them and actively promoted railroad efforts.

Charles Mason, judge in the corrupt Half-Breed partition settlement, became president of the Peoria and Oquawka Railroad. Hugh T. Reid, also involved in the Half-Breed partition, and former attorney for Joseph Smith helped to develop the Keokuk and Missouri railroad.[449] Though temporarily prosperous and active in railroad projects in Iowa, David Kilbourne eventually became mayor of Keokuk. Later, however, Keokuk was devastated commercially after overinvesting in railroad projects. Without links at Warsaw or Nauvoo, they had no access to Eastern cities and could not compete with others with eastern states access. The prophetic utterances of Joseph Smith to Calvin A. Warren regarding the future of Warsaw, should he not heed the instructions, came to pass. It was not built up, as was planned by Mark Aldrich and Warren's other associates. Judge Richard M. Young was later appointed as the commissioner of the US General Land Office in Washington, DC.

An Engraver's Warning of the Conspiracy

The 1852 book *History of the Mormons or Latter-day Saints: With Memoirs of the Life and Death of Joseph Smith, The American Mahomet*, published by Miller, Orton, and Mulligan, contained a poignant illustration with a key message of the conspiracy to murder Joseph Smith. In the preface, the author stated the illustrations are representations of events "derived from authentic sources, having been drawn from the rude sketches, or minute descriptions, of persons to whom the spots were familiar, and who were, in many cases, eyewitnesses of the incidents depicted."[450] The engraver, "N. Orr" of New York, researched the events of the Martyrdom and created an engraving capturing for future generations insights as to the conspiracy leaders.

This illustration depicts three militia soldiers observing the events of the Martyrdom while making no effort to stop the atrocity. Had Mr. Orr been aware of the trial proceedings, he would have known the three militia officers involved: Colonel Levi Williams, Major Mark Aldrich, and Captain William Grover. This image was reprinted and appeared in various other publications for many years following their original book editions.

17: What If?

What if the *Nauvoo Expositor* had never been published? What if the evil designs of the various conspiracy groups threatening Joseph Smith and the Saints had continued to be thwarted? What if the Saints had fully embraced the doctrine of Zion and sought first and foremost the building of the kingdom of God?

To expand the scope of his campaign, the Prophet Joseph Smith called upon his eloquent friend William Phelps to assist in the drafting of "The Voice of Truth." He was planning for the power of truth, elaborated in the new pamphlet, to be broadcast by an army of three hundred electioneering missionaries still in the field.

The message in the preface was one of a solemn and heartfelt warning to all the noble citizens of America. It was written as a call to action to protect this great land of promise from the powermongers conniving to usurp man's God-given rights. These enemies were not lurking in the shadows but prosecuted their evil deeds in full view in the coveted positions of political and economic institutions.

> But, gentle reader, the "Voice of Truth" is like one crying in the midst of a great city at midnight—Fire! Fire! Fire!

> The sanctuaries of religion are on fire; the temple of liberty is on fire; the nation is on fire; the world is on fire, and the great mobs of the whole earth, . . . through the black clouds of vengeance . . . are an all sufficient signal, that towns, cities, nations and kingdoms, will be sacked, pillaged and plundered, and "but few men left." Fear has seized upon all hearts, while the "nobles of the land" instead of exclaiming, "to your tents O Israel!" and watch, for thieves, are now gambling for your rights among the tombs of your illustrious fathers! They also are "rioting" and reveling in the sanctum sanctorum of freedom. . . . Exclaiming, "I know your cause is just. But government has no power to do anything for you!
>
> In such an awful dilemma; upon the eve of such a tempest of trouble: as a messenger that only escaped alone to tell thee, "The Voice of Truth," composed of facts, to favor the people, is sent forth to open the eyes, unstop the ears and quicken the senses of wise men to arise in the panoply of virtuous patriots, and save the nation from ruin and disgrace, and themselves from the ravages of wrath! . . . What say the people?[451]

What was Joseph referring to when he acknowledged his divine mission? "I calculate to be one of the instruments of setting up the kingdom of Daniel by the word of the Lord, and I intend to lay a foundation that will revolutionize the whole world."[452]

With the efforts of members in Nauvoo and the electioneering missionaries, the message of "The Voice of Truth" would have been republished by national newspapers. The flagrant violations of state and federal law in regards to the indefensible Extermination Order and the lack of due process to all the Mormon victims would have been held in public view with dismay. Outrage against the conduct of Judge Austin King and his vendetta with the Mormons for the unfortunate death of his sister's husband, while engaged in criminal conduct, should have ended his political career. The parable of the importunate widow would have made justice manifest.

Congress would have to investigate. The flagrant land takeovers by 1844 would have been well documented in Jackson County and in the northern counties of Missouri. The multitude of examples of abuse fostered by Senator Benton through Finis Ewing would have been exposed. The corruption of the preemption deadline, occurring while the Mormon leaders were captive, would have been obvious to investigators. The sinister ploy in preventing the Mormons from bidding on the Prudhomme landing site would also have been brought to light. The Mormons would have prevailed in their petition hearings.

During his visit in 1841, Francis Scott Key indicated that it was their belief that Joseph Smith prophesied that they would receive the entire Half-Breed Tract of land, consisting of 119,000 acres. The Chouteaus later lost their case on the Dubuque Spanish land grant. The Reddick heirs also later lost their Spanish land grant claim in the US Supreme Court, temporarily. In regards to the Montrose litigation between the Reddick heirs and the New York Land Company, the fraudulent conduct of the New York Land Company in misrepresenting the Mormon settlers and owners as being their "landlord" would have entirely changed the case prosecution. The Mormons would have been able to settle directly with the Reddick heirs.

With the excessive costs of paying the Mormons for their improvements required by law, the Reddick heirs could have negotiated with the Mormons for joint use of the steamboat landing and the rest of the square mile property. The need to pay for improvements on the other Half-Breed Tract lands was an immense problem for the New York and St. Louis Land Companies and the other partition participants. Rather than have to pay the Mormon owners and wait for the ability to sell the lots, the Mormon leaders would have been able to negotiate for allocated lands. For many of the same reasons, and because of a lack of funds, the New York Land Company, in 1844, would likely have negotiated a sale of their entire 41 percent holdings of the 119,000 acres.

The fraudulent conduct by the New York Land Company would have become public knowledge. The lands of the half-breed tenants wanting to sell—such as Mary Tolman and the other claimants involved with Galland, comprising the pre-partnership agreement of 1836 of twenty thousand dollars (which lands were legally conveyed to the Mormons in their 1839 purchase from Galland)—would have provided the means for the Mormons to sue for the overturn of the partition agreement and subsequent reallocation involving a legitimate Mormon distribution, or the Mormons could have negotiated portions of the forty-one shares previously allocated to the New York Land Company.

This problem, plus the challenge of having to pay for improvements, would have encouraged settlement from the New York Land Company leaders and administrators. The settlement would have resulted in substantial holdings for the Mormons in Nashville, Keokuk, and along the Mississippi River and Des Moines River shore lines.

Similarly, the Mormons would have been able to oppose the partition agreement or take over the St. Louis Land Company holdings pertaining to the Isaac Antaya lands that Isaac Campbell had sold to the Mormon, and then fraudulently used again in the partition allocation.

The Hugh Reid versus Webster ruling was reversed by the Supreme Court in 1850, thus disallowing Reid's actions on behalf of his client: the New York Land Company. Reid had secured nearly all the Half-Breed Tract through Sherriff Hawkins Taylor for which he had paid only $2,885 in January 1842. Public notice of the Sheriff's sale had not been handled properly. The general public, and in particular the Mormons, already occupied much of the lands and should have been notified. At the time of the sheriff's sale, Hugh Reid was the attorney for the New York Land Company and, by their joint conduct in concealing notice of the sheriff's sale, would have cast the appearance of collusion. The hypocrisy of Hugh Reid in secretly securing the Mormon lands while representing them in legal matters would have brought outrage.

The various Half-Breed Tract lawsuits, and later Kilbourne versus Claggett lawsuit, would have been exposed and Kilbourne's immoral and illegal conduct revealed. This would also implicate the New York and the St. Louis Land Company's leadership in their corrupt practices.

All of these cases were to be heard before Chief Justice Roger Taney, the brother-in-law to Francis Scott Key, who died in 1843. Links between Justice Taney and Senator Benton could also draw unwanted scrutiny.

With proceeds from the redress petitions, Mormons would hold key commercial and residential property in Jackson, Daviess, Caldwell, and Carroll Counties in Missouri and throughout Lee County, Iowa, and Hancock County, Illinois. Prior debt arrangement for these properties could have been better negotiated due to the new leverage for the Mormons.

In July 1845, William Thomas, as administrator for the deceased Joseph Duncan, was made the president of the Warsaw Land Company.

Thomas was charged with securing the funds due the federal government, based on Duncan's surety bonds to his brother-in-law. Mormons could have purchased those lands in Warsaw held by Aldrich, Barrett, and Duncan and had intended to do that previously.

With the adverse attention drawn to Barrett and the plan he had with Governor Duncan, while they were both in key positions of trust, he would likely have abandoned his ambitions there and sold his holdings in Iowa as well. Aldrich, having lost his interest in Warsaw land development, left his wife and family and moved to California in 1849.

After fraudulent conduct and other illegal and immoral treatments against the Mormons were brought to light, the Mormons likely would have held dominant ownership position over all four corners of the Des Moines Rapids (Montrose, Nauvoo, Keokuk, and Warsaw). With such an enviable position, the Mormons, with their allies, could have created a virtual monopoly on Mississippi traffic in both directions and from both sides of the river. After completion of the canal, the method preferred by Joseph Smith, they could have created a successful commercial "Nauvoo Emporium." Perhaps this was the intent of the revelation given to Joseph Smith regarding the hub and spokes between Nauvoo and Iowa across the river.

Over time, it was concluded that the plan suggested by Lee and other engineers to clear a fifty-foot wide channel through the Spanish Chute proved ineffective in remedying the problems. In 1848, Samuel Curtis, a retired US Army engineer, planned a canal through the Des Moines Rapids but failed to secure funding. It took two decades before another effort was launched at building a canal in Keokuk to bypass the Rapids. That canal was finally completed in 1877. With funds from the redress petitions, members could have invested in the Curtis plan.

By divine intervention, the Saints could have experienced a type of "reverse honeycomb effect." The greedy conduct of all the enemy conspirators attempting to take advantage of the Mormons would have resulted in the forfeitures of the lands they seized, plus their improvements back to the former and lawful Mormon owners. To advance the cause of Zion, the Church would have been invited in multiple key improvement project networks of the Chouteaus and the former Benton allies as they withdrew.

In a state Committee of Finance report in January 1843 sent to the US Senate, the values of the Illinois and Michigan Canal were extolled in terms of annual revenues from imports and exports to be earned through Lake Michigan,

> What amount of revenues will the canal yield? It requires . . . little consideration to perceive that there is no other work in the Union, perhaps none in the world . . . with the same number of miles of artificial navigation, opens a trade between territories so . . . rich in agricultural and mineral products. It will complete the water communication between the east and the west. The whole territory lying on the great lakes, so rapidly advancing in population and wealth, with the whole valley of the Illinois, the Mississippi and its tributaries, will be brought into commercial intercourse. In addition to the immense amount of agricultural products which it would carry to market, there would be large items of lumber, salt, coal, lead, merchandise, and . . . goods from the east, to the whole valley of the upper Mississippi, and the groceries of the south, &c.[453]

Plans were in place concerning the Wabash Canal and Wabash River access to Lake Erie. With the support of the Mormon population and some of the proceeds of the Missouri redress petitions, the means could have been provided to reinvigorate efforts previously stalled on the Des Moines Rapids, Northern Cross, and Alton Springfield Railroads. With the Des Moines Rapids Railroad in place, the crane concept at the steamboat landings would have successfully provided an improved solution to the Des Moines Rapids problem and provided substantial revenues for the Mormon and non-Mormon operators.

The northern transport route, proposed by the Illinois legislature to Warsaw, would have aided the "Nauvoo Emporium." It would have begun at the New York City port, continued up the Hudson through the Erie Canal, and linking through the Great Lakes down the Illinois and Michigan Canal to Beardstown and by rail to Quincy, Carthage, Warsaw, and Nauvoo.

If Calvin Warren had accepted Joseph Smith's offer in December 1841 to join together with the support of eastern investors, massive labor and investment resources could have been secured to advance the many planned internal improvement projects. If Warren would have forsaken his evil partners as directed, the Missouri and Iowa opportunities, combined with the various eastern projects and access points, could have accelerated the transcontinental transportation network that was just developing to the Pacific Ocean. With the success of the Saints in benefitting from the redress petitions and the Iowa lands, and with the adverse attention given his former allies, Warren would have more likely joined with the Saints as partners.

The 1820 Stephen Long Expedition from Pittsburgh to the Rocky Mountains demonstrated the potential that could have linked the planned Ohio River connections to Madison, Indiana, connected with the already constructed Madison to Indianapolis railroad and adding Indianapolis to Lafayette extension. With support from the Mormons and Calvin Warren, Isaac Morris, and the Quincy and Springfield promoters, the Northern Cross Railroad should have been completed which would have been able to link with the Lafayette to Madison, Indiana Railroad connection. The various problems associated with steamboat traffic between Madison, Indiana, and the Mississippi River could have been alleviated by rerouting the steamboat cargoes at Madison and continuing by rail to the Mississippi River.

The bridge plan across the Mississippi River in Hancock County along the proposed Des Moines Rapids Railroad Line, promoted by Adolphus Allen and his Des Moines Bridge Associates presented to Congress, over time would likely have been adopted as a better option than the eventual first railroad bridge location near Rock Island. Allen was already acquainted with the Mormons and had previously offered to sell lands to the Saints. With joint support from the Mormons along the proposed path of the Des Moines Rapids Railroad, and continuing on to Quincy as was considered, Calvin Warren and his associates and the Mormon leadership could have forged a powerful commercial enterprise base.

Further, with the support of Abraham Lincoln and his Springfield supporters, the Alton Springfield Railroad could have been constructed much sooner as an important appendage to the Northern Cross Railroad. This addition would have added access for St. Louis to the eastern improvements. The National Cumberland Road was progressing to southern Illinois. Plans were already established to link this highway to intersecting roads to Warsaw and Nauvoo. The Nauvoo Emporium then would also have benefited immensely from this rural feeder network of agricultural products to further stimulate commerce at the ever-expanding Mormon metropolis.

In 1844, Joseph Smith was considering new settlement areas for the Church, in addition to the Great Basin in Utah. He contemplated settlements in Vancouver, San Francisco, and southern California. Joseph sent a memorial to Congress, asking to lead volunteers to the Oregon and Texas Territories. After Brigham Young arrived in the Salt Lake Valley, he soon began colonizing efforts to the "Mormon Corridor" region to link with southern California to provide a Pacific Ocean international seaport access and to link the Salt Lake Valley to San Francisco.

With the Church supporting the four corners of the Des Moines Rapids region, efforts could have escalated in establishing railroad transport following the Des Moines River and on to Council Bluffs, as Benton and Chouteau had planned. With these direct connections to Council Bluffs, the transcontinental railroad plans following the Platte River to the Rocky Mountains could have begun much sooner.

Senator Benton menaced the Saints for interfering with his "Road to India" plan emanating from the Jefferson and Astor discussions in 1808. Completions of the massive railroad and highway transcontinental projects could have been achieved much earlier than they did. Investors in alliance with Mormon leaders could have advanced earlier preparations.

The Prophet had set the foundation for the transportation pillar centered in Nauvoo and in Jackson County, Missouri, to link with the various major internal improvement projects of the other states to the East sea coast and eventually to connect to the Pacific Coast. Further development was underway to expand commerce to Texas. With Mormon leadership support, the quest to build up the kingdom of God in Texas could have been achieved, thus linking with Lyman White's efforts when he took the Wisconsin Pinery members to settle Texas.

Joseph anticipated the kingdom spoken of by Daniel would create a world revolution. This was to include a global transportation revolution far beyond what John Jacob Astor, President Jefferson, and Senator Benton had envisioned. Joseph Smith had set the foundation for the commerce pillar centered in the trade for silver and gold with

Santa Fe, Mexico, through trade with the merchants in Independence, Missouri. This trade would have greatly expanded. The gold and silver thus obtained would have served as bank specie to complete what Joseph had intended for the Kirtland Bank and the Bank of Monroe, Michigan. As other foreign economies were destined to struggle, the Mormon Zion could have prospered with its increasing gold and silver reserves to create a global commerce revolution far beyond what Senator Benton planned.

With the canal and dam development projects implemented, water power would have spurred new mills and factories. As foreign nations suffered economicly, unemployment of skilled craftsmen and laborers soared, leaving many families destitute. The Mormon Zion was to gather these converts to build the long awaited kingdom of God. This plan, if allowed to develop, would have created an agricultural and manufacturing global revolution. The Enoch Prophecy could have been fulfilled in Joseph's lifetime. The pursuit of building a dam on the Mississippi and a canal to avoid the perils of the Des Moines Rapids was visionary for Joseph Smith in 1843.

The creation of the Nauvoo Power Company was likewise a progressive pursuit by the Saints, even though they had to abandon the project and sell the lands in 1846. Two years later, David W. Kilbourne, General Samuel Curtis, and others pursued Joseph's lead and secured through the legislature the Navigation & Hydraulic Company of the Mississippi Rapids. Hiram Barney strongly promoted the project in the East. Barney later married the daughter of David Kilbourne. President Lincoln appointed Hiram Barney collector of the ports at New York. In 1913, the largest hydroelectric dam in the world was constructed at Keokuk. After its completion, the river was raised several feet and covered the small island near Montrose. The Montrose and Nauvoo steamboat landing sites became submerged, as they remain today.

In 1844, Henry Brown published *The History of Illinois: From Its First Discovery and Settlement to the Present Time.* He attached the famed Colton map to this book. That map highlighted the internal improvement projects planned at the time and laid out the scenario of this "what if?" potential.

With the accumulation of attention placed on Senator Benton, his political career could have ended in disgrace. He lost Senate reelection for another term in 1851 because of the defections of previous

Central Clique allies. The dissension amongst their ranks that had already surfaced a few years earlier could have accelerated and drawn greater scrutiny to the corrupt practices of the Central Clique leadership, ending their political chokehold in the state sooner.

The Missouri legislature, after tabling the hearings regarding the Mormon war in late 1838, justified their actions because the nature of the evidence against the Mormons was *ex parte*. They admitted that Judge King's court documentary evidence pertained to a preliminary hearing only; as such, witnesses had not been cross examined, or the defendants afforded basic protections. Clearly, defense witnesses had been intimidated from testifying. The adverse attention that would have been directed to the conduct of Judge King, coupled with the humiliation to Missouri and the massive burden of funding the Mormon petition settlements he exposed the state and the federal government to, would likely have ended his public career.

A return of the Mormons to Jackson County, the plains of Kansas, and the northern counties would have secured, and then expanded, their previous commercial endeavors. Supplying the fur trade, the Indian tribes and the Santa Fe merchants would have linked the "Nauvoo Emporium" with the "Jackson County Emporium" and *entrepôt* networks. Through these efforts, the vision of Joseph Smith in Nauvoo could have been fully realized. "There is a wheel, Nauvoo is the hub."[454] Stakes and temples were to follow along the economic trade routes. The focus of Joseph Smith to the evils of "Democracy, Whiggery and Cliquery" would have challenged corruption under the guise of party devotion. In 1845, the "Apostles Proclamation" provisions could have been achieved. (Doctrine and Covenants 124 could have been realized.)

> And now, O ye kings, rulers, and people of the Gentiles, . . . You are not only required to repent and obey the gospel in its fulness, and thus become members or citizens of the kingdom of God; but you are also hereby commanded, in the name of Jesus Christ, to put your silver and gold, your ships and steam-vessels, your railroad trains and your horses, chariots, camels, mules, and litters, into active use for the fulfillment of these purposes. For be it known unto you, that the only salvation which remains for the Gentiles, is for them to be identified in the same covenant, and to worship at the same altar with Israel. In short, they must come to the same standard; for there shall be one Lord, and his name one, and He shall be king over all the earth.

> And now, O ye kings, rulers, presidents, governors, judges, legislators, nobles, lords, and rich men of the earth, will you leave us to struggle alone, and to toil unaided in so great a work? Or will you share in the labours, toils, sacrifices, honours, and blessings of the same? . . .
>
> Have you not the same interest in it that we have? Is it not sent forth to renovate the world—to enlighten the nations—to cover the earth with light, knowledge, truth, union, peace, and love? And thus usher in the great millennium or Sabbath of rest, so long expected and sought for by all good men? We bear testimony that it is; and the fulfillment of our words will establish their truth to millions yet unborn, while there are those now living upon the earth who will live to see the consummation. . . .
>
> Know, assuredly, that whether you come to the help of the Saints in this great work, or whether you make light of this message, and withhold your aid and co-operation, it is all the same as to the success and final triumph of the work; for it is the work of the great God—for which his word and oath have been pledged from before the foundation of the world. And the same promise and oath have been renewed unto man from the beginning, down through each succeeding dispensation, and confirmed again by his own voice out of the heavens in the present age; therefore he is bound to fulfill it, and to overcome every obstacle. . . .
>
> The loss will therefore be on their own part, and not on the part of God or of his Saints, should the people neglect their duty in the great work of modern restoration. . . .
>
> Let the government . . . continue to gather together, and to colonize the tribes and remnants of Israel [the Indians], . . . protect them . . . to bring them to the knowledge of their Israelitish origin, and of the fullness of the gospel which was revealed to, and written by their forefathers on this land, the record of which has now come to light. . . .
>
> Let them also come on with their gold, and silver, and goods, and workmen, to establish manufactories and business of all kinds, for the building up of the city, and for the employment and support of the poor, and thus strengthen . . . those who have borne the burden . . . in laying the foundation of the kingdom of God, and moving on the work.[455]

In the end, the Creator's hand was manifest in Missouri, Illinois, and Iowa. Those determined to fight against Joseph Smith and the cause of Zion were thwarted in their selfish ambitions. Had the members been more faithful and committed, the gains of those fighting the Saints could have been forfeited back and fulfilled the Enoch Prophecy. Because they failed, future generations will be tasked to bring to pass a Zion people.

What can be learned from Joseph and the challenges he faced to build the future Zion and kingdom of God?

Presently, many are still concerned with government corruption and abuse at all levels. At the county and state levels and especially in our national institutions of Congress, the Supreme Court, and executive departments, many feel they are no longer fairly represented. A return of persecution is feared as more pressure is levied against religious leaders to forsake long-held values supported by scripture and succumb to pressures for secular governance and compliance. Joseph Smith in his "Voice of Truth" pamphlet addressed many of the key issues we struggle with today. His call to all patriots to unite to defeat the evils of government still applies. He targeted government abuse when used to favor select groups at the public expense. He clearly defined the proper role of government was to support the four pillars of economic prosperity (transportation, commerce, manufacturing, and agriculture) for all citizens equally.

Before his death, Governor Thomas Ford included in his history of Illinois:

> The Christian world . . . may have cause to fear its rapid increase. . . . At the death of the prophet, fourteen years after the first Mormon Church was organized, the Mormons in all the world numbered about two hundred thousand souls [a half million according to their statistics]; a number equal, perhaps, to the number of Christians, when the Christian Church was of the same age. It is to be feared that, in course of a century, some fitted man like Paul, some splendid orator, . . . may succeed in breathing a new life into this modern Mahometanism, and make the name of the martyred Joseph ring as loud, and stir the souls of men as much, as the mighty name of Christ itself. Sharon, Palmyra, Manchester, Kirtland, Far West, Adamon Diahmon, Ramus, Nauvoo, and the Carthage Jail, may become holy and venerable names, places of classic interest, in another age; like Jerusalem, the Garden of Gethsemane, the Mount of Olives, and Mount Calvary to the Christian, and Mecca and Medina to the Turk. And in that event, the author of this history feels degraded by the reflection, that the humble governor of an obscure State, who would otherwise be forgotten in a few years,

stands a fair chance, like Pilate and Herod, by their official connection with the true religion, of being dragged down to posterity with an immortal name, hitched on to the memory of a miserable impostor. There may be those whose ambition would lead them to desire an immortal name in history, even in those humbling terms. I am not one of that number.[456]

Appendix: Overview of Church Persecution Groups

St. Louis Junto (later the St. Louis Land Company): Initial leading members of the Junto included the St. Louis Chouteau family, Superintendent William Clark, and Senator Thomas Benton. Closely aligned with them were the Chouteau family network, consisting of Francois Chouteau in Jackson County, Missouri, and several brothers, all engaged in the fur trade with most of the Indian tribes west of the Mississippi River.

About 1836, Isaac Campbell formed the St. Louis Land Company to purchase land in the Iowa Half-Breed Tract. With them was Edward Brooks of St. Louis, representing the heirs of Thomas Reddick involved in legal disputes regarding a square mile of land in Montrose. Hugh White was a steamship captain living in St. Louis, who sold land in Nauvoo to the Mormons. He was a brother-in-law to Isaac Campbell. It appears the St. Louis Land Company committed fraud against Mormon land owners in Iowa Territory. He sold land acquired from Isaac Antaya (Antaga) to the Mormons, and then used the same lands as a claim in the partition agreement that gave the St. Louis Land Company members reallocated lands in Iowa Territory. They feared getting exposed by the Mormons for their illegal conduct. Later George T. M.

Davis acted as attorney for the Chouteaus and was actively involved with many of the St. Louis Chamber of Commerce members.

Merchants of Independence, Missouri: The Jackson County court held the first sale of town lots for Independence in July 1827. Merchants involved in the Santa Fe trade purchased twenty-five of the entire seventy lots initially sold. These merchants included Lilburn Boggs, Samuel Owens, James Aull, various Flournoy brothers, S. V. Noland, Richard Fristoe, and others who participated in the secret constitution that forced the Mormons out of Jackson County. These merchants were also involved in selling to the Indian tribes to get their government annuity funds and to other fur traders.

The Mormons began competing with the Independence merchants in the Santa Fe trade. Mormons also were friendly to the Indians and were expected to jeopardize the monopoly on that trade as well. Lilburn Boggs and Samuel Owens were the primary leaders of the alliance of Independence merchants. Owens also worked in various capacities with the St. Louis Junto through Francois Chouteau. They were fearful that the Mormons might return. Francois Chouteau wrote in 1836 that they were willing to fight the Mormons to the end. After the Mormons were forced out, Owens and others took over the lands of Francois Chouteau and formed the "Town of Kansas" to control the merchant trade along the Missouri and surrounding areas. They feared Joseph Smith would prevail in the redress petitions, as he continually pressed the matter. If successful, the Mormons could reclaim lands and improvements forceably taken from them. Some feared criminal prosecution for their conduct.

New York Land Company: Formed as a partnership in October 1836 to purchase land in the Iowa Half-Breed Tract. Isaac Galland was the initial local partner in charge of operations for the company. He was replaced by David Kilbourne. The New York Land Company was in lawsuit with the Reddick heirs concerning the valuable land in Montrose, which included the steamship landing site there.

The company committed fraud against the Mormon land owners in Iowa Territory who purchased their lands from Isaac Galland. Galland had purchased rights from half-breed claimants, such as Mary Tolman, before becoming a partner in the New York Land Company. After joining them, Galland was to transfer his prior land claims to the New York Land Company but did not sign them over. He had disputes with the New York Land Company and withdrew from the partnership, taking his prior land claims with him, which was not contested by the other principals. After selling the land involved with his prior land claims to Mormons, the New York Land Company used Galland's prior land claims in the partition agreement, which constituted a large portion of their 41 percent cumulative land holding. Nearly twenty thousand acres of land that was sold to the Mormons in the Iowa Territory was reallocated in the partition agreement, resulting in a total disenfranchisement of the Iowa Mormon lands. They had the most to fear in getting exposed by the Mormons for their illegal conduct. Similarly, the Montrose lands were in dispute with Galland's sale with the Mormons on lands he secured prior to the partnership.

Warsaw Land Company and Railroad Commissioners: The Warsaw Land Company was formed by Mark Aldrich. John Vineyard, who married the sister of Samuel Owens, laid out the lands in Warsaw for sale by the land company. Samuel's sister was Mary Owens, who was for a while engaged to Abraham Lincoln. Governor Joseph Duncan and Fund Commissioner Richard F. Barrett later joined the venture. Duncan served as president of the Warsaw Land Company until his death in 1844.

Twelve internal improvements leaders were involved in the plot to murder Joseph Smith. Nine anti-Mormon leaders were associated with railroad plans. Seven were state-approved commissioners for the Des Moines Rapids Railroad or Peoria and Warsaw and Wabash Railroad: Mark Aldrich, David Matthews, John Montague, William Abernathy, Joel Catlin, Calvin Warren, and Walter Bagby. Thomas Sharp took over for John Wilcox as Warsaw Railroad commissioner when he married his widow. William Grover was the railroad engineer. Three anti-Mormon leaders were involved in the turnpike or state roads, including Colonel Levi Williams, John Atherton, and Valentine Wilson.

In 1839, the Des Moines Rapids Railroad was authorized by the state, with Mark Aldrich, Joseph Duncan, Richard Barrett, Calvin Warren, and Isaac Morris all associated with the Warsaw Land Company. Isaac Galland was also a commissioner. The railroad route would connect Warsaw to Nauvoo right up to the steamboat landing sites through the heart of Nauvoo. Like other land speculators in the area, they paid too much for their Warsaw land but sold to others at higher prices, with high expectations that various anticipated internal improvement projects would make the area from Warsaw to Carthage, Rushville, and Beardstown extremely prosperous. After 1843, when the Illinois and Michigan Canal received renewed funding because of the efforts of Governor Ford, they expected other projects would be renewed, and they could finally sell their lands profitably.

Central Clique (Boonslick Democracy): John Sappington, a close friend of Senator Benton, was the patriarch of this group. His sons-in-law, Miles Meredith and Claybourne Fox, were also leaders. The active participants of this clique, who took part in active opposition to the Church, included Senator Benton, Governor Lilburn Boggs, Governor Thomas Reynolds, Judge Austin King, and Captain Sterling Price.

At the time of the Extermination Order, most of the state offices were held by active Central Clique members: governor, lieutenant governor, Speaker of the House, Speaker of the Senate, and Supreme Court justices. The Central Clique acted aggressively to prequalify candidates who supported Senator Benton.

The corrupt conspiracy escalated when these groups joined together in the plot to murder Joseph Smith. Samuel Owens's family relationships and John Bennett's associates aided the efforts.

Endnotes

1. George T. M. Davis, *Autobiography of the Late Colonel George T. M. Davis* (New York City: Jenkins & McCowan, 1891), 80. The name of this meeting was identified by George T. M. Davis in his autobiographical papers.

2. "Stephen Markham letter to Wilford Woodruff from Fort Supply" (Salt Lake City: LDS Church History Library). The context of this letter was included in *History of the Church.*

3. Joseph Smith and William Phelps, "The Voice of Truth" (Nauvoo: printed by John Taylor, 1844), reprint, 34.

4. "Stephen Markham letter to Wilford Woodruff from Fort Supply" (Salt Lake City: LDS Church History Library).

5. George T. M. Davis, *Autobiography of the Late Colonel George T. M. Davis*, 80–81.

6. Joseph Smith, *History of the Church of Jesus Christ of Latter-day Saints*, Vol. 6 (Salt Lake City: Deseret Book, 1978), 587–88.

7. Thomas Ford, *A History of Illinois, from Its Commencement as a State in 1818 to 1847* (Chicago: S. C. Griggs & Company, 1854), 354.

8. Joseph Smith and William Phelps, "The Voice of Truth," 34.
9. Joseph Smith, *History of the Church of Jesus Christ of Latter-day Saints*, Vol. 5, 422.
10. Joseph Smith and William Phelps, "The Voice of Truth," 55.
11. Ibid., 58.
12. Joseph Smith, *History of the Church of Jesus Christ of Latter-day Saints*, Vol. 6, 365.
13. Peter Stark, *Astoria John Jacob Astor and Thomas Jefferson's Lost Pacific Empire* (New York City: HarperCollins Publishers, 2014), 17.
14. Ibid.
15. Ibid., 19–20.
16. Ibid., 20–21.
17. Shirley Christian, *Before Lewis and Clark* (New York: Farrar, Straus, and Giroux, LLC., 2004), 196–97.
18. Albert Watkins, *Publications of the Nebraska State Historical Society*, Vol. 20 (Lincoln: University of Nebraska Press, 1922), 3–5.
19. William Nisbet Chambers, *Old Bullion Benton* (Boston: Atlantic Monthly Press, 1956), 66.
20. Robert Nelson, *Enemy of the Saints* (Baltimore: Publishamerica, 2011), 44.
21. William Nisbet Chambers, *Old Bullion Benton*, 90.
22. Ibid., 72.
23. Ibid., 72–73.
24. Ibid.
25. Ibid., 70–71.
26. Ibid., 81.
27. Ibid., 88–89, as printed in *St. Louis Enquirer*, June 1819.

28. Ken S. Mueller, *Senator Benton and the People* (Dekalb: Northern Illinois University Press, 2014), 183.
29. William Nisbet Chambers, *Old Bullion Benton*, 100.
30. Thomas Hart Benton, *Thirty Years View*, Vol. 1 (New York City: D. Appleton and Company, 1856), reprint, 13.
31. Ibid., 14.
32. William Nisbet Chambers, *Old Bullion Benton*, 110–11.
33. Kristie C. Wolferman, *The Osage in Missouri* (Columbia: University of Missouri Press, 1997), 101.
34. Ibid.
35. David Lavender, *The Fist in the Wilderness* (Lincoln: University of Nebraska Press, 1964), 337.
36. John E. Sunder, *Joshua Pilcher: Fur Trader and Indian Agent* (Norman: University of Oklahoma Press, 1968), 40–41.
37. The passion for Benton regarding the "Road to India," and his endearment to Jefferson, was elaborated by his daughter Jesse Benton Fremont. See John C. Fremont, *Memoirs of My Life* Vol. 1. A bronze statue of Benton is located in St. Louis. He is depicted with his hand pointing west. On the pedestal is engraved, "There is the East; there is the Road to India."
38. Thomas Hart Benton, *Thirty Years View*, Vol. 1, 54.
39. William Nisbet Chambers, *Old Bullion Benton*, 128–29.
40. Ibid., 128.
41. Kate L. Gregg, *The Road to Santa Fe* (Albuquerque: University of New Mexico Press, 1995), 212–13.
42. Ibid., 213.
43. Harold H. Schuler, *Fort Pierre Chouteau* (Vermillion: University of South Dakota Press, 1990), 9.
44. Stan Hoig, *The Chouteaus First Family of the Fur Trade* (Albuquerque: University of New Mexico Press, 2008), 67–71, 129–32.

45. Thomas Hart Benton, *Thirty Years View*, Vol. 1, 109.

46. John E. Sunder, *Joshua Pilcher Fur Trader and Indian Agent*, 60–69.

47. William Patrick O'Brien, *Merchants of Independence* (Kirksville: Truman State University Press, 2014), 149–50.

48. Robert Nelson, *Enemy of the Saints*, 40.

49. Ibid., 14.

50. Rhoda Wooldridge, *Fort Osage Opening of the American West* (Independence: Independence Press, 1983), 79–80.

51. Robert Nelson, *Enemy of the Saints*, 44–45.

52. Dorothy Brandt Marra, *Cher Oncle, Cher Papa* (Kansas City: Western Historical Manuscript Collection, 2001) 69–70.

53. The point that Samuel C. Owens and the Aull brothers filled the leadership void because of the death of the Mexican trader Samuel Lamme was presented by William Patrick O'Brien, *Merchants of Independence*, 121.

54. Harold H. Schuler, *Fort Pierre Chouteau*, 100–1.

55. Susan Easton Black, "Isaac Galland: Both Sides of the River," *Nauvoo Journal* (Fall 1996), 5.

56. Landon Y. Jones, *William Clark and the Shaping of the West* (New York City: Farrar, Straus, and Giroux, 2004), 299.

57. Ibid., 299–300.

58. Ibid., 300–1.

59. Parley P. Pratt, *Autobiography of Parley Parker Pratt* (New York: Russell Brothers, 1874), 58–60.

60. Ibid.

61. Jay H. Buckley, *William Clark: Indian Diplomat* (Norman: University of Oklahoma Press, 2008), 221, 223.

62. Church Education System, *Church History in the Fulness of Times Student Manual* (Salt Lake City: the Church of Jesus Christ of

Latter-day Saints, 2003), 86–88. Copy of letter from Oliver Cowdery to William Clark, February 14, 1831, in William Clark letter book.

63. Landon Y. Jones, *William Clark and the Shaping of the West*, 307.

64. William Phelps, *Evening and Morning Star*, August 1832.

65. *A History of David Pettegrew*, (Provo, Utah: Harold B. Lee Library) 11.

66. Ibid., 13–14.

67. Ibid., 12–13.

68. Joseph Smith, *History of the Church of Jesus Christ of Latter-day Saints*, Vol. 1, 316.

69. *A History of David Pettegrew,* 16.

70. Ibid., 17.

71. Joseph Smith, *History of the Church of Jesus Christ of Latter-day Saints*, Vol. 1, 376.

72. Church Education System, *Church History in the Fulness of Times Student Manual*, 129.

73. Robert Nelson, *Enemy of the Saints*, 68.

74. Samuel Owens wrote to Pierre Chouteau in St. Louis on October 5, 1833, describing a shipment he had taken on behalf of Francis Chouteau of a large sum of money transported by him and his partners—the Aulls—on the steamboat *John Nelson*. Owens was the primary liaison for the St. Louis Junto in the western region. His services were sought by Francois Chouteau, the local representative. Owens accepted the dominance of the Chouteau network. He joined their pursuits to extend trade to the Rocky Mountains and beyond. The more successful they were in their pursuits, the greater the potential for mercantile engagements extended to him and his partners. Owens and Francois Chouteau, representing the St. Louis Junto, were linked in their mission to rid the area of the Mormon settlers.

75. Joseph Fielding Smith, *Essentials in Church History* (Salt Lake City: Deseret Book, 1979), 136.

76. US Army Corp of Engineers, *Kansas City District Blue River Channel Project Kansas City, Missouri,* 31.

77. Agent Cummins is mentioned a few times in the Francois Chouteau letters to his father-in-law, Pierre Menard. See Dorothy Brandt Marra, *Cher Oncle, Cher Papa.*

78. There are Benton token coins with his image and this phrase, but it is unknown when they were created. More than likely, these were created long after Benton died. However, the sentiment still reflects that this was a key attitude of Senator Benton.

79. Ken S. Mueller, *Senator Benton and the People*, 108.

80. Louis Cortambert, *The Bulletin: Missouri Historical Society*, April 1963, 207–9; from the contemporary account given by the Frenchman Louis Cortambert in his article "Journey to the Land of the Osages 1835–36." In his report, he gave the following account while in Independence: "Two or three times I was asked a question that I did not understand very well: 'Aren't you one of the Mormons?' I answered no, just at random; it is a good thing that I did not answer yes. The Mormons are a religious sect who were also impelled by some instinct or other to go to the West. They cast their eyes on the country around Independence, the New Jerusalem. Several articles of their doctrine, notably the abolition of slavery, tended to turn the settlers against them. But what gave the finishing touch to irritating the almost completely mercantile population of Independence was this: the Mormons, wishing to devote themselves to commerce and at the same time to agriculture, had brought in a considerable quantity of merchandise; since they were in need of country produce for their subsistence, they offered the neighboring farmers their merchandise in exchange, in place of money. The farmers, finding the merchandise of good quality and cheap, turned to the Mormons, and the other shops were neglected. Hence a general market town insurrection against the new sectarians. A political coloration was given

to the affair, and the Jacksonians, or Democrats, who are in the great majority in Jackson County, of which Independence is the county seat, organized a regular persecution of the Mormons. These unfortunate people were besieged in their houses, basely mistreated, and finally turned out. But they did not consider themselves beaten; They reappeared at independence, well armed and headed by a courageous leader. The settlers proposed to come to terms if the Mormons were willing to lay down their arms. To this they consented. Their treacherous enemies then got the upper hand again, and the Mormons again saw themselves obliged to withdraw from the place. They applied to the Governor of the State (and) to President Jackson, in order to obtain justice; the Governor, the President, sent them back to the Circuit Court, composed of men who had contributed to their expulsion. Nevertheless, they have not renounced New Jerusalem."

81. *A History of David Pettegrew*, 17–18.

82. US Army Corp of Engineers, *Kansas City District Blue River Channel Project Kansas City, Missouri,* 31.

83. *A History of David Pettegrew*, 19.

84. Ibid., 20.

85. Ibid., 14.

86. Church Education System, *Church History in the Fulness of Times Student Manual*, 131.

87. Horace Strong Rawson, *A Short Sketch or Biography of Horace Strong Rawson,* unpublished history.

88. Thomas M. Spencer, *Missouri Mormon Experience* (Columbia: University of Missouri Press, 2010), 12.

89. Roger D. Launius, *Alexander William Doniphan* (Columbia: University of Missouri Press, 1997), 17, footnote 43.

90. Thomas M. Spencer, *Missouri Mormon Experience*, 12.

91. Ibid.

92. Joseph Smith, *History of the Church of Jesus Christ of Latter-day Saints*, Vol. 2, 84–86.

93. *Times and Seasons*, January 15, 1846, 1090–91.

94. Ibid., 1092.

95. Church Education System, *Church History in the Fulness of Times Student Manual*, 148.

96. Ibid.

97. *Times and Seasons*, January 15, 1846, 1092.

98. Brigham H. Roberts, *The Missouri Persecutions* (Provo: Maasai, Inc., 2001), reprint, 170.

99. Glenn Rawson and Dennis Lyman, *The Mormon Wars* (American Fork, Covenant Communications, Inc., 2014), 42.

100. Robert E. Shalhope, *Sterling Price: Portrait of a Southerner* (Columbia: University of Missouri Press, 1971), 18.

101. Thomas M. Spencer, *Missouri Mormon Experience*, 35, 47.

102. Ibid., 35–36.

103. Dorothy Brandt Marra, *Cher Oncle, Cher Papa*, 156.

104. Stan Hoig, *The Chouteaus First Family of the Fur Trade*, 182.

105. Joseph Smith, *History of the Church of Jesus Christ of Latter-day Saints*, Vol. 2, 449–50.

106. Dorothy Brandt Marra, *Cher Oncle, Cher Papa*, 157–58.

107. Joseph Smith, *History of the Church of Jesus Christ of Latter-day Saints*, Vol. 2, 461–62.

108. Leland H. Gentry, "The Land Question at Adam-ondi-Ahman," *BYU Studies* 26, No. 2 (1986), 4.

109. Dorothy Brandt Marra, *Cher Oncle, Cher Papa*, 161.

110. Ibid., 168–69.

111. Joseph Smith Jr., *Scriptory Book*, May 18, 1838 (Salt Lake City: Church History Library). See also Dean C. Jessee, *The Papers of*

Joseph Smith, 2 vols. (Salt Lake City: Deseret Book, 1989–92), 2:243. Referenced by Jeffrey N. Walker, "Mormon Land Rights in Caldwell and Daviess Counties and the Mormon Conflict of 1838," *BYU Studies* 47, No. 1 (2008).

112. Shirley Christian, *Before Lewis and Clark*, 299.

113. John H. Krenkel, *Illinois Internal Improvements 1818–48* (Cedar Rapids: The Torch Press, 1958), 32.

114. Leon L. Lamet, *History of Hancock County, Illinois* (Warsaw Township), 577.

115. Gene V. Glendinning, *The Chicago & Alton Railroad* (DeKalb: Northern Illinois University Press, 2002), 9.

116. "Laws of the State of Illinois Passed by the Ninth General Assembly at Their First Session, Commencing December 1, 1834, and Ending February 13, 1835," reprint, 98–99, 223–29.

117. Ibid. The Winchester Jacksonville Railroad Act was omitted from the printed laws and inserted in the printed laws of the next session: "Incorporation Laws of the State of Illinois, Begun Day 6 of December, 1836," reprint, 150–52.

118. Donald F. Carmony, *Indiana 1816–50: The Pioneer Era* (Indianapolis: Indiana Historical Society,1998), 193–96.

119. Ibid., 357–58.

120. "Laws of the State of Illinois Passed," 1836, 77.

121. Ibid., 76.

122. Henry Brown, *The History of Illinois, from Its First Discovery and Settlement to the Present Time* (New York City: J. Winchester, New World Press, 1844), 424.

123. Copies of the deed information included in an unmarked folder at the Warsaw Illinois Public Library.

124. John Wilson Million, *State Aid to Railways in Missouri* (Chicago: University of Chicago Press, 1896), reprint, 25.

125. Jessica M. Lepler, *The Many Panics of 1837* (New York: Cambridge University Press, 2013) 47.

126. Ibid.

127. Ibid., 49.

128. Ibid., 60.

129. Elizabeth Putnam, *The Life and Services of Joseph Duncan, Governor of Illinois, 1834–38* (Springfield: Illinois State Historical Society, 1921), reprint, 153.

130. Ibid., 154.

131. John H. Krenkel, *Illinois Internal Improvements 1818–48*, 79.

132. "Incorporation Laws of the State of Illinois Passed at a Session of the General Assembly, Begun Day 6 of December, 1836," reprint, 30–31.

133. Document on file at the Abraham Lincoln Presidential Library, manuscript: "Joseph Duncan Document number SC 431."

134. Deed transcription at Warsaw Public Library in Mark Aldrich unmarked folders.

135. James William Putnam, *The Illinois and Michigan Canal* (Chicago: The University of Chicago Press, 1918) Reprint, 38–40.

136. Elizabeth Putnam, *The Life and Services of Joseph Duncan, Governor of Illinois, 1834–38*, 169.

137. David Herbert Donald, *Lincoln* (New York City: Touchstone; Simon & Schuster, 1996), 42–43.

138. Dale Thomas, *Lincoln's Old Friends of Menard County, Illinois* (Charleston: The History Press, 2012), 62–63.

139. David Herbert Donald, *Lincoln*, 52.

140. Roy P. Basler, *The Collected Works of Abraham Lincoln*, Vol. 1 (New Brunswick: Rutgers University Press, 1953), 32–33.

141. Gene V. Glendinning, *The Chicago & Alton Railroad*, 9.

142. Dale Thomas, *Lincoln's Old Friends of Menard County, Illinois*, 47.

143. Mark Aldrich sold land to Richard F. Barrett and Joseph Duncan on July 28, 1836. Their deed referred to a plan.

144. Dale Thomas, *Lincoln's Old Friends of Menard County, Illinois*, 81. References as its source: Fehrenbacher, "Abraham Lincoln," *Speeches and Writings*, Vol. 1, 7–8.

145. Roy P. Basler, *The Collected Works of Abraham Lincoln*, Vol. 1, 76.

146. Dale Thomas, *Lincoln's Old Friends of Menard County, Illinois*, 91. References as its source: Fehrenbacher, "Abraham Lincoln," *Speeches and Writings*, Vol. 1, 19.

147. Roy P. Basler, *The Collected Works of Abraham Lincoln*, Vol. 1, 94–95.

148. Dale Thomas, *Lincoln's Old Friends of Menard County, Illinois*, 94. References as its source: Fehrenbacher, "Abraham Lincoln," *Speeches and Writings*, Vol. 1, 39.

149. Ibid., 94–95. References as its source: Fehrenbacher, "Abraham Lincoln," *Speeches and Writings*, Vol. 1, 39.

150. Roy P. Basler, *The Collected Works of Abraham Lincoln*, Vol. 1, 122–23.

151. Wayne C. Temple, *Lincoln's Connections with the Illinois & Michigan Canal* (Springfield: Illinois Bell, 1986), 11.

152. Richard Lawrence Miller, *Lincoln and His World: The Early Years, Birth to Illinois Legislature*, 316. References August 25, 1838 issue.

153. Ibid.

154. Ibid., 325.

155. Ibid.

156. Ibid.

157. Edgar R. Harlan, "Dr. Galland's Account of the Half-Breed Tract," *Annals of Iowa*, Vol. 10, No. 6 (Des Moines, July 1912), 452–54.

158. Ibid., 452–53.

159. George T. M. Davis, *Autobiography of the Late Colonel George T. M. Davis*, 47–48.

160. "Incorporation Laws of the State of Illinois (Tenth General Assembly)," reprint, 17.

161. Twenty-Fifth Congress, Second Session, Senate Bill 259, March 5, 1838, 8, 23; original copy of the bill in author's possession.

162. Twenty-Fifth Congress, Second Session, Senate Bill, March 12, 1838, presented by Senator Thomas Benton.

163. Ibid. Another reference has the bill presented by Henry Clay.

164. Landon Y. Jones, *William Clark and the Shaping of the West*, 333.

165. House of Representatives; Thirty-Third Congress, First Session. Ex. Doc. No. 104. "Des Moines and Rock River Rapids, in the Mississippi River." Letter from the Secretary of War. Inspection Report of Colonel S. H. Long, May 20, 1854, 64; document in author's possession.

166. Ibid., 63.

167. "Incorporation Laws of the State of Illinois," 75, in "An Act to Incorporate the Des Moines Rapids Railroad Company, "February 19, 1839.

168. Ibid.

169. J. Young Scammon, *State of Illinois, Supreme Court Records* (information taken from various depositions in James Doyle versus Joseph Teas, December 1843 term; the case was heard at the October 1842 term before Judge Stephen A. Douglas), Classic Reprint Series, 202–68.

170. John H. Krenkel, *Illinois Internal Improvements 1818–48*, 94–97.

171. David W. Kilbourne, "Strictures on Dr. I. Galland's pamphlet, entitled 'Villainy Exposed,' with some account of his transactions in lands in the Sac and Fox Reservations, in Lee County, Iowa" (Fort Madison, Iowa, 1850), 8.

172. Ibid.

173. Albert Watkins, *Publications of the Nebraska State Historical Society*, Vol. 20, 79–80.

174. Michael Dickey, *Arrow Rock Crossroads of the Missouri Frontier* (Arrow Rock: the Friends of Arrow Rock, Inc., 2004), 84.

175. Glenn Rawson and Dennis Lyman, *The Mormon Wars*, 53.

176. Brandon G. Kinney, *The Mormon War* (Yardley, Pennsylvania: Westholme Publishing, LLC., 2011), 91–92, 98.

177. Ibid., 96–97.

178. Leland H. Gentry and Todd M. Compton, *Fire and Sword* (Salt Lake City: Greg Kofford Books, 2011), 179–80.

179. "Document containing the correspondence, orders, &c. in relation to the disturbances with the Mormons: and the evidence given before the Hon. Austin A. King, Missouri Office of the Secretary of State, Missouri General Assembly (1840–41)," Fayette, Missouri, 20.

180. Ibid., 15–16.

181. Copy of the order included in the *Senate Journals of the State of Missouri* for December 6, 1838, 101.

182. *Niles National Register*, Baltimore, Maryland, October 13, 1838 (which included reprints of statements from the Columbia Patriot of September 12 and the text of Price's Commission notice to the people of Chariton), 103.

183. Ibid.

184. Ibid.

185. Michael Dickey, *Arrow Rock Crossroads of the Missouri Frontier*, 84.

186. "Document containing the correspondence, orders, &c. in relation to the disturbances with the Mormons," 95; date corrected as October 23, 1838.

187. Roger D. Launius, *Alexander William Doniphan*, 63.

188. Ibid., 64.

189. "Letter of Governor Boggs," Executive Department, City of Jefferson, November 19, 1838. To General John B. Clark. In the records of the 1841 Missouri General Assembly, 81.

190. Parley P. Pratt, *Autobiography of Parley Parker Pratt*, 229–30.

191. Roger D. Launius, *Alexander William Doniphan*, 66–67.

192. Ibid., 67.

193. Joseph Smith, *History of the Church of Jesus Christ of Latter-day Saints*, Vol. 3, 420.

194. Ibid., 421. See also Glenn Rawson and Dennis Lyman, *The Mormon Wars* (American Fork, Covenant Communications, Inc., 2014), 69–70.

195. Leland H. Gentry and Todd M. Compton, *Fire and Sword*, 495; quote from "Letter from the Editor, A. B. Chambers," *Missouri Republican Daily* (February 8, 1839).

196. Ibid.

197. Ibid.

198. *Senate Journals of the State of Missouri* (Jefferson City, 1838), 134.

199. Robert E. Shalhope, *Sterling Price: Portrait of a Southerner*, 28.

200. Robert E. Shalhope, *Sterling Price: Portrait of a Southerner*, 27–28.

201. Gordon A. Madsen, Jeffrey N. Walker, and John W. Welch, "Sustaining the Law," *BYU Studies* (Provo: Utah, 2014), 528.

202. Minutes of the meeting in Carroll County on July 30 were published in the *Missouri Republican*, dated August 18,1838, and reprinted in *Publications of the Nebraska State Historical Society*, Vol. 20, 79–80.

203. "Revised Statutes of the State of Missouri 1835 Crimes and Punishments," Article 1, Sections 4 and 5; copy in author's possession). This was referred to by Joseph Smith in his publication, "A Friendly Hint to Missouri" and included in the publication of "The Voice of Truth" in 1844.

204. Ibid.

205. William Nisbet Chambers, *Old Bullion Benton*, 235–36.

206. Ken S. Mueller, *Senator Benton and the People*, 175.

207. Roger D. Launius, *Alexander William Doniphan*, 71.

208. Joseph Smith, *History of the Church of Jesus Christ of Latter-day Saints*, Vol. 3, 292.

209. *Niles National Register*, Baltimore, Maryland, February 20, 1841.

210. Richard Lawrence Miller, *Lincoln and His World: The Early Years, Birth to Illinois Legislature* (Mechanicsburg: Stackpole Books, 2008), 316.

211. Ibid., 317.

212. Ibid.

213. Ibid., 316.

214. Ibid.

215. Ibid.

216. Ibid.

217. Joseph Smith, *History of the Church of Jesus Christ of Latter-day Saints*, Vol. 3, 342, 275.

218. David W. Kilbourne, "Strictures on Dr. I. Galland's pamphlet, entitled 'Villainy Exposed,'" 9.

219. Joseph Smith, *History of the Church of Jesus Christ of Latter-day Saints*, Vol. 3, 348–49.

220. Lyndon W. Cook, "Isaac Galland—Mormon Benefactor," *BYU Studies* 19 (1979), 261–84; quoting from letter "Isaac Galland to Samuel B. Swasey," July 22, 1839.

221. *The Joseph Smith Papers, Journals*, Vol. 1 (Salt Lake City, The Church Historians Press, 2008), 345.

222. Kessinger Legacy Reprints, *Letter from the Governor, Enclosing a Communication from Richard M. Young, as Agent of the State*

of Illinois, for Negotiating Loans for the Illinois And Michigan Canal (1841), 14.

223. Lyndon W. Cook, "Isaac Galland—Mormon Benefactor," *BYU Studies* 19, 261–84.

224. Richard Lawrence Miller, *Lincoln and His World: The Early Years, Birth to Illinois Legislature*, 404.

225. D. N. White (Editor), *Western World*, Vol. 1, No. 1, May 13, 1840.

226. Joseph Smith, *History of the Church of Jesus Christ of Latter-day Saints*, Vol. 4, 177–78.

227. *US Senate Journal* for January 25 ,1838; Twenty-Fifth Congress, Second Session, begun December 4, 1837; Congressional Edition, Vol. 313, 173.

228. *US Senate Journal* for December 17, 1838.

229. Dallin H. Oaks and Joseph I. Bentley, "Joseph Smith And Legal Process: In the Wake of the Steamboat Nauvoo," *BYU Studies* 19 (Winter 1979), 167–99.

230. James L. Kimball Jr., "A Wall to Defend Zion: The Nauvoo Charter" *BYU Studies*, Vol. 15 (Summer 1975), 495.

231. Glen Leonard, *Nauvoo: A Place of Peace, a People of Promise* (Salt Lake City: Deseret Book, 2002), 105–6.

232. James L. Kimball Jr., "A Wall to Defend Zion: The Nauvoo Charter," 495.

233. Copy of the letter in receipt of payment from Pierre Chouteau, McKenzie, and Benjamin Clapp, written January 30, 1840, for legal work regarding the Pavilion and Griffith versus Tanner. Original letter is included in the *Pierre Chouteau Papers*. A copy was downloaded on the Internet.

234. Donald L. Enders, "A Dam for Nauvoo: An Attempt to Industrialize the City," *BYU Studies* 18, No. 2 (Winter 1978), 246–47.

235. Dennis Rowley, "Nauvoo: A River Town" *BYU Studies* 18 (Winter 1978), 264–65. See also Joseph Smith, *History of the Church of Jesus Christ of Latter-day Saints*, Vol. 4, 297.

236. Richard Lawrence Miller, *Lincoln and His World: The Early Years, Birth to Illinois Legislature*, 411.

237. Ibid., 411–12.

238. Ibid., 412.

239. Joseph Smith, *History of the Church of Jesus Christ of Latter-day Saints*, Vol. 4, 367–71.

240. Ibid.

241. Irene D. Neu, *Erastus Corning: Merchant and Finacier*, 1794–1872 (Ithaca: Cornell University Press, 1960; Fall Creek Books, 2010), 137.

242. *Iowa Journal of History*, Vol. 13 (Iowa City: The State Historical Society of Iowa, 1915), 248–49.

243. Sina Dubovoy, *The Lost World of Francis Scott Key* (Bloomington, Indiana: WestBow Press, 2014), 449, 451, 596–97.

244. Ibid., 449.

245. Letter from Francis Scott Key to Hiram Barney, May 2, 1841.

246. Letter from Francis Scott Key to Hiram Barney, May 6, 1841.

247. Letter from Francis Scott Key to Hiram Barney, May 12, 1841.

248. This lawsuit was finally settled by the Supreme Court in favor of Edward Brooks and the Reddick heirs in 1852. At the time, Benton's friend Judge Taney was still the Chief Justice of the Supreme Court who ruled on this legislation. Taney was the brother-in-law of Francis Scott Key, who had helped the New York Land claim develop the partition plan. After Key's death, Lewis Barney and the New York Land Company refused to give Key's widow much of a settlement. This could have affected a bias of Chief Justice Taney.

249. US Supreme Court, No. 154, 1861; "Clagett versus Kilbourne," transcript of records, 11–12.

250. Ibid., 14.

251. Ibid.

252. Sina Dubovoy, *The Lost World of Francis Scott Key*, 449, 451, 596–97.

253. Ibid.

254. Ibid., 449.

255. Ibid., 452.

256. Ibid., 456.

257. Sina Dubovoy, *The Lost World of Francis Scott Key*, 456–57.

258. Ibid., 461–71.

259. Warren A. Jennings, "Two Iowa Postmasters View Nauvoo; Anti-Mormon Letters to the Governor of Missouri," *BYU Studies*, Vol. 11 (1971), 275–92.

260. Timothy R. Mahoney, *Provincial Lives Middle-class Experience in the Antebellum Middle West* (New York City: Cambridge University Press, 1999), 76–77.

261. Ibid., 76–79.

262. Joseph Smith, *History of the Church of Jesus Christ of Latter-day Saints*, Vol. 4, 311–12.

263. Isaac Galland "Doctor Isaac Galland's reply to various falsehood, misstatement and misrepresentations, concerning the Latter-day Saints, reproachfully called Mormons"(Philadelphia: July 13, 1841).

264. Ibid.

265. Joseph Smith, *History of the Church of Jesus Christ of Latter-day Saints*, Vol. 4, 416–17.

266. Ibid., 417.

267. John C. Bennett, *The History of the Saints; or an Expose of Joe Smith and Mormonism* (Boston: Leland & Whiting, 1842) 99–100.

268. Ibid., 100–2.

269. The revelations of Joseph Smith regarding Iowa lands were later published in Doctrine and Covenants 125.

270. The public disclosure of Galland renouncing his partnership involvement came from David Kilbourne himself in 1850 in his pamphlet: "Strictures on Dr. I Galland's pamphlet, entitled, 'Villainy Exposed,'" published at Fort Madison and printed at the Statesman Office in 1850. In this article, Kilbourne quoted the notice published in the *Iowa Territorial Gazette*, Vol. 2, No. 41, dated April 27, 1839, 8.

271. Isaac Galland "Doctor Isaac Galland's reply to various falsehood, misstatement and misrepresentations."

272. This was confirmed by Edward Brooks in a later deposition, in which he testified, "I always understood that the claim of Dr. Galland as a Half-Breed claimant was as an individual, and sole owner, and not as a member or Agent of the New York Company and consequently was antagonistic to the New York Company." Brooks further stated, "In 1840 the claims or titles to the Half-Breed Tract were in an unsettled condition, and Dr. Gallands titles were considered as good as any body elses." See Jacob Van Der Zee, "The Oldest Land Titles in the State of Iowa," *Iowa Journal of History and Politics*, Vol. 13 (1915), reprint, page 247–49.

273. US Supreme Court, No. 154, 1861; "Clagett versus Kilbourne," transcript of records, 14.

274. The entire listing of the lands reassigned to the 101 claimants was published in court documents in the case of Clagett versus Kilbourne in US Supreme Court, No. 238, settled in 1861. These records show that each of the 101 claimants were allocated portions of land in Keokuk and Nashville and other random sections of land by lottery. Through this process, all 119,000 acres of land in the Half-Breed Tract were reassigned to the new

owners. The entire lands of the Mormons sold by Isaac Galland of nearly twenty thousand acres were reallocated to the 101 claimants as of October 6, 1841.

275. *The History of Lee County Iowa* (Chicago: Western Historical Company, 1879), 730. In a section regarding Isaac Campbell, the article states that Campbell "purchased the first claim ever sold, from Isaac Antaya; . . . in 1838, he disposed of his remaining interest in the Half-Breed Tract, consisting of one-thirteenth part of 119,000 acres of Half-Breed lands to Dr. Galland, a man named Knight and Joseph Smith, the Mormon Prophet, for the sum of $14,000; of this amount, $2,000 was paid down, in old chairs, horses, carriages, etc.; he failed to take a mortgage on the lands to secure the payment of the balance and lost the whole amount; he still holds the notes of Galland, Knight and Smith as souvenirs."

276. "Decree Partition of the Half-Breed Tract in Lee County, Iowa, 1840," *Annals of Iowa*, Vol. 14, No. 6 (Fall Issue 1924), 424–60. This decree partition was rendered by Charles Mason, Chief Justice of the Iowa Supreme Court.

277. US Supreme Court documents: 49 US 223 and 8 How. 223, 12 L. Ed. 1056, which eventually was appealed to the Supreme Court. Samuel Marsh, William E. Lee, and Edward C. Delavan (plaintiffs in error) versus Edward Brooks and Virgina C., his wife, formerly Virgina C. Reddick, Charles Billou (defendants in error).

278. Joseph Smith, *History of the Church of Jesus Christ of Latter-day Saints*, Vol. 4, 444–45.

279. Ibid., 487.

280. *Times and Seasons*, January 1, 1842, 651.

281. Ibid.

282. A. B. Chambers, *Proceedings of the St. Louis Chamber of Commerce, in Relation to the Improvement of the Navigation of the Mississippi River: And Its Principal Tributaries and the St. Louis Harbor* (St. Louis: Chambers & Knapp, 1842), reprint, 14–23.

283. Ibid.

284. Ibid.

285. Ibid.

286. Joseph Smith, *History of the Church of Jesus Christ of Latter-day Saints*, Vol. 4, 543.

287. James L. Kimball Jr., "A Wall to Defend Zion: The Nauvoo Charter," 517–18.

288. *Wilford Woodruff Journal*, February 17, 1841.

289. Parley P. Pratt, *Millennial Star*, 1:57; referenced in *BYU Studies* 15 (Summer 1975), 518–19.

290. Joseph Smith, *History of the Church of Jesus Christ of Latter-day Saints*, Vol. 5, 1–2.

291. Original license document held at Church History Library, Salt Lake City, Utah. August 22, 1842.

292. Warren A. Jennings, "Two Iowa Postmasters View Nauvoo; Anti-Mormon Letters to the Governor of Missouri," 275–92.

293. Andrew F. Smith, *The Saintly Scoundrel* (Urbana: University of Illinois Press, 1997), 104.

294. Joseph Smith, *History of the Church of Jesus Christ of Latter-day Saints*, Vol. 5, 3–4.

295. Andrew F. Smith, *The Saintly Scoundrel*, 86–87 and referencing *Times and Seasons* 3 (July 1, 1842), 841.

296. William Smith, *The Wasp* 1 (May 21, 1842).

297. Joseph Smith, *History of the Church of Jesus Christ of Latter-day Saints*, Vol. 5, 42–44.

298. Andrew F. Smith, *The Saintly Scoundrel*, 93–94.

299. Joseph Smith, *History of the Church of Jesus Christ of Latter-day Saints*, Vol. 5, 61.

300. Warren A. Jennings, "Two Iowa Postmasters View Nauvoo; Anti-Mormon Letters to the Governor of Missouri," 275–92.

301. Thomas C. Sharp, *Warsaw Signal*, July 23, 1842.

302. George R. Gayler, "A Social, Economic, and Political Study of the Mormons in Western Illinois, 1839–1846; a Reevalution" (unpublished PhD dissertation, Indiana University, 1955).

303. Referenced in Andrew F. Smith, *The Saintly Scoundrel*, 99.

304. Printed in the *Illinois Register* on July 3, 1843.

305. *Iowa Journal of History*, Vol. 13 (Iowa City: the State Historical Society of Iowa, 1915) 245.

306. Ibid., 245–49. Edward Brooks was later deposed and indicated that he never understood by what right they claimed to be landlords. He also verified: "the Decree Title which was engendered in fraud and brought forward in iniquity, has given, by general consent of the parties interested as Half-Breed Claimants some shadow of title, and possession and the statutes of limitation may eventually settle the half Breed Title among themselves, yet that title will not stand the legal test of trial in Courts against outsiders." Edward Brooks also claimed in the deposition, "In 1840 the claims or titles to the Half-Breed Tract were in an unsettled condition, and Dr. Gallands titles were considered as good as any body elses."

307. "Letter of Joseph Duncan to George T. M. Davis," June 14, 1842, held at the Abraham Lincoln Presidential Library at Springfield, Document SC 431.

308. Joseph Smith, *History of the Church of Jesus Christ of Latter-day Saints*, Vol. 5, 60.

309. Ibid., 334–35.

310. Ibid., 162.

311. Ibid., 335.

312. David W. Kilbourne, "Strictures on Dr. I. Galland's pamphlet, entitled 'Villainy Exposed.'" David Kilbourne stated that the Remmick transaction with Galland occurred in January 1842. Eventually, Remmick sued Galland in St. Louis regarding the transaction, but the courts acquitted him (pages 15, 17–18).

That suggests that Galland had proof that his Iowa land dealings were separate from those of the New York Land Company and were never signed over to the company principals.

313. Joseph Smith, *History of the Church of Jesus Christ of Latter-day Saints*, Vol. 5, 335.

314. Ibid., 266.

315. Ibid.

316. If this John C. Walsh was the same John Walsh of St. Louis who was a partner in the St. Louis Land Company and a stockholder of the St. Louis Hotel Company, he would have been interested in taking over the Nauvoo House if the note payees defaulted. John Walsh and his brother Edward were influential with Senator Benton and the St. Louis elite.

317. Warren A. Jennings, "Two Iowa Postmasters View Nauvoo; Anti-Mormon Letters to the Governor of Missouri," 284.

318. Ibid., 284–85.

319. Thomas Ford, *A History of Illinois, from Its Commencement as a State in 1818 to 1847*, 270–71.

320. Ibid., 274.

321. Joseph Smith, *History of the Church of Jesus Christ of Latter-day Saints*, Vol. 5, 206.

322. Thomas Ford, *A History of Illinois, from Its Commencement as a State in 1818 to 1847*, 372.

323. Ibid., 295–97.

324. Joseph Smith, *History of the Church of Jesus Christ of Latter-day Saints*, Vol. 5, 382–83.

325. Ibid., 382; Vol. 6, 464.

326. Ibid., 422.

327. Lyndon W. Cook, "Isaac Galland—Mormon Benefactor," *BYU Studies* 19, 261–84.

328. LeGrand L. Baker, *Murder of the Mormon Prophet* (Salt Lake City: Eborn Books, 2006), 102–4.

329. Joseph Smith, *History of the Church of Jesus Christ of Latter-day Saints*, Vol. 6, 4.

330. Ibid., 4–7.

331. Joseph Smith, *History of the Church of Jesus Christ of Latter-day Saints*, Vol. 1, 374; from the manifesto of the mob dated in July 1833 at Jackson County, Missouri.

332. Joseph Smith, *History of the Church of Jesus Christ of Latter-day Saints*, Vol. 6, 7.

333. See the entire history of the case in 49 US 223 and 8 How. 223, 12 L. Ed. 1056, which eventually was appealed to the Supreme Court. Samuel Marsh, William E. Lee, and Edward C. Delavan (plaintiffs in error) versus Edward Brooks and Virgina C., his wife, formerly Virgina C. Reddick, Charles Billou (defendants in error).

334. Thomas Ford, *A History of Illinois, from Its Commencement as a State in 1818 to 1847*, 372.

335. Donald L. Enders, "A Dam for Nauvoo: An Attempt to Industrialize the City," 249–50.

336. See Robert Wicks and Fred Foister, *Junius and Joseph* (Logan: Utah State University Press, 2005) for greater background regarding John C. Elliott as a deputy marshall.

337. Joseph Smith, *History of the Church of Jesus Christ of Latter-day Saints*, Vol. 6, 122.

338. Ibid., 117–29.

339. Robert Wicks and Fred Foister, *Junius and Joseph*, 70–74; Joseph Smith, *History of the Church of Jesus Christ of Latter-day Saints*, Vol. 6, 122–48 (various references).

340. C. H. McClure, *Early Opposition to Thomas Hart Benton* (Columbia: the State Historical Society of Missouri, 1916), 172–73.

341. B. J. Scammon, *Reports of Cases Argued and Determined in the Supreme Court of the State of Illinois*, Vol. 5 (St. Louis: W. J. Gilbert, Publisher,1869), Classic Reprint Edition, 202–68.

342. See Missouri Department of Mental Health website, from the "Archives—by Henry V. "Hank" Guhleman, MD." Also referenced in *Dictionary of Missouri Biography*, 647.

343. Warren A. Jennings, "Two Iowa Postmasters View Nauvoo; Anti-Mormon Letters to the Governor of Missouri," 275–92.

344. Robert S. Wicks and Fred R. Foister, *Junius and Joseph*, 70.

345. Ibid., 69.

346. Ibid.

347. In 1839, Davis represented the Chouteaus in a lawsuit regarding their steamship *Pavilion*.

348. See Robert S. Wicks and Fred R. Foister, *Junius and Joseph*, for a detailed account.

349. Robert S. Wicks and Fred R. Foister, *Junius and Joseph*, 7.

350. Joseph Smith and William Phelps, "The Voice of Truth"; correspondence with John C. Calhoun, 22.

351. Ibid., 23.

352. Joseph Smith, *History of the Church of Jesus Christ of Latter-day Saints*, Vol. 6, 188.

353. Scott H. Faulring, *The Diaries and Journals of Joseph Smith* (Salt Lake City, Signature Books, 1989), 443–44.

354. Joseph Smith and William Phelps, "The Voice of Truth," 30.

355. Ibid., 32–34.

356. Ibid., 36.

357. Joseph Smith, *History of the Church of Jesus Christ of Latter-day Saints*, Vol. 6, 222.

358. Scott H. Faulring, *The Diaries and Journals of Joseph Smith*, 447.

359. Joseph Smith and William Phelps, "The Voice of Truth," 42.

360. Joseph Smith, *History of the Church of Jesus Christ of Latter-day Saints*, Vol. 6, 225.

361. Ibid., 243.

362. Scott H. Faulring, *The Diaries and Journals of Joseph Smith*, 457.

363. Joseph Smith and William Phelps, "The Voice of Truth," 45–46. Also confirmed in "Revised Statutes of the State of Missouri 1835 Crimes and Punishments," drafted by Judge Austin King.

364. Joseph Smith, *History of the Church of Jesus Christ of Latter-day Saints*, Vol. 6, 256.

365. See Scott H. Faulring, *The Diaries and Journals of Joseph Smith*, 457–58.

366. Joseph Smith, *History of the Church of Jesus Christ of Latter-day Saints*, Vol. 6, 275–76.

367. Ibid., 248.

368. Ibid.

369. Ibid., 278–79.

370. Scott H. Faulring, *The Diaries and Journals of Joseph Smith*, 468.

371. Joseph Smith and William Phelps, "The Voice of Truth," 46–47.

372. Ibid., 48–50.

373. Referenced in House of Representatives Bill, Twenty-Ninth Congress, First Session No. 432, in regards to Pierre Chouteau Jr., dated March 14, 1846. In this ruling, the Spanish land claim of the Dubuque Mines for Pierre Chouteau were denied. (A copy of the original bill is in the author's possession.)

374. John E. Sunder, *Joshua Pilcher Fur Trader and Indian Agent*, 170–72.

375. Robert S. Wicks and Fred R. Foister, *Junius and Joseph*, 116.

376. Ibid.

377. Ibid.

378. Ibid., 117.

379. Joseph Smith, *History of the Church of Jesus Christ of Latter-day Saints*, Vol. 6, 363–65.

380. Joseph Smith and William Phelps, "The Voice of Truth," 55–56.

381. Ibid., 58.

382. Joseph Smith, *History of the Church of Jesus Christ of Latter-day Saints*, Vol. 6, 365.

383. Joseph Smith, *History of the Church of Jesus Christ of Latter-day Saints*, Vol. 7, 136.

384. Thomas C. Sharp, *Warsaw Signal*, May 29, 1844, 2.

385. John E. Hallwas and Roger D. Launius, *Cultures in Conflict* (Logan: Utah State University Press, 1995), 155.

386. John E. Hallwas and Roger D. Launius, *Cultures in Conflict*, 161–62.

387. Melba Porter Hay, *Papers of Henry Clay*, Vol. 10 (Lexington: the University Press of Kentucky, 1991), 70.

388. Thomas Ford, *A History of Illinois, from Its Commencement as a State in 1818 to 1847*, 324.

389. Ibid., 324.

390. Joseph Smith, *History of the Church of Jesus Christ of Latter-day Saints*, Vol. 6, footnote 228—pages 3–7 regarding the September 1843 anti-Mormon meeting at Carthage, where the various resolutions were established.

391. Thomas Ford, *A History of Illinois, from Its Commencement as a State in 1818 to 1847*, 339 (footnote). Governor Ford, in his account, admitted he had his own plan to rid the state of Mormons.

392. Ibid., 330–31.

393. Ibid., 333, 342.

394. Ibid., 339–49. This conspiracy plan was confirmed by Governor Ford in his biography. Ford's earlier acceptance of the planned march on Nauvoo and the direct involvement of the leaders of the anti-Mormons, as well as their plans to assassinate Ford, were admitted by Thomas Ford himself. Ford stated, "The Mormons had been represented to me as a lawless, infatuated, and fanatical people, not governed by the ordinary motives which influence the rest of mankind. If so, most likely an exterminating war would ensue, and the whole land would be covered with desolation. . . . As for myself, I was well convinced that those, whoever they were, who assassinated the Smiths, meditated in turn my assassination by the Mormons . . . that the murder must be committed whilst the governor was at Nauvoo" (348–49).

395. Ibid., 342. In his own words, Governor Ford was involved in the conspiracy to attempt to force the Mormons from Illinois.

396. George T. M. Davis, *Autobiography of the Late Colonel George T. M. Davis*, 80–81. In his account, he identified the meeting.

397. "Stephen Markham letter to Wilford Woodruff from Fort Supply" (Salt Lake City: LDS Church History Library).

398. George T. M. Davis, *Autobiography of the Late Colonel George T. M. Davis*, 80–81. This sentiment was expressed in his autobiography and account of the Martyrdom.

399. Copy of the letter in receipt of payment from Pierre Chouteau, McKenzie, and Benjamin Clapp, written January 30, 1840, for legal work regarding the Pavilion and Griffith versus Tanner. Original letter is included in the *Pierre Chouteau Papers*. A copy was downloaded on the Internet.

400. George T. M. Davis, *Autobiography of the Late Colonel George T. M. Davis*, 80–81.

401. Joseph Smith, *History of the Church of Jesus Christ of Latter-day Saints*, Vol. 6, 587–88.

402. Dallin H. Oaks and Marvin S. Hill, *Carthage Conspiracy*, (Urbana: University of Illinois Press, 1979), 155.

403. See Robert S. Wicks and Fred R. Foister, *Junius and Joseph*, for further details.

404. Dallin H. Oaks and Marvin S. Hill, *Carthage Conspiracy*, 156.

405. Richard Barrett was appointed by the state as fund commissioner to "take charge of all that part of the Northern Cross Railroad, situate between Springfield and the Illinois River," February 27, 1841 (Illinois statutes). Joseph Duncan was appointed a commissioner for the Jacksonville and Meredocia Railroad on February 5, 1835 (Illinois statutes), 321.

406. George T. M. Davis, *Autobiography of the Late Colonel George T. M. Davis*, 80–81.

407. Thomas Ford, *A History of Illinois, from Its Commencement as a State in 1818 to 1847*, 366. Ford confirmed their hiding rendezvous point.

408. Warren A. Jennings, "The Lynching of an American Prophet," *BYU Studies* 40, No. 1 (2001), 207–11.

409. Ibid., 212–13.

410. George T. M. Davis, *An Authentic Account of the Massacre of Joseph Smith, the Mormon Prophet, and Hyrum Smith, His Brother* (St. Louis: Chambers & Knapp, 1844), 3–4

411. Ibid., 40–41.

412. Dale Thomas, *Lincoln's Old Friends of Menard County Illinois*, 105; referencing their source as Allen, *History of Kentucky*, 383–84.

413. William Nisbet Chambers, *Old Bullion Benton*, 263 [by 1845, Benton still owed Pierre Chouteau five thousand dollars (304)].

414. Ken S. Mueller, *Senator Benton and the People*, 208–9.

415. *Times and Seasons*, Vol. 5 No. 15; August 15, 1844, 619.

416. US Supreme Court, Webster versus Reid, 52 US 437 (1850), 52 US 437 and How. Joseph Webster (plaintiff in error) versus Hugh T. Reid.

417. Ibid.

418. John H. Krenkel, *Illinois Internal Improvements 1818–48*, 186–88.

419. Donald L. Enders, "A Dam for Nauvoo: An Attempt to Industrialize the City," 252–54.

420. Ibid.

421. US Supreme Court, Webster versus Reid, 52 US 437 (1850), 52 US 437 and How. Joseph Webster (plaintiff in error) versus Hugh T. Reid.

422. See Dallin H. Oaks and Marvin S. Hill, *Carthage Conspiracy*, for further details.

423. "Great Wabash River. Resolutions of the Legislature of Illinois, Relative to the Great Wabash River." Twenty-Eighth Congress, Second Session, Docket No. 109. The state resolution was provided to the US Congress as it involved multi-state issues and financing. William A. Richardson signed as state Speaker of the House of Representatives.

424. Robert S. Wicks and Fred R. Foister, *Junius and Joseph*, 72.

425. Gordon A. Madsen, Jeffrey N. Walker, and John W. Welch, "Sustaining the Law," 539.

426. Dallin H. Oaks and Marvin S. Hill, *Carthage Conspiracy*, 99.

427. Ibid., 101.

428. Ibid.

429. Ibid., 97–101.

430. Ibid., 117–19.

431. Ibid., 119.

432. Ibid., 120, 138.

433. Ibid., 119.

434. "Stephen Markham letter to Wilford Woodruff from Fort Supply" (Salt Lake City: LDS Church History Library).

435. Dallin H. Oaks and Marvin S. Hill, *Carthage Conspiracy*, 41, 45 (footnote).

436. Melba Porter Hay, *Papers of Henry Clay*, 349.

437. Dallin H. Oaks and Marvin S. Hill, *Carthage Conspiracy*, 38, 45 (footnote). Writs issued for William Law, Robert and Charles Foster, and "the whole guard that was placed over the Smiths."

438. Ibid., 185.

439. Ibid., 193–94. Reverend B. F. Morris confirmed this in his letter to the *Warsaw Signal*.

440. Robert Flanders, *Nauvoo Kingdom on the Mississippi* (Urbana: University of Illinois Press, 1975), 331.

441. Ibid., 331–32.

442. Ibid., 329.

443. John E. Hallwas and Roger D. Launius, *Cultures in Conflict*, 304–5.

444. J. M. Reid, *Sketches and Anecdotes of the Old Settlers and New Comers* (Keokuk, 1876), reprint, 46–49.

445. Warren A. Jennings, "The Lynching of an American Prophet," 214–16.

446. US Supreme Court: Samuel Marsh, William E. Lee, and Edward C. Delavan (plaintiffs in error) versus Edward Brooks and Virginia C. (his wife), formerly Virginia C. Reddick, Charles Billou, and Frances E. (his wife), formerly Frances E. Reddick, Walter J. Reddick, and Dabney C. Reddick by Eliza M. Reddick—their guardian, heirs at law of Thomas F. Reddick, deceased (defendants in error). Settled January 1850 term. 49 US 223, 8 How. 223, 12 L. Ed. 1056.

447. Timothy R. Mahoney, *Provincial Lives Middle-Class Experience in the Antebellum Middle West* (New York City: Cambridge University Press, 1999), 74. The original bill is held at the Huntington Library, San Marino, California.

448. Glenn Rawson and Dennis Lyman, *The Mormon Wars*, 81–85.

449. Timothy R. Mahoney, *Provincial Lives Middle-Class Experience in the Antebellum Middle West*, 220–27.

450. Miller, Orton, and Mulligan, *History of the Mormons or Latter-day Saints, with Memoirs of the Life and Death of Joseph Smith, the American Mahomet* (Auburn and Buffalo: Miller, Orton, and Mulligan, 1854), iv.

451. Joseph Smith and William Phelps, "The Voice of Truth," preface.

452. Joseph Smith, *History of the Church of Jesus Christ of Latter-day Saints*, Vol. 6, 365.

453. "Documents Relating to the Illinois and Michigan Canal," US Congress; 115, reprint, 16.

454. Joseph Smith, *History of the Church of Jesus Christ of Latter-day Saints*, Vol. 5, 296.

455. Parley P. Pratt, *Proclamation of the Twelve Apostles to All the Kings of the World* (Liverpool: published by Wilford Woodruff, 1845); original in author's possession.

456. Thomas Ford, *A History of Illinois, from Its Commencement as a State in 1818 to 1847*, 359–60.

About the Author

Mark Goodmansen currently resides at South Jordan, Utah. He graduated *cum laude* at the University of Utah in accounting, became a certified public accountant, and served as a business and marketing executive for various companies. His other passion is history. His style blends key aspects of LDS Church history with contemporary people and events prominent in American history. Active in family history research since his teenage years, he has written three books on early ancestors. Mark and his wife, Margene, have four children and twelve grandchildren. For additional information regarding *Conspiracy at Carthage* or to contact the author, visit his website, which includes, blogs, charts, maps, and copies of historical documents.

SCAN to visit

WWW.MARKGOODMANSEN.COM

0 26575 18502 7